BOOKS BY RICHARD A. FALK

Law, Morality, and War in the Contemporary World
The Role of Domestic Courts in the International Legal Order
Security in Disarmament
(editor, with R. J. Barnet)
The Strategy of World Order, 4 volumes
(editor, with Saul H. Mendlovitz)
Legal Order in a Violent World
Neutralization and World Politics
(with Cyril E. Black, Klaus Knorr, and Oran Young)
International Law and Organization
(editor, with Wolfram Hanrieder)
The Vietnam War and International Law, 2 volumes (editor)
The Status of Law in International Society
The Future of the International Legal Order, 2 volumes to
date (editor, with Cyril E. Black)
This Endangered Planet

BOOKS BY GABRIEL KOLKO

The Roots of American Foreign Policy
*The Politics of War: The World and United States Foreign
Policy, 1943–1945*
Railroads and Regulation, 1877–1916
*The Triumph of Conservatism: A Reinterpretation of American
History, 1900–1916*
*Wealth and Power in America: An Analysis of Social Class and
Income Distribution*

BOOKS BY ROBERT JAY LIFTON

Boundaries: Psychological Man in Revolution
History and Human Survival
*Revolutionary Immortality: Mao Tse-tung and the Chinese Cul-
tural Revolution*
Death in Life: Survivors of Hiroshima
*Thought Reform and the Psychology of Totalism: A Study of
"Brainwashing" in China*
Birds
Edited
America and the Asian Revolutions
The Woman in America

CRIMES OF WAR

CRIMES
OF WAR

A legal, political-documentary, and psychological inquiry into the responsibility of leaders, citizens, and soldiers for criminal acts in wars

EDITED BY

RICHARD A. FALK
GABRIEL KOLKO
AND
ROBERT JAY LIFTON

Random House New York

Acknowledgment is gratefully extended to the following for permission
to reprint from their works:

Bertrand Russell Peace Foundation Ltd., London: From the Erich Wulff
testimony in *Against the Crime of Silence.*

Bobbs-Merrill Company, Inc.: From *Chemical and Biological Warfare,*
by Seymour M. Hersh. Copyright © 1958 by Seymour M. Hersh.

Dell Publishing Co.: From *Cat's Cradle,* by Kurt Vonnegut, Jr.

George Braziller, Inc.: From the Introduction by Jean-Paul Sartre to
The Question, by Henri Alleg. Copyright © 1958 by George Braziller,
Inc.

The Guardian: From "Our Own Reporter" and "Saigon 'Falsifying'
Casualty Figures," January 30, 1970.

Alfred A. Knopf, Inc.: From *The Military Half,* by Jonathan Schell.
Copyright © 1968 by Jonathan Schell. Originally appeared in *The New
Yorker* in slightly different form.

Liberation Magazine: From "American Atrocities in Vietnam," by Eric
Norden, February, 1966.

The Macmillan Company: From *Night Flight to Hanoi,* by Daniel Berrigan, S. J. Copyright © 1968 by Daniel Berrigan, S.J.

TO ALL VICTIMS
OF THE WAR IN INDOCHINA

EDITORS' STATEMENT

In the aftermath of the My Lai disclosures in November of 1969 we came together on several occasions to discuss the significance of the event. We had been familiar with the United States' widespread commission of war crimes in Vietnam, but My Lai brought the issue before the public, at least briefly, in decisive and dramatic fashion. This book represents our joint effort to contribute to an American response to the awesome fact that war crimes have been and are being committed in our name. Indeed, it is increasingly plausible to join with Jean-Paul Sartre and others in conceiving of the entire war—or any massive counterinsurgency campaign by outside forces relying upon modern weaponry—as one all-embracing war crime.

We believe that all societies have the capacity to commit and authorize war crimes or other varieties of atrocity. But certain situations and pressures heighten this potentiality to such an extent as virtually to drag human beings across a threshold of inevitability. We write with a particular concern for the GI, who is being compelled to serve in the nation's armed forces under circumstances of severe danger and stress, and whose unseen, distant commanders and political leaders order him into situations where the commission of war crimes is a normal incident of military behavior. We are disturbed that some GIs politically and legally vulnerable to prosecution will be punished solely to shield both our leaders and the general citizenry from any shared sense of responsibility for the course and conduct of the war. These GIs are being prosecuted mainly to sustain an image of self-righteousness and decency on the part of those who have initiated, planned, and are continuing to carry out the vicious tactics of battle that have long been a daily part of this war.

We offer this book in the conviction that the struggle for moral clarification on the broadest basis is crucial for America and Americans, and that the issue of war crimes confronts each of us with a profound challenge—"After such knowledge, what forgiveness?" The challenge seems to us to call for response, action, and a sense of moral urgency, first about the present but extending also to war-linked criminality—and the criminality of war itself—in the past and in the possible future. In this spirit, we are devoting our royalties from this book to the work of the Education/Action Conference on U.S. Crimes of War in Vietnam.

We are indebted to Stewart Meacham, Rev. Richard Fernandez, and Francine Gray for joining with us in discussion and action on these matters in ways that contributed greatly to the emergence of this book; and to Jonathan Lear and Claudia Cords for invaluable research assistance. Alice Mayhew, our editor at Random House, has been a spiritual as well as an intellectual part of this project almost from its inception. She has shared our dilemmas of selection, and our decisions to leave out a number of "obvious" (because well-known) essays and commentaries in favor of others ordinarily less accessible to an American audience.

RICHARD A. FALK
GABRIEL KOLKO
ROBERT JAY LIFTON

CONTENTS

THE QUESTION OF WAR CRIMES
Richard A. Falk

ON THE AVOIDANCE OF REALITY
Gabriel Kolko

BEYOND ATROCITY
Robert Jay Lifton

THE QUESTION OF WAR CRIMES: A STATEMENT OF PERSPECTIVE

Richard A. Falk

During a discussion period after a talk I gave at a mass meeting in support of the October Moratorium against the Vietnam War (1969), a student from the audience asked: "If what you have said is accurate, then do you favor punishing our political and military leaders as war criminals? If not, why not?"

Even at the time I appreciated the difficulty of finding an adequate answer for the question, and proceeded to respond as follows: "Although the United States Government is waging an illegal war of aggression by criminal means in Vietnam, it would not be practical or even desirable to prosecute our leaders as war criminals. It would not be practical because there does not seem to be any way to constitute a tribunal that would be capable of apprehending the accused defendants and subjecting them to prosecution. It would not be desirable because such a drastic effort to repudiate the political leadership of this country would lead to a divisive kind of domestic turmoil at a time when we needed desperately to move beyond the awful years of involvement in Vietnam by undertaking more constructive tasks at home and abroad."

Such a response didn't, even at the time, satisfy me. It felt inconsistent with the search for serious restraints upon the international behavior of governmental officials and it went against the most basic teaching of the Nuremberg Judgment, namely, that by punishing the leaders of Germany for war crimes after World War II a precedent was laid down that would be relied upon in the future. To conclude, as I had, that the United States was waging a war of aggression against North Vietnam and was guilty of the systematic commission of war crimes on a massive scale in South Vietnam, and yet to shrink back from the conclusion that where there are crimes there are also criminals, seemed to involve a very dubious kind of intellectual casuistry. But worse than this, such a preference for exemption with regard to American officials seemed to confirm the most cynical criticisms of the Nuremberg concept as a hypocritical enactment of "victors' justice" disguised beneath the pieties of legal ritual. Why was Nuremberg good for Germany and international law, but some new trial of American leaders undesirable? There is no satisfactory reply to such a question. It is possible, but evasive, to retreat again to the arguments of practicality by contending that the discussion is ridiculous without some serious prospect that the international community could get together to form such a tribunal and reach an agreement on the need to prosecute some American leaders responsible for the war. World public opinion, although it has generally opposed the war, has not called for a war crimes tribunal, and most governments, aside from the socialist group, have been unwilling to impose responsibility for the war on the United States Government, let alone call for a war crimes tribunal. Without a world consensus, there is no possible way to convene a new war crimes tribunal, or even to set up an inquiry into allegations and evidence. Besides, the persistence of warfare in world affairs and the vitality of sovereign prerogatives has made it clear that it would be premature to impose criminal responsibility on leaders of governments who are guilty of war crimes. Since World War II there has been a virtual abandonment of any effort to impose criminal responsibility on states which have been identified by the international community as an "aggressor." China has been condemned by the United Nations as an "aggressor" because it sent "volunteers" to fight on behalf of North Korea in the Korean War, but no one has ever proposed that Chinese action was a suitable occasion for Nuremberg treatment. Indeed, labeling China as an aggressor has probably set back the cause of world peace by putting the UN on one side in a central political dispute in which neither side can claim victory or virtue entirely for itself.

Soviet invasions of Hungary in 1956 and Czechoslovakia in 1968, the British-French-Israeli Suez Campaign of 1956, and American action in the Dominican Republic in 1965 illustrate the inability of the UN to protect victims of aggression against encroachment by powerful states. The danger of nuclear war has also limited the capacity of powerful states to oppose and pass judgment upon one another. International society is deeply divided, the most powerful governments possess huge stockpiles of nuclear weapons, and the central institutions of the world have little influence on diplomacy. In such a world setting it is almost absurd to talk about the relevance of Nuremberg, except with regard to possible military action taken by South Africa. It is true that South Africa's racial policies of apartheid are abhorrent to all major governments and that a South African "war of aggression," if it takes place, might generate a credible campaign to prosecute its government leaders as war criminals. But beyond this special case there is no general disposition to establish an effective criminal law to enforce prohibitions upon illegal recourse to and conduct of war.

The disclosures of Son My sharpened my attitudes on these matters to a large extent. I became convinced that it was essential to expose the criminal essence of the Vietnam War as it was being waged by the United States Government. I became convinced that we needed to understand that crimes were being committed in our name and on our behalf in Vietnam and that it was essential to oppose the attempt by the Nixon Administration to separate the Son My massacre from the overall conduct of the war. To shoot women and children at point-blank range in a peasant village is so obviously an atrocity that it need not even be demonstrated to constitute a specific war crime, although of course it does. But to send B-52 sorties against populated areas day after day, and to destroy vast areas of cropland by herbicides in a hungry country, are official policies that are just as clearly criminal as what our leaders have repudiated when they joined in the condemnation of Songmy. To train the Green Berets to engage in political assassination on a large scale in Operation Phoenix or to turn over prisoners to the South Vietnamese for routine torture is also criminal behavior. In the face of this gigantic official effort at mystification about the character of the war, one part of which consists of the military trials of Calley and his colleagues, will produce greater confusion than ever among the American people. Pub-

lic opinion polls have revealed that only a small percentage of
Americans—under 15 percent—thought that Lieutenant Calley should have been prosecuted for shooting a group of helpless civilians to death, an apparent indication that the public,
at least, fails to distinguish between what Lieutenant Calley
did and the overall character of the war.

After Son My became known, a great deal of interest cen-
tered on the war crimes issue for several weeks. And then the
question was again virtually forgotten except by a few intellectuals and religious leaders on the fringe of the mainstream
of thought in America. The war continued as before, and after
the invasion of Cambodia on April 30, 1970, entered an entirely new phase. On May 3 the National Guard killed four
white students during anti-war demonstrations on the campus
of Kent State University, and a few days later some state police
killed two black students who were peacefully present in their
dormitory at Jackson State College in Jackson, Mississippi.
Such events further exposed a wide and growing gap between
the rulers and one sector of the ruled in American society, and
suggested to many moderate citizens that the time to engage in
political action had finally arrived.

But it is not enough to get out of Vietnam, or even to understand that to enter Vietnam and be unable to end the war represents a gigantic failure of the American government to ad-
just its behavior to either political or moral reality. There is a
further truth that needs to be understood—namely, that our
government was engaged all along in a criminal enterprise in
Vietnam and that our population was, by and large, unable to
perceive this actuality.

In the face of this widespread insensitivity to the behavior
of our civilian and military rulers, I changed my mind about
the relevance of the war crimes question to American society. I
believe that it is vitally important to appreciate the extent to
which the Vietnam War has displayed the capacity of our government to operate beyond the restraints of law without provoking much of a negative reaction, except among the young.
Just as Son My exposed the *criminality* of battlefield practice

in Vietnam, the Cambodian invasion exposed the *illegitimacy* of the war in relation to the Constitution. The President has gradually usurped the war-declaring role of Congress without encountering much resistance. Moral decay is evident whenever a society loses belief in itself to the extent of abandoning its own proudest traditions without even an awareness of what is happening.

We cannot hope to avoid the destruction of the Republic without knowledge and awareness of the peril. Many young men of conscience have refused to fight in Vietnam, and have accepted prison or exile as a consequence, thereby bearing solemn witness to our fallen condition. Often this act of individual refusal has been based upon an explicit or implicit acceptance of the Nuremberg teaching that human beings have obligations that may transcend their duty to obey the dictates of their own state. Indeed the most important positive contribution of Nuremberg may have been to give citizens an argument to interpose between themselves and the criminal conduct of their government. As yet, our courts have refused even to listen to such arguments. Indeed, in the *Mitchell* decision, one of the earliest Vietnam cases based on the Nuremberg argument, the District Court judge dismissed the defense as "tommyrot," and affirmed a five-year jail sentence for draft resistance. Most courts have merely disallowed the defense as "irrelevant" and have ruled the war to be "a political question" beyond judicial purview. By so deciding, courts have refused to acknowledge the existence of positive international law rules prohibiting aggressive war (the Kellogg-Briand Pact and the UN Charter) and the punishment of war crimes (the Nuremberg and Tokyo Judgments). As a result an individual is caught in a hopeless situation between two conflicting obligations—the norms against helping aggressive war and the norms against disobeying national authority in which courts have a protective role. Mr. Justice Roberts in a dissent to the *Korematsu* decision expressed the conventional wisdom on the subject when he wrote: "I had supposed that if a citizen was constrained by two laws, or two orders having the force of law, and obedience to one would violate the other, to punish him for violation of either would deny him due process of law. And I had supposed that under these circumstances a conviction for violating one of the orders could not stand." 323 U.S. 214–248, at 232 (1944) The Constitution makes validly ratified treaties part of the "supreme law of the land" and the U.S. Supreme Court has often declared that domestic courts should apply rules of international law whenever relevant to the adjudication of a controversy. Therefore, the draft resister or the serviceman who opposes the war by an appeal to international law deserves, at least, his day in court. To deny judicial redress in such circumstances is to shatter any belief in the capacity of our legal system to secure justice.

Any serious concern with war crimes tends to weaken the link between man and the state and to place a certain limit upon the absolute pretensions of state sovereignty. Perhaps it may not be too naïve to believe that the prolonged agony of Vietnam is but a revelation of the twilight of the sovereign state, especially by its demonstration of the diminishing capacity of a government to command the blind allegiance of its population for purposes of aggressive war-making. Of course, unpopular and unsuccessful wars have encountered domestic resistance before, but today, especially in the United States, a war is fought under the lengthening shadows cast over human destiny by the nuclear arms race and by the growing realization that modern technology is pushing the world toward the brink of ecological collapse. We are living, in other words, in an apocalyptic age in which the permanent end of human life has become a normal and frequent topic of conversation. Under such circumstances, there is no genuine prospect for revival without drastic change in our attitudes, behavior, and institutions.

No area of change is more important than is the elimination of the war system from human affairs. The success of such an enterprise of elimination may well determine whether the human species can overcome this challenge to its survival. One way of response is to repudiate criminal acts of war and criminal wars, and to understand that illegal war policies are indeed crimes just as clearly as are domestic acts of murder and theft.

It may now be worth returning to the question, Should we punish our leaders as war criminals? My answer to this question today would still probably be negative, largely because there is such a wide chasm between the claim and the prospect of satisfying it and because the punishment of criminals does not serve mankind well. Punishment may itself be little more than authorized crime, as when a helpless prisoner is kept in a cage or sent to his death by the premeditated acts of his executioner. Surely, there is no evidence that the punishments imposed at Nuremberg helped to deter future war crimes. The whole endeavor—as a formal activity—seemed limited to the special circumstances of complete victory surrounding the end of World War II, not likely to be repeated in an ideologically divided world of nuclear powers. Also the endeavor seemed flawed by the refusal to extend the war crimes concept to cover activity of the victors, such as the mass bombings of Dresden, Tokyo, or Hiroshima or the mistreatment of civilians and prisoners in Eastern Europe.

The purpose of defining activity as criminal is to draw an outer boundary around what is permissible. Once a boundary has been drawn and it is exceeded, then there is a proper occasion for repudiation. Draft resisters and a few other citizens refused to follow the government across the boundaries of criminality in Vietnam. The rest of us have remained unaccountably blind toward the existence and violation of such boundaries. We must ask ourselves, Why?

I see, then, the issue of war crimes as crucially related to the development of a realistic political consciousness. The importance of the criminal concept is to reinforce a boundary—to paint the limiting condition of state behavior in bold colors—not to provide a foundation for punishment and retribution. We have almost no evidence to vindicate the impulse to punish wrongdoers. Punishment does not seem to rehabilitate the criminals, deter future crime, or raise the consciousness of the group that inflicts the punishment. And especially in relation to war, the identification of leaders as "the criminals" tends to exempt the supporting population. The rulers who fail to resist are part of the criminal process that makes it possible for governments to wage illegal wars. These rulers are representatives whose rulership should be repudiated, if at all possible, as soon as the boundaries of crime are crossed.

The importance, then, of the inquiry into war crimes is to discover the erosion of the criminal boundaries and the need to restore their claims upon our actions. We need, in other words, to educate ourselves to the point that we know that waging aggressive war and committing illegal acts of war are war crimes. We also need to reorient our sense of citizenship toward the position that it is disloyal for citizens to abet the crimes of their government. As well, we need to make our governors sensitive to the criminal boundaries that restrict the exercise of political power. On this basis we can learn from the long experience of the Vietnam War.

ON THE AVOIDANCE OF REALITY
Gabriel Kolko

The twentieth century has been so full of tragedy and barbarism that it is natural for a historian to be reluctant to attach some unique significance to American war crimes in Vietnam. Yet both for the world, and most certainly for the U.S., the war the American Government has been waging in Vietnam is distinctive and without parallel. The openly justified, systematic, and continuous effort at the destruction of a population of an entire nation by an external enemy is quite rare in modern history. The Nazis carried on such a policy against the Jews, and it was far more "successful" on its own terms because European Jewry, unlike the Vietnamese, was unable or unwilling to resist. But the essential difference is that the Nazis concealed from the German masses their genocidal efforts, which they attempted to hide for fear civilization's taboos regarding mass murder might damn them in the eyes of their own people. In Vietnam, the U.S. Government has no shame about the effects of its warfare. The daily press and TV have for years revealed everything one needs to know about the magnitude of the horror and the consequences of the war.

The real question of war crimes in the Vietnam War is no longer the facts themselves but rather the justification Washington has employed for its systematic terror. And, above all, it is the failure and seeming unwillingness of the American people to translate their knowledge of specific inhumanities and events, of the countless Son Mys, into a larger political perception of the objective of American foreign policy or a comprehension of the essential human and moral significance of the war in Vietnam. For the absence of a far greater sense of abhorrence, one based essentially on empathy with the sufferings of the Vietnamese rather than only with that of unwilling American boys sent to die in a distant land, potentially marks a moral and political immunization of a nation that has far greater significance for the future of American society and politics than I for one care to imagine.

It is not possible to refer to a "public" response to the Vietnam War and crimes Washington commits on its behalf, for American society is not, and has never been, an undifferentiated mass. The U.S. is a nation of powerful and powerless, rich and poor, white and black, and complex as well as simple variations of class strata and castes, and a great many Americans have also been victims of violence and oppression at home. There are also men and women of good will who remain, either out of perverse choice or genuine naïveté, ignorant of the horrors and significance of Vietnam, and such powerless individuals may be found taking every conceivable position on the future of the war.

The inability of such individuals to define the war for what it is, but their desire also to retain a capacity to express a sense of outrage and their unwillingness to grasp an ideology that makes a virtue or justifiable necessity of reality, is both a political and moral fact we must confront. Robert Lifton will consider here the psychological dimensions and moral immunization of such Americans. I wish briefly to discuss yet another aspect of this common but essential problem of why the great mass of Americans—good, powerless, and institutionally guiltless people—have not yet defined the Vietnam War as an intrinsically criminal undertaking or joined to a far greater extent the opposition and resistance to it.

Essentially, most Americans have neither the ideological or intellectual perceptions, much less a descriptively accurate language of politics, capable of characterizing the social and human consequences of their government's foreign policy. This is true of the average man as well as of the typical academic. Candor is far less palatable than paying obeisance to an abstract commitment to "truth" that ruffles no sensibilities or interests. Accuracy is reserved in the universities for the crimes and follies of other nations, not for our own. Other nations are called imperialist, but I know of no text on American diplomacy published in this country that is willing to so describe the omnivorous policies of the U.S. in this century, or even to substitute another concept that conveys this reality. So too with "body counts" in Vietnam, which trumpet the death inflicted each day or in each battle on those caught in America's mechanized death maw. Americans do not probe the significance of what their rulers are doing because they have been educated from the beginning, in universities as well as grade schools, to avoid universal categories of explanation which also describe social and historical phenomena in this country as well as in Europe. The United States duns itself into believing—which most politicians generally do with the greatest sincerity even if they are in power—that somehow it is uniquely "open," "liberal," "rational," and most certainly not predatory. Aberrations from conduct and goals consistent with such a society are regarded as errors and scarcely as the essence of the game. In brief, the nation has for some decades been intellectually and culturally mystified in a drugging official ideology of liberalism, one that historians are obligated to dissect and microscopically describe before most individuals are willing to perceive the real nature of the socially diseased and destructive organism. At the time of this writing, also, there is no widely accepted comprehensive alternative model of what American society and capitalism truly are at home and abroad.

This liberal myopia immunizes most Americans to the dominant political facts, experiences, and trends of our age—to war, repression, and war crimes everywhere. Such illusions become a defense against reality as well as a means for its perpetuation, and this mentality makes it impossible for many citizens to recognize war crimes in Vietnam just as they cannot perceive racism and repression at home—and generalize upon it in a manner that leads to fundamentally new alternative visions of society or political strategies. For once the conventional wisdom that blocks out a clear vision of reality is pushed aside, opening our view to the meaning and causes of our malaise at home and the terror and misery America inflicts abroad, then we also close the door on the seemingly easy, but in reality futile, widely accepted means of solving problems—which is to say, we fundamentally doubt the official theory of the American political process and the requisites for changing it. At that point, we have attained the precondition for ceasing to pain-lessly, rationally seeking to transform power with reason, peti-tions, and electoral charades.

To fully comprehend American war crimes in Vietnam, therefore, is to understand the war, the reasons why the U.S. became involved in Vietnam in the first place, and the sources and objectives of American power in the world today. Hence Americans, including many who oppose the war, reject con-sidering the barbarism in Vietnam as intrinsic to Washington's confrontation with the Third World in modern times, much less as simply one more variation of the only role the United States is capable of playing in a world in upheaval and revolu-tion. Apart from the psychological blocks and terror, for Americans to confront war crimes in Vietnam is not merely to examine the degradation and perversity that the war has re-vealed in their soldiers, but also the human and moral conse-quences of American power as much of the outside world now regards it.

Most Americans are still incapable of such a searing reap-praisal of their cherished assumptions and vision of society, which will come, if at all, only in response to internal crises at home which they themselves must experience. However, the Son My massacre, which was the most publicized and dramatic example of the war's criminal nature, was met by some Ameri-cans not with shock, silence, or confusion but with accolades. After all, Son My was so bestial that once it was revealed even the Pentagon reluctantly stigmatized those alleged to be re-sponsible for it. The rather triumphant welcome various politi-cal and veteran organizations gave Lieutanant Calley reveals that terror and barbarism have their followers and admirers at home as well as in Vietnam. Conventional liberal wisdom can-not tell us what this implies for the future of American society, just as it cannot anticipate war crimes as a routine outcome of American efforts abroad or police and courts at home that are repressive and corrupt. We should not dismiss lightly the Ya-hoos who welcome Calley, or who regard student radicals and black militants as something other than human. For they evoke the dread thought that the same men who urge maximum violence in Vietnam, and to whom the present Administration caters in the hope of winning their political backing and also because of a very real consensus both share, may someday bring home even more of Vietnam than we have hitherto experienced. For the exercise of repression as a principle, once admitted, is limited only by the interests and stakes involved and the power and resolve of the potential executioners.

Son My and the war crimes in Vietnam, therefore, have told us much about the intrinsic nature of that war, about the frightful dimensions of American power as applied today, its implications for our own future, and how liberal theory has disarmed our comprehension of such realities. But if it has caused the realities to move blindingly into our vision, and the advocates of terror to surface along with them, we should not ignore the more impersonal, mechanistic aspects of the Vietnam War and the condition of our society, for the true architects of terror are respectable men of manners and conventional views who calculate and act from behind desks and computers rather than in villages in the field. For like virtually everything the U.S. has done in Vietnam, Son My and the endless parallel crimes were programmed—and predictable.

If violence is random and of short duration, and quite purposeless, it may be based on personal idiosyncracies and guilt. Individual decisions then become the rule. But the U.S. effort in Vietnam is grounded on former Secretary of Defense McNamara's concepts of cost effectiveness, which weighs firepower and available resources against political-military needs and objectives. To pay for such a vast undertaking, and rationalize expenditures to Congress, violence is carefully calculated and its intended outcome translated into military and economic terms, with the relative "body counts" becoming a vital measure of results. Such mechanized, dehumanizing slaughter assumes mass death, from the air, from artillery shells, in fields and prisons.

In the following pages the reader may judge for himself the quality and objectives of Washington's policies in Vietnam.

Any consistent and careful survey of the daily press over a period of time will probably produce sufficient facts to reach the same estimate of reality. Indeed, for some readers the facts in this volume may sound familiar, even stale. Yet the understanding of their significance is not likely to be so widely accepted. And for this reason we must again ask ourselves: How did conventional wisdom and theory prepare us to predict and explain America's torture of a whole nation in an intense sea of fire and death?

The landscape doesn't change much. For days and days you see just about nothing. It's unfamiliar—always unfamiliar. Even when you go back to the same place, it's unfamiliar. And it makes you feel as though, well, there's nothing left in the world but this. . . . You have the illusion of going great distances and traveling, like hundreds of miles . . . and you end up in the same place because you're only a couple of miles away. . . . But you feel like it's not all real. It couldn't possibly be. We couldn't still be in this country. We've been walking for days. . . . You're in Vietnam and they're using real bullets. . . . Here in Vietnam they're actually shooting people for no reason. . . . Any other time you think, It's such an extreme. Here you can go ahead and shoot them for nothing. . . . As a matter of fact it's even . . . smiled upon, you know. Good for you. Everything is backwards. That's part of the kind of unreality of the thing. To the "grunt" [infantryman] this isn't backwards. He doesn't understand. . . . But something [at My Lai 4] was missing. Something you thought was real that would accompany this. It wasn't there. . . . There was something missing in the whole business that made it seem like it really wasn't happening. . . .

American GI's recollections of
My Lai (personal interview)

BEYOND ATROCITY
Robert Jay Lifton, M.D.

When asked to speak at a number of recent occasions, I have announced my title as "On Living in Atrocity." To be sure, neither I nor anyone else lives there all or even most of the time. But at this moment, in mid-1970, an American investigator of atrocity finds himself dealing with something that has become, for his countrymen in general, a terrible subterranean image that can be neither fully faced nor wished away. There is virtue in bringing that image to the surface.

In one sense, no matter what happens in the external world, personal atrocity, for everyone, begins at birth. It can also be said that some of us have a special nose for atrocity. Yet I can remember very well, during the early stirrings of the academic peace movement taking place around Harvard University during the mid- and late 1950s—about two hundred years ago, it now seems—how hard it was for us to *feel* what might happen at the other end of a nuclear weapon. Whatever one's nose for atrocity, there are difficulties surrounding the imaginative act of coming to grips with it.

After six months of living and working in Hiroshima, studying the human effects of the first atomic bomb, I found that these difficulties were partly overcome and partly exacerbated. On the one hand I learned all too well to feel what happened at the other end of an atomic bomb. But on the other hand I became impressed with the increasing gap we face between our technological capacity for perpetrating atrocities and our imaginative ability to confront their full actuality. Yet the attempt to narrow that gap can be enlightening, even liberating. For me Hiroshima was a profoundly "radicalizing" experience —not in any strict ideological sense but in terms of fundamental issues of living and dying, of how one lives, how one may die.

Whatever the contributing wartime pressures, Hiroshima looms as a paradigm of technological atrocity. Each of the major psychological themes of Hiroshima survivors—death immersion, psychic numbing, residual guilt—has direct relationship to its hideously cool and vast technological character. The specific technology of the bomb converted the brief moment of exposure into a lifelong encounter with death—through the sequence of the survivor's early immersion in massive and grotesque death and dying, his experiencing or witnessing bizarre and frequently fatal acute radiation effects during the following weeks and months, his knowledge of the increased incidence over the years of various forms (always fatal) of leukemia and cancer, and finally his acquisition of a death-tainted group identity, an "identity of the dead" or shared sense of feeling emotionally bound both to those killed by the bomb and to the continuing worldwide specter of nuclear genocide.

The experience of psychic numbing, or emotional desensitization—what some survivors called "paralysis of the mind"—

was a necessary defense against feeling what they clearly knew to be happening. But when one looks further into the matter one discovers that those who made and planned the use of that first nuclear weapon—and those who today make its successors and plan their use—require their own form of psychic numbing. They too cannot afford to feel what they cognitively know would happen.

Victims and victimizers also shared a sense of guilt, expressed partly in a conspiracy of silence, a prolonged absence of any systematic attempt to learn about the *combined* physical and psychic assaults of the bomb on human beings. Survivors felt guilty about remaining alive while others died, and also experienced an amorphous sense of having been part of—having imbibed—the overall evil of the atrocity. The perpetrators of Hiroshima (and those in various ways associated with them) —American scientists, military and political leaders, and ordinary people—felt their own forms of guilt, though, ironically, in less tangible form than that of victims. Yet one cannot but wonder to what extent Hiroshima produced in Americans (and others) a guilt-associated sense that, If we could do this we could do anything; and, Anyone could do anything to us; in other words, an anticipatory sense of unlimited atrocity.

If these are lessons of Hiroshima, one has to learn them personally. My own immersion in massive death during investigations in that city, though much more privileged and infinitely less brutal, will nonetheless be as permanent as that of Hiroshima survivors themselves; as in their case, it has profoundly changed my relationship to my own death as well as to all collective forms of death that stalk us. I had a similarly personal lesson regarding psychic numbing. During my first few interviews in Hiroshima I felt overwhelmed by the grotesque horrors described to me, but within the short space of a week or so this feeling gave way to a much more comfortable sense of myself as a psychological investigator, still deeply troubled by what he heard but undeterred from his investigative commitment. This kind of partial, task-oriented numbing now strikes me as inevitable and, in that situation, useful, yet at the same time potentially malignant in its implications.

By "becoming" a Hiroshima survivor (as anyone who opens himself to the experience must), while at the same time remaining an American, I shared something of both victim's and victimizer's sense of guilt. This kind of guilt by identification has it pitfalls, but I believe it to be one of the few genuine psychological avenues to confrontation of atrocity. For these three psychological themes are hardly confined to Hiroshima: death immersion, psychic numbing, and guilt are a psychic trinity found in all atrocity.

Hiroshima also taught me the value and appropriateness of what I would call the apocalyptic imagination. The term offends our notions of steadiness and balance. But the technological dimensions of contemporary atrocity seem to me to require that we attune our imaginations to processes that are apocalyptic in the full dictionary meaning of the word—processes that are "wildly unrestrained" and "ultimately decisive," that involve "forecasting or predicting the ultimate destiny of the world in the shape of future events" and "foreboding imminent disaster of final doom."

In the past this kind of imagination has been viewed as no more than the "world-ending" delusion of the psychotic patient. But for the people of Hiroshima the "end of the world" —or something very close to it—became part of the actuality of their experience. Thus one survivor recalled: "My body seemed all black, everything seemed dark, dark all over . . . then I thought, 'The world is ending.' " And another: "The feeling I had was that everyone was dead . . . . I thought this was the end of Hiroshima—of Japan—of humankind." Those witnessing Nazi mass murder—the greatest of all man's atrocities to date—called forth similar images, though they could usually perceive that the annihilating process was in some way selective (affecting mainly Jews or anti-Nazis, or other specific groups). As Hiroshima took me to Auschwitz and Treblinka, however, I was struck mostly by the similarities and parallels in the overall psychology of atrocity.

Yet similar end-of-the-world impressions have been recorded

in connection with "God-made" atrocities, as in the case of survivors' accounts of the plagues of the Middle Ages:

> How will posterity believe that there has been a time when without the lightings of heaven or the fires of earth, without wars or other visible slaughter, not this or that part of the earth, but well-nigh the whole globe, has remained without inhabitants. . . . We should think we were dreaming if we did not with our eyes, when we walk abroad, see the city in mourning with funerals, and returning to our home, find it empty, and thus know that what we lament is real.

The plagues were God-made not only in the sense of being a mysterious and deadly form of illness outside of man's initiation or control, but also because they could be comprehended as part of a God-centered cosmology. To be sure scenes like the above strained people's belief in an ordered universe and a just God, but their cosmology contained enough devils, enough flexibility, and enough depth of imprint to provide, if not a full "explanation" of holocaust, at least a continuing psychic framework within which to go on living. In contrast, Hiroshima and Auschwitz were initiated and carried out by men upon men, and at a time when old cosmologies had already lost much of their hold and could provide little explanatory power. Survivors were left with an overwhelming sense of dislocation and absurdity: like the GI quoted earlier in relationship to My Lai, something for them was "missing"—namely, meaning or a sense of reality. With Hiroshima and Auschwitz now part of man's historical experience, it is dangerously naïve to insist that our imaginative relationship to world-destruction can remain unchanged—that we can continue to make a simple-minded distinction between psychotic proclivity for, and "normal" avoidance of, that image.

Yet whatever the force of external events, there must be a subjective, imaginative component to the perceived "end of the world." Hiroshima survivors had to call forth early inner images of separation and helplessness, of stasis and annihilation, images available from everyone's infancy and childhood, but to some with greater force than to others. There is therefore a danger, not just for Hiroshima survivors but for all of us, of being trapped in such images, bound by a psychic sense of doom to the point of being immobilized and totally unable or unwilling to participate in essential day-by-day struggles to counter atrocity and prevent the collective annihilation imagined.

Psychological wisdom, then, seems to lie in neither wallowing in, nor numbing ourselves to, our imaginings of apocalypse. A simple example of the constructive use of the apocalyptic imagination is recorded by Eugene Rabinowitch, from the beginning an articulate leader in scientists' anti-atomic-bomb movements. Rabinowitch describes how, when walking down the streets of Chicago during the spring of 1945, he looked up at the city's great buildings and suddenly imagined a holocaust in which skyscrapers crumbled. He then vowed to redouble his efforts to prevent that kind of event from happening by means of the scientists' petition he and others were drawing up to head off the dropping of an atomic bomb, without warning, on a populated area. The effort of course failed, but this kind of apocalyptic imagination—on the part of Rabinowitch, Leo Szilard, and Bertrand Russell among others—has made it possible for at least a small minority of men and women to name and face the true conditions of our existence.* For we live in the shadow of the ultimate atrocity, of the potentially terminal revolution—and if that term is itself a contradiction, the same contradiction is the central fact of our relationship to death and life.

We perpetrate and experience the American atrocity at My Lai in the context of these apocalyptic absurdities and dislocations. The GI's quoted description suggests not only that atrocity can be a dreamlike affair (in this sense, resembling the quoted passage about the plague), but that it is committed by men living outside of ordinary human connection, outside of

* Betrand Russell had earlier exhibited the dangers of the apocalyptic imagination when he advocated that we threaten to drop atomic bombs on Russia in order to compel her to agree to a system of international control of nuclear weapons.

both society and history. My Lai was acted out by men who had lost their bearings, men wandering about in both a military and psychic no-man's land. The atrocity itself can be seen as a grotesquely paradoxical effort to put straight this crooked landscape, to find order and significance in disorder and absurdity. There is at the same time an impulse to carry existing absurdity and disorder to their logical extreme, as if both to transcend and demonstrate that aberrant existential state.

Atrocities are committted by desperate men—in the case of My Lai, men victimized by the absolute contradictions of the war they were asked to fight, by the murderous illusions of their country's policy. Atrocity, then, is a perverse quest for meaning, the end result of a spurious sense of mission, the product of false witness.

To say that American military involvement in Vietnam is itself a crime is also to say that it is an atrocity-producing situation. Or to put the matter another way, My Lai illuminates, as nothing else has, the essential nature of America's war in Vietnam. The elements of this atrocity-producing situation include an advanced industrial nation engaged in a counterinsurgency action in an underdeveloped area, against guerrillas who merge with the people—precisely the elements which Jean-Paul Sartre has described as inevitably genocidal. In the starkness of its murders and the extreme dehumanization experienced by victimizers and imposed on victims, My Lai reveals to us how far America has gone along the path of deadly illusion.

Associated with this deadly illusion are three psychological patterns as painful to the sensitized American critic of the war as they are self-evident. The first is the principle of atrocity building upon atrocity, because of the need to deny the atrocity-producing situation. In this sense My Lai itself was a product of earlier, smaller My Lais; and it was followed not by an ending of the war but by the American extension of the war into Laos and Cambodia.

The second principle involves the system of non-responsibility. One searches in vain for a man or group of men who

will come forward to take the blame or even identify a human
source of responsibility for what took place: from those who
fired the bullets at My Lai (who must bear some responsibility,
but were essentially pawns and victims of the atrocity-producing situation, and are now being made scapegoats as well) ; to
the junior-grade officers who gave orders to do the firing and
apparently did some of it themselves; to the senior-grade officers who seemed to have ordered the operation; to the highest
military and civilian planners in Vietnam, the Pentagon, and
the White House who set such policies as that of a *"permanent
free-fire zone"* (which, according to Richard Hammer, means,
"in essence . . . that any Americans operating within it had,
basically, a license to kill and any Vietnamese living within it
had a license to be killed") and made even more basic decisions about continuing and even extending the war; to the
amorphous conglomerate of the American people who presumably chose, or at least now tolerate, the aforementioned as their
representatives. The atrocity-producing situation, at least in
this case, depends upon what Masao Maruyama has called a
"system of non-responsibility." Situation and system alike are
characterized by a technology and a technicized bureaucracy
unchecked by sensate human minds.

The third and perhaps most terrible pattern is the psychology of nothing happening. General Westmoreland gives way
to General Abrams, President Johnson to President Nixon, a
visibly angry student generation to one silent with rage—and
the war, the atrocity-producing situation, continues to grind
out its thousands of recorded and unrecorded atrocities. To be
more accurate, something does happen—the subliminal American perception of atrocity edges toward consciousness, making
it more difficult but, unfortunately, not impossible to defend
and maintain the atrocity-producing situation. The widespread feeling of being *stuck in atrocity* contributes, in ways
we can now hardly grasp, to a national sense of degradation
and a related attraction to violence. For nothing is more conducive to collective rage and totalism than a sense of being
bound to a situation perceived to be both suffocating and evil.

Atrocity in general, and My Lai in particular, brings its perpetrators—even a whole nation—into the realm of existential evil. That state is exemplified by what another GI described to me as a working definition of the enemy in Vietnam: "If it's dead, it's VC—because it's dead. If it's dead, it *had* to be VC. And of course, a corpse couldn't defend itself anyhow." When at some future moment, ethically sensitive historians get around to telling the story of the Vietnam War—assuming that there will be ethically sensitive (or for that matter, any) historians around—I have no doubt that they will select the phenomenon of the "body count" as the perfect symbol of America's descent into evil. What better represents the numbing, brutalization, illusion (most of the bodies, after all, turn out to be those of civilians), grotesque competition (companies and individuals vie for the highest body counts), and equally grotesque technicizing (progress lies in the *count*) characteristic of the overall American crime of war in Vietnam.

My Lai is rather unusual in one respect. It combines two kinds of atrocity: technological overkill (of unarmed peasants by Americans using automatic weapons), and a more personal, face-to-face gunning-down of victims at point-blank range. This combination lends the incident particular psychic force, however Americans may try to fend off awareness of its implications. A participating GI could characterize My Lai as "just like a Nazi-type thing" (as recorded in Seymour Hersh's book, *My Lai 4*), a characterization made by few if any pilots or crewmen participating in the more technologically distanced killings of larger numbers of Vietnamese civilians from the air.

The sense of being associated with existential evil is new to Americans. This is so partly because such perceptions have been suppressed in other atrocity-producing situations, but also because of the humane elements of American tradition that contribute to a national self-image of opposing, through use of force if necessary, just this kind of "Nazi-type thing." The full effects of the war in Vietnam upon this self-image are at this point unclear. The returns from My Lai are not yet in. Perhaps they never are for atrocity. But I for one worry about a society that seems to absorb, with some questioning but without fundamental self-examination, first Hiroshima and now My Lai.

For there is always a cost. Atrocities have a way of coming home. The killings by National Guardsmen of Kent State students protesting the extension of the war in Cambodia reflect the use of violence in defense of illusion and denial of evil—and the killings of blacks at Augusta, Georgia, and of black students at Jackson State in Mississippi reflect more indirectly that atmosphere. Indeed there is a real danger that the impulse to preserve illusion and deny evil could carry America beyond Vietnam and Cambodia into some form of world-destroying nuclear confrontation. In this sense, as well as in its relationship to existential evil, My Lai symbolized a shaking of the American foundations—a bitterly mocking perversion of what was left of the American dream. Like Hiroshima and Auschwitz, My Lai is a revolutionary event: its total inversion of moral standards raises fundamental questions about the institutions and national practices of the nation responsible for it.

The problem facing Americans now is, What do we do with our atrocities? Do we simply try our best to absorb them by a kind of half-admission which denies their implications and prevents genuine confrontation? That is the classical method of governments for dealing with documented atrocities, and it is clearly the method now being used by the United States Government and military in its legal trials of individuals. Those who did the shooting and those who covered up the event are being labeled aberrant and negligent, so that the larger truth of the atrocity-producing situation can be avoided. The award of a Pulitzer Prize to Seymour Hersh for his journalistic feat in uncovering the story of My Lai and telling it in detail would seem to be a step in the direction of that larger truth. Yet one cannot but fear that such an award—as in the case of the National Book Award I received for my work on Hiroshima—can serve as a form of conscience-salving, token recognition in place of confrontation. Surely more must be faced throughout American society, more must be articulated and given form by leaders and ordinary people, if this atrocity is to contribute to a national process of illumination instead of merely one of further degradation.

I am struck by how little my own profession has had to say about the matter—about the way in which aberrant *situations* can produce collective disturbance and mass murder. The psychiatry and psychohistory I would like to envisage for the future would put such matters at its center. That ideal profession would also encourage its practitioners to combine ethical involvement with professional skills in ways that could simultaneously shed light upon such crimes of war and contribute to the transformation our country so desperately requires. In dealing with our dislocations we need to replace the false witness of atrocity with the genuine witness of new and liberating forms and directions. The task, then, is to confront atrocity in order to move beyond it.

A Legal
Framework

International law has evolved over several centuries a set of minimum rules governing the conduct of warfare. These rules were accepted as limits upon the concept of military necessity and were enforced by military commissions against violators. More recently, actually since the efforts at the end of World War I to prosecute Kaiser Wilhelm as a war criminal, there has been a growing set of demands that political leaders responsible for the violation of the laws of war be prosecuted as war criminals.

In 1928 the United States took the lead in organizing a treaty to prohibit recourse to war except in situations of self-defense. The Kellogg-Briand Pact made it illegal to wage aggressive war, and this legal development served as the foundation for the indictment of German and Japanese political and military leaders for war crimes at the end of World War II. The Nuremberg Judgment stands, above all, for the proposition that "the supreme crime" is to wage an aggressive war against another country.

In this section we have collected some of the formal material bearing on the growth of criminal responsibility in relation both to the *conduct of warfare* and *recourse to war*.

The Declaration of St. Petersburg in 1868 was made by the principal European governments. Note the concern with the prohibition of weapons of war that cause unnecessary suffering to their victims.

THE DECLARATION OF ST. PETERSBURG, 1868

On the proposition of the Imperial Cabinet of Russia, an International Military Commission having assembled at St. Petersburg in order to examine into the expediency of forbidding the use of certain projectiles in time of war between civilized nations, and that Commission, having by common agreement fixed the technical limits at which the necessities of war ought to yield to the requirements of humanity, the Undersigned are authorized by the orders of their Governments to declare as follows:

Considering that the progress of civilization should have

the effect of alleviating as much as possible the calamities of war;

That the only legitimate object which States should endeavor to accomplish during war is to weaken the military forces of the enemy;

That for this purpose it is sufficient to disable the greatest possible number of men;

That this object would be exceeded by the employment of arms which uselessly aggravate the sufferings of disabled men, or render their death inevitable;

That the employment of such arms would, therefore, be contrary to the laws of humanity;

The Contracting Parties engage mutually to renounce, in case of war among themselves, the employment by their military or naval troops of any projectile of a weight below 400 grammes, which is either explosive or charged with fulminating or inflammable substances. . . .

The Hague Conventions of 1899 and 1907 were the outcome of diplomatic conferences that attracted great attention. These various treaties created a comprehensive basis for a modern law of war, embodying the main precepts of prior uncodified state practice that had in many instances attained the status of customary international law. The main ideas underlying the Hague approach were to work out rules and procedures that would eliminate *unnecessary suffering* by participants in war (e.g., by providing for humane treatment, based on mutuality, for prisoners and wounded soldiers) and maintain, to the extent possible, the immunity of noncombatants and of nonmilitary targets.

Modern military technology (bombardment, submarine warfare, blockade) and doctrine ("total war") placed growing pressure on the Hague approach. Nevertheless, the norms and standards embodied in the Hague Conventions are still binding as treaty rules, except to the extent that later treaties have taken their place (e.g., Geneva Conventions of 1949) and are a valuable insight into ideas of limits on permissible conduct of war that prevailed at an earlier time in world affairs. Note that rules making behavior by *governments illegal* should not be confused with rules making certain kinds of violations of law a matter of *individual criminal responsibility*.

HAGUE CONVENTION ON LAND WARFARE, 1907

His Majesty the German Emperor, King of Prussia; [etc.]:

Seeing that, while seeking means to preserve peace and prevent armed conflicts between nations, it is likewise necessary to bear in mind the case where the appeal to arms has been brought about by events which their care was unable to avert;

Animated by the desire to serve, even in this extreme case, the interests of humanity and the ever progressive needs of civilization;

Thinking it important, with this object, to revise the general laws and customs of war, either with a view to defining them with greater precision or to confining them within such limits as would mitigate their severity as far as possible;

Have deemed it necessary to complete and explain in certain particulars the work of the First Peace Conference, which, following on the Brussels Conference of 1874, and inspired by the ideas dictated by a wise and generous forethought, adopted provisions intended to define and govern the usages of war on land.

According to the views of the high contracting Parties, these provisions, the wording of which has been inspired by the desire to diminish the evils of war, as far as military requirements permit, are intended to serve as a general rule of conduct for the belligerents in their mutual relations and in their relations with the inhabitants.

It has not, however, been found possible at present to concert regulations covering all the circumstances which arise in practice;

On the other hand, the high contracting Parties clearly do not intend that unforeseen cases should, in the absence of a written undertaking, be left to the arbitrary judgment of military commanders.

Until a more complete code of the laws of war has been issued, the high contracting Parties deem it expedient to declare that, in cases not included in the Regulations adopted by them, the inhabitants and the belligerents remain under the protection and the rule of the principles of the law of nations, as they result from the usages established among civilized peoples, from the laws of humanity, and the dictates of the public conscience.

They declare that it is in this sense especially that Articles 1 and 2 of the Regulations adopted must be understood.

The high contracting Parties, wishing to conclude a *fresh* Convention to this effect, have appointed the following as their plenipotentiaries:

[Here follow the names of plenipotentiaries.]

Who, after having deposited their full powers, found in good and due form, have agreed upon the following:

ARTICLE 1

The contracting Powers shall issue instructions to their armed land forces which shall be in conformity with the Regulations respecting the laws and customs of war on land, annexed to the present Convention.

ARTICLE 2

The provisions contained in the Regulations referred to in Article 1, as well as in the present Convention, do not apply except between contracting Powers, and then only if all the belligerents are parties to the Convention.

ARTICLE 3

A belligerent party which violates the provisions of the said Regulations shall, if the case demands, be liable to pay compensation. It shall be responsible for all acts committed by persons forming part of its armed forces.

ARTICLE 4

The present Convention, duly ratified, shall as between the contracting Powers, be substituted for the Convention of the 29th July, 1899, respecting the laws and customs of war on land.

The Convention of 1899 remains in force as between the Powers which signed it, and which do not also ratify the present Convention. . . .

REGULATIONS RESPECTING THE LAWS AND CUSTOMS OF WAR ON LAND
SECTION I.—ON BELLIGERENTS
CHAPTER I.—THE QUALIFICATIONS OF BELLIGERENTS

ARTICLE 1

The laws, rights, and duties of war apply not only to armies, but also to militia and volunteer corps fulfilling the following conditions:

1. To be commanded by a person responsible for his subordinates;

2. To have a fixed distinctive emblem recognizable at a distance;

3. To carry arms openly; and

4. To conduct their operations in accordance with the laws and customs of war.

In countries where militia or volunteer corps constitute the army, or form part of it, they are included under the denomination "army."

ARTICLE 2

The inhabitants of a territory which has not been occupied, who, on the approach of the enemy, spontaneously take up arms to resist the invading troops without having had time to organize themselves in accordance with Article 1, shall be regarded as belligerents if they carry arms openly and if they respect the laws and customs of war.

ARTICLE 3

The armed forces of the belligerent parties may consist of combatants and non-combatants. In the case of capture by the enemy, both have a right to be treated as prisoners of war.

CHAPTER II.—PRISONERS OF WAR

ARTICLE 4

Prisoners of war are in the power of the hostile Government, but not of the individuals or corps who capture them.

They must be humanely treated.

All their personal belongings, except arms, horses, and military papers, remain their property.

ARTICLE 5

Prisoners of war may be interned in a town, fortress, camp, or other place, and bound not to go beyond certain fixed limits; but they can not be confined except as an indispensable measure of safety and only while the circumstances which necessitate the measure continue to exist. . . .

ARTICLE 8

Prisoners of war shall be subject to the laws, regulations, and orders in force in the army of the State in whose power they are. Any act of insubordination justifies the adoption towards them of such measures of severity as may be considered necessary.

Escaped prisoners who are retaken before being able to rejoin their own army or before leaving the territory occupied by the army which captured them are liable to disciplinary punishment.

Prisoners who, after succeeding in escaping, are again taken prisoners, are not liable to any punishment on account of the previous flight. . . .

SECTION II.—HOSTILITIES

CHAPTER I.—MEANS OF INJURING THE ENEMY, SIEGES, AND BOMBARDMENTS

ARTICLE 22

The right of belligerents to adopt means of injuring the enemy is not unlimited.

ARTICLE 23

In addition to the prohibitions provided by special Conventions, it is especially forbidden—

(a.) To employ poison or poisoned weapons;

(b.) To kill or wound treacherously individuals belonging to the hostile nation or army;

(c.) To kill or wound an enemy who, having laid down his arms, or having no longer means of defence, has surrendered at discretion;

(d.) To declare that no quarter will be given;

(e.) To employ arms, projectiles, or material calculated to cause unnecessary suffering;

(f.) To make improper use of a flag of truce, of the national flag or of the military insignia and uniform of the enemy, as well as the distinctive badges of the Geneva Convention;

(g.) To destroy or seize the enemy's property, unless such

destruction or seizure be imperatively demanded by the necessities of war;

(*h.*) To declare abolished, suspended, or inadmissible in a court of law the rights and actions of the nationals of the hostile party.

A belligerent is likewise forbidden to compel the nationals of the hostile party to take part in the operations of war directed against their own country, even if they were in the belligerent's service before the commencement of the war.

ARTICLE 24

Ruses of war and the employment of measures necessary for obtaining information about the enemy and the country are considered permissible.

ARTICLE 25

The attack or bombardment, by whatever means, of towns, villages, dwellings, or buildings which are undefended is prohibited.

ARTICLE 26

The officer in command of an attacking force must, before commencing a bombardment, except in cases of assault, do all in his power to warn the authorities.

ARTICLE 27

In sieges and bombardments all necessary steps must be taken to spare, as far as possible, buildings dedicated to religion, art, science, or charitable purposes, historic monuments, hospitals, and places where the sick and wounded are collected, provided they are not being used at the time for military purposes.

It is the duty of the besieged to indicate the presence of such buildings or places by distinctive and visible signs, which shall be notified to the enemy beforehand.

ARTICLE 28

The pillage of a town or place, even when taken by assault, is prohibited. . . .

The Versailles Treaty at the end of World War I imposed on Germany responsibility for the war. Germany was restricted in its freedom of action, German society was expected to pay reparations as an expression of its collective responsibility, and Kaiser Wilhelm—if he had been captured—was to have been prosecuted as a war criminal. The Versailles solution has often been criticized as causing resentment in Germany that was part of the climate conducive to the rise of Nazism and the embrace of a foreign policy based on military conquest and racial superiority.

VERSAILLES TREATY, 1918: PROVISIONS ON REPARATIONS AND FOR SANCTIONS ON KAISER WILHELM II

The Allied and Associated Powers publicly arraign William II of Hohenzollern, formerly German Emperor, for a supreme offence against international morality and the sanctity of treaties.

A special tribunal will be constituted to try the accused, thereby assuring him the guarantees essential to the right of defence. It will be composed of five judges, one appointed by each of the following Powers: namely, the United States of America, Great Britain, France, Italy and Japan.

In its decision the tribunal will be guided by the highest motives of international policy, with a view to vindicating the solemn obligations of international undertakings and the validity of international morality. It will be its duty to fix the punishment which it considers should be imposed.

The Allied and Associated Powers will address a request to the Government of the Netherlands for the surrender to them of the ex-Emperor in order that he may be put on trial.

The German Government recognizes the right of the Allied and Associated Powers to bring before military tribunals persons accused of having committed acts in violation of the laws and customs of war. Such persons shall, if found guilty, be sentenced to punishments laid down by law. This provision will apply notwithstanding any proceedings or prosecution before a tribunal in Germany or in the territory of her allies.

The German Government shall hand over to the Allied and Associated Powers, or to such one of them as shall so request, all persons accused of having committed an act in violation of the laws and customs of war, who are specified either by name or by the rank, office or employment which they held under the German authorities.

Persons guilty of criminal acts against the nationals of one of the Allied and Associated Powers will be brought before the military tribunals of that Power.

Persons guilty of criminal acts against the nationals of more than one of the Allied and Associated Powers will be brought before military tribunals composed of members of the military tribunals of the Powers concerned.

In every case the accused will be entitled to name his own counsel.

The German Government undertakes to furnish all documents and information of every kind, the production of which may be considered necessary to ensure the full knowledge of the incriminating acts, the discovery of offenders and the just appreciation of responsibility.

The Allied and Associated Governments affirm and Germany accepts the responsibility of Germany and her allies for causing all the loss and damage to which the Allied and Associated Governments and their nationals have been subjected as a consequence of the war imposed upon them by the aggression of Germany and her allies.

The Geneva Protocol represents an early repudiation of poison gas as a legitimate weapon of war. The United States has not yet ratified this treaty, although President Nixon, in November, 1969 (see statement below), recommended that the United States Senate give its consent to the ratification of the Geneva Protocol. A controversial question is whether the Protocol covers nonlethal poison gases and herbicides such as have been extensively relied upon by the United States throughout the Vietnam War.

GENEVA PROTOCOL ON POISON GAS
AND BACTERIOLOGICAL WARFARE, 1925

The undersigned plenipotentiaries, in the name of their respective Governments:

Whereas the use in war of asphyxiating, poisonous or other gases, and of all analogous liquids materials or devices, has been justly condemned by the general opinion of the civilized world; and

Whereas the prohibition of such use has been declared in Treaties to which the majority of Powers of the world are Parties; and

To the end that this prohibition shall be universally accepted as a part of International Law, binding alike the conscience and the practice of nations;

DECLARE:

That the High Contracting Parties, so far as they are not already Parties to Treaties prohibiting such use, accept this prohibition, agree to extend this prohibition to the use of bacteriological methods of warfare and agree to be bound as between themselves according to the terms of this declaration.

The High Contracting Parties will exert every effort to induce other States to accede to the present Protocol. Such accession will be notified to the Government of the French Republic, and by the latter to all signatory and acceding Powers, and will take effect on the date of the notification by the Government of the French Republic.

The present Protocol, of which the French and English texts are both authentic, shall be ratified as soon as possible. It shall bear today's date.

The ratifications of the present Protocol shall be addressed to the Government of the French Republic, which will at once notify the deposit of such ratification to each of the signatory and acceding Powers.

The Kellogg-Briand Pact of 1928 is the most fundamental norm underlying the movement to punish wars of aggression as international crimes. It has not been possible, despite many attempts, to reach an agreed definition of what constitutes "aggression" or "self-defense." Some critics of the war crimes approach to political leaders have argued that this failure of definition makes it highly arbitrary to impose responsibility on leaders of defeated nations.

THE PACT OF PARIS (KELLOGG-BRIAND PACT), 1928

The President of the German Reich, the President of the United States of America, His Majesty the King of the Belgians, the President of the French Republic, His Majesty the King of Great Britain, Ireland and the British Dominions beyond the Seas, Emperor of India, His Majesty the King of Italy, His Majesty the Emperor of Japan, the President of the Republic of Poland, the President of the Czechoslovak Republic,

Deeply sensible of their solemn duty to promote the welfare of mankind;

Persuaded that the time has come when a frank renunciation of war as an instrument of national policy should be made to the end that the peaceful and friendly relations now existing between their peoples may be perpetuated;

Convinced that all changes in their relations with one another should be sought only by pacific means and be the result of a peaceful and orderly process, and that any signatory Power which shall hereafter seek to promote its national interests by resort to war should be denied the benefits furnished by this Treaty;

Hopeful that, encouraged by their example, all the other nations of the world will join in this humane endeavor and by adhering to the present Treaty as soon as it comes into force bring their peoples within the scope of its beneficent provisions, thus uniting the civilized nations of the world in a common renunciation of war as an instrument of their national policy; . . . .

ARTICLE I

The High Contracting Parties solemnly declare in the names of their respective peoples that they condemn recourse to war for the solution of international controversies, and renounce it as an instrument of national policy in their relations with one another.

ARTICLE II

The High Contracting Parties agree that the settlement or solution of all disputes or conflicts of whatever nature or of whatever origin they may be, which may arise among them, shall never be sought except by pacific means.

ARTICLE III

The present Treaty shall be ratified by the High Contracting Parties named in the Preamble in accordance with their respective constitutional requirements, and shall take effect as between them as soon as all their several instruments of ratification shall have been deposited at Washington.

This Treaty shall, when it has come into effect as prescribed in the preceding paragraph, remain open as long as may be necessary for adherence by all the other Powers of the world. Every instrument evidencing the adherence of a Power shall be deposited at Washington and the Treaty shall immediately upon such deposit become effective as between the Power thus adhering and the other Powers parties hereto.

It shall be the duty of the Government of the United States to furnish each Government named in the Preamble and every Government subsequently adhering to this Treaty with a certified copy of the Treaty and of every instrument of ratification or adherence. It shall also be the duty of the Government of the United States telegraphically to notify such Governments immediately upon the deposit with it of each instrument of ratification or adherence.

In faith whereof the respective Plenipotentiaries have signed this Treaty in the French and English languages both texts having equal force, and hereunto affix their seals.

Done at Paris, the twenty-seventh day of August in the year one thousand nine hundred and twenty-eight.

The Geneva Conventions of 1949 attempted to update and make systematic the humanitarian side of the law of war. The four separate conventions deal with the treatment of prisoners, the protection of civilians, and the rendering of help to wounded soldiers, and were negotiated without publicity by technical experts. In this respect, the Geneva Conventions should be contrasted with the Hague Conventions, which were regarded at the time as major political events. Article 3 is common to the four Geneva Conventions and represents an effort to extend some coverage of humanitarian international law to conditions of civil war, that is, to warfare in which the opposing parties may not be governments of separate sovereign states. This is an important rule, especially as warfare in the nuclear age tends so often to take the form of internal struggles for political control.

PROVISIONS FROM THE GENEVA CONVENTIONS ON THE LAW OF WAR, 1949

ARTICLE 3

In the case of armed conflict not of an international character occurring in the territory of one of the High Contracting Parties, each Party to the conflict shall be bound to apply, as a minimum, the following provisions:

(1) Persons taking no active part in the hostilities, including members of armed forces who have laid down their arms and those placed *hors de combat* by sickness, wounds, detention, or any other cause, shall in all circumstances be treated humanely, without any adverse distinction founded on race, color, religion or faith, sex, birth or wealth, or any other similar criteria.

To this end the following acts are and shall remain prohibited at any time and in any place whatsoever with respect to the above-mentioned persons:

(a) violence to life and person, in particular murder of all kinds, mutilation, cruel treatment and torture;

    (*b*) taking of hostages;

    (*c*) outrages upon personal dignity, in particular humiliating and degrading treatment;

    (*d*) the passing of sentences and the carrying out of executions without previous judgment pronounced by a regularly constituted court, affording all the judicial guarantees which are recognised as indispensable by civilized peoples.

(2) The wounded and sick shall be collected and cared for.

An impartial humanitarian body, such as the International Committee of the Red Cross, may offer its services to the Parties to the conflict.

The Parties to the conflict should further endeavour to bring into force, by means of special agreements, all or part of the other provisions of the present Convention.

The application of the preceding provisions shall not affect the legal status of the Parties to the conflict.

The Genocide Convention of 1949 is a direct result of the German treatment of the Jews during World War II. It is notable in its prohibition of behavior by a government against its own population. In this sense, South Africa's treatment of its black population seems genocidal, as did the efforts by the Lon Nol regime to organize the destruction of ethnic Vietnamese citizens living in Cambodia. Some observers have called counterinsurgency warfare genocidal if practiced on a large scale in a Third World country (see Sartre selection, page 534).

THE GENOCIDE CONVENTION, 1949

The Contracting Parties,

Having considered the declaration made by the General Assembly of the United Nations in its resolution 96 (I) dated 11 December 1946 that genocide is a crime under international law, contrary to the spirit and aims of the United Nations and condemned by the civilized world;

Recognizing that at all periods of history genocide has inflicted great losses on humanity; and

Being convinced that, in order to liberate mankind from such an odious scourge, international co-operation is required:

Hereby agree as hereinafter provided:

Article I

The Contracting Parties confirm that genocide, whether committed in time of peace or in time of war, is a crime under international law which they undertake to prevent and to punish.

ARTICLE II

In the present Convention, genocide means any of the following acts committed with intent to destroy, in whole or in part, a national, ethical, racial or religious group, as such:

(*a*) Killing members of the group;

(*b*) Causing serious bodily or mental harm to members of the group;

(*c*) Deliberately inflicting on the group conditions of life calculated to bring about its physical destruction in whole or in part;

(*d*) Imposing measures intended to prevent births within the group;

(*e*) Forcibly transferring children of the group to another group.

ARTICLE III

The following acts shall be punishable:

(*a*) Genocide;

(*b*) Conspiracy to commit genocide;

(*c*) Direct and public incitement to commit genocide;

(*d*) Attempt to commit genocide;

(*e*) Complicity in genocide.

ARTICLE IV

Persons committing genocide or any of the other acts of enumerated in article III shall be punished, whether they are constitutionally responsible rulers, public officials or private individuals.

ARTICLE V

The Contracting Parties undertake to enact, in accordance with their respective Constitutions, the necessary legislation to give effect to the provisions of the present Convention and, in particular, to provide effective penalties for persons guilty of genocide or any of the other acts enumerated in article III.

ARTICLE VI

Persons charged with genocide or any of the other acts enumerated in article III shall be tried by a competent tribunal of the State in the territory of which the act was committed, or by such international penal tribunal as may have jurisdiction with respect to those Contracting Parties which shall have accepted its jurisdiction.

ARTICLE VII

Genocide and the other acts enumerated in article III shall not be considered as political crimes for the purpose of extradition.

The Contracting Parties pledge themselves in such cases to grant extradition in accordance with their laws and treaties in force.

ARTICLE VIII

Any Contracting Party may call upon the competent organs of the United Nations to take such action under the Charter of the United Nations as they consider appropriate for the prevention and suppression of acts of genocide or any of the other acts enumerated in article III.

ARTICLE IX

Disputes between the Contracting Parties relating to the interpretation, application or fulfilment of the present Convention, including those relating to the responsibility of a State for genocide or any of the other acts enumerated in article III, shall be submitted to the International Court of Justice at the request of any of the parties to the dispute.

ARTICLE X

The present Convention, of which the Chinese, English, French, Russian and Spanish texts are equally authentic, shall bear the date of . . .

ARTICLE XI

The present Convention shall be open until 31 December 1949 for signature on behalf of any Member of the United Nations and of any non-member State to which an invitation to sign has been addressed by the General Assembly.

The present Convention shall be ratified, and the instruments of ratification shall be deposited with the Secretary-General of the United Nations.

After 1 January 1950, the present Convention may be acceded to on behalf of any Member of the United Nations and of any non-member State which has received an invitation as aforesaid.

Instruments of accession shall be deposited with the Secretary-General of the United Nations.

ARTICLE XII

Any Contracting Party may at any time, by notification addressed to the Secretary-General of the United Nations, extend the application of the present Convention to all or any of the territories for the conduct of whose foreign relations that Contracting Party is responsible.

ARTICLE XIII

On the day when the first twenty instruments of ratification or accession have been deposited, the Secretary-General shall draw up a *procès-verbal* and transmit a copy of it to each Member of the United Nations and to each of the non-member States contemplated in article XI.

The present Convention shall come into force on the ninetieth day following the date of deposit of the twentieth instrument of ratification or accession.

Any ratification or accession effected subsequent to the latter date shall become effective on the ninetieth day following the deposit of the instrument of ratification or accession.

ARTICLE XIV

The present Convention shall remain in effect for a period of ten years as from the date of its coming into force.

It shall thereafter remain in force for successive periods of five years for such Contracting Parties as have not denounced it at least six months before the expiration of the current period.

Denunciation shall be effected by a written notification addressed to the Secretary-General of the United Nations.

ARTICLE XV

If, as a result of denunciations, the number of Parties to the present Convention should become less than sixteen, the Convention shall cease to be in force as from the date on which the last of these denunciations shall become effective.

ARTICLE XVI

A request for the revision of the present Convention may be made at any time by any Contracting Party by means of a notification in writing addressed to the Secretary-General.

The General Assembly shall decide upon the steps, if any, to be taken in respect of such request.

ARTICLE XVII

The Secretary-General of the United Nations shall notify all Members of the United Nations and the non-member States contemplated in article XI of the following:

(a) Signatures, ratifications and accessions received in accordance with article XI;

(b) Notifications received in accordance with article XII;

(c) The date upon which the present Convention comes into force in accordance with article XIII;

(d) Denunciations received in accordance with article XIV;

(e) The abrogation of the Convention in accordance with article XV;

(f) Notifications received in accordance with article XVI.

ARTICLE XVIII

The original of the present Convention shall be deposited in the archives of the United Nations.

A certified copy of the Convention shall be transmitted to all Members of the United Nations and to the non-member States contemplated in article XI.

ARTICLE XIX

The present Convention shall be registered by the Secretary-General of the United Nations on the date of its coming into force.

B

Resolution relating to the study by the International Law Commission of the question of an international criminal jurisdiction

The General Assembly,

Considering that the discussion of the Convention on the Prevention and Punishment of the Crime of Genocide has raised the question of the desirability and possibility of having persons charged with genocide tried by a competent international tribunal,

Considering that, in the course of development of the international community, there will be an increasing need of an international judicial organ for the trial of certain crimes under international law,

Invites the International Law Commission to study the desirability and possibility of establishing an international judicial organ for the trial of persons charged with genocide or other crimes over which jurisdiction will be conferred upon that organ by international conventions;

Requests the International Law Commission in carrying out this task to pay attention to the possibility of establishing a Criminal Chamber of the International Court of Justice.

The next selection is a resolution passed by the UN General Assembly declaring that the use of nuclear weapons would be a violation of the Charter and a crime against mankind. These weapons were used against Hiroshima and Nagasaki at the end of World War II, but did not lead to any criminal indictments. It seems reasonable to assume that if Germany, rather than the United States, had dropped atomic bombs on populated states, then the German defendants would have been held criminally responsible. Five survivors of Hiroshima did persuade a Japanese district court to hold that the atomic attack violated international law. This decision—known as the *Shimoda* case—is one of the major documents of the nuclear age.* Incidentally, the United States voted against this resolution in the General Assembly and has opposed efforts to withdraw legitimacy from nuclear weapons. A resolution of the General Assembly can be regarded in different ways, as a mere recommendation of the organ or as an expression of the legislative mood of the organized international community.

GENERAL ASSEMBLY RESOLUTION 1653 (XVI) ON THE PROHIBITION OF NUCLEAR WARFARE, 1961

The General Assembly,

Mindful of its responsibility under the Charter of the United Nations in the maintenance of international peace and security, as well as in the consideration of principles governing disarmament,

Gravely concerned that, while negotiations on disarmament have not so far achieved satisfactory results, the armaments race, particularly in the nuclear and thermo-nuclear fields, has reached a dangerous stage requiring all possible precautionary measures to protect humanity and civilization from the hazard of nuclear and thermo-nuclear catastrophe,

Recalling that the use of weapons of mass destruction, causing unnecessary human suffering, was in the past prohibited, as being contrary to the laws of humanity and to the principles of international law, by international declarations and binding agreements, such as the Declaration of St. Petersburg of

* For text see Falk and Mendlovitz, eds., *The Strategy of World Order*, Vol. I, pp. 314–359.

1868, the Declaration of the Brussels Conference of 1874, the Conventions of The Hague Peace Conferences of 1899 and 1907, and the Geneva Protocol of 1925, to which the majority of nations are still parties,

Considering that the use of nuclear and thermo-nuclear weapons would bring about indiscriminate suffering and destruction to mankind and civilization to an even greater extent than the use of those weapons declared by the aforementioned international declarations and agreements to be contrary to the laws of humanity and a crime under international law,

Believing that the use of weapons of mass destruction, such as nuclear and thermo-nuclear weapons, is a direct negation of the high ideals and objectives which the United Nations has been established to achieve through the protection of succeeding generations from the scourge of war and through the preservation and promotion of their cultures,

1. *Declares that:*

(*a*) The use of nuclear and thermo-nuclear weapons is contrary to the spirit, letter and aims of the United Nations and, as such, a direct violation of the Charter of the United Nations;

(*b*) The use of nuclear and thermo-nuclear weapons would exceed even the scope of war and cause indiscriminate suffering and destruction to mankind and civilization and, as such, is contrary to the rules of international law and to the laws of humanity;

(*c*) The use of nuclear and thermo-nuclear weapons is a war directed not against an enemy or enemies alone but also against mankind in general, since the peoples of the world not involved in such a war will be subjected to all the evils generated by the use of such weapons;

(*d*) Any State using nuclear and thermo-nuclear weapons is to be considered as violating the Charter of the United Nations, as acting contrary to the laws of humanity and as committing a crime against mankind and civilization;

2. *Requests* the Secretary-General to consult the Governments of Member States to ascertain their views on the possi-

bility of convening a special conference for signing a convention on the prohibition of the use of nuclear and thermo-nuclear weapons for war purposes and to report on the results of such consultation to the General Assembly at its seventeenth session.

GENERAL ASSEMBLY RESOLUTION 2603 (XXIV) ON PROHIBITING THE USE OF CHEMICAL AND BIOLOGICAL METHODS OF WARFARE

THE GENERAL ASSEMBLY,

Considering that chemical and biological methods of warfare have always been viewed with horror and been justly condemned by the international community,

Considering that these methods of warfare are inherently reprehensible, because their effects are often uncontrollable and unpredictable and may be injurious without distinction to combatants and non-combatants and because any use would detail a serious risk of escalation,

Recalling that successive international instruments have prohibited or sought to prevent the use of such methods of warfare,

Noting specifically in this regard:

(*a*) That the majority of States then in existence adhered to the Protocol for the Prohibition of the Use in War of Asphyxiating, Poisonous or Other Gases, and of Bacteriological Methods of Warfare, signed at Geneva on 17 June 1925,

(*b*) That since then further States have become Parties to that Protocol,

(*c*) That yet other States have declared that they will abide by its principles and objectives,

(*d*) That these principles and objectives have commanded broad respect in the practice of States,

(*e*) That the General Assembly, without any dissenting vote, has called for the strict observance by all States of the principles and objectives of the Geneva Protocol,

Recognizing therefore, in the light of all the above circumstances, that the Geneva Protocol embodies the generally recognized rules of international law prohibiting the use in international armed conflicts of all biological and chemical methods of warfare, regardless of any technical developments,

Mindful of the report of the Group of Experts, appointed by the Secretary-General under General Assembly resolution 2454 A (XXIII) of 20 December 1968, on chemical and bacteriological (biological) weapons and the effects of their possible use,

Considering that this report and the foreword to it by the Secretary-General add further urgency for an affirmation of these rules and for dispelling, for the future, any uncertainty as to their scope and, by such affirmation, assure the effectiveness of the rules and enable all States to demonstrate their determination to comply with them,

Declares as contrary to the generally recognized rules of international law, as embodied in the Protocol for the Prohibition of the Use in War of Asphyxiating, Poisonous or Other Gases, and of Bacteriological Methods of Warfare, signed at Geneva on 17 June 1925, the use in international armed conflicts of:

(*a*) Any chemical agents of warfare—chemical substances, whether gaseous, liquid or solid—which might be employed because of their direct toxic effects on man, animals or plants;

(*b*) Any biological agents of warfare—living organisms, whatever their nature, or infective material derived from them —which are intended to cause disease or death in man, animals or plants, and which depend for their effects on their ability to multiply in the person, animal or plant attacked.

Mr. Nixon's statement in 1969 should be compared with the U.S. stand on nuclear weapons and with the conduct of the Indochina War. It should also be understood as a positive effort to cap one part of the volcano.

STATEMENT BY PRESIDENT NIXON ON CHEMICAL AND BIOLOGICAL WEAPONS, 1969

Soon after taking office I directed a comprehensive study of our chemical and biological defense policies and programs. There had been no such review in over fifteen years. As a result, objectives and policies in this field were unclear and programs lacked definition and direction.

Under the auspices of the National Security Council, the Departments of State and Defense, the Arms Control and Disarmament Agency, the Office of Science and Technology, the intelligence community, and other agencies worked closely together on this study for over six months. These government efforts were aided by contributions from the scientific community through the President's Scientific Advisory Committee.

This study has now been completed and its findings carefully considered by the National Security Council. I am now reporting the decisions taken on the basis of this review.

Chemical Warfare Program

As to our chemical warfare program, the United States:

—Reaffirms its oft-repeated renunciation of the first use of lethal chemical weapons.

—Extends this renunciation to the first use of incapacitating chemicals.

Consonant with these decisions, the administration will submit to the Senate, for its advice and consent to ratification, the Geneva Protocol of 1925, which prohibits the first use in war of "asphyxiating, poisonous or other gases and of bacteriological methods of warfare." The United States has long supported the principles and objectives of this protocol. We take this step toward formal ratification to reinforce our continuing advocacy of international constraints on the use of these weapons.

Biological Research Program

Biological weapons have massive, unpredictable, and potentially uncontrollable consequences. They may produce global epidemics and impair the health of future generations. I have therefore decided that:

—The United States shall renounce the use of lethal biological agents and weapons and all other methods of biological warfare.

—The United States will confine its biological research to defensive measures, such as immunization and safety measures.

—The Department of Defense has been asked to make recommendations as to the disposal of existing stocks of bacteriological weapons.

In the spirit of these decisions, the United States associates itself with the principles and objectives of the United Kingdom draft convention, which would ban the use of biological methods of warfare. We will seek, however, to clarify specific provisions of the draft to assure that necessary safeguards are included.

The provisions of the U. S. Army Field Manual indicate the extent to which American soldiers are held criminally accountable for compliance with the laws of war. Such provisions are highly relevant to the indictment of men who engage in battlefield atrocities. These provisions do not, however, concern the status of crimes by higher officials who make the decision to initiate warfare and to pursue battlefield tactics. The provisions of the Field Manual, if applied to low-level perpetrators of war crimes, might serve the larger purpose of providing scapegoats for policies whose real architects are allowed to live among us as esteemed citizens, and even leaders.

PROVISIONS FROM THE U. S. ARMY FIELD MANUAL, The Law of Land Warfare, 1956

[Excerpts]

CHAPTER 1 / BASIC RULES AND PRINCIPLES

Section I. GENERAL

1. Purpose and Scope

The purpose of this Manual is to provide authoritative guidance to military personnel on the customary and treaty law applicable to the conduct of warfare on land and to relationships between belligerents and neutral States. Although certain of the legal principles set forth herein have application to warfare at sea and in the air as well as to hostilities on land, this Manual otherwise concerns itself with the rules peculiar to naval and aerial warfare only to the extent that such rules have some direct bearing on the activities of land forces.

This Manual is an official publication of the United States Army. However, those provisions of the Manual which are neither statutes nor the text of treaties to which the United States is a party should not be considered binding upon courts and tribunals applying the law of war. However, such provisions are of evidentiary value insofar as they bear upon questions of custom and practice.

2. Purposes of the Law of War

The conduct of armed hostilities on land is regulated by the law of land warfare which is both written and unwritten. It is inspired by the desire to diminish the evils of war by:

a. Protecting both combatants and noncombatants from unnecessary suffering;

b. Safeguarding certain fundamental human rights of persons who fall into the hands of the enemy, particularly prisoners of war, the wounded and sick, and civilians; and

c. Facilitating the restoration of peace.

3. Basic Principles

a. Prohibitory Effect. The law of war places limits on the exercise of a belligerent's power in the interests mentioned in paragraph 2 and requires that belligerents refrain from employing any kind or degree of violence which is not actually necessary for military purposes and that they conduct hostilities with regard for the principles of humanity and chivalry.

The prohibitory effect of the law of war is not minimized by "military necessity" which has been defined as that principle which justifies those measures not forbidden by international law which are indispensable for securing the complete submission of the enemy as soon as possible. Military necessity has been generally rejected as a defense for acts forbidden by the customary and conventional laws of war inasmuch as the latter have been developed and framed with consideration for the concept of military necessity.

b. Binding on States and Individuals. The law of war is binding not only upon States as such but also upon individuals and, in particular, the members of their armed forces.

4. Sources

The law of war is derived from two principal sources:

a. Lawmaking Treaties (or Conventions), such as the Hague and Geneva Conventions.

b. Custom. Although some of the law of war has not been incorporated in any treaty or convention to which the United States is a party, this body of unwritten or customary law is firmly established by the custom of nations and well defined by recognized authorities on international law.

Lawmaking treaties may be compared with legislative enactments in the national law of the United States and the customary law of war with the unwritten Anglo-American common law. . . .

7. Force of the Law of War

a. Technical Force of Treaties and Position of the United States. Technically, each of the lawmaking treaties regarding the conduct of warfare is, to the extent established by its terms, binding only between the States that have ratified or acceded to, and have not thereafter denounced (withdrawn from), the treaty or convention and is binding only to the extent permitted by the reservations, if any, that have accompanied such ratification or accession on either side. The treaty provisions quoted in this manual in bold-face type are contained in treaties which have been ratified without reservation, except as otherwise noted, by the United States.

These treaty provisions are in large part but formal and specific applications of general principles of the unwritten law. While solemnly obligatory only as between the parties thereto, they may be said also to represent modern international public opinion as to how belligerents and neutrals should conduct themselves in the particulars indicated.

For these reasons, the treaty provisions quoted herein will be strictly observed and enforced by United States forces without regard to whether they are legally binding upon this country. Military commanders will be instructed which, if any, of the written rules herein quoted are not legally binding as between the United States and each of the States immediately concerned, and which, if any, for that reason are not for the time being to be observed or enforced.

b. Force of Treaties Under the Constitution. Under the Constitution of the United States, treaties constitute part of the "supreme Law of the Land" (art. VI, clause 2). In consequence, treaties relating to the law of war have a force equal to that of laws enacted by the Congress. Their provisions must be observed by both military and civilian personnel with the same strict regard for both the letter and spirit of the law which is required with respect to the Constitution and statutes enacted in pursuance thereof.

c. Force of Customary Law. The unwritten or customary law of war is binding upon all nations. It will be strictly observed by United States forces, subject only to such exceptions as shall have been directed by competent authority by way of legitimate reprisals for illegal conduct of the enemy (see par. 497). The customary law of war is part of the law of the United States and, insofar as it is not inconsistent with any treaty to which this country is a party or with a controlling executive or legislative act, is binding upon the United States, citizens of the United States, and other persons serving this country. . . .

CHAPTER 8 / REMEDIES FOR VIOLATION OF INTERNATIONAL LAW; WAR CRIMES

Section II. CRIMES UNDER INTERNATIONAL LAW

498. Crimes Under International Law

Any person, whether a member of the armed forces or a civilian, who commits an act which constitutes a crime under international law is responsible therefor and liable to punishment. Such offenses in connection with war comprise:

    a. Crimes against peace.

    b. Crimes against humanity.

    c. War crimes.

Although this manual recognizes the criminal responsibility of individuals for those offenses which may comprise any of the foregoing types of crimes, members of the armed forces will normally be concerned only with those offenses constituting "war crimes."

499. War Crimes

The term "war crime" is the technical expression for a violation of the law of war by any person or persons, military or civilian. Every violation of the law of war is a war crime.

500. Conspiracy, Incitement, Attempts, and Complicity

Conspiracy, direct incitement, and attempts to commit, as well as complicity in the commission of, crimes against peace, crimes against humanity, and war crimes are punishable.

501. Responsibility for Acts of Subordinates

In some cases, military commanders may be responsible for war crimes committed by subordinate members of the armed forces, or other persons subject to their control. Thus, for instance, when troops commit massacres and atrocities against the civilian population of occupied territory or against prisoners of war, the responsibility may rest not only with the actual perpetrators but also with the commander. Such a responsibility arises directly when the acts in question have been committed in pursuance of an order of the commander concerned. The commander is also responsible if he has actual knowledge, or should have knowledge, through reports received by him or through other means, that troops or other persons subject to his control are about to commit or have committed a war crime and he fails to take the necessary and reasonable steps to insure compliance with the law of war or to punish violators thereof. . . .

Section III. PUNISHMENT OF WAR CRIMES

505. Trials

a. Nature of Proceeding. Any person charged with a war crime has the right to a fair trial on the facts and law.

b. Rights of Accused. Persons accused of "grave breaches" of the Geneva Conventions of 1949 are to be tried under conditions no less favorable than those provided by Article 105 and those following (par. 181 and following) of *GPW (GWS, art. 49; GWS Sea, art. 50; GPW, art. 129; GC, art. 146, 4th par. only; par. 506 herein.)*

c. Rights of Prisoners of War. Pursuant to Article 85, *GPW* (par. 161) , prisoners of war accused of war crimes benefit from the provisions of *GPW,* especially Articles 82–108 (pars. 158–184) .

d. How Jurisdiction Exercised. War crimes are within the jurisdiction of general courts-martial *(UCMJ, Art. 18)* , military commissions, provost courts, military government courts, and other military tribunals *(UCMJ, Art. 21)* of the United States, as well as of international tribunals.

e. Law Applied. As the international law of war is part of the law of the land in the United States, enemy personnel charged with war crimes are tried directly under international law without recourse to the statutes of the United States. However, directives declaratory of international law may be promulgated to assist such tribunals in the performance of their function. (See pars. 506 and 507.)

506. Suppression of War Crimes

a. Geneva Conventions of 1949. The Geneva Conventions of 1949 contain the following common undertakings:

The High Contracting Parties undertake to enact any legislation necessary to provide effective penal sanctions for persons committing, or ordering to be committed, any of the grave breaches of the present Convention defined in the following Article.

Each High Contracting Party shall be under the obligation to search for persons alleged to have committed, or to have ordered to be committed, such grave breaches, and shall bring such persons, regardless of their nationality, before its own courts. It may also, if it prefers, and in accordance with the provisions of its own legislation, hand such persons over for trial to another High Contracting Party concerned, provided such High Contracting Party has made out a *prima facie* case.

Each High Contracting Party shall take measures necessary for the suppression of all acts contrary to the provisions of the present Convention other than the grave breaches defined in the following Article.

In all circumstances, the accused persons shall benefit by safeguards of proper trial and defence, which shall not be less favourable than those provided by Article 105 and those following of the Geneva Convention relative to the Treatment of Prisoners of War of August 12, 1949. (*GWS, art. 49; GWS Sea, art. 50; GPW, art. 129; GC, art. 146.*)

b. Declaratory Character of Above Principles. The principles quoted in *a*, above, are declaratory of the obligations of belligerents under customary international law to take measures for the punishment of war crimes committed by all persons, including members of a belligerent's own armed forces.

c. Grave Breaches. "Grave breaches" of the Geneva Conventions of 1949 and other war crimes which are committed by enemy personnel or persons associated with the enemy are tried and punished by United States tribunals as violations of international law.

If committed by persons subject to United States military law, these "grave breaches" constitute acts punishable under the Uniform Code of Military Justice. Moreover, most of the acts designated as "grave breaches" are, if committed within the United States, violations of domestic law over which the civil courts can exercise jurisdiction.

507. Universality of Jurisdiction

a. Victims of War Crimes. The jurisdiction of United States military tribunals in connection with war crimes is not limited to offenses committed against nationals of the United States but extends also to all offenses of this nature committed against nationals of allies and of cobelligerents and stateless persons.

b. Persons Charged with War Crimes. The United States normally punishes war crimes as such only if they are committed by enemy nationals or by persons serving the interests of the enemy State. Violations of the law of war committed by persons subject to the military law of the United States will usually constitute violations of the Uniform Code of Military Justice and, if so, will be prosecuted under that Code. Violations of the law of war committed within the United States by other persons will usually constitute violations of federal or state criminal law and preferably will be prosecuted under such law (see pars. 505 and 506). Commanding officers of United States troops must insure that war crimes committed by members of their forces against enemy personnel are promptly and adequately punished.

508. Penal Sanctions

The punishment imposed for a violation of the law of war must be proportionate to the gravity of the offense. The death penalty may be imposed for grave breaches of the law. Corporal punishment is excluded. Punishments should be deterrent, and in imposing a sentence of imprisonment it is not necessary to take into consideration the end of the war, which does not of itself limit the imprisonment to be imposed.

509. Defense of Superior Orders

a. The fact that the law of war has been violated pursuant to an order of a superior authority, whether military or civil, does not deprive the act in question of its character of a war crime, nor does it constitute a defense in the trial of an accused individual, unless he did not know and could not reasonably have been expected to know that the act ordered was unlawful. In all cases where the order is held not to constitute a defense to an allegation of war crime, the fact that the individual was acting pursuant to orders may be considered in mitigation of punishment.

b. In considering the question whether a superior order constitutes a valid defense, the court shall take into consideration the fact that obedience to lawful military orders is the duty of every member of the armed forces; that the latter cannot be expected, in conditions of war discipline, to weigh scrupulously the legal merits of the orders received; that certain rules of warfare may be controversial; or that an act otherwise amounting to a war crime may be done in obedience to orders conceived as a measure of reprisal. At the same time it must be borne in mind that members of the armed forces are bound to obey only lawful orders *(e.g., UCMJ, Art. 92)* .

510. Government Officials

The fact that a person who committed an act which constitutes a war crime acted as the head of a State or as a responsible government official does not relieve him from responsibility for his act.

511. Acts Not Punished in Domestic Law

The fact that domestic law does not impose a penalty for an act which constitutes a crime under international law does not relieve the person who committed the act from responsibility under international law.

The whole conception of war crimes gained prominence after World War II when the victorious Allied powers together prosecuted and judged the principal surviving German war leaders at Nuremberg. There has been a revival of interest in the Nuremberg idea since the Vietnam War. North Vietnam threatened at one time to prosecute captured American pilots as war criminals; Bertrand Russell organized a tribunal of inquiry which passed judgment on the American leadership responsible for executing war policies in Vietnam; and draft resisters and other opponents of the war in the United States have generally based their positions, in part at least, on the Nuremberg idea of complicity in a criminal war and in crimes of war.

In this section we offer some central materials arising out of the efforts after World War II to hold leaders of Germany and Japan responsible for war crimes. The questions raised after World War II in relation to war crimes are a very relevant part of the present discussion. The position of the United States Government has changed. After World War II the United States took the lead in urging that the action against the German and Japanese leaders and wrongdoers would create a precedent for the future. What opinions are held today about the wisdom of such a precedent? Who are the criminals? What means are available for their apprehension and punishment?

The first three short selections are all part of the buildup to Nuremberg after World War II. Of particular interest is President Roosevelt's appeal to the German people to collect evidence of war crimes that might be of use in postwar prosecutions.

THE MOSCOW DECLARATION ON GERMAN ATROCITIES, 1943

The United Kingdom, the United States and the Soviet Union have received from many quarters evidence of atrocities, massacres and cold-blooded mass executions which are being perpetrated by the Hitlerite forces in the many countries they have overrun and from which they are now being steadily expelled. The brutalities of Hitlerite domination are no new thing and all the peoples or territories in their grip have suffered from the worst form of government by terror. What is new is that many of these territories are now being redeemed by the advancing armies of the liberating Powers and that in their desperation, the recoiling Hitlerite Huns are redoubling their ruthless cruelties. This is now evidenced with particular clearness by monstrous crimes of the Hitlerites on the territory of the Soviet Union which is being liberated from the Hitlerites, and on French and Italian territory.

Accordingly, the aforesaid three allied Powers, speaking in the interests of the thirty-two [thirty-three] United Nations, hereby solemnly declare and give full warning of their declaration as follows:

At the time of the granting of any armistice to any government which may be set up in Germany, those German officers and men and members of the Nazi party who have been responsible for, or have taken a consenting part in the above atrocities, massacres and executions, will be sent back to the countries in which their abominable deeds were done in order that they may be judged and punished according to the laws of these liberated countries and of the free governments which will be created therein. Lists will be compiled in all possible detail from all these countries having regard especially to the invaded parts of the Soviet Union, to Poland and Czechoslovakia, to Yugoslavia and Greece, including Crete and other islands, to Norway, Denmark, the Netherlands, Belgium, Luxemburg, France and Italy.

Thus, the Germans who take part in wholesale shootings of Italian officers or in the execution of French, Dutch, Belgian or Norwegian hostages or of Cretan peasants, or who have shared in the slaughters inflicted on the people of Poland or in territories of the Soviet Union which are now being swept clear of the enemy, will know that they will be brought back to the scene of their crimes and judged on the spot by the peoples whom they have outraged. Let those who have hitherto not imbrued their hands with innocent blood beware lest they join the ranks of the guilty, for most assuredly the three allied Powers will pursue them to the uttermost ends of the earth and will deliver them to their accusers in order that justice may be done.

The above declaration is without prejudice to the case of the major criminals, whose offences have no particular geographical localisation and who will be punished by the joint decision of the Governments of the Allies.

(Signed) :   Roosevelt

Churchill

Stalin

STATEMENT BY PRESIDENT ROOSEVELT
ON GERMAN WAR CRIMES, 1944

The United Nations are fighting to make a world in which tyranny and aggression cannot exist; a world based upon freedom, equality and justice; a world in which all persons regardless of race, color or creed may live in peace, honor and dignity.

In the meantime in most of Europe and in parts of Asia the systematic torture and murder of civilians—men, women and children—by the Nazis and the Japanese continue unabated. In areas subjugated by the aggressors innocent Poles, Czechs, Norwegians, Dutch, Danes, French, Greeks, Russians, Chinese, Filipinos—and many others—are being starved or frozen to death or murdered in cold blood in a campaign of savagery.

The slaughters of Warsaw, Lidice, Kharkov and Nanking— the brutal torture and murder by the Japanese, not only of civilians but of our own gallant American soldiers and fliers— these are startling examples of what goes on day by day, year in and year out, wherever the Nazis and the Japs are in military control—free to follow their barbaric purpose.

In one of the blackest crimes of all history—begun by the Nazis in the day of peace and multiplied by them a hundred times in time of war—the wholesale systematic murder of the Jews of Europe goes on unabated every hour. As a result of the events of the last few days hundreds of thousands of Jews, who while living under persecution at least found a haven from death in Hungary and the Balkans, are now threatened with annihilation as Hitler's forces descend more heavily upon these lands. That these innocent people, who have already survived a decade of Hitler's fury, should perish on the very eve of triumph over the barbarism which their persecution symbolizes, would be a major tragedy.

It is therefore fitting that we should again proclaim our determination that none who participate in these acts of savagery shall go unpunished. The United Nations have made it clear that they will pursue the guilty and deliver them up in order that Justice be done. That warning applies not only to the leaders but also to their functionaries and subordinates in Germany and in the satellite countries. All who knowingly take part in the deportation of Jews to their death in Poland or Norwegians and French to their death in Germany are equally guilty with the executioner. All who share the guilt shall share the punishment.

Hitler is committing these crimes against humanity in the name of the German people. I ask every German and every man everywhere under Nazi domination to show the world by his action that in his heart he does not share these insane criminal desires. Let him hide these pursued victims, help them to get over their borders, and do what he can to save them from the Nazi hangman. I ask him also to keep watch, and to record the evidence that will one day be used to convict the guilty.

In the meantime, and until the victory that is now assured is won, the United States will persevere in its efforts to rescue the victims of brutality of the Nazis and the Japs. In so far as the necessity of military operations permit this Government will use all means at its command to aid the escape of all intended victims of the Nazi and Jap executioner—regardless of race or religion or color. We call upon the free peoples of Europe and Asia temporarily to open their frontiers to all victims of oppression. We shall find havens of refuge for them, and we shall find the means for their maintenance and support until the tyrant is driven from their homelands and they may return.

In the name of justice and humanity let all freedom loving people rally to this righteous undertaking.

OPENING STATEMENT AT NUREMBERG BY THE CHIEF U. S. PROSECUTOR, JUSTICE ROBERT H. JACKSON, 1945

May it please your honors, the privilege of opening the first trial in history for crimes against the peace of the world imposes a grave responsibility. The wrongs which we seek to condemn and punish have been so calculated, so malignant and so devastating, that civilization cannot tolerate their being ignored because it cannot survive their being repeated. That four great nations, flushed with victory and stung with injury, stay the hand of vengeance and voluntarily submit their captive enemies to the judgment of the law is one of the most significant tributes that Power ever has paid to Reason.

This Tribunal, while it is novel and experimental, is not the product of abstract speculations nor is it created to vindicate legalistic theories. This inquest represents the practical effort of four of the most mighty of nations, with the support of fifteen more, to utilize International Law to meet the greatest menace of our times—aggressive war. The common sense of mankind demands that law shall not stop with the punishment of petty crimes by little people. It must also reach men who possess themselves of great power and make deliberate and concerted use of it to set in motion evils which leave no home in the world untouched. It is a cause of this magnitude that the United Nations will lay before Your Honors.

In the prisoners' dock sit twenty-odd broken men. Reproached by the humiliation of those they have led almost as bitterly as by the desolation of those they have attacked, their personal capacity for evil is forever past. It is hard now to perceive in these miserable men as captives the power by which as Nazi leaders they once dominated much of the world and terrified most of it. Merely as individuals, their fate is of little consequence to the world.

What makes this inquest significant is that these prisoners represent sinister influences that will lurk in the world long after their bodies have returned to dust. They are living symbols of racial hatreds, of terrorism and violence, and of the arrogance and cruelty of power. They are symbols of fierce nationalisms and of militarism, of intrigue and war-making which have embroiled Europe generation after generation, crushing its manhood, destroying its homes, and impoverishing its life. They have so identified themselves with the philosophies they conceived and with the forces they directed that any tenderness to them is a victory and an encouragement to all the evils which are attached to their names. Civilization can afford no compromise with the social forces which would gain renewed strength if we deal ambiguously or indecisively with the men in whom those forces now precariously survive.

What these men stand for we will patiently and temperately disclose. We will give you undeniable proofs of incredible events. The catalogue of crimes will omit nothing that could be conceived by a pathological pride, cruelty, and lust for power. These men created in Germany, under the "Führer-prinzip," a National Socialist despotism equaled only by the dynasties of the ancient East. They took from the German people all those dignities and freedoms that we hold natural and inalienable rights in every human being. The people were compensated by inflaming and gratifying hatreds toward those who were marked as "scapegoats." Against their opponents, including Jews, Catholics, and free labor, the Nazis directed such a campaign of arrogance, brutality, and annihilation as the world has not witnessed since the pre-Christian ages. They excited the German ambition to be a "master race," which of course implies serfdom for others. They led their people on a mad gamble for domination. They diverted social energies and resources to the creation of what they thought to be an invincible war machine. They overran their neighbors. To sustain the "master race" in its war-making, they enslaved millions of human beings and brought them into Germany, where these hapless creatures now wander as "displaced persons." At length bestiality and bad faith reached such excess that they aroused the sleeping strength of imperiled Civilization. Its united efforts have ground the German war machine to fragments. But the struggle has left Europe a liberated yet prostrate land where a demoralized society struggles to survive. These are the fruits of the sinister forces that sit with these defendants in the prisoners' dock.

In justice to the nations and the men associated in this prosecution, I must remind you of certain difficulties which may leave their mark on this case. Never before in legal history has an effort been made to bring within the scope of a single litigation the developments of a decade, covering a whole Continent, and involving a score of nations, countless individuals, and innumerable events. Despite the magnitude of the task, the world has demanded immediate action. This demand has had to be met, though perhaps at the cost of finished craftsmanship. In my country, established courts, following familiar procedures, applying well-thumbed precedents, and dealing with the legal consequences of local and limited events seldom commence a trial within a year of the event in litigation. Yet less than eight months ago today the courtroom in which you sit was an enemy fortress in the hands of German SS troops. Less than eight months ago nearly all our witnesses and documents were in enemy hands. The law had not been codified, no procedures had been established, no Tribunal was in existence, no usable courthouse stood here, none of the hundreds of tons of official German documents had been examined, no prosecuting staff had been assembled, nearly all the present defendants were at large, and the four prosecuting powers had not yet joined in common cause to try them. I should be the last to deny that the case may well suffer from incomplete researches and quite likely will not be the example of professional work which any of the prosecuting nations would normally wish to sponsor. It is, however, a completely adequate case to the judgment we shall ask you to render, and its full development we shall be obliged to leave to historians.

Before I discuss particulars of evidence, some general considerations which may affect the credit of this trial in the eyes of the world should be candidly faced. There is a dramatic disparity between the circumstances of the accusers and of the accused that might discredit our work if we should falter, in even minor matters, in being fair and temperate.

Unfortunately, the nature of these crimes is such that both prosecution and judgment must be by victor nations over vanquished foes. The world-wide scope of the aggressions carried out by these men has left but few real neutrals. Either the victors must judge the vanquished or we must leave the defeated to judge themselves. After the first World War, we learned the futility of the latter course. The former high station of these defendants, the notoriety of their acts, and the adaptability of their conduct to provoke retaliation make it hard to distinguish between the demand for a just and measured retribution, and the unthinking cry for vengeance which arises from the anguish of war. It is our task, so far as humanly possible, to draw the line between the two. We must never forget that the record on which we judge these defendants today is the record on which history will judge us tomorrow. To pass these defendants a poisoned chalice is to put it to our own lips as well. We must summon such detachment and intellectual integrity to our task that this trial will commend itself to posterity as fulfilling humanity's aspirations to do justice.

At the very outset, let us dispose of the contention that to put these men to trial is to do them an injustice entitling them to some special consideration. These defendants may be hard pressed but they are not ill-used. Let us see what alternative they would have to being tried.

More than a majority of these prisoners surrendered to or were tracked down by forces of the United States. Could they expect us to make American custody a shelter for our enemies against the just wrath of our Allies? Did we spend American lives to capture them only to save them from punishment? Under the principles of the Moscow Declaration, those suspected war criminals who are not to be tried internationally must be turned over to individual governments for trial at the scene of their outrages. Many less responsible and less culpable American-held prisoners have been and will be turned over to other United Nations for local trial. If these defendants should succeed, for any reason, in escaping the condemnation of this Tribunal, or if they obstruct or abort this trial, those who are American-held prisoners will be delivered up to our continental Allies. For these defendants, however, we have set up an International Tribunal and have undertaken the burden of participating in a complicated effort to give them fair and dispassionate hearings. That is the best-known protection to any man with a defense worthy of being heard.

If these men are the first war leaders of a defeated nation to be prosecuted in the name of the law, they are also the first to be given a chance to plead for their lives in the name of the law. Realistically, the Charter of this Tribunal, which gives them a hearing, is also the source of their only hope. It may be that these men of troubled conscience, whose only wish is that the world forget them, do not regard a trial as a favor. But they do have a fair opportunity to defend themselves—a favor which these men, when in power, rarely extended to their fellow countrymen. Despite the fact that public opinion already condemns their acts, we agree that here they must be given a presumption of innocence, and we accept the burden of proving criminal acts and the responsibility of these defendants for their commission.

When I say that we do not ask for convictions unless we prove crime, I do not mean mere technical or incidental transgression of international conventions. We charge guilt on planned and intended conduct that involves moral as well as legal wrong. And we do not mean conduct that is a natural and human, even if illegal, cutting of corners, such as many of us might well have committed had we been in the defendants' positions. It is not because they yielded to the normal frailties of human beings that we accuse them. It is their abnormal and inhuman conduct which brings them to this bar.

We will not ask you to convict these men on the testimony of their foes. There is no count of the Indictment that cannot be proved by books and records. The Germans were always meticulous record keepers, and these defendants had their share of the Teutonic passion for thoroughness in putting things on paper. Nor were they without vanity. They arranged frequently to be photographed in action. We will show you their own films. You will see their own conduct and hear their own voices as these defendants re-enact for you, from the screen, some of the events in the course of the conspiracy.

We would also make clear that we have no purpose to incriminate the whole German people. We know that the Nazi Party was not put in power by a majority of the German vote. We know it came to power by an evil alliance between the most extreme of the Nazi revolutionists, the most unrestrained of the German reactionaries, and the most aggressive of the German militarists. If the German populace had willingly accepted the Nazi program, no Stormtroopers would have been needed in the early days of the Party and there would have been no need for concentration camps or the Gestapo, both of which institutions were inaugurated as soon as the Nazis gained control of the German state. Only after these lawless innovations proved successful at home were they taken abroad. . . .

A failure of these Nazis to heed, or to understand the force and meaning of this evolution in the legal thought of the world is not a defense or a mitigation. If anything, it aggravates their offense and makes it the more mandatory that the law they have flouted be vindicated by juridical application to their lawless conduct. Indeed, by their own law—had they heeded any law—these principles were binding on these defendants. Article 4 of the Weimar Constitution provided that "the generally accepted rules of International Law are to be considered as binding integral parts of the law of the German Reich." Can there be any doubt that the outlawry of aggressive war was one of the "generally accepted rules of International Law" in 1939?

Any resort to war—to any kind of a war—is a resort to means that are inherently criminal. War inevitably is a course of killings, assaults, deprivations of liberty, and destruction of property. An honestly defensive war is, of course, legal and saves those lawfully conducting it from criminality. But inherently criminal acts cannot be defended by showing that those who committed them were engaged in a war, when war itself is illegal. The very minimum legal consequence of the treaties making aggressive wars illegal is to strip those who incite or wage them of every defense the law ever gave, and to leave war-makers subject to judgment by the usually accepted principles of the law of crimes.

But if it be thought that the Charter, whose declarations concededly bind us all, does contain new law I still do not shrink from demanding its strict application by this Tribunal. The rule of law in the world, flouted by the lawlessness incited by these defendants, had to be restored at the cost to my country of over a million casualties, not to mention those of other nations. I cannot subscribe to the perverted reasoning that society may advance and strengthen the rule of law by the expenditure of morally innocent lives but that progress in the law may never be made at the price of morally guilty lives.

It is true, of course, that we have no judicial precedent for the Charter. But International Law is more than a scholarly collection of abstract and immutable principles. It is an outgrowth of treaties and agreements between nations and of accepted customs. Yet every custom has its origin in some single act, and every agreement has to be initiated by the action of some state. Unless we are prepared to abandon every principle of growth for International Law, we cannot deny that our own day has the right to institute customs and to conclude agreements that will themselves become sources of a newer and strengthened International Law. International Law is not capable of development by the normal processes of legislation for there is no continuing international legislative authority. Innovations and revisions in International Law are brought about by the action of governments designed to meet a change in circumstances. It grows, as did the Common Law, through decisions reached from time to time in adapting settled principles to new situations. The fact is that when the law evolves by the case method, as did the Common Law and as International Law must do if it is to advance at all, it advances at the expense of those who wrongly guessed the law and learned too late their error. The law, so far as International Law can be decreed, had been clearly pronounced when these acts took place. Hence, I am not disturbed by the lack of judicial precedent for the inquiry we propose to conduct.

The events I have earlier recited clearly fall within the standards of crimes, set out in the Charter, whose perpetrators this Tribunal is convened to judge and punish fittingly. The standards for war crimes and crimes against humanity are too familiar to need comment. There are, however, certain novel problems in applying other precepts of the Charter which I should call to your attention. . . .

The American dream of a peace and plenty economy, as well as the hopes of other nations, can never be fulfilled if those nations are involved in a war every generation so vast and devastating as to crush the generation that fights and burden the generation that follows. But experience has shown that wars are no longer local. All modern wars become world wars eventually. And none of the big nations at least can stay out. If we cannot stay out of wars, our only hope is to prevent wars.

I am too well aware of the weaknesses of juridical action alone to contend that in itself your decision under this Charter can prevent future wars. Judicial action always comes after the event. Wars are started only on the theory and in the confidence that they can be won. Personal punishment, to be suffered only in the event the war is lost, will probably not be a sufficient deterrent to prevent a war where the war-makers feel the chances of defeat to be negligible.

But the ultimate step in avoiding periodic wars, which are inevitable in a system of international lawlessness, is to make statesmen responsible to law. And let me make clear that while this law is first applied against German aggressors, the law includes, and if it is to serve a useful purpose it must condemn, aggression by any other nations, including those which sit here now in judgment. We are able to do away with domestic tyranny and violence and aggression by those in power against the rights of their own people only when we make all men answerable to the law. This trial represents mankind's desperate effort to apply the discipline of the law to statesmen who have used their powers of state to attack the foundations of the world's peace and to commit aggressions against the rights of their neighbors.

The usefulness of this effort to do justice is not to be measured by considering the law or your judgment in isolation. This trial is part of the great effort to make the peace more secure. One step in this direction is the United Nations organization, which may take joint political action to prevent war if possible, and joint military action to insure that any nation which starts a war will lose it. This Charter and this trial, implementing the Kellogg-Briand Pact, constitute another step in the same direction—juridical action of a kind to ensure that those who start a war will pay for it personally.

While the defendants and the prosecutors stand before you as individuals, it is not the triumph of either group alone that is committed to your judgment. Above all personalities there are anonymous and impersonal forces whose conflict makes up much of human history. It is yours to throw the strength of the law back of either the one or the other of these forces for at least another generation. What are the real forces that are contending before you?

No charity can disguise the fact that the forces which these defendants represent, the forces that would advantage and delight in their acquittal, are the darkest and most sinister forces in society—dictatorship and oppression, malevolence and passion, militarism and lawlessness. By their fruits we best know them. Their acts have bathed the world in blood and set civilization back a century. They have subjected their European neighbors to every outrage and torture, every spoliation and deprivation that insolence, cruelty, and greed could inflict. They have brought the German people to the lowest pitch of wretchedness, from which they can entertain no hope of early deliverance. They have stirred hatreds and incited domestic violence on every continent. These are the things that stand the dock shoulder to shoulder with these prisoners.

The real complaining party at your bar is Civilization. In all our countries it is still a struggling and imperfect thing. It does not plead that the United States, or any other country, has been blameless of the conditions which made the German people easy victims to the blandishments and intimidations of the Nazi conspirators.

But it points to the dreadful sequence of aggressions and crimes I have recited, it points to the weariness of flesh, the exhaustion of resources, and the destruction of all that was beautiful or useful in so much of the world, and to greater potentialities for destruction in the days to come. It is not necessary among the ruins of this ancient and beautiful city, with untold members of its civilian inhabitants still buried in its rubble, to argue the proposition that to start or wage an aggressive war has the moral qualities of the worst of crimes. The refuge of the defendants can be only their hope that International Law will lag so far behind the moral sense of mankind that conduct which is crime in the moral sense must be regarded as innocent in law.

Civilization asks whether law is so laggard as to be utterly helpless to deal with crimes of this magnitude by criminals of this order of importance. It does not expect that you can make war impossible. It does expect that your juridical action will put the forces of International Law, its precepts, its prohibitions and, most of all, its sanctions, on the side of peace, so that men and women of good will in all countries may have "leave to live by no man's leave, underneath the law."

The Nuremberg Judgment is the prime document embodying the approach of international law to the problems of war crimes. Note that at Nuremberg the defendants were charged with three categories of crime: (1) war of aggression; (2) war crimes relevant to battlefield conduct; and (3) crimes against humanity (i.e., genocidal acts against the Jews and others). The Tribunal rejected category (3) because no prior legal rules of prohibition were in existence.

THE NUREMBERG JUDGMENT, 1946

[Excerpts]

This indictment charges the defendants with crimes against peace by the planning, preparation, initiation, and waging of wars of aggression, which were also wars in violation of international treaties, agreements, and assurances; with war crimes; and with crimes against humanity. The defendants are also charged with participating in the formulation or execution of a common plan or conspiracy to commit all these crimes. The Tribunal was further asked by the prosecution to declare all the named groups or organizations to be criminal within the meaning of the Charter. . . .

The Tribunal now turns to the consideration of the crimes against peace charged in the indictment. Count one of the indictment charges the defendants with conspiring or having a common plan to commit crimes against peace. Count two of the indictment charges the defendants with committing specific crimes against peace by planning, preparing, initiating, and waging wars of aggression against a number of other States. It will be convenient to consider the question of the existence of a common plan and the question of aggressive war together, and to deal later in this judgment with the question of the individual responsibility of the defendants.

The charges in the indictment that the defendants planned and waged aggressive wars are charges of the utmost gravity. War is essentially an evil thing. Its consequences are not confined to the belligerent states alone, but affect the whole world.

To initiate a war of aggression, therefore, is not only an international crime; it is the supreme international crime differing only from other war crimes in that it contains within itself the accumulated evil of the whole.

The first acts of aggression referred to in the indictment are the seizure of Austria and Czechoslovakia; and the first war of aggression charged in the indictment is the war against Poland begun on the 1st September 1939.

Before examining that charge it is necessary to look more closely at some of the events which preceded these acts of aggression. The war against Poland did not come suddenly out of an otherwise clear sky; the evidence has made it plain that this war of aggression, as well as the seizure of Austria and Czechoslovakia, was premeditated and carefully prepared, and was not undertaken until the moment was thought opportune for it to be carried through as a definite part of the preordained scheme and plan.

For the aggressive designs of the Nazi Government were not accidents arising out of the immediate political situation in Europe and the world; they were a deliberate and essential part of Nazi foreign policy.

From the beginning, the National Socialist movement claimed that its object was to unite the German people in the consciousness of their mission and destiny, based on inherent qualities of race, and under the guidance of the Fuehrer.

For its achievement, two things were deemed to be essential: The disruption of the European order as it had existed since the Treaty of Versailles, and the creation of a Greater Germany beyond the frontiers of 1914. This necessarily involved the seizure of foreign territories.

War was seen to be inevitable, or at the very least, highly probable, if these purposes were to be accomplished. The German people, therefore, with all their resources, were to be organized as a great political-military army, schooled to obey without question any policy decreed by the State. . . .

The invasion of Austria was a premeditated aggressive step in furthering the plan to wage aggressive wars against other countries. As a result Germany's flank was protected, that of Czechoslovakia being greatly weakened. The first step had been taken in the seizure of "Lebensraum"; many new divisions of trained fighting men had been acquired; and with the seizure of foreign exchange reserves the rearmament program had been greatly strengthened. . . .

It was contended before the Tribunal that the annexation of Austria was justified by the strong desire expressed in many quarters for the union of Austria and Germany; that there were many matters in common between the two peoples that made this union desirable; and that in the result the object was achieved without bloodshed.

These matters, even if true, are really immaterial, for the facts plainly prove that the methods employed to achieve the object were those of an aggressor. The ultimate factor was the armed might of Germany ready to be used if any resistance was encountered. Moreover, none of these considerations appear from the Hossbach account of the meetings of the 5th November 1937, to have been the motives which actuated Hitler; on the contrary, all the emphasis is there laid on the advantage to be gained by Germany in her military strength by the annexation of Austria. . . .

The conference of the 5th November 1937, made it quite plain that the seizure of Czechoslovakia by Germany had been definitely decided upon. The only question remaining was the selection of the suitable moment to do it. . . .

On the 31st August 1938, Hitler approved a memorandum by Jodl dated 24th August 1938, concerning the timing of the order for the invasion of Czechoslovakia and the question of defense measures. This memorandum contained the following:

"Operation Gruen will be set in motion by means of an 'incident' in Czechoslovakia, which will give Germany provocation for military intervention. The fixing of the *exact time* for this incident is of the utmost importance."

These facts demonstrate that the occupation of Czechoslovakia had been planned in detail long before the Munich conference.

In the month of September 1938, the conferences and talks with military leaders continued. In view of the extraordinarily critical situation which had arisen, the British Prime Minister, Mr. Chamberlain, flew to Munich and then went to Berchtesgaden to see Hitler. On the 22d September Mr. Chamberlain met Hitler for further discussions at Bad Godesberg. On the 26th September 1938, Hitler said in a speech in Berlin, with reference to his conversation:

"I assured him, moreover, and I repeat it here, that when this problem is solved there will be no more territorial problems for Germany in Europe; and I further assured him that from the moment when Czechoslovakia solves its other problems, that is to say, when the Czechs have come to an arrangement with their other minorities, peacefully and without oppression, I will be no longer interested in the Czech State, and that as far as I am concerned I will guarantee it. We don't want any Czechs."

On the 29th September 1938, after a conference between Hitler and Mussolini and the British and French Prime Ministers in Munich, the Munich Pact was signed, by which Czechoslovakia was required to acquiesce in the cession of the Sudetenland to Germany. The "piece of paper" which the British Prime Minister brought back to London, signed by himself and Hitler, expressed the hope that for the future Britain and Germany might live without war. That Hitler never intended to adhere to the Munich Agreement is shown by the fact that a little later he asked the defendant Keitel for information with regard to the military force which in his opinion would be required to break all Czech resistance in Bohemia and Moravia. Keitel gave his reply on the 11th October 1938. On the 21st October 1938, a directive was issued by Hitler, and countersigned by the defendant Keitel, to the armed forces on their future tasks, which stated:

"Liquidation of the remainder of Czechoslovakia. It must be possible to smash at any time the remainder of Czechoslovakia if her policy should become hostile towards Germany."

On the 14th March 1939, the Czech President Hacha and

his Foreign Minister Chvalkovsky came to Berlin at the suggestion of Hitler, and attended a meeting at which the defendants von Ribbentrop, Goering, and Keitel were present, with others. The proposal was made to Hacha that if he would sign an agreement consenting to the incorporation of the Czech people in the German Reich at once Bohemia and Moravia would be saved from destruction. He was informed that German troops had already received orders to march and that any resistance would be broken with physical force. The defendant Goering added the threat that he would destroy Prague completely from the air. Faced by this dreadful alternative, Hacha and his Foreign Minister put their signature to the necessary agreement at 4:30 in the morning, and Hitler and Ribbentrop signed on behalf of Germany.

On the 15th March, German troops occupied Bohemia and Moravia, and on the 16th March the German decree was issued incorporating Bohemia and Moravia into the Reich as a protectorate, and this decree was signed by the defendants von Ribbentrop and Frick.

By March 1939 the plan to annex Czechoslovakia, which had been discussed by Hitler at the meeting of the 5th November 1937, had been accomplished. The time had now come for the German leaders to consider further acts of aggression, made more possible of attainment because of that accomplishment.

On the 23d May 1939, a meeting was held in Hitler's study in the new Reich Chancellery in Berlin. Hitler announced his decision to attack Poland and gave his reasons, and discussed the effect the decision might have on other countries. . . .

Following the occupation of Bohemia and Moravia by Germany on the 15th March 1939, which was a flagrant breach of the Munich Agreement, Great Britain gave an assurance to Poland on the 31st March 1939, that in the event of any action which clearly threatened Polish independence, and which the Polish Government accordingly considered it vital to resist with their national forces, Great Britain would feel itself bound at once to lend Poland all the support in its power. The French Government took the same stand. It is interesting to note in this connection, that one of the arguments frequently presented by the defense in the present case is that the defendants were induced to think that their conduct was not in breach of international law by the acquiescence of other powers. The declarations of Great Britain and France showed, at least, that this view could be held no longer.

On the 3d April 1939, a revised OKW directive was issued to the armed forces, which after referring to the question of Danzig made reference to Fall Weiss (the military code name for the German invasion of Poland) and stated:

"The Fuehrer has added the following directions to Fall Weiss: (1) Preparations must be made in such a way that the operation can be carried out at any time from the 1st September 1939 onwards. (2) The High Command of the Armed Forces has been directed to draw up a precise timetable for Fall Weiss and to arrange by conferences the synchronized timings between the three branches of the Armed Forces."

On the 11th April 1939, a further directive was signed by Hitler and issued to the armed forces, and in one of the annexes to that document the words occur:

"Quarrels with Poland should be avoided. Should Poland, however, adopt a threatening attitude toward Germany, 'a final settlement' will be necessary, notwithstanding the pact with Poland. The aim is then to destroy Polish military strength, and to create in the east a situation which satisfies the requirements of defense. The Free State of Danzig will be incorporated into Germany at the outbreak of the conflict at the latest. Policy aims at limiting the war to Poland, and this is considered possible in view of the internal crisis in France, and British restraint as a result of this." . . .

After all attempts to persuade Germany to agree to a settlement of her dispute with Poland on a reasonable basis had failed, Hitler, on the 31st August, issued his final directive, in which he announced that the attack on Poland would start in the early morning of the 1st September, and gave instructions as to what action would be taken if Great Britain and France should enter the war in defense of Poland.

In the opinion of the Tribunal, the events of the days immediately preceding the 1st September 1939, demonstrate the determination of Hitler and his associates to carry out the declared intention of invading Poland at all costs, despite appeals from every quarter. With the ever increasing evidence before him that this intention would lead to war with Great Britain and France as well, Hitler was resolved not to depart from the course he had set for himself. The Tribunal is fully satisfied by the evidence that the war initiated by Germany against Poland on the 1st September 1939, was most plainly an aggressive war, which was to develop in due course into a war which embraced almost the whole world, and resulted in the commission of countless crimes, both against the laws and customs of war, and against humanity.

. . . [I]t is clear that as early as October 1939 the question of invading Norway was under consideration. The defense that has been made here is that Germany was compelled to attack Norway to forestall an Allied invasion, and her action was therefore preventive.

It must be remembered that preventive action in foreign territory is justified only in case of "an instant and overwhelming necessity for self-defense leaving no choice of means and no moment of deliberation." (The *Caroline* Case, *Moore's Digest of International Law*, Vol. II, p. 412.) How widely the view was held in influential German circles that the Allies intended to occupy Norway cannot be determined with exactitude. Quisling asserted that the Allies would intervene in Norway with the tacit consent of the Norwegian Government. The German Legation at Oslo disagreed with this view, although the Naval Attaché at that Legation shared it. . . .

[W]hen the plans for an attack on Norway were being made they were not made for the purpose of forestalling an imminent Allied landing, but, at the most, that they might prevent an Allied occupation at some future date.

When the final orders for the German invasion of Norway were given, the diary of the Naval Operations Staff for March 23, 1940, records:

"A mass encroachment by the English into Norwegian territorial waters . . . is not to be expected at the present time."

And Admiral Assmann's entry for March 26 says:

"British landing in Norway not considered serious."

Documents which were subsequently captured by the Germans are relied on to show that the Allied plan to occupy harbors and airports in western Norway was a definite plan, although in all points considerably behind the German plans under which the invasion was actually carried out. These documents indicate that an altered plan had been finally agreed upon on March 20, 1940, that a convoy should leave England on April 5, and that mining in Norwegian waters would begin the same day; and that on April 5 the sailing time had been postponed until April 8. But these plans were not the cause of the German invasion of Norway. Norway was occupied by Germany to afford her bases from which a more effective attack on England and France might be made, pursuant to plans prepared long in advance of the Allied plans which are now relied on to support the argument of self-defense.

It was further argued that Germany alone could decide, in accordance with the reservations made by many of the Signatory Powers at the time of the conclusion of the Kellogg-Briand Pact, whether preventive action was a necessity, and that in making her decision her judgment was conclusive. But whether action taken under the claim of self-defense was in fact aggressive or defensive must ultimately be subject to investigation and adjudication if international law is ever to be enforced. . . .

The Charter defines as a crime the planning or waging of war that is a war of aggression or a war in violation of international treaties. The Tribunal has decided that certain of the defendants planned and waged aggressive wars against ten nations, and were therefore guilty of this series of crimes. This makes it unnecessary to discuss the subject in further detail, or even to consider at any length the extent to which these aggressive wars were also "wars in violation of international treaties, agreements, or assurances." . . .

The jurisdiction of the Tribunal is defined in the Agreement and Charter, and the crimes coming within the jurisdiction of the Tribunal, for which there shall be individual responsibility, are set out in Article 6. The law of the Charter is decisive, and binding upon the Tribunal.

The making of the Charter was the exercise of the sovereign legislative power by the countries to which the German Reich unconditionally surrendered; and the undoubted right of these countries to legislate for the occupied territories has been recognized by the civilized world. The Charter is not an arbitrary exercise of power on the part of the victorious nations, but in the view of the Tribunal, as will be shown, it is the expression of international law existing at the time of its creation; and to that extent is itself a contribution to international law.

The Signatory Powers created this Tribunal, defined the law it was to administer, and made regulations for the proper conduct of the trial. In doing so, they have done together what any one of them might have done singly; for it is not to be doubted that any nation has the right thus to set up special courts to administer law. With regard to the constitution of the court, all that the defendants are entitled to ask is to receive a fair trial on the facts and law.

The Charter makes the planning or waging of a war of aggression or a war in violation of international treaties a crime; and it is therefore not strictly necessary to consider whether and to what extent aggressive war was a crime before the execution of the London Agreement. But in view of the great importance of the questions of law involved, the Tribunal has heard full argument from the prosecution and the defense, and will express its view on the matter.

It was urged on behalf of the defendants that a fundamental principle of all law—international and domestic—is that there can be no punishment of crime without a preexisting law. *"Nullum crimen sine lege, nulla poena sine lege."* It was submitted that *ex post facto* punishment is abhorrent to the law of all civilized nations, that no sovereign power had made aggressive war a crime at the time the alleged criminal acts were committed, that no statute had defined aggressive war, that no penalty had been fixed for its commission, and no court had been created to try and punish offenders.

In the first place, it is to be observed that the maxim *nullum crimen sine lege* is not a limitation of sovereignty, but is in general a principle of justice. To assert that it is unjust to punish those who in defiance of treaties and assurances have attacked neighboring states without warning is obviously untrue, for in such circumstances the attacker must know that he is doing wrong, and so far from it being unjust to punish him, it would be unjust if his wrong were allowed to go unpunished. Occupying the positions they did in the government of Germany, the defendants, or at least some of them must have known of the treaties signed by Germany, outlawing recourse to war for the settlement of international disputes; they must have known that they were acting in defiance of all international law when in complete deliberation they carried out their designs of invasion and aggression. On this view of the case alone, it would appear that the maxim has no application to the present facts.

This view is strongly reinforced by a consideration of the state of international law in 1939, so far as aggressive war is concerned. The General Treaty for the Renunciation of War of August 27, 1928, more generally known as the Pact of Paris or the Kellogg-Briand Pact, was binding on sixty-three nations, including Germany, Italy, and Japan at the outbreak of war in 1939. . . .

The question is, what was the legal effect of this pact? The nations who signed the pact or adhered to it unconditionally condemned recourse to war for the future as an instrument of policy, and expressly renounced it. After the signing of the pact, any nation resorting to war as an instrument of national policy breaks the pact. In the opinion of the Tribunal, the solemn renunciation of war as an instrument of national policy necessarily involves the proposition that such a war is illegal in international law; and that those who plan and wage such a war, with its inevitable and terrible consequences, are committing a crime in so doing. War for the solution of international controversies undertaken as an instrument of national policy certainly includes a war of aggression, and such a war is therefore outlawed by the pact. As Mr. Henry L. Stimson, then Secretary of State of the United States, said in 1932:

"War between nations was renounced by the signatories of the Kellogg-Briand Treaty. This means that it has become throughout practically the entire world . . . an illegal thing. Hereafter, when engaged in armed conflict, either one or both of them must be termed violators of this general treaty law. . . . We denounce them as law breakers."

But it is argued that the pact does not expressly enact that such wars are crimes, or set up courts to try those who make such wars. To that extent the same is true with regard to the laws of war contained in the Hague Convention. The Hague Convention of 1907 prohibited resort to certain methods of waging war. These included the inhumane treatments of prisoners, the employment of poisoned weapons, the improper use of flags of truce, and similar matters. Many of these prohibitions had been enforced long before the date of the Convention; but since 1907 they have certainly been crimes, punishable as offenses against the laws of war; yet the Hague Convention nowhere designates such practices as criminal, nor is any sentence prescribed, nor any mention made of a court to try and punish offenders. For many years past, however, military tribunals have tried and punished individuals guilty of violating the rules of land warfare laid down by this Convention. In the opinion of the Tribunal, those who wage aggressive war are doing that which is equally illegal, and of much greater moment than a breach of one of the rules of the Hague Convention. In interpreting the words of the pact, it must be remembered that international law is not the product of an international legislature, and that such international agreements as the Pact of Paris have to deal with general principles of law, and not with administrative matters of procedure. The law of war is to be found not only in treaties, but in the customs and practices of states which gradually obtained universal recognition, and from the general principles of justice applied by jurists and practiced by military courts. This law is not static, but by continued adaptation follows the needs of a changing world. Indeed, in many cases treaties do no more than express and define for more accurate reference the principles of law already existing.

The view which the Tribunal takes of the true interpretation of the pact is supported by the international history which preceded it. In the year 1923 the draft of a Treaty of Mutual Assistance was sponsored by the League of Nations. In Article I the treaty declared "that aggressive war is an international crime," and that the parties would "undertake that no one of them will be guilty of its commission." The draft treaty was submitted to twenty-nine states, about half of whom were in favor of accepting the text. The principal objection appeared to be in the difficulty of defining the acts which would constitute "aggression," rather than any doubt as to the criminality of aggressive war. The preamble to the League of Nations 1924 Protocol for the Pacific Settlement of International Disputes ("Geneva Protocol"), after "recognising the solidarity of the members of the international community," declared that "a war of aggression constitutes a violation of this solidarity and is an international crime." It went on to declare that the contracting parties were "desirous of facilitating the complete application of the system provided in the Covenant of the League of Nations for the pacific settlement of disputes between the states and of ensuring the repression of international crimes." The Protocol was recommended to the members of the League of Nations by a unanimous resolution in the Assembly of the 48 members of the League. These members included Italy and Japan, but Germany was not then a member of the League.

Although the Protocol was never ratified, it was signed by the leading statesmen of the world, representing the vast majority of the civilized States and peoples, and may be regarded as strong evidence of the intention to brand aggressive war as an international crime.

At the meeting of the Assembly of the League of Nations on the 24th September 1927, all the delegations then present (including the German, the Italian, and the Japanese) unanimously adopted a declaration concerning wars of aggression. The preamble to the declaration stated:

"The Assembly: Recognizing the solidarity which unites the community of nations;

"Being inspired by a firm desire for the maintenance of general peace;

"Being convinced that a war of aggression can never serve as a means of settling international disputes, and is in consequence an international crime . . ."

The unanimous resolution of the 18th February 1928, of twenty-one American republics at the sixth (Havana) Pan-American Conference, declared that "war of aggression constitutes an international crime against the human species."

All these expressions of opinion, and others that could be cited, so solemnly made, reinforce the construction which the Tribunal placed upon the Pact of Paris, that resort to a war of aggression is not merely illegal, but is criminal. The prohibition of aggressive war demanded by the conscience of the world, finds its expression in the series of Pacts and Treaties to which the Tribunal has just referred.

It is also important to remember that Article 227 of the Treaty of Versailles provided for the constitution of a special tribunal, composed of representatives of five of the Allied and Associated Powers which had been belligerents in the First World War opposed to Germany, to try the former German Emperor "for a supreme offence against international morality and the sanctity of treaties." The purpose of this trial was expressed to be "to vindicate the solemn obligations of international undertakings, and the validity of international morality." In Article 228 of the Treaty, the German Government expressly recognized the right of the Allied Powers "to bring before military tribunals persons accused of having committed acts in violation of the laws and customs of war."

It was submitted that international law is concerned with the actions of sovereign States, and provides no punishment for individuals; and further, that where the act in question is an act of State, those who carry it out are not personally responsible, but are protected by the doctrine of the sovereignty of the State. In the opinion of the Tribunal, both these submissions must be rejected. That international law imposes duties and liabilities upon individuals as well as upon states has long been recognized. In the recent case of Ex parte Quirin (1942, 317 U.S. 1, 63 S.Ct. 2), before the Supreme Court of the United States, persons were charged during the war with landing in the United States for purposes of spying and sabotage. The late Chief Justice Stone, speaking for the court, said:

"From the very beginning of its history this Court has applied the law of war as including that part of the law of nations which prescribes for the conduct of war, the status, rights, and duties of enemy nations as well as enemy individuals."

He went on to give a list of cases tried by the courts, where individual offenders were charged with offences against the laws of nations, and particularly the laws of war. Many other authorities could be cited, but enough has been said to show that individuals can be punished for violations of international law. Crimes against international law are committed by men, not by abstract entities, and only by punishing individuals who commit such crimes can the provisions of international law be enforced.

The provisions of Article 228 of the Treaty of Versailles already referred to illustrate and enforce this view of individual responsibility.

The principle of international law, which, under certain circumstances, protects the representatives of a State, cannot be applied to acts which are condemned as criminal by international law. The authors of these acts cannot shelter themselves behind their official position in order to be freed from punishment in appropriate proceedings. Article 7 of the Charter expressly declares:

"The official position of defendants, whether as heads of State, or responsible officials in government departments, shall not be considered as freeing them from responsibility, or mitigating punishment."

On the other hand the very essence of the Charter is that individuals have international duties which transcend the national obligations of obedience imposed by the individual State. He who violates the laws of war cannot obtain immunity while acting in pursuance of the authority of the State if the State in authorizing action moves outside its competence under international law.

It was also submitted on behalf of most of these defendants that in doing what they did they were acting under the orders of Hitler, and therefore cannot be held responsible for the acts committed by them in carrying out these orders. The Charter specifically provides in Article 8:

"The fact that the defendant acted pursuant to order of his Government or of a superior shall not free him from responsibility, but may be considered in mitigation of punishment."

The provisions of this Article are in conformity with the law of all nations. That a soldier was ordered to kill or torture in violation of the international law of war has never been recognized as a defense to such acts of brutality, though, as the Charter here provides, the order may be urged in mitigation of the punishment. The true test, which is found in varying degrees in the criminal law of most nations, is not the existence of the order, but whether moral choice was in fact possible. . . .

The evidence relating to war crimes has been overwhelming, in its volume and its detail. It is impossible for this judgment adequately to review it, or to record the mass of documentary and oral evidence that has been presented. The truth remains that war crimes were committed on a vast scale, never before seen in the history of war. They were perpetrated in all the countries occupied by Germany, and on the high seas, and were attended by every conceivable circumstance of cruelty and horror. There can be no doubt that the majority of them arose from the Nazi conception of "total war," with which the aggressive wars were waged. For in this conception of "total war" the moral ideas underlying the conventions which seek to make war more humane are no longer regarded as having force or validity. Everything is made subordinate to the overmastering dictates of war. Rules, regulations, assurances, and treaties, all alike, are of no moment; and so, freed from the restraining influence of international law, the aggressive war is conducted by the Nazi leaders in the most barbaric way. Accordingly, war crimes were committed when and wherever the Fuehrer and his close associates thought them to be advantageous. They were for the most part the result of cold and criminal calculation.

On some occasions war crimes were deliberately planned long in advance. In the case of the Soviet Union, the plunder of the territories to be occupied, and the ill-treatment of the civilian population, were settled in minute detail before the attack was begun. As early as the autumn of 1940, the invasion of the territories of the Soviet Union was being considered. From that date onwards, the methods to be employed in destroying all possible opposition were continuously under discussion.

Similarly, when planning to exploit the inhabitants of the occupied countries for slave labor on the very greatest scale, the German Government conceived it as an integral part of the war economy, and planned and organized this particular war crime down to the last elaborate detail.

Other war crimes, such as the murder of prisoners of war who had escaped and been recaptured, or the murder of commandos or captured airmen, or the destruction of the Soviet commissars, were the result of direct orders circulated through the highest official channels.

The Tribunal proposes, therefore, to deal quite generally with the question of war crimes, and to refer to them later when examining the responsibility of the individual defendants in relation to them. Prisoners of war were ill-treated and tortured and murdered, not only in defiance of the well-established rules of international law, but in complete disregard of the elementary dictates of humanity. Civilian populations in occupied territories suffered the same fate. Whole populations were deported to Germany for the purposes of slave labor upon defense works, armament production and similar tasks connected with the war effort. Hostages were taken in very large numbers from the civilian populations in all the occupied countries, and were shot as suited the German purposes. Public and private property was systematically plundered and pillaged in order to enlarge the resources of Germany at the expense of the rest of Europe. Cities and towns and villages were wantonly destroyed without military justification or necessity. . . .

The Law Relating to War Crimes and Crimes Against Humanity

. . . The Tribunal is of course bound by the Charter, in the definition which it gives both of war crimes and crimes against humanity. With respect to war crimes, however, as has already been pointed out, the crimes defined by Article 6, section (b), of the Charter were already recognized as war crimes under international law. They were covered by Articles 46, 50, 52, and 56 of the Hague Convention of 1907, and Articles 2, 3, 4, 46, and 51 of the Geneva Convention of 1929. That violation of these provisions constituted crimes for which the guilty individuals were punishable is too well settled to admit of argument.

But it is argued that the Hague Convention does not apply in this case, because of the "general participation" clause in Article 2 of the Hague Convention of 1907. That clause provided:

"The provisions contained in the regulations (rules of land warfare) referred to in Article 1 as well as in the present convention do not apply except between contracting powers, and then only if all the belligerents are parties to the convention."

Several of the belligerents in the recent war were not parties to this convention.

In the opinion of the Tribunal it is not necessary to decide this question. The rules of land warfare expressed in the convention undoubtedly represented an advance over existing international law at the time of their adoption. But the convention expressly stated that it was an attempt "to revise the general laws and customs of war," which it thus recognized to be then existing, but by 1939 these rules laid down in the convention were recognized by all civilized nations, and were regarded as being declaratory of the laws and customs of war which are referred to in Article 6 (b) of the Charter.

A further submission was made that Germany was no longer bound by the rules of land warfare in many of the territories occupied during the war, because Germany had completely subjugated those countries and incorporated them into the German Reich, a fact which gave Germany authority to deal with the occupied countries as though they were part of Germany. In the view of the Tribunal it is unnecessary in this case to decide whether this doctrine of subjugation, dependent as it is upon military conquest, has any application where the subjugation is the result of the crime of aggressive war. The doctrine was never considered to be applicable so long as there was an army in the field attempting to restore the occupied countries to their true owners, and in this case, therefore, the doctrine could not apply to any territories occupied after the 1st September 1939. As to the war crimes committed in Bohemia and Moravia, it is a sufficient answer that these territories were never added to the Reich, but a mere protectorate was established over them.

With regard to crimes against humanity, there is no doubt whatever that political opponents were murdered in Germany before the war, and that many of them were kept in concentration camps in circumstances of great horror and cruelty. The policy of terror was certainly carried out on a vast scale, and in many cases was organized and systematic. The policy of persecution, repression, and murder of civilians in Germany before the war of 1939, who were likely to be hostile to the Government, was most ruthlessly carried out. The persecution of Jews during the same period is established beyond all doubt. To constitute crimes against humanity, the acts relied on before the outbreak of war must have been in execution of, or in connection with, any crime within the jurisdiction of the Tribunal. The Tribunal is of the opinion that revolting and horrible as many of these crimes were, it has not been satisfactorily proved that they were done in execution of, or in connection with, any such crime. The Tribunal therefore cannot make a general declaration that the acts before 1939 were crimes against humanity within the meaning of the Charter, but from the beginning of the war in 1939 war crimes were committed on a vast scale, which were also crimes against humanity; and insofar as the inhumane acts charged in the indictment, and committed after the beginning of the war, did not constitute war crimes, they were all committed in execution of, or in connection with, the aggressive war, and therefore constituted crimes against humanity.

The Nuremberg Principles provide us with the most authoritative summary of what was decided at Nuremberg. This summary was fully consistent with the unanimous opinion of the Membership of the United Nations that the Nuremberg Judgment represented a desirable development in international law (see General Assembly Resolution 95 [I]). The Principles were formulated by the International Law Commission, a specialized body of technical experts, at the request of the General Assembly.

THE NUREMBERG PRINCIPLES, 1946

1. Principles of International Law Recognized in the Charter of the Nuremberg Tribunal and in the Judgment of the Tribunal

As formulated by the International Law Commission, June–July 1950.

Principle I

Any person who commits an act which constitutes a crime under international law is responsible therefor and liable to punishment.

Principle II

The fact that internal law does not impose a penalty for an act which constitutes a crime under international law does not relieve the person who committed the act from responsibility under international law.

Principle III

The fact that a person who committed an act which constitutes a crime under international law acted as Head of State or responsible government official does not relieve him from responsibility under international law.

Principle IV

The fact that a person acted pursuant to order of his Government or of a superior does not relieve him from responsibility under international law, provided a moral choice was in fact possible to him.

Principle V

Any person charged with a crime under international law has the right to a fair trial on the facts and law.

Principle VI

The crimes hereinafter set out are punishable as crimes under international law:

a. Crimes against peace:

(i) Planning, preparation, initiation or waging of a war of aggression or a war in violation of international treaties, agreements or assurances;

(ii) Participation in a common plan or conspiracy for the accomplishment of any of the acts mentioned under (i).

b. War crimes:

Violations of the laws or customs of war which include, but are not limited to, murder, ill-treatment or deportation to slave-labour or for any other purpose of civilian population of or in occupied territory, murder or ill-treatment of prisoners of war or persons on the seas, killing of hostages, plunder of public or private property, wanton destruction of cities, towns, or villages, or devastation not justified by military necessity.

c. Crimes against humanity:

Murder, extermination, enslavement, deportation and other inhuman acts done against any civilian population, or persecutions on political, racial or religious grounds, when such acts are done or such persecutions are carried on in execution of or in connexion with any crime against peace or any war crime.

Principle VII

Complicity in the commission of a crime against peace, a war crime, or a crime against humanity as set forth in Principle VI is a crime under international law.

The Tokyo trials against Japanese war leaders have attracted far less attention than did the German prosecutions. From a legal point of view, the Japanese trials are more significant in many ways. The tribunal consisted of Allied powers other than the Big Four. The Government of Japan was viewed in less demoniac terms than was the Nazi regime. Dissenting opinions resulted that questioned the whole idea of proceeding against the military and civilian leaders of a defeated nation. Justice Pal from India went on to question the concept of "aggression" from a legal, political, and moral point of view. His opinion indicts the Western policies of exploitation as the basis of the conflict and, thereby, anticipates the whole anticolonial mood which was to become such an important aspect of the postwar period.

THE JUDGMENT IN THE TOKYO WAR CRIMES TRIAL, 1948

[Excerpt from main judgment]

CHAPTER I. ESTABLISHMENT AND PROCEEDINGS OF THE TRIBUNAL

The Tribunal was established in virtue of and to implement the Cairo Declaration of the 1st of December, 1943, the Declaration of Potsdam of the 26th of July, 1945, the Instrument of Surrender of the 2nd of September, 1945, and the Moscow Conference of the 26th of December, 1945. . . .

The Declaration of Potsdam . . . was made by the President of the United States of America, the President of the National Government of the Republic of China, and the Prime Minister of Great Britain and later adhered to by the Union of Soviet Socialist Republics. Its principal relevant provisions are:

"Japan shall be given an opportunity to end this war.

"There must be eliminated for all time the authority and influence of those who have deceived and misled the people of Japan into embarking on world conquest, for we insist that a new order of peace, security and justice will be impossible until irresponsible militarism is driven from the world. . . .

"We do not intend that the Japanese people shall be enslaved as a race or destroyed as a nation, but stern justice shall be meted out to all war criminals including those who have visited cruelties upon our prisoners.". . .

CHAPTER II. THE LAW

(a) *Jurisdiction of the Tribunal*

In our opinion the law of the Charter is decisive and binding on the Tribunal. This is a special tribunal set up by the Supreme Commander under authority conferred on him by the Allied Powers. It derives its jurisdiction from the Charter. In this trial its members have no jurisdiction except such as is to be found in the Charter. The Order of the Supreme Commander, which appointed the members of the Tribunal, states: "The responsibilities, powers, and duties of the members of the Tribunal are set forth in the Charter thereof. . . ." In the result, the members of the Tribunal, being otherwise wholly without power in respect to the trial of the accused, have been empowered by the documents, which constituted the Tribunal and appointed them as members, to try the accused but subject always to the duty and responsibility of applying to the trial the law set forth in the Charter.

The foregoing expression of opinion is not to be taken as supporting the view, if such view be held, that the Allied Powers or any victor nations have the right under international law in providing for the trial and punishment of war criminals to enact or promulgate laws or vest in their tribunals powers in conflicts with recognized international law or rules of principles thereof. In the exercise of their right to create tribunals for such a purpose and in conferring powers upon such tribunals belligerent powers may act only within the limits of international law.

The substantial grounds of the defence challenge to the

jurisdiction of the Tribunal to hear and adjudicate upon the charges contained in the Indictment are the following:

(1) The Allied Powers acting through the Supreme Commander have no authority to include in the Charter of the Tribunal and to designate as justiciable "Crimes against Peace" (Article 5 (a)) ;

(2) Aggressive war is not per se illegal and the Pact of Paris of 1928 renouncing war as an instrument of national policy does not enlarge the meaning of war crimes nor constitute war a crime;

(3) War is the act of a nation for which there is no individual responsibility under international law;

(4) The provisions of the Charter are "ex post facto" legislation and therefore illegal;

(5) The Instrument of Surrender which provides that the Declaration of Potsdam will be given effect imposes the condition that Conventional War Crimes are recognized by international law at the date of the Declaration (26 July 1945) would be the only crimes prosecuted;

(6) Killings in the course of belligerent operations except in so far as they constitute violations of the rules of warfare or the laws and customs of war are the normal incidents of war and are not murder;

(7) Several of the accused being prisoners of war are triable by court martial as provided by the Geneva Convention of 1929 and not by this Tribunal.

Since the law of the Charter is decisive and binding upon it this Tribunal is formally bound to reject the first four of the above seven contentions advanced for the Defence but in view of the great importance of the questions of law involved the Tribunal will record its opinion on these questions.

After this Tribunal had in May 1946 dismissed the defence motions and upheld the validity of its Charter and its jurisdiction thereunder, stating that the reasons for this decision would be given later, the International Military Tribunal sitting at Nuremberg delivered its verdicts on the first of October 1946. . . .

Prisoners taken in war and civilian internees are in the power of the Government which captures them. This was not always the case. For the last two centuries, however, this position has been recognized and the customary law to this effect was formally embodied in the Hague Convention No. IV in 1907 and repeated in the Geneva Prisoners of War Convention of 1929. Responsibility for the care of prisoners of war and of civilian internees (all of whom we will refer to as "prisoners") rests therefore with the Government having them in possession. This responsibility is not limited to the duty of mere maintenance but extends to the prevention of mistreatment. In particular, acts of inhumanity to prisoners which are forbidden by the customary law of nations as well as by conventions are to be prevented by the Government having responsibility for the prisoners.

In the discharge of these duties to prisoners Governments must have resort to persons. Indeed the Governments responsible, in this sense, are those persons who direct and control the functions of Government. In this case and in the above regard we are concerned with the members of the Japanese Cabinet. The duty to prisoners is not a meaningless obligation cast upon a political abstraction. It is a specific duty to be performed in the first case by those persons who constitute the Government. In the multitude of duties and tasks involved in modern government there is of necessity an elaborate system of subdivision and delegation of duties. In the case of the duty of Governments to prisoners held by them in time of war those persons who constitute the Government have the principal and continuing responsibility for their prisoners, even though they delegate the duties of maintenance and protection to others.

In general the responsibility for prisoners held by Japan may be stated to have rested upon:

(1) Members of the Government;
(2) Military or Naval Officers in command of formations having prisoners in their possession;
(3) Officials in those departments which were concerned with the well-being of prisoners;

(4) Officials, whether civilian, military, or naval, having direct and immediate control of prisoners.

It is the duty of all those on whom responsibility rests to secure proper treatment of prisoners and to prevent their illtreatment by establishing and securing the continuous and efficient working of a system appropriate for these purposes. Such persons fail in this duty and become responsible for illtreatment of prisoners if:

(1) They fail to establish such a system.
(2) If having established such a system, they fail to secure its continued and efficient working.

Each of such persons has a duty to ascertain that the system is working and if he neglects to do so he is responsible. He does not discharge his duty by merely instituting an appropriate system and thereafter neglecting to learn of its application. An Army Commander or a Minister of War, for example, must be at the same pains to ensure obedience to his orders in this respect as he would in respect of other orders he has issued on matters of the first importance.

Nevertheless, such persons are not responsible if a proper system and its continuous efficient functioning be provided for and conventional war crimes be committed unless:

(1) They had knowledge that such crimes were being committed, and having such knowledge they failed to take such steps as were within their power to prevent the commission of such crimes in the future, or
(2) They are at fault in having failed to acquire such knowledge.

If such a person had, or should, but for negligence or supineness, have had such knowledge he is not excused for inaction if his Office required or permitted him to take any action to prevent such crimes. On the other hand it is not enough for the exculpation of a person, otherwise responsible, for him to show that he accepted assurances from others more directly associated with the control of the prisoners if having regard to the position of those others, to the frequency of reports of such crimes, or to any other circumstances he should have been put upon further enquiry as to whether those assurances were true or untrue. That crimes are notorious, numerous and widespread as to time and place are matters to be considered in imputing knowledge.

A member of a Cabinet which collectively, as one of the principal organs of the Government, is responsible for the care of prisoners is not absolved from responsibility if, having knowledge of the commission of the crimes in the sense already discussed, and omitting or failing to secure the taking of measures to prevent the commission of such crimes in the future, he elects to continue as a member of the Cabinet. This is the position even though the Department of which he has the charge is not directly concerned with the care of prisoners. A Cabinet member may resign. If he has knowledge of ill-treatment of prisoners, is powerless to prevent future ill-treatment, but elects to remain in the Cabinet thereby continuing to participate in its collective responsibility for protection of prisoners he willingly assumes responsibility for any ill-treatment in the future.

Army or Navy Commanders can, by order, secure proper treatment and prevent ill-treatment of prisoners. So can Ministers of War and of the Navy. If crimes are committed against prisoners under their control, of the likely occurrence of which they had, or should have had, knowledge in advance, they are responsible for those crimes. If, for example, it be shown that within the units under his command conventional war crimes have been committed of which he knew or should have known, a commander who takes no adequate steps to prevent the occurrence of such crimes in the future will be responsible for such future crimes.

Departmental Officials having knowledge of ill-treatment of prisoners are not responsible by reason of their failure to resign; but if their functions included the administration of the system of protection of prisoners and if they had or should have had knowledge of crimes and did nothing effective, to the extent of their powers, to prevent their occurrence in the future then they are responsible for such future crimes. . . .

Under the heading of "Crimes Against Peace" the Charter names five separate crimes. These are planning, preparation, initiation and waging aggressive war or a war in violation of international law, treaties, agreements or assurances; to these four is added the further crime of participation in a common plan or conspiracy for the accomplishment of any of the foregoing. The Indictment was based upon the Charter and all the above crimes were charged in addition to further charges founded upon other provisions of the Charter.

A conspiracy to wage aggressive or unlawful war arises when two or more persons enter into an agreement to commit that crime. Thereafter, in furtherance of the conspiracy, follows planning and preparing for such war. Those who participate at this stage may be either original conspirators or later adherents. If the latter adopt the purpose of the conspiracy and plan and prepare for its fulfillment they become conspirators. For this reason, as all the accused are charged with the conspiracies, we do not consider it necessary in respect of those we may find guilty of conspiracy to enter convictions also for planning and preparing. In other words, although we do not question the validity of the charges we do not think it necessary in respect of any defendants who may be found guilty of conspiracy to take into consideration or to enter convictions upon Counts 6 to 17 inclusive.

A similar position arises in connection with the counts of initiating and waging aggressive war. Although initiating aggressive war in some circumstances may have another meaning, in the Indictment before us it is given the meaning of commencing the hostilities. In this sense it involves the actual waging of the aggressive war. After such a war has been initiated or has been commenced by some offenders others may participate in such circumstances, as to become guilty of waging the war. This consideration, however, affords no reason for registering convictions on the counts of initiating as well as of waging aggressive war. We propose therefore to abstain from consideration of Counts 18 to 26 inclusive.

Counts 37 and 38 charge conspiracy to murder. Article 5,

sub-paragraphs (b) and (c) of the Charter, deal with Conventional War Crimes and Crimes against Humanity. In sub-paragraph (c) of Article 5 occurs this passage: "Leaders, organizers, instigators and accomplices participating in the formulation or execution of a common plan or conspiracy to commit any of the foregoing crimes are responsible for all acts performed by any person in execution of such plan." A similar provision appeared in the Nuremberg Charter although there it was an independent paragraph and was not, as in our Charter, incorporated in sub-paragraph (c). The context of this provision clearly relates it exclusively to sub-paragraph (a), Crimes against Peace, as that is the only category in which a "common plan or conspiracy" is stated to be a crime. It has no application to Conventional War Crimes and Crimes against Humanity as conspiracies to commit such crimes are not made criminal by the Charter of the Tribunal. The Prosecution did not challenge this view but submitted that the counts were sustainable under Article 5 (a) of the Charter. It was argued that the waging of aggressive war was unlawful and involved unlawful killing which is murder. From this it was submitted further that a conspiracy to wage war unlawfully was a conspiracy also to commit murder. The crimes triable by this Tribunal are those set out in the Charter. Article 5 (a) states that a conspiracy to commit the crimes therein specified is itself a crime. The crimes, other than conspiracy, specified in Article 5 (a) are "planning, preparation, initiating or waging" of a war of aggression. There is no specification of the crime of conspiracy to commit murder by the waging of aggressive war or otherwise. We hold therefore that we have no jurisdiction to deal with charges of conspiracy to commit murder as contained in Counts 37 and 38 and decline to entertain these charges.

[EXCERPT FROM DISSENTING OPINION, JUDGE RÖLING (NETHERLANDS)]

. . . The Charter, in art. 5, sub. 2, refers to crimes against peace. With regard to the question as to whether international law acknowledges, or did acknowledge, this crime, it must be borne in mind that the word "crime" in international law, as in domestic law, may indicate concepts of quite different nature.

In international law, "crime" covers acts of espionage and war-treason, honored on one side of the border, punished on the other, as well as acts morally and legally condemned in all civilized nations, as, e. g., the torture of prisoners of war.

In his "Report to the President" Justice Jackson, who signed the London Agreement on behalf of the Government of the United States, qualified the crime of making unjustifiable war "the crime which comprehends all lesser crimes." The Nuremberg Judgment referred to the crime of initiating a war of aggression as "the supreme international crime differing only from other war crimes in that it contains within itself the accumulated evil of the whole."

The chief prosecutor in Tokyo, in his summation, spoke of the crime against peace as "the vilest," and many occasions could be cited on which the prosecution denied any difference of character between the crimes mentioned in art. 5, subs. a, b, and c.

Considering, at this point, "crime" in the meaning of a vile act, violating the law in such a way that punishment has to be inflicted so as to maintain legal order, the question has to be answered as to whether or not the "crime against peace" is such a crime according to existing international law.

It will not be necessary to enumerate those authorities in the field of international law who recognize that, until the era of the League of Nations and the Pact of Paris, the waging of war was a sovereign right of states. . . .

The question is whether in positive international law, which accepted war as a sovereign right of nations, any change has been brought about by the Covenant, the Resolutions of the League of Nations, the resolutions of other international institutions, and the Kellogg-Briand Pact. . . .

[The Assembly of the League declared in 1927:] " (1) That all wars of aggression are, and shall always be, prohibited.

(2) That every pacific means must be employed to settle disputes, of every description, which may arise between States. "The Assembly declares that the State Members of the League are under an obligation to conform to these principles."

What could be the significance of such a declaration? Nations, being living entities, change. Changed conditions require changes in relations. Thus, conflicts among nations find their origin in their very nature. These conflicts demand solution. This may be done by peaceful means, but, if peaceful means do not provide the solution, the only alternative left is war. In the maintenance of peace, it is therefore essential to find pacific means for the solution of conflicts. When those means have been found, "outlawry of war" may follow logically. To ban war before the means for the solution of conflicts have been found would, in practice, merely amount to the maintenance of the status quo. . . .

The Pact of Paris, signed on behalf of sixty-three nations, among those Japan, appears to be the only real basis for a different conception with regard to the jus ad bellum. It is questionable, however, whether it did in fact bring about such a change that aggressive war became a vile crime. The Pact itself provides only the one sanction that states waging war in violation of the Pact "should be denied the benefits furnished by this Treaty." (Preamble.) But hardly any mention was made (before the Second World War), by those who interpreted this Pact, of the consequence that aggressive war is criminal, and involves individual responsibility.

The essential significance of the Pact is undoubtedly contained in Article 2, where the contracting parties agree
"that the settlement and solution of all disputes or conflicts of whatever nature, or of whatever origin they may be, which may arise among them, shall never be sought except by pacific means."
The bare text, however, does not fully disclose the expressed design of the parties. Examination of the preparatory work reveals what is equivalent to an additional explanatory article,

in a definite acknowledgment that the agreement should not curtail the freedom of the signatories to have recourse to defensive measures. . . .

But how far does self-defense go? The problem of self-defense in itself is most complicated. How it was understood in the United States at the time when the Kellogg-Briand Pact was proposed and accepted, can be learned from the statements made in Congress before its ratification. Senator Borah went so far as to maintain that it was a fact that every nation reserved the right to employ force to protect its nationals when their lives might be endangered in foreign lands. Secretary of State Kellogg declared that the reservation of the right of self-defense meant "that this Government has a right to take such measures as it believes necessary to the defense of the country, *or to prevent things that might endanger the country.*" (Italics supplied.) . . .

This reservation makes it extremely difficult, if not impossible, to prove a breach of the Pact. The reasoning of the Nuremberg Judgment on this point seems to be almost a *petitio principii*, where it says:

"Whether action taken under the claim of self-defense was in fact aggressive or defensive must ultimately be subject to investigation and adjudication if international law is ever to be enforced." . . .

Secretary of State Kellogg, explaining the Pact to the U.S. Senate Committee on Foreign Relations, stated on December 7, 1928:

"I knew that this Government, at least, would never agree to submit to any tribunal the question of self-defense, and I do not think any of them would." (Record, p. 4)

Senator Borah, who played such an influential part before the Briand-Kellogg Pact was ratified by the American Senate, stated at the beginning of the discussions in the Senate:

"The only censor—and these things we may understand and frankly admit—the only censor or criticising power of a nation exercising the right of self-defense, if it does not exercise it upon true principle, is the power of public opinion. There being no super-government, no tribunal to which [to] appeal, and no one willing to create a super-government, and no authority otherwise to pass upon the matter, that is the only judge that we can rely upon to censor this part of the treaty. I know of no other tribunal to which we can appeal for the rectitude of nations in the exercise of this right of self-defense."

The principal question in relation to the above is: Did the Pact of Paris make aggressive war an international crime for which individuals can be held responsible? . . .

Neither the lofty phrases used in resolutions, nor the ambiguous Pact of Paris outlawed war in the sense that waging an illegal war did become criminal in the ordinary sense. . . .

One may see in the Pact of Paris the denial of the sovereign right of nations to go to war at will and the expression of the willingness "to renounce war as a means of national policy." To read more in it would leave unanswered the question why no provisions were made for the inevitable legal consequences of the new viewpoint. . . .

From the above, it follows that "crimes against peace" were not regarded true crimes before the London Agreement, and were not considered as such before the end of 1943.

The question has to be faced and answered whether the concept of these crimes was, and could be, created as such by the London Agreement of August 8, 1945, or by the Charter for the IMTFE. . . .

The dreadfulness of World War II may have made us realize the necessity of preventing wars in the future. But we need not discuss here whether the horror of the atomic bomb opened our eyes to the criminality of Japanese aggression.

These horrors of World War II may compel the nations to take the legal steps to achieve the maintenance of peace. This has not been done to date. Consequently, apart from the question as to whether, according to international law, victorious powers, either in a mutual treaty or by order of their Supreme Commander, could bring about a change in the legal situation of aggressive war, the relations of the nations did not change in the sense that even at this moment every illegal war could be qualified as a vile crime.

Positive international law, as existing at this moment, compels us to interpret the "crime against peace," as mentioned in the Charter, in a special way. It may be presupposed that the Allied nations did not intend to create rules in violation of international law. This indicates that the Charter should be interpreted so that it is in accordance with International Law.

There is no doubt that powers victorious in a *bellum justum,* and as such responsible for peace and order thereafter, have, according to international law, the right to counteract elements constituting a threat to that newly established order, and are entitled, as a means of preventing the recurrence of gravely offensive conduct, to seek and retain the custody of the pertinent persons. Napoleon's elimination offers a precedent. . . .

Crime in international law is applied to concepts with different meanings. Apart from those indicated above, it can also indicate acts comparable to political crimes in domestic law, where the decisive element is the danger rather than the guilt, where the criminal is considered an enemy rather than a villain, and where the punishment emphasizes the political measure rather than the judicial retribution.

In this sense should be understood the "crime against peace," referred to in the Charter. In this sense the crime against peace, as formulated in the Charter, is in accordance with international law. It goes without saying that this conception of the character of the "crime" has certain consequences with regard to the appropriate "punishment.". . .

As long as the dominant principle in the crime against peace is the dangerous character of the individual who committed this crime, the punishment should only be determined by considerations of security.

In this case, this means that no capital punishment should be given to anyone guilty of the crime against peace only. . . .

In this trial, together with the Nuremberg Trial, the first in which aggression-as-a-crime is at stake, it is not necessary to draw a sharp line between aggression and defense. Here, as the evidence shows, we are dealing with wars which can be called wars of conquest, wars of illegal expansion. These wars of conquest certainly come within the scope of illegal aggression, whatever definition might be given. The question whether the impulses which led to those wars of conquest did, perhaps, originate partly in the defensive sphere, may here be left out of discussion. Insight in the genesis of the crime has but limited importance, as it is not so much retribution for the offense by punishment of the perpetrators which is here being sought, as a measure for protection by elimination of dangerous persons.

[EXCERPT FROM DISSENTING OPINION, JUDGE PAL (INDIA)]

. . . The accused at the earliest possible opportunity expressed their apprehension of injustice in the hands of the Tribunal as at present constituted.

The apprehension is that the Members of the Tribunal being representatives of the Nations which defeated Japan and which are accusers in this action, the accused cannot expect a fair and impartial trial at their hands and consequently the Tribunal as constituted should not proceed with this trial. . . .

The judges are here no doubt from the different victor nations, but they are here in their personal capacities. One of the essential factors usually considered in the selection of members of such tribunals is moral integrity. This of course embraces more than ordinary fidelity and honesty. It includes "a measure of freedom from prepossessions, a readiness to face the consequences of views which may not be shared, a devotion to judicial processes, and a willingness to make the sacrifices which the performance of judicial duties may involve." The accused persons here have not challenged the constitution of the tribunal on the ground of any shortcoming in any of the members of the tribunal in these respects. The Supreme Commander seems to have given careful and anxious thought to this aspect of the case and there is a provision in the Charter itself permitting the judges to decline to take part in the trial if for any reason they consider that they should not do so.

Ordinarily, on an objection like the one taken in this connection, the judges themselves might have expressed their unwillingness to take upon themselves the responsibility. Administration of justice demands that it should be conducted in such a way as not only to assure that justice is done but also to create the impression that it is being done. In the classic language of Lord Hewart, Lord Chief Justice of England, "It is not merely of some importance, but it is of fundamental importance that justice should not only be done but should manifestly and undoubtedly be seen to be done. . . . Nothing is to be done which creates even a suspicion that there has been an improper interference with the course of justice." The fear of miscarriage of justice is constantly in the mind of all who are practically or theoretically concerned with the law and especially with the dispensation of criminal law. The special difficulty as to the rule of law governing this case, taken with the ordinary uncertainty as to how far our means are sufficient to detect a crime and coupled further with the awkward possibilities of bias created by racial or political factors, makes our position one of very grave responsibility. The accused cannot be found fault with, if, in these circumstances, they entertain any such apprehension, and I, for myself, fully appreciate the basis of their fear. We cannot condemn the accused if they apprehend, in their trial by a body as we are, any possible interference of emotional factors with objectivity.

We cannot overlook or underestimate the effect of the influence stated above. They may indeed operate even unconsciously. We know how unconscious processes may go on in the mind of anyone who devotes his interest and his energies to finding out how a crime was committed, who committed it, and what were the motives and psychic attitude of the criminal. Since these processes may remain unobserved by the conscious part of the personality and may be influenced only indirectly and remotely by it, they present permanent pitfalls to objective and sound judgment—always discrediting the integrity of human justice. But in spite of all such obstacles it is human justice with which the accused must rest content. . . .

With these observations I persuade myself to hold that this objection of the accused need not be upheld. . . .

The so-called trial held according to the definition of crime now given by the victors obliterates the centuries of civilization which stretch between us and the summary slaying of the defeated in a war. A trial with law thus prescribed will only be a sham employment of legal process for the satisfaction of a thirst for revenge. It does not correspond to any idea of justice. Such a trial may justly create the feeling that the setting up of a tribunal like the present is much more a political than a legal affair, an essentially political objective having thus been cloaked by a juridical appearance. Formalized vengeance can bring only an ephemeral satisfaction, with every probability of ultimate regret; but vindication of law through genuine legal process alone may contribute substantially to the "re-establishment of order and decency in international relations.". . .

The Allied Powers have nowhere given the slightest indication of their intention to assume any power which does not belong to them in law. It is therefore pertinent to inquire what is the extent of the lawful authority of a victor over the vanquished in international relations. I am sure no one in this twentieth century would contend that even now this power is unlimited in respect of the person and the property of the defeated. Apart from the right of reprisal, the victor would no doubt have the right of punishing persons who had violated the laws of war. But to say that the victor can define a crime at his will and then punish for that crime would be to revert back to those days when he was allowed to devastate the occupied country with fire and sword, appropriate all public and private property therein, and kill the inhabitants or take them away into captivity. . . .

Under international law, as it now stands, a victor nation or a union of victor nations would have the authority to establish a tribunal for the trial of war criminals, but no authority to legislate and promulgate a new law of war crimes. When such a nation or group of nations proceeds to promulgate a Charter for the purpose of the trial of war criminals, it does so only under the authority of international law and not in exercise of any sovereign authority. I believe, even in relation to the defeated nationals or to the occupied territory, a victor nation is not a sovereign authority.

At any rate the sovereignty is recognized by the civilized world to have been limited in this respect by the international law at least in respect of its power over the prisoners of war within its custody. . . .

Whatever view of the legality or otherwise of a war may be taken, victory does not invest the victor with unlimited and undefined power now. International laws of war define and regulate the rights and duties of the victor over the individuals of the vanquished nationality. In my judgment, therefore, it is beyond the competence of any victor nation to go beyond the rules of international law as they exist, give new definitions of crimes and then punish the prisoners for having committed offense according to this new definition. This is really not a norm in abhorrence of the retroactivity of law: It is something more substantial. To allow any nation to do that will be to allow usurpation of power which international law denies that nation.

Keeping all this in view my reading of the Charter is that it does not purport to define war crimes; it simply enacts what matters will come up for trial before the Tribunal, leaving it to the Tribunal to decide, with reference to the international law, what offense, if any, has been committed by the persons placed on trial. . . .

I believe the Tribunal, established by the Charter, is not set up in a field unoccupied by any law. If there is such a thing

as international law, the field where the Tribunal is being
established is already occupied by that law and that law will
operate at least until its operation is validly ousted by any
authority. Even the Charter itself derives its authority from
this international law. In my opinion it cannot override the
authority of this law and the Tribunal is quite competent, under the authority of this international law, to question the
validity or otherwise of the provisions of the Charter. At any
rate unless and until the Charter expressly or by necessary
implication overrides the application of international law,
that law shall continue to apply and a Tribunal validly established by a Charter under the authority of such international
law will be quite competent to investigate the question
whether any provision of the Charter is or is not ultra vires.
The trial itself will involve this question. Its specific remit-
tance for investigation by the Charter will not be required. . . .

It is not the prosecution case that "war," irrespective of its
character, became a crime in international law. Their case is
that a war possessing the alleged character was made illegal
and criminal in international law and that consequently persons provoking such criminal war by such acts of planning,
etc., committed a crime under international law.

Two principal questions therefore arise here for our decision, namely:

1. Whether the wars of the alleged character became criminal in international law.

2. Assuming wars of the alleged character to be criminal in
international law, whether the individuals functioning as alleged here would incur any criminal responsibility in international law. . . .

The atom bomb during the Second World War, it is said,
has destroyed selfish nationalism and the last defense of isolationism more completely than it razed an enemy city. It is believed that it has ended one age and begun another—the new
and unpredictable age of soul.

"Such blasts as leveled Hiroshima and Nagasaki on August 6 and 9, 1945, never occurred on earth before—nor in the sun or stars, which burn from sources that release their energy much more slowly than does Uranium." [So said John J. O'Neill, the Science Editor, New York Herald Tribune.] "In a fraction of a second the atomic bomb that dropped on Hiroshima altered our traditional economic, political, and military values. It caused a revolution in the technique of war that forces immediate reconsideration of our entire national defense problem."

Perhaps these blasts have brought home to mankind "that every human being has a stake in the conduct not only of national affairs but also of world affairs." Perhaps these explosives have awakened within us the sense of unity of mankind,—the feeling that:

> "We are a unity of humanity, linked to all our fellow human beings, irrespective of race, creed or color, by bonds which have been fused unbreakably in the diabolical heat of those explosions."

All this might have been the result of these blasts. But certainly these feelings were non-existent at the time when the bombs were dropped. I, for myself, do not perceive any such feeling of broad humanity in the justifying words of those who were responsible for their use. As a matter of fact, I do not perceive much difference between what the German Emperor is alleged to have announced during the First World War in justification of the atrocious methods directed by him in the conduct of that war and what is being proclaimed after the Second World War in justification of these inhuman blasts.

I am not sure if the atom bombs have really succeeded in blowing away all the pre-war humbugs; we may be just dreaming. It is yet to be seen how far we have been alive to the fact that the world's present problems are not merely the more complex reproductions of those which have plagued us since 1914; that the new problems are not merely old national problems with world implications, but are real world problems and problems of humanity.

There is no doubt that the international society, if any, has been taken ill. Perhaps the situation is that the nations of the international group are living in an age of transition to a planned society.

But that is a matter for the future and perhaps is only a dream.

The dream of all students of world politics is to reduce the complex interplay of forces to a few elementary constants and variables by the use of which all the past is made plain and even the future stands revealed in lucid simplicity. Let us hope it is capable of realization in actual life. I must, however, leave this future to itself with the remark that this future prospect will not in the least be affected even if the existing law be not strained so as to fix any criminal responsibility for state acts on the individual authors thereof in order to make the criminality of states more effective. The future may certainly rely on adequate future provisions in this respect made by the organizers of such future.

During and after the present war, many eminent authors have come forward with contributions containing illuminating views on the subject of "War Criminals—Their Prosecution and Punishment." None of these books and none of the prosecutions professed to be prompted by any desire for retaliation. Most of these contributors claim to have undertaken the task because "miscarriage of justice" after World War I shocked them very much, particularly because such failure was ascribable to the instrumentality of jurists who deserved the epithets of being "stiff-necked conceptualists," "strict constructionists," and men "afflicted with an ideological rigor mortis." These Jurists, it is said, by giving the appearance of legality and logic to arguments based on some unrealistic, outworn and basically irrelevant technicality, caused the greatest confusion in the minds of ordinary laymen with regard to the problems of war criminals. These, it is claimed, were the chief present-day obstacles to the just solution of the problem and these authors have done their best to remove such obstacles and to supply "not a mere textbook on some remote technically intricate phrase of a branch of law," but "a weapon with which to enforce respect for the tenets of international law with its underlying principles of international justice."

Some of these authors have correctly said that law is not merely a conglomeration of human wisdom in the form of rules to be applied wherever and whenever such rules, like pieces in a jigsaw puzzle, may fit in. "Law is instead a dynamic human force regulating behaviour between man and man and making the existence and continuity of human society possible."

Its chief characteristic is that it stems from man's reasonableness and from his innate sense of justice.

"Stability and consistency are essential attributes of rules of law, no doubt,"

says such an author:

"Precedent is the *sine qua non* of an orderly legal system. But one must be certain that the precedent has undoubted relevancy and complete applicability to the new situation or to the given set of facts. And if applicable precedent is not available, a new precedent must be formed, for at all times law must seek to found itself on common sense and must strive for human justice."

With all respect to these learned authors, there is a very big assumption in all these observations when made in connection with international law. In our quest for international law are we dealing with an entity like national societies completely brought under the rule of law? Or, are we dealing with an inchoate society in a stage of its formation? It is a society where only that rule has come to occupy the position of law which has been unanimously agreed upon by the parties concerned. Any new precedent made will not be the law safeguarding the peace-loving law-abiding members of the Family of Nations, but will only be a precedent for the future victor against the future vanquished. Any misapplication of a doubtful legal doctrine here will threaten the very formation of the much coveted Society of Nations, will shake the very foundation of any future international society.

Law is a dynamic human force only when it is the law of

an organized society; when it is to be the sum of the conditions of social co-existence with regard to the activity of the community and of the individual. Law stems from a man's reasonableness and from his innate sense of justice. But what is that law? And is international law of that character? . . . .

In my judgment no category of war became a crime in international life up to the date of commencement of the world war under our consideration. Any distinction between just and unjust war remained only in the theory of the international legal philosphers. The Pact of Paris did not affect the character of war and failed to introduce any criminal responsibility in respect of any category of war in international life. No war became an illegal thing in the eye of international law as a result of this Pact. War itself, as before, remained outside the province of law, its conduct only having been brought under legal regulations. No customary law developed so as to make any war a crime. International community itself was not based on a footing which would justify the introduction of the conception of criminality in international life. . . .

The question of introduction of the conception of crime in international life requires to be examined from the viewpoint of the social utility of punishment. At one time and another different theories justifying punishment have been accepted for the purpose of national systems. These theories may be described as (1) Reformatory, (2) Deterrent, (3) Retributive and (4) Preventive. "Punishment has been credited with reforming the criminal into a law-abiding person, deterring others from committing the crime for which previous individuals were punished, making certain that retribution would be fair and judicious, rather than in the nature of private revenge, and enhancing the solidarity of the group by the collective expression of its disapproval of the law-breaker." Contemporary criminologists give short shrift to these arguments. I would however proceed on the footing that punishment can produce one or the other of the desired results.

So long as the international organization continues at the

stage where the trial and punishment for any crime remains available only against the vanquished in a lost war, the introduction of criminal responsibility cannot produce the deterrent and the preventive effects.

The risk of criminal responsibility incurred in planning an aggressive war does not in the least become graver than that involved in the possible defeat in the war planned.

I do not think any one would seriously think of reformation in this respect through the introduction of such a conception of criminal responsibility in international life. Moral attitudes and norms of conduct are acquired in too subtle a manner for punishment to be a reliable incentive even where such conduct relates to one's own individual interest. Even a slight knowledge of the processes of personality-development should warn us against the old doctrine of original sin in a new guise. If this is so, even when a person acts for his own individual purposes, it is needless to say that when the conduct in question relates, at least in the opinion of the individual concerned, to his national cause, the punishment meted out, or criminal responsibility imposed by the victor nation, can produce very little effect. Fear of being punished by the future possible victor for violating a rule which that victor may be pleased then to formulate would hardly elicit any appreciation of the values behind that norm.

In any event, this theory of reformation, in international life, need not take the criminal responsibility beyond the State concerned. The theory proceeds on this footing. If a person does a wrong to another, he does it from an exaggeration of his own personality, and this aggressiveness must be restrained and the person made to realize that his desires do not rule the world, but that the interests of the community are determinative. Hence, punishment is designed to be the influence brought to bear on the person in order to bring to his consciousness the conditionality of his existence, and to keep it within its limits. This is done by the infliction of such suffering as would cure the delinquent of his individualistic excess. For this purpose, an offending State itself can be effectively punished. Indeed the punishment can be effective only if the delinquent State as such is punished.

In my opinion it is inappropriate to introduce criminal responsibility of the agents of a state in international life for the purpose of retribution. Retribution, in the proper sense of the term, means the bringing home to the criminal the legitimate consequences of his conduct, legitimate from the ethical standpoint. This would involve the determination of the degree of his moral responsibility, a task that is an impossibility for any legal Tribunal even in national life. Conditions of knowledge, of training, of opportunities for moral development, of social environment generally and of motive fall to be searched out even in justifying criminal responsibility on this ground in national life. In international life many other factors would fall to be considered before one can justify criminal responsibility on this retributive theory.

The only justification that remains for the introduction of such a conception in international life is revenge, a justification which all those who are demanding this trial are disclaiming. . . .

After giving my anxious and careful consideration to the reasons given by the prosecution as also to the opinions of the various authorities I have arrived at the conclusion:

1. That no category of war became criminal or illegal in international life;

2. That the individuals comprising the government and functioning as agents of that government incur no criminal responsibility in international law for the acts alleged;

3. That the international community has not as yet reached a stage which would make it expedient to include judicial process for condemning and punishing either states or individuals.

I have not said anything about the alleged object of the Japanese plan or conspiracy. I believe no one will seriously contend that domination of one nation by another became a crime in international life. Apart from the question of legality or otherwise of the means designed to achieve this object it must be held that the object itself was not yet illegal or criminal in international life. In any other view, the entire international community would be a community of criminal races. At least many of the powerful nations are living this sort of life and if these acts are criminal then the entire international community is living that criminal life, some actually committing the crime and others becoming accessories after the fact in these crimes. No nation has as yet treated such acts as crimes and all the powerful nations continue close relations with the nations that had committed such acts. . . .

We need not stop here to consider whether a static conception of peace is at all justifiable in international relations. I am not sure if it is possible to create "peace" once for all, and if there can be status quo which is to be eternal. At any rate in the present state of international relations such a static idea of peace is absolutely untenable. Certainly, dominated nations of the present day status quo cannot be made to submit to eternal domination only in the name of peace. International law must be prepared to face the problem of bringing within juridical limits the politico-historical evolution of mankind which up to now has been accomplished chiefly through war. War and other methods of self-help by force can be effectively excluded only when this problem is solved, and it is only then that we can think of introducing criminal responsibility for efforts at adjustment by means other than peaceful. Before the introduction of criminal responsibility for such efforts the international law must succeed in establishing rules for effecting peaceful changes. Until then there can hardly be any justification for any direct and indirect attempt at maintaining, in the name of humanity and justice, the very status quo which might have been organized and hitherto maintained only by force by pure opportunist "Have and Holders," and which, we know, we cannot undertake to vindicate. The part of humanity which has been lucky enough to enjoy political freedom can now well afford to have the deterministic ascetic outlook of life, and may think of peace in terms of political status quo. But every part of humanity has not been equally lucky and a considerable part is still haunted by the wishful thinking about escape from political dominations. To them the present age is faced with not only the menace of totalitarianism but also the actual plague of imperialism. They have not as yet been in a position to entertain a simple belief in a valiant god struggling to establish a real democratic order in the Universe. They know how the present state of things came into being. A swordsman may genuinely be eager to return the weapon to its scabbard at the earliest possible moment after using it successfully for his gain, if he can keep his spoil without having to use it any more. But, perhaps one thing which you cannot do with weapons like bayonets and swords is that you cannot sit on them. . . .

It may be suggested, as has very often been done in course of this trial, that simply because there might be robbers untried and unpunished it would not follow that robbing is no crime and a robber placed under trial for robbery would gain nothing by showing that there are other robbers in the world who are going unpunished. This is certainly sound logic when we know for certain that robbery is a crime. When, however, we are still to determine whether or not a particular act in a particular community is or is not criminal, I believe it is a pertinent enquiry how the act in question stands in relation to the other members of the community and how the community looks upon the act when done by such other members.

Before we can decide which meaning should be attached to the words "aggressor," "aggression" and "aggressive," we must decide which of the views as to a certain category of war having become criminal is being accepted by us. It is needless to say that we are now proceeding on the assumption that a certain category of war is a crime under the international law. . . .

There is yet another difficult matter that must enter into our consideration in this connection. We must not overlook the system of Power Politics prevailing in international life. It will be a pertinent question whether or not self-defense or self-protection would include maintenance of a nation's position in the system. The accused in the present case claim such defensive character also for their action in the Pacific.

As, in my opinion, the Pact of Paris left the parties themselves to be the judge of the condition of self-defense, I would only insist upon there having been bona fide belief in the existence of some sufficient objective condition.

A war to secure domination of certain territories as alleged in the indictment would perhaps constitute a breach of the Pact of Paris, if such a measure cannot be justified by the party adopting it on the grounds indicated above. But I have already given my view of the Pact. So far as the question of criminal liability, either of the state or of the state agents, is concerned, I have already given my conclusion in the negative.

I would only like to observe once again that the so-called Western interests in the Eastern Hemisphere were mostly founded on the past success of these western people in "transmuting violence into commercial profit." The inequity, of course, was of their fathers who had had recourse to the sword for this purpose. But perhaps it is right to say that "the man of violence cannot both genuinely repent of his violence and permanently profit by it.". . .

The Kaiser Wilhelm II was credited with a letter to the Austrian Kaiser Franz Joseph in the early days of that war, wherein he stated as follows:

"My soul is torn, but everything must be put to fire and sword; men, women and children and old men must be slaughtered and not a tree or house be left standing. With these methods of terrorism, which are alone capable of affecting a people as degenerate as the French, the war will be over in two months, whereas if I admit considerations of humanity it will be prolonged for years. In spite of my repugnance I have therefore been obliged to choose the former system."

This showed his ruthless policy, and this policy of indiscriminate murder to shorten the war was considered to be a crime.

In the Pacific war under our consideration, if there was anything approaching what is indicated in the above letter of the German Emperor, it is the decision coming from the allied powers to use the atom bomb. Future generations will judge this dire decision. History will say whether any outburst of popular sentiment against usage of such a new weapon is irrational and only sentimental and whether it has become legitimate by such indiscriminate slaughter to win the victory by breaking the will of the whole nation to continue to fight. We need not stop here to consider whether or not "the atom bomb comes to force a more fundamental searching of the nature of warfare and of the legitimate means for the pursuit of military objectives." It would be sufficient for my present purpose to say that if any indiscriminate destruction of civilian life and property is still illegitimate in warfare, then, in the Pacific war, this decision to use the atom bomb is the only near approach to the directives of the German Emperor during the First World War and of the Nazi leaders during the Second World War. Nothing like this could be traced to the credit of the present accused. . . .

Some years later, Israel located Adolph Eichmann living a se-
cluded life in Argentina. He was abducted by Israeli agents
and brought forcibly to Israel for trial as a war criminal. Eichmann had been in charge of carrying out "the final solution"
by which the Jewish population under German control was to
be exterminated. Many criticisms were directed against the
Eichmann trial. Israel had not existed at the time of Eichmann's crimes, no acts had been committed on Israeli territory,
and there was no prospect of a fair trial. We include here a
short excerpt from the judgment that bears on the main concerns of this book.

THE DECISION IN THE EICHMANN CASE, 1961

[Excerpts]

11. But we have also perused the sources of international law,
including the numerous authorities mentioned by learned
Counsel in his comprehensive written brief upon which he
based his oral pleadings, and by the learned Attorney-General
in his comprehensive oral pleadings, and failed to find any
foundation for the contention that Israel law is in conflict
with the principles of international law. On the contrary, we
have reached the conclusion that the law in question conforms
to the best traditions of the law of nations.

The power of the State of Israel to enact the law in question
or Israel's "right to punish" is based, with respect to the offences in question, from the point of view of international
law, on a dual foundation: The universal character of the
crimes in question and their specific character as being designed to exterminate the Jewish people. In what follows we
shall deal with each of these two aspects separately.

12. The abhorrent crimes defined in this law are crimes not
under Israel law alone. These crimes which afflicted the whole
of mankind and shocked the conscience of nations are grave
offences against the law of nations itself (*delicta juris gen-
tium*). Therefore, so far from international law negating or
limiting the jurisdiction of countries with respect to such

crimes, in the absence of an International Court the international law is in need of the judicial and legislative authorities of every country, to give effect to its penal injunctions and to bring criminals to trial. The authority and jurisdiction to try crimes under international law are *universal*. . . .

16. We have said that the crimes dealt with in this case are not crimes under Israel law alone, but are in essence offences against the law of nations. Indeed, the crimes in question are not a figment of the imagination of the legislator who enacted the law for the punishment of Nazis and Nazi collaborators, but have been stated and defined in that law according to a precise pattern of international laws and conventions which define crimes under the law of nations. The "crime against the Jewish people" is defined on the pattern of the genocide crime defined in the "Convention for the prevention and punishment of genocide" which was adopted by the United Nations Assembly on 9.12.48. The "crime against humanity" and the "war crime" are defined on the pattern of crimes of identical designations defined in the Charter of the International Military Tribunal (which is the Statute of the Nuremberg Court) annexed to the Four-Power Agreement of 8.8.45 on the subject of the trial of the principal war criminals (the London Agreement), and also in Law No. 10 of the Control Council of Germany of 20.12.45. The offence of "membership of a hostile organization" is defined by the pronouncement in the judgment of the Nuremberg Tribunal, according to its Charter, to declare the organizations in question as "criminal organisations," and is also patterned on the Council of Control Law No. 10. For purposes of comparison we shall set forth in what follows the parallel articles and clauses side by side. [Comparison omitted]. . . .

17. The crime of "genocide" was first defined by Raphael Lemkin in his book *Axis Rule in Occupied Europe* (1944) in view of the methodical extermination of peoples and populations, and primarily the Jewish people by the Nazis and their satellites (after the learned author had already moved, at the Madrid 1933 International Congress for the Consolidation of

International Law, that the extermination of racial, religious or social groups be declared "a crime against international law"). On 11.12.46 after the International Military Tribunal pronounced its judgment against the principal German criminals, the United Nations Assembly, by its Resolution No. 96 (I), unanimously declared that "genocide" is a crime against the law of nations. . . .

19. In the light of the recurrent affirmation by the United Nations in the 1946 Assembly resolution and in the 1948 convention, and in the light of the advisory opinion of the International Court of Justice, there is no doubt that genocide has been recognized as a crime under international law in the full legal meaning of this term, and at that *ex tunc;* that is to say: the crimes of genocide which were committed against the Jewish people and other peoples were crimes under international law. It follows therefore, in the light of the acknowledged principles of international law, that the jurisdiction to try such crimes is universal. . . .

30. We have discussed at length the international character of the crimes in question because this offers the broadest possible, though not the only, basis for Israel's jurisdiction according to the law of nations. No less important from the point of view of international law is the special connection the State of Israel has with such crimes, seeing that the people of Israel (Am Israel) —the Jewish people (Ha'am Ha'yehudi—to use the term in the Israel legislation) —constituted the target and the victim of most of the crimes in question. The State of Israel's "right to punish" the accused derives, in our view, from two cumulative sources: a universal source (pertaining to the whole of mankind) which vests the right to prosecute and punish crimes of this order in every State within the family of nations; and a specific or national source which gives the victim nation the right to try any who assault their existence. . . .

33. When the question is presented in its widest form, as stated above, it seems to us that there can be no doubt as to what the answer will be. The "linking point" between Israel

and the accused (and for that matter between Israel and any person accused of a crime against the Jewish people under this Law) is striking and glaring in a "crime manifest against the Jewish people," a crime that postulates an intention to exterminate the Jewish people in whole or in part. Indeed, even without such specific definition—and it must be noted that the draft law had only defined "crimes against humanity" and "war crimes" (Bills of Law of the year 5710 No. 36, p. 119) —there was a subsisting "linking point," seeing that most of the Nazi crimes of this kind were perpetrated against the Jewish people; but viewed in the light of the definition of "crime against the Jewish people," the legal position is clearer. The "crime against the Jewish people," as defined in the Law, constitutes in effect an attempt to exterminate the Jewish people, or a partial extermination of the Jewish people. If there is an effective link (and not necessarily an identity) between the State of Israel and the Jewish people, then a crime intended to exterminate the Jewish people has a very striking connection with the State of Israel. . . .

The *Yamashita* trial involved the prosecution of a Japanese general by an American military commission. General Yamashita was charged with responsibility for war crimes committed by his soldiers in the closing weeks of Japanese occupation of the Philippines. General Yamashita was not accused of having committed or authorized the acts for which he was charged, or even to have had specific knowledge of their occurrence. The decision by the Supreme Court upholding a death sentence is of extreme interest in relation to the Vietnam War and, in particular, in relation to the trial of Lieutenant Calley and his associates for the massacre at My Lai. There are two kinds of relevant inquiry: (1) If the *Yamashita* precedent is authentic, then why not demand the prosecution of General Westmoreland or General Abrams? (2) Was General Yamashita being made a scapegoat for acts that he did not approve of and could not have prevented?

IN THE MATTER OF YAMASHITA, 1945

[*Excerpts*]

Mr. Chief Justice Stone delivered the opinion of the Court.

No. 61 Miscellaneous is an application for leave to file a petition for writs of habeas corpus and prohibition in this Court. No. 672 is a petition for certiorari to review an order of the Supreme Court of the Commonwealth of the Philippines (28 USCA § 349, 8 FCA title 28, § 349), denying petitioner's application to that court for writs of habeas corpus and prohibition. As both applications raise substantially like questions, and because of the importance and novelty of some of those presented, we set the two applications down for oral argument as one case.

*[5]

*From the petitions and supporting papers it appears that prior to September 3, 1945, petitioner was the Commanding General of the Fourteenth Army Group of the Imperial Japanese Army in the Philippine Islands. On that date he surrendered to and became a prisoner of war of the United States

Army Forces in Baguio, Philippine Islands. On September 25th, by order of respondent, Lieutenant General Wilhelm D. Styer, Commanding General of the United States Army Forces, Western Pacific, which command embraces the Philippine Islands, petitioner was served with a charge prepared by the Judge Advocate General's Department of the Army, purporting to charge petitioner with a violation of the law of war. On October 8, 1945, petitioner, after pleading not guilty to the charge, was held for trial before a military commission of five Army officers appointed by order of General Styer. The order appointed six Army officers, all lawyers, as defense counsel. Throughout the proceedings which followed, including those before this Court, defense counsel have demonstrated their professional skill and resourcefulness and their proper zeal for the defense with which they were charged. . . .

The charge. Neither Congressional action nor the military orders constituting the commission authorized it to place petitioner on trial unless the charge preferred against him is of a violation of the law of war. The charge, so far as now relevant, is that petitioner, between October 9, 1944, and September 2, 1945, in the Philippine Islands, "while commander of armed forces of Japan at war with the United States of America and its allies, unlawfully disregarded and failed to discharge his

*[14]

duty as commander to *control the operations of the members of his command, permitting them to commit brutal atrocities and other high crimes against people of the United States and of its allies and dependencies, particularly the Philippines; and he . . . thereby violated the laws of war."

Bills of particulars, filed by the prosecution by order of the commission, allege a series of acts, one hundred and twenty-three in number, committed by members of the forces under petitioner's command during the period mentioned. The first item specifies the execution of "a deliberate plan and purpose to massacre and exterminate a large part of the civilian population of Batangas Province, and to devastate and destroy public, private and religious property therein, as a result of which more than 25,000 men, women and children, all unarmed non-combatant civilians, were brutally mistreated and killed, without cause or trial, and entire settlements were devastated and destroyed wantonly and without military necessity." Other items specify acts of violence, cruelty and homicide inflicted upon the civilian population and prisoners of war, acts of wholesale pillage and the wanton destruction of religious monuments.

It is not denied that such acts directed against the civilian population of an occupied country and against prisoners of war are recognized in international law as violations of the law of war. Articles 4, 28, 46, and 47, Annex to Fourth Hague Convention, 1907, 36 Stat 2277, 2296, 2303, 2306, 2307. But it is urged that the charge does not allege that petitioner has either committed or directed the commission of such acts, and consequently that no violation is charged as against him. But this overlooks the fact that the gist of the charge is an unlawful breach of duty by petitioner as an army commander to control the operations of the members of his command by "permitting them to commit" the extensive and widespread atrocities specified. The question then is whether the law of war imposes on an army commander a duty to take such appropriate measures as are within his power to control the troops under his command for the prevention of the specified acts which are violations of the law of war and which are likely to attend the occupation of hostile territory by an uncontrolled soldiery, and whether he may be charged with personal responsibility for his failure to take such measures when violations result. That this was the precise issue to be tried was made clear by the statement of the prosecution at the opening of the trial.

It is evident that the conduct of military operations by troops whose excesses are unrestrained by the orders or efforts of their commander would almost certainly result in violations which it is the purpose of the law of war to prevent. Its purpose to protect civilian populations and prisoners of war from brutality would largely be defeated if the commander of an invading army could with impunity neglect to take reasonable measures for their protection. Hence the law of war presupposes that its violation is to be avoided through the control of the operations of war by commanders who are to some extent responsible for their subordinates.

This is recognized by the Annex to Fourth Hague Convention of 1907, respecting the laws and customs of war on land. Article 1 lays down as a condition which an armed force must fulfill in order to be accorded the rights of lawful belligerents, that it must be "commanded by a person responsible for his subordinates." 36 Stat 2295. Similarly Article 19 of the Tenth Hague Convention, relating to bombardment by naval vessels, provides that commanders in chief of the belligerent vessels "must see that the above Articles are properly carried out." 36 Stat 2389. And Article 26 of the Geneva Red Cross Convention of 1929, 47 Stat 2074, 2092, for the amelioration of the condition of the wounded and sick in armies in the field, makes it "the duty of the commanders-in-chief of the belligerent armies to provide for the details of execution of the foregoing articles, [of the convention] as well as for the unforeseen cases." And, finally, Article 43 of the Annex of the Fourth Hague Convention, 36 Stat 2306, requires that the commander of a force occupying enemy territory, as was petitioner, "shall take all the measures in his power to restore, and ensure, as far as possible, public order and safety, while respecting, unless absolutely prevented, the laws in force in the country."

These provisions plainly imposed on petitioner, who at the time specified was military governor of the Philippines, as well as commander of the Japanese forces, an affirmative duty to take such measures as were within his power and appropriate in the circumstances to protect prisoners of war and the civilian population. This duty of a commanding officer has heretofore been recognized, and its breach penalized by our own military tribunals.[3] A like principle has been applied so as to

---

[3] Failure of an officer to take measures to prevent murder of an inhabitant of an occupied country committed in his presence. Gen. Orders No. 221, Hq. Div. of the Philippines, August 17, 1901. And in Gen. Orders

impose liability on the United States in international arbitrations. Case of Jennaud [sic], 3 Moore, International Arbitrations, 3000; Case of "The Zafiro," 5 Hackworth, Digest of International Law, 707.

We do not make the laws of war but we respect them so far as they do not conflict with the commands of Congress or the Constitution. There is no contention that the present charge, thus read, is without the support of evidence, or that the commission held petitioner responsible for failing to take measures which were beyond his control or inappropriate for a

*[17]

commanding officer to take in the circumstances.⁴ * We do not here appraise the evidence on which petitioner was convicted. We do not consider what measures, if any, petitioner took to prevent the commission, by the troops under his command, of the plain violations of the law of war detailed in the bill of particulars, or whether such measures as he may have taken were appropriate and sufficient to discharge the duty imposed upon him. These are questions within the peculiar competence of the military officers composing the commission and were for it to decide. See Smith v. Whitney, 116 US 167, 178, 29 L ed 601, 604, 6 S Ct 570. It is plain that the charge on which petitioner was tried charged him with a breach of his duty to control the operations of the members of his command, by permitting them to commit the specified atrocities. This was enough to require the commission to hear evidence

---

No. 264, Hq. Div. of the Philippines, September 9, 1901, it was held that an officer could not be found guilty for failure to prevent a murder unless it appeared that the accused had "the power to prevent" it.

⁴ In its findings the commission took account of the difficulties "faced by the accused, with respect not only to the swift and overpowering advance of American forces, but also to errors of his predecessors, weakness in organization, equipment, supply . . . , training, communication, discipline and morale of his troops," and "the tactical situation, the character, training and capacity of staff officers and subordinate commanders, as well as the traits of character . . . of his troops." It nonetheless found that petitioner had not taken such measures to control his troops as were "required by the circumstances." We do not weigh the evidence. We merely hold that the charge sufficiently states a violation against the law of war, and that the commission, upon the facts found, could properly find petitioner guilty of such a violation.

tending to establish the culpable failure of petitioner to perform the duty imposed on him by the law of war and to pass upon its sufficiency to establish guilt.

Obviously charges of violations of law of war triable before a military tribunal need not be stated with the precision of a common law indictment. Cf. Collins v. McDonald, supra (258 US 420, 66 L ed 696, 42 S Ct 326). But we conclude that the allegations of the charge, tested by any reasonable standard, adequately allege a violation of the law of war and that the commission had authority to try and decide the issue which it raised. Cf. Dealy v. United States, 152 US 539, 38 L ed 545, 14 S Ct 680; Williamson v. United States, 207 US 425, 447, 52 L ed 278, 290, 28 S Ct 163; Glasser v. United States, 315 US 60, 66, 86 L ed 680, 697, 62 S Ct 457, and cases cited. . . .

Mr. Justice Murphy, dissenting.

The significance of the issue facing the Court today cannot be over-emphasized. An American military commission has been established to try a fallen military commander of a conquered nation for an alleged war crime. The authority for such action grows out of the exercise of the power conferred upon Congress by Article 1, § 8, cl 10 of the Constitution to "define and punish . . . Offenses against the Law of Nations . . ." The grave issue raised by this case is whether a military commission so established and so authorized may disregard the procedural rights of an accused person as guaranteed by the Constitution, especially by the due process clause of the Fifth Amendment.

The answer is plain. The Fifth Amendment guarantee of due process of law applies to "any person" who is accused of a crime by the Federal Government or any of its agencies. No exception is made as to those who are accused of war crimes or as to those who possess the status of an enemy belligerent. Indeed, such an exception would be contrary to the whole philosophy of human rights which makes the Constitution the great living document that it is. The immutable rights of the individual, including those secured by the due process clause of the Fifth Amendment, belong not alone to the members of those nations that excel on the battlefield or that subscribe to the democratic ideology. They belong to every person in the world, victor or vanquished, whatever may be his race, color or beliefs. They rise above any status of belligerency or outlawry. They survive any popular passion or frenzy of the moment. No court or legislature or executive, not even the

*[27]

mightiest *army in the world, can ever destroy them. Such is the universal and indestructible nature of the rights which the due process clause of the Fifth Amendment recognizes and protects when life or liberty is threatened by virtue of the authority of the United States.

The existence of these rights, unfortunately, is not always respected. They are often trampled under by those who are motivated by hatred, aggression or fear. But in this nation individual rights are recognized and protected, at least in regard to governmental action. They cannot be ignored by any branch of the Government, even the military, except under the most extreme and urgent circumstances.

The failure of the military commission to obey the dictates of the due process requirements of the Fifth Amendment is apparent in this case. The petitioner was the commander of an army totally destroyed by the superior power of this nation. While under heavy and destructive attack by our forces, his troops committed many brutal atrocities and other high crimes. Hostilities ceased and he voluntarily surrendered. At that point he was entitled, as an individual protected by the due process clause of the Fifth Amendment, to be treated fairly and justly according to the accepted rules of law and procedure. He was also entitled to a fair trial as to any alleged crimes and to be free from charges of legally unrecognized crimes that would serve only to permit his accusers to satisfy their desires for revenge.

A military commission was appointed to try the petitioner for an alleged war crime. The trial was ordered to be held in territory over which the United States has complete sovereignty. No military necessity or other emergency demanded the suspension of the safeguards of due process. Yet petitioner was rushed to trial under an improper charge, given insufficient time to prepare an adequate defense, deprived of the benefits of some of the most elementary rules of evidence and summarily sentenced to be hanged. In all this needless and unseemly haste there was no serious attempt to charge or to prove that he committed a recognized violation of the laws of war. He was not charged with personally participating in the acts of atrocity or with ordering or condoning their commission. Not even knowledge of these crimes was attributed to him. It was simply alleged that he unlawfully disregarded and failed to discharge his duty as commander to control the operations of the members of his command, permitting them to commit the acts of atrocity. The recorded annals of warfare and the established principles of international law afford not the slightest precedent for such a charge. This indictment in effect permitted the military commission to make the crime whatever it willed, dependent upon its biased view as to petitioner's duties and his disregard thereof, a practice reminiscent of that pursued in certain less respected nations in recent years.

In my opinion, such a procedure is unworthy of the traditions of our people or of the immense sacrifices that they have made to advance the common ideals of mankind. The high feelings of the moment doubtless will be satisfied. But in the sober afterglow will come the realization of the boundless and dangerous implications of the procedure sanctioned today. No one in a position of command in an army, from sergeant to general, can escape those implications. Indeed, the fate of some future President of the United States and his chiefs of staff and military advisers may well have been sealed by this decision. But even more significant will be the hatred and ill-will growing out of the application of this unprecedented procedure. That has been the inevitable effect of every method of punishment disregarding the element of personal culpability. The effect in this instance, unfortunately, will be magnified infinitely for here we are dealing with the rights of man on an international level. To subject an enemy belligerent to an unfair trial, to charge him with an unrecognized crime, or to vent on him our retributive emotions only antagonizes the enemy nation and hinders the reconciliation necessary to a peaceful world.

That there were brutal atrocities inflicted upon the helpless Filipino people, to whom tyranny is no stranger, by Japanese armed forces under the petitioner's command is undeniable. Starvation, execution or massacre without trial, torture, rape, murder and wanton destruction of property were foremost among the outright violations of the laws of war and of the conscience of a civilized world. That just punishment should be meted out to all those responsible for criminal acts of this nature is also beyond dispute. But these factors do not answer the problem in this case. They do not justify the abandonment of our devotion to justice in dealing with a fallen enemy commander. To conclude otherwise is to admit that the enemy has lost the battle but has destroyed our ideals.

War breeds atrocities. From the earliest conflicts of recorded history to the global struggles of modern times inhumanities, lust and pillage have been the inevitable by-products of man's resort to force and arms. Unfortunately, such despicable acts have a dangerous tendency to call forth primitive impulses of vengeance and retaliation among the victimized peoples. The satisfaction of such impulses in turn breeds resentment and fresh tension. Thus does the spiral of cruelty and hatred grow.

If we are ever to develop an orderly international community based upon a recognition of human dignity it is of the utmost importance that the necessary punishment of those guilty of atrocities be as free as possible from the ugly stigma of revenge and vindictiveness. Justice must be tempered by compassion rather than by vengeance. In this, the first case involving this momentous problem ever to reach this Court, our responsibility is both lofty and difficult. We must insist, within the confines of our proper jurisdiction, that the highest standards of justice be applied in this trial of an enemy commander conducted under the authority of the United States.

Otherwise stark retribution will be free to masquerade in a cloak of false legalism. And the hatred and cynicism engendered by that retribution will supplant the great ideals to which this nation is dedicated.

This Court fortunately has taken the first and most important step toward insuring the supremacy of law and justice in the treatment of an enemy belligerent accused of violating the laws of war. Jurisdiction properly has been asserted to inquire "into the cause of restraint of liberty" of such a person. 28 USCA § 452, 8 FCA title 28, § 452. Thus the obnoxious doctrine asserted by the Government in this case, to the effect that restraints of liberty resulting from military trials of war criminals are political matters completely outside the arena of judicial review, has been rejected fully and unquestionably. This does not mean, of course, that the foreign affairs and policies of the nation are proper subjects of judicial inquiry. But when the liberty of any person is restrained by reason of the authority of the United States the writ of habeas corpus is available to test the legality of that restraint, even though direct court review of the restraint is prohibited. The conclusive presumption must be made, in this country at least, that illegal restraints are unauthorized and unjustified by any foreign policy of the Government and that commonly accepted juridical standards are to be recognized and enforced. On that basis judicial inquiry into these matters may proceed within its proper sphere.

The determination of the extent of review of war trials calls for judicial statesmanship of the highest order. The ultimate nature and scope of the writ of habeas corpus are within the discretion of the judiciary unless validly circumscribed by Congress. Here we are confronted with a use of the writ under circumstances novel in the history of the Court. For my own part, I do not feel that we should be confined by the traditional lines of review drawn in connection with the use of the writ by ordinary criminals who have direct access to the judiciary in the first instance. Those held by the military lack any such access; consequently the judicial review available by habeas corpus must be wider than usual in order that proper standards of justice may be enforceable.

But for the purposes of this case I accept the scope of review recognized by the Court at this time. As I understand it, the following issues in connection with war criminal trials are reviewable through the use of the writ of habeas corpus: (1) whether the military commission was lawfully created and had authority to try and to convict the accused of a war crime; (2) whether the charge against the accused stated a violation of the laws of war; (3) whether the commission, in admitting certain evidence, violated any law or military command defining the commission's authority in that respect; and (4) whether the commission lacked jurisdiction because of a failure to give advance notice to the protecting power as required by treaty or convention.

The Court, in my judgment, demonstrates conclusively that the military commission was lawfully created in this instance and that petitioner could not object to its power to try him for a recognized war crime. Without pausing here to discuss the third and fourth issues, however, I find it impossible to agree that the charge against the petitioner stated a recognized violation of the laws of war.

It is important, in the first place, to appreciate the background of events preceding this trial. From October 9, 1944, to September 2, 1945, the petitioner was the Commanding General of the 14th Army Group of the Imperial Japanese Army, with headquarters in the Philippines. The reconquest of the Philippines by the armed forces of the United States began approximately at the time when the petitioner assumed this command. Combined with a great and decisive sea battle, an invasion was made on the island of Leyte on October 20, 1944. "In the six days of the great naval action the Japanese position in the Philippines had become extremely critical. Most of the serviceable elements of the Japanese Navy had been committed to the battle with disastrous results. The strike had miscarried, and General MacArthur's land wedge was firmly implanted in the vulnerable flank of the enemy.

. . . There were 260,000 Japanese troops scattered over the Philippines but most of them might as well have been on the other side of the world so far as the enemy's ability to shift them to meet the American thrusts was concerned. If General MacArthur succeeded in establishing himself in the Visayas where he could stage, exploit, and spread under cover of overwhelming naval and air superiority, nothing could prevent him from overrunning the Philippines." Biennial Report of the Chief of Staff of the United States Army, July 1, 1943, to June 30, 1945, to the Secretary of War, p 74.

By the end of 1944 the island of Leyte was largely in American hands. And on January 9, 1945, the island of Luzon was invaded. "Yamashita's inability to cope with General MacArthur's swift moves, his desired reaction to the deception measures, the guerrillas, and General Kenney's aircraft combined to place the Japanese in an impossible situation. The enemy was forced into a piecemeal commitment of his troops." Id. p 78. It was at this time and place that most of the alleged atrocities took place. Organized resistance around Manila ceased on February 23. Repeated land and air assaults pulverized the enemy and within a few months there was little left of petitioner's command except a few remnants which had gathered for a last stand among the precipitous mountains.

As the military commission here noted, "The Defense established the difficulties faced by the Accused with respect not only to the swift and overpowering advance of American forces, but also to the errors of his predecessors, weaknesses in organization, equipment, supply with especial reference to food and gasoline, training, communication, discipline and morale of his troops. It was alleged that the sudden assignment of Naval and Air Forces to his tactical command presented almost insurmountable difficulties. This situation was followed, the Defense contended, by failure to obey his orders to withdraw troops from Manila, and the subsequent massacre of unarmed civilians, particularly by Naval forces. Prior to the Luzon Campaign, Naval forces had reported to a separate ministry in the Japanese Government and Naval Commanders may not have been receptive or experienced in this instance with respect to a joint land operation under a single commander who was designated from the Army Service."

The day of final reckoning for the enemy arrived in August, 1945. On September 3, the petitioner surrendered to the United States Army at Baguio, Luzon. He immediately became a prisoner of war and was interned in prison in conformity with the rules of international law. On September 25, approximately three weeks after surrendering, he was served with the charge in issue in this case. Upon service of the charge he was removed from the status of a prisoner of war and placed in confinement as an accused war criminal. Arraignment followed on October 8 before a military commission specially appointed for the case. Petitioner pleaded not guilty. He was also served on that day with a bill of particulars alleging 64 crimes by troops under his command. A supplemental bill alleging 59 more crimes by his troops was filed on October 29, the same day that the trial began. No continuance was allowed for preparation of a defense as to the supplemental bill. The trial continued uninterrupted until December 5, 1945. On December 7 petitioner was found guilty as charged and was sentenced to be hanged.

The petitioner was accused of having "unlawfully disregarded and failed to discharge his duty as commander to control the operations of the members of his command, permitting them to commit brutal atrocities and other high crimes." The bills of particular further alleged that specific acts of atrocity were committed by "members of the armed forces of Japan under the command of the accused." Nowhere was it alleged that the petitioner personally committed any of the atrocities, or that he ordered their commission, or that he had any knowledge of the commission thereof by members of his command.

The findings of the military commission bear out this absence of any direct personal charge against the petitioner. The commission merely found that atrocities and other high crimes "have been committed by members of the Japanese

armed forces under your command . . . that they were not
sporadic in nature but in many cases were methodically supervised by Japanese officers and noncommissioned officers . . .
that during the period in question you failed to provide effective control of your troops as was required by the circumstances."

In other words, read against the background of military
events in the Philippines subsequent to October 9, 1944, these
charges amount to this: "We, the victorious American forces,
have done everything possible to destroy and disorganize your
lines of communication, your effective control of your personnel, your ability to wage war. In those respects we have
succeeded. We have defeated and crushed your forces. And
now we charge and condemn you for having been inefficient in
maintaining control of your troops during the period when
we were so effectively besieging and eliminating your forces
and blocking your ability to maintain effective control. Many
terrible atrocities were committed by your disorganized troops.
Because these atrocities were so widespread we will not bother
to charge or prove that you committed, ordered or condoned
any of them. We will assume that they must have resulted
from your inefficiency and negligence as a commander. In
short, we charge you with the crime of inefficiency in controlling your troops. We will judge the discharge of your
duties by the disorganization which we ourselves created in
large part. Our standards of judgment are whatever we wish to
make them."

Nothing in all history or in international law, at least as
far as I am aware, justifies such a charge against a fallen
commander of a defeated force. To use the very inefficiency
and disorganization created by the victorious forces as the
primary basis for condemning officers of the defeated armies
bears no resemblance to justice or to military reality.

International law makes no attempt to define the duties of
a commander of an army under constant and overwhelming
assault; nor does it impose liability under such circumstances
for failure to meet the ordinary responsibilities of command.

The omission is understandable. Duties, as well as ability to control troops, vary according to the nature and intensity of the particular battle. To find an unlawful deviation from duty under battle conditions requires difficult and speculative calculations. Such calculations become highly untrustworthy when they are made by the victor in relation to the actions of a vanquished commander. Objective and realistic norms of conduct are then extremely unlikely to be used in forming a judgment as to deviations from duty. The probability that vengeance will form the major part of the victor's judgment is an unfortunate but inescapable fact. So great is that probability that international law refuses to recognize such a judgment as a basis for a war crime, however fair the judgment may be in a particular instance. It is this consideration that undermines the charge against the petitioner in this case. The indictment permits, indeed compels, the military commission of a victorious nation to sit in judgment upon the military strategy and actions of the defeated enemy and to use its conclusions to determine the criminal liability of an enemy commander. Life and liberty are made to depend upon the biased will of the victor rather than upon objective standards of conduct.

The Court's reliance upon vague and indefinite references in certain of the Hague Conventions and the Geneva Red Cross Convention is misplaced. Thus the statement in Article 1 of the Annex to Hague Convention No. IV of October 18, 1907, 36 Stat. 2277, 2295, to the effect that the laws, rights and duties of war apply to military and volunteer corps only if they are "commanded by a person responsible for his subordinates," has no bearing upon the problem in this case. Even if it has, the clause "responsible for his subordinates" fails to state to whom the responsibility is owed or to indicate the type of responsibility contemplated. The phrase has received differing interpretations by authorities on international law. In Oppenheim, *International Law* (6th ed rev by Lauterpacht, 1940, vol 2, p 204, fn 3) it is stated that "The meaning of the word 'responsible' . . . is not clear. It probably means 'responsible to some higher authority,' whether the person is appointed from above or elected from below; . . ." Another authority has stated that the word "responsible" in this particular context means "presumably to a higher authority," or "possibly it merely means one who controls his subordinates and who therefore can be called to account for their acts" Wheaton, *International Law* (7th ed by Keith, 1944, p 172, fn 30). Still another authority, Westlake, *International Law* (1907, Part II, p 61), states that "probably the responsibility intended is nothing more than a capacity of exercising effective control." Finally, Edmonds and Oppenheim, *Land Warfare* (1912, p 19, ¶ 22), state that it is enough "if the commander of the corps is regularly or temporarily commissioned as an officer or is a person of position and authority. . . ." It seems apparent beyond dispute that the word "responsible" was not used in this particular Hague Convention to hold the commander of a defeated army to any high standard of efficiency when he is under destructive attack; nor was it used to impute to him any criminal responsibility for war crimes committed by troops under his command under such circumstances.

The provisions of the other conventions referred to by the Court are on their face equally devoid of relevance or significance to the situation here in issue. Neither Article 19 of Hague Convention No. X, 36 Stat 2371, 2389, nor Article 26 of the Geneva Red Cross Convention of 1929, 47 Stat 2074, 2092, refers to circumstances where the troops of a commander commit atrocities while under heavily adverse battle conditions. Reference is also made to the requirement of Article 43 of the Annex to Hague Convention No. IV, 36 Stat 2295, 2306, that the commander of a force occupying enemy territory "shall take all the measures in his power to restore, and ensure, as far as possible, public order and safety, while respecting, unless absolutely prevented, the laws in force in the country." But the petitioner was more than a commander of a force occupying enemy territory. He was the leader of an army under constant and devastating attacks by a superior re-invading force. This provision is silent as to the responsibilities of a commander under such conditions as that.

Even the laws of war heretofore recognized by this nation fail to impute responsibility to a fallen commander for excesses committed by his disorganized troops while under attack. Paragraph 347 of the War Department publication, *Basic Field Manual, Rules of Land Warfare,* FM 27–10 (1940), states the principal offenses under the laws of war recognized by the United States. This includes all of the atrocities which the Japanese troops were alleged to have committed in this instance. Originally this paragraph concluded with the statement that "The commanders ordering the commission of such acts, or under whose authority they are committed by their troops, may be punished by the belligerent into whose hands they may fall." The meaning of the phrase "under whose authority they are committed" was not clear. On November 15, 1944, however, this sentence was deleted and a new paragraph was added relating to the personal liability of those who violate the laws of war. Change 1, FM 27–10. The new paragraph 345.1 states that "Individuals and organizations who violate the accepted laws and customs of war may be punished therefor. However, the fact that the acts complained of were done pursuant to order of a superior or government sanction may be taken into consideration in determining culpability, either by way of defense or in mitigation of punishment. The person giving such orders may also be punished." From this the conclusion seems inescapable that the United States recognizes individual criminal responsibility for violations of the laws of war only as to those who commit the offenses or who order or direct their commission. Such was not the allegation here. Cf. Article 67 of the Articles of War, 10 USC § 1539, 11 FCA title 10, § 1539.

There are numerous instances, especially with reference to the Philippine Insurrection in 1900 and 1901, where commanding officers were found to have violated the laws of war by specifically ordering members of their command to commit atrocities and other war crimes. Francisco Frani, GO 143,

Dec. 13, 1900, Hq Div Phil; Eugenio Fernandez and Juan Soriano, GO 28, Feb. 6, 1901, Hq Div Phil; Ciriaco Cabungal, GO 188, Jul. 22, 1901, Hq Div Phil; Natalio Valencia, GO 221, Aug. 17, 1901, Hq Div Phil; Aniceta Angeles, GO 246, Sept. 2, 1901, Hq Div Phil; Francisco Braganza, GO 291, Sept. 26, 1901, Hq Div Phil; Lorenzo Andaya, GO 328, Oct. 25, 1901, Hq Div Phil. And in other cases officers have been held liable where they knew that a crime was to be committed, had the power to prevent it and failed to exercise that power. Pedro Abad Santos, GO 130, June 19, 1901, Hq Div Phil. Cf. Pedro A. Cruz, GO 264, Sept. 9, 1901, Hq Div Phil. In no recorded instance, however, has the mere inability to control troops under fire or attack by superior forces been made the basis of a charge of violating the laws of war.

The Government claims that the principle that commanders in the field are bound to control their troops has been applied so as to impose liability on the United States in international arbitrations. Case of Jeannaud (1880), 3 Moore, International Arbitrations (1898) 3000; Case of The Zafiro (1910), 5 Hackworth, Digest of International Law (1943) 707. The difference between arbitrating property rights and charging an individual with a crime against the laws of war is too obvious to require elaboration. But even more significant is the fact that even these arbitration cases fail to establish any principle of liability where troops are under constant assault and demoralizing influences by attacking forces. The same observation applies to the common law and statutory doctrine, referred to by the Government, that one who is under a legal duty to take protective or preventive action is guilty of criminal homicide if he wilfully or negligently omits to act and death is proximately caused. State v. Harrison, 107 NJL 213, 152 A 867; State v. Irvine, 126 La 434, 52 So 567; Holmes, *Common Law*, p 278. No one denies that inaction or negligence may give rise to liability, civil or criminal. But it is quite another thing to say that the inability to control troops under highly competitive and disastrous battle conditions renders one guilty of a war crime in the absence of personal culpability. Had there been some element of knowledge or direct connection with the atrocities the problem would be entirely different. Moreover, it must be remembered that we are not dealing here with an ordinary tort or criminal action; precedents in those fields are of little if any value. Rather we are concerned with a proceeding involving an international crime, the treatment of which may have untold effects upon the future peace of the world. That fact must be kept uppermost in our search for precedent.

The only conclusion I can draw is that the charge made against the petitioner is clearly without precedent in international law or in the annals of recorded military history. This is not to say that enemy commanders may escape punishment for clear and unlawful failures to prevent atrocities. But that punishment should be based upon charges fairly drawn in light of established rules of international law and recognized concepts of justice.

But the charge in this case, as previously noted, was speedily drawn and filed but three weeks after the petitioner surrendered. The trial proceeded with great dispatch without allowing the defense time to prepare an adequate case. Petitioner's rights under the due process clause of the Fifth Amendment were grossly and openly violated without any justification. All of this was done without any thorough investigation and prosecution of those immediately responsible for the atrocities, out of which might have come some proof or indication of personal culpability on petitioner's part. Instead the loose charge was made that great numbers of atrocities had been committed and that petitioner was the commanding officer; hence he must have been guilty of disregard of duty. Under that charge the commission was free to establish whatever standard of duty on petitioner's part that it desired. By this flexible method a victorious nation may convict and execute any or all leaders of a vanquished foe, depending upon the prevailing degree of vengeance and the absence of any objective judicial review.

At a time like this when emotions are understandably high

it is difficult to adopt a dispassionate attitude toward a case of this nature. Yet now is precisely the time when that attitude is most essential. While peoples in other lands may not share our beliefs as to due process and the dignity of the individual, we are not free to give effect to our emotions in reckless disregard of the rights of others. We live under the Constitution, which is the embodiment of all the high hopes and aspirations of the new world. And it is applicable in both war and peace. We must act accordingly. Indeed, an uncurbed spirit of revenge and retribution, masked in formal legal procedure for purposes of dealing with a fallen enemy commander, can do more lasting harm than all of the atrocities giving rise to that spirit. The people's faith in the fairness and objectiveness of the law can be seriously undercut by that spirit. The fires of nationalism can be further kindled. And the hearts of all mankind can be embittered and filled with hatred, leaving forlorn and impoverished the noble ideal of malice toward none and charity to all. These are the reasons that lead me to dissent in these terms.

Mr. Justice Rutledge, dissenting.

Not with ease does one find his views at odds with the Court's in a matter of this character and gravity. Only the most deeply felt convictions could force one to differ. That reason alone leads me to do so now, against strong considerations for withholding dissent.

More is at stake than General Yamashita's fate. There could be no possible sympathy for him if he is guilty of the atrocities for which his death is sought. But there can be and should be justice administered according to law. In this stage of war's aftermath it is too early for Lincoln's great spirit, best lighted in the Second Inaugural, to have wide hold for the treatment of foes. It is not too early, it is never too early, for the nation steadfastly to follow its great constitutional traditions, none older or more universally protective against unbridled power than due process of law 1 1 the trial and punishment of men, that is, of all men, whether citizens, aliens, alien enemies or enemy belligerents. It can become too late.

This long-held attachment marks the great divide between our enemies and ourselves. Theirs was a philosophy of universal force. Ours is one of universal law, albeit imperfectly made flesh of our system and so dwelling among us. Every departure weakens the tradition, whether it touches the high or the low, the powerful or the weak, the triumphant or the conquered. If we need not or cannot be magnanimous, we can keep our own law on the plane from which it has not descended hitherto and to which the defeated foes' never rose. . . .

The *Korematsu* decision concerns a review by the U.S. Supreme Court of the charge that the relocation of ethnic Japanese in "camps" during World War II was inconsistent with the Constitution. Such a question has great importance in evaluating the claim of the victor to be conducting a just war and to have the moral standing to pass judgment on the crimes of a defeated nation. The *Korematsu* decision also bears witness to the link between American racism and war. Ethnic Germans were not subject to any comparable procedures of coercive quarantine during the course of World War II.

KOREMATSU V. UNITED STATES, 1944

[Excerpt from Opinion of the Court]

Mr. Justice Black delivered the opinion of the Court:

The petitioner, an American citizen of Japanese descent, was convicted in a Federal District Court for remaining in San Leandro, California, a "Military Area," contrary to Civilian Exclusion Order No. 34 of the Commanding General of the Western Command, U. S. Army, which directed that after May 9, 1942, all persons of Japanese ancestry should be excluded from that area. No question was raised as to petitioner's loyalty to the United States. The Circuit Court of Appeals affirmed, and the importance of the constitutional question involved caused us to grant certiorari. 321 US 760, 88 L ed 1058, 64 S Ct 786.

It should be noted, to begin with, that all legal restrictions which curtail the civil rights of a single racial group are immediately suspect. That is not to say that all such restrictions are unconstitutional. It is to say that courts must subject them to the most rigid scrutiny. Pressing public necessity may sometimes justify the existence of such restrictions; racial antagonism never can.

In the instant case prosecution of the petitioner was begun by information charging violation of an Act of Congress, of March 21, 1942, 56 Stat 173, c 191, 18 USCA § 97a, 7 FCA title 78, § 97a, which provides that ". . . whoever shall enter, remain in, leave, or commit any act in any military area or military zone prescribed, under the authority of an Executive order of the President, by the Secretary of War, or by any military commander designated by the Secretary of War, contrary to the restrictions applicable to any such area or zone or contrary to the order of the Secretary of War or any such military commander, shall, if it appears that he knew or should have known of the existence and extent of the restrictions or order and that his act was in violation thereof, be guilty of a misdemeanor and upon conviction shall be liable to a fine of not to exceed $5,000 or to imprisonment for not more than one year, or both, for each offense."

Exclusion Order No. 34, which the petitioner knowingly and admittedly violated, was one of a number of military orders and proclamations, all of which were substantially based upon Executive Order No. 9066, 7 Fed Reg 1407. That order, issued after we were at war with Japan, declared that "the successful prosecution of the war requires every possible protection against espionage and against sabotage to national-defense material, national-defense premises, and national-defense utilities. . . ."

One of the series of orders and proclamations, a curfew order, which like the exclusion order here was promulgated pursuant to Executive Order 9066, subjected all persons of Japanese ancestry in prescribed West Coast military areas to remain in their residences from 8 P.M. to 6 A.M. As is the case with the exclusion order here, that prior curfew order was designed as a "protection against espionage and against sabotage." In Hirabayashi v. United States, 320 US 81, 87 L ed 1774, 63 S Ct 1375, we sustained a conviction obtained for violation of the curfew order. The Hirabayashi conviction and this one thus rest on the same 1942 Congressional Act and the same basic executive and military orders, all of which orders were aimed at the twin dangers of espionage and sabotage.

The 1942 Act was attacked in the Hirabayashi Case as an unconstitutional delegation of power; it was contended that the curfew order and other orders on which it rested were beyond the war powers of the Congress, the military authorities and of the President, as Commander in Chief of the Army; and finally that to apply the curfew order against none but citizens of Japanese ancestry amounted to a constitutionally prohibited discrimination solely on account of race. To these questions, we gave the serious consideration which their importance justified. We upheld the curfew order as an exercise of the power of the government to take steps necessary to prevent espionage and sabotage in an area threatened by Japanese attack.

In the light of the principles we announced in the Hirabayashi Case, we are unable to conclude that it was beyond the war power of Congress and the Executive to exclude those of Japanese ancestry from the West Coast war area at the time they did. True, exclusion from the area in which one's home is located is a far greater deprivation than constant confinement to the home from 8 P.M. to 6 A.M. Nothing short of apprehension by the proper military authorities of the gravest imminent danger to the public safety can constitutionally justify either. But exclusion from a threatened area, no less than curfew, has a definite and close relationship to the prevention of espionage and sabotage. The military authorities, charged with the primary responsibility of defending our shores, concluded that curfew provided inadequate protection and ordered exclusion. They did so, as pointed out in our Hirabayashi opinion, in accordance with congressional authority to the military to say who should, and who should not, remain in the threatened areas.

In this case the petitioner challenges the assumptions upon which we rested our conclusions in the Hirabayashi Case. He also urges that by May 1942, when Order No. 34 was promulgated, all danger of Japanese invasion of the West Coast had disappeared. After careful consideration of these contentions we are compelled to reject them.

Here, as in the Hirabayashi Case, supra (320 US at p 99, 87 L ed 1785, 63 S Ct 1375), "we cannot reject as unfounded the judgment of the military authorities and of Congress that there were disloyal members of that population, whose number and strength could not be precisely and quickly ascertained. We cannot say that the war-making branches of the Government did not have ground for believing that in a critical hour such persons could not readily be isolated and separately dealt with, and constituted a menace to the national defense and safety, which demanded that prompt and adequate measures be taken to guard against it."

Like curfew, exclusion of those of Japanese origin was deemed necessary because of the presence of an unascertained number of disloyal members of the group, most of whom we have no doubt were loyal to this country. It was because we could not reject the finding of the military authorities that it was impossible to bring about an immediate segregation of the disloyal from the loyal that we sustained the validity of the curfew order as applying to the whole group. In the instant case, temporary exclusion of the entire group was rested by the military on the same ground. The judgment that exclusion of the whole group was for the same reason a military imperative answers the contention that the exclusion was in the nature of group punishment based on antagonism to those of Japanese origin. That there were members of the group who retained loyalties to Japan has been confirmed by investigations made subsequent to the exclusion. Approximately five thousand American citizens of Japanese ancestry refused to swear unqualified allegiance to the United States and to renounce allegiance to the Japanese Emperor, and several thousand evacuees requested repatriation to Japan.

We uphold the exclusion order as of the time it was made and when the petitioner violated it. Cf. Chastleton Corp v. Sinclair, 264 US 543, 547, 68 L ed 841, 843, 44 S Ct 405; Block v. Hirsh, 256 US 135, 154, 155, 65 L ed 865, 870, 871, 41 S Ct 458, 16 ALR 165. In doing so, we are not unmindful of the hardships imposed by it upon a large group of American citizens. Cf. Ex parte Kawato, 317 US 69, 73, 87 L ed 58, 61,

63 S Ct 115. But hardships are part of war, and war is an aggregation of hardships. All citizens alike, both in and out of uniform, feel the impact of war in greater or lesser measure. Citizenship has its responsibilities as well as its privileges, and in time of war the burden is always heavier. Compulsory exclusion of large groups of citizens from their homes, except under circumstances of direst emergency and peril, is inconsistent with our basic governmental institutions. But when under conditions of modern warfare our shores are threatened by hostile forces, the power to protect must be commensurate with the threatened danger. . . .

It is said that we are dealing here with the case of imprisonment of a citizen in a concentration camp solely because of his ancestry, without evidence or inquiry concerning his loyalty and good disposition towards the United States. Our task would be simple, our duty clear, were this a case involving the imprisonment of a loyal citizen in a concentration camp because of racial prejudice. Regardless of the true nature of the assembly and relocation centers—and we deem it unjustifiable to call them concentration camps with all the ugly connotations that term implies—we are dealing specifically with nothing but an exclusion order. To cast this case into outlines of racial prejudice, without reference to the real military dangers which were presented, merely confuses the issue. Korematsu was not excluded from the Military Area because of hostility to him or his race. He *was* excluded because we are at war with the Japanese Empire, because the properly constituted military authorities feared an invasion of our West Coast and felt constrained to take proper security measures, because they decided that the military urgency of the situation demanded that all citizens of Japanese ancestry be segregated from the West Coast temporarily, and finally, because Congress, reposing its confidence in this time of war in our military leaders— as inevitably it must—determined that they should have the power to do just this. There was evidence of disloyalty on the part of some, the military authorities considered that the need for action was great, and time was short. We cannot—by availing ourselves of the calm perspective of hindsight—now say that at that time these actions were unjustified.

Affirmed. . . .

[EXCERPT FROM DISSENTING OPINION OF MR. JUSTICE ROBERTS]

Mr. Justice Roberts:

I dissent, because I think the indisputable facts exhibit a clear violation of Constitutional rights.

This is not a case of keeping people off the streets at night as was Hirabayashi v. United States, 320 US 81, 87 L ed 1774, 63 S Ct 1375, nor a case of temporary exclusion of a citizen from an area for his own safety or that of the community, nor a case of offering him an opportunity to go temporarily out of an area where his presence might cause danger to himself or to his fellows. On the contrary, it is the case of convicting a citizen as a punishment for not submitting to imprisonment in a concentration camp, based on his ancestry, and solely because of his ancestry, without evidence or inquiry concerning his loyalty and good disposition toward the United States. If this be a correct statement of the facts disclosed by this record, and facts of which we take judicial notice, I need hardly labor the conclusion that constitutional rights have been violated. . . .

The obvious purpose of the orders made, taken together, was to drive all citizens of Japanese ancestry into Assembly Centers within the zones of their residence, under pain of criminal prosecution.

The predicament in which the petitioner thus found himself was this: He was forbidden, by Military Order, to leave the zone in which he lived; he was forbidden, by Military Order, after a date fixed, to be found within that zone unless he were in an Assembly Center located in that zone. General De-Witt's report to the Secretary of War concerning the program of evacuation and relocation of Japanese makes it entirely clear, if it were necessary to refer to that document— and, in the light of the above recitation, I think it is not—that an Assembly Center was a euphemism for a prison. No person within such a center was permitted to leave except by Military Order.

In the dilemma that he dare not remain in his home, or voluntarily leave the area, without incurring criminal penalties, and that the only way he could avoid punishment was to go to an Assembly Center and submit himself to military imprisonment, the petitioner did nothing.

June 12, 1942, an Information was filed in the District Court for Northern California charging a violation of the Act of March 21, 1942, in that petitioner had knowingly remained within the area covered by Exclusion Order No. 34. A demurrer to the information having been overruled, the petitioner was tried under a plea of not guilty and convicted. Sentence was suspended and he was placed on probation for five years. We know, however, in the light of the foregoing recitation, that he was at once taken into military custody and lodged in an Assembly Center. We further knew that, on March 18, 1942, the President had promulgated Executive Order No. 9102 establishing the War Relocation Authority under which so-called Relocation Centers, a euphemism for concentration camps, were established pursuant to cooperation between the military authorities of the Western Defense Command and the Relocation Authority, and that the petitioner has been confined either in an Assembly Center, within the zone in which he had lived or has been removed to a Relocation Center where, as the facts disclosed in Ex parte Endo (No. 70 of this Term [323 US 283, post, 243, 65 S Ct 208]) demonstrate, he was illegally held in custody.

The Government has argued this case as if the only order outstanding at the time the petitioner was arrested and informed against was Exclusion Order No. 34 ordering him to leave the area in which he resided, which was the basis of the information against him. That argument has evidently been effective. The opinion refers to the Hirabayashi Case, supra, to show that this court has sustained the validity of a curfew order in an emergency. The argument then is that exclusion from a given area of danger, while somewhat more sweeping than a curfew regulation, is of the same nature—a temporary expedient made necessary by a sudden emergency. This, I think, is a substitution of an hypothetical case for the case actually before the court. I might agree with the court's disposition of the hypothetical case. The liberty of every American citizen freely to come and to go must frequently, in the face of sudden danger, be temporarily limited or suspended. The civil authorities must often resort to the expedient of excluding citizens temporarily from a locality. The drawing of fire lines in the case of a conflagration, the removal of persons from the area where a pestilence has broken out, are familiar examples. If the exclusion worked by Exclusion Order No. 34 were of that nature the Hirabayashi Case would be authority for sustaining it.

But the facts above recited, and those set forth in Ex parte Endo, supra, show that the exclusion was but a part of an overall plan for forceable detention. This case cannot, therefore, be decided on any such narrow ground as the possible validity of a Temporary Exclusion Order under which the residents of an area are given opportunity to leave and go elsewhere in their native land outside the boundaries of a military area. To make the case turn on any such assumption is to shut our eyes to reality.

As I have said above, the petitioner, prior to his arrest, was faced with two diametrically contradictory orders given sanction by the Act of Congress of March 21, 1942. The earlier of those orders made him a criminal if he left the zone in which he resided; the later made him a criminal if he did not leave.

I had supposed that if a citizen was constrained by two laws, or two orders having the force of law, and obedience to one would violate the other, to punish him for violation of either would deny him due process of law. And I had supposed that under these circumstances a conviction for violating one of the orders could not stand.

We cannot shut our eyes to the fact that had the petitioner attempted to violate Proclamation No. 4 and leave the military area in which he lived he would have been arrested and tried and convicted for violation of Proclamation No. 4. The two conflicting orders, one which commanded him to stay and the other which commanded him to go, were nothing but a cleverly devised trap to accomplish the real purpose of the military authority, which was to lock him up in a concentration camp. The only course by which the petitioner could avoid arrest and prosecution was to go to that camp according to instructions to be given him when he reported at a Civil Control Center. We know that is the fact. Why should we set up a figmentary and artificial situation instead of addressing ourselves to the actualities of the case?

The stark realities are met by the suggestion that it is lawful to compel an American citizen to submit to illegal imprisonment on the assumption that he might, after going to the Assembly Center, apply for his discharge by suing out a writ of habeas corpus, as was done in the Endo Case, supra. The answer, of course, is that where he was subject to two conflicting laws he was not bound, in order to escape violation of one or the other, to surrender his liberty for any period. Nor will it do to say that the detention was a necessary part of the process of evacuation, and so we are here concerned only with the validity of the latter.

Again it is a new doctrine of constitutional law that one indicted for disobedience to an unconstitutional statute may not defend on the ground of the invalidity of the statute but must obey it though he knows it is no law and, after he has suffered the disgrace of conviction and lost his liberty by sentence, then, and not before, seek, from within prison walls, to test the validity of the law.

Moreover, it is beside the point to rest decision in part on the fact that the petitioner, for his own reasons, wished to remain in his home. If, as is the fact, he was constrained so to do, it is indeed a narrow application of constitutional rights to ignore the order which constrained him, in order to sustain his conviction for violation of another contradictory order.

I would reverse the judgment of conviction.

[EXCERPT FROM DISSENTING OPINION OF
MR. JUSTICE MURPHY]

Mr. Justice Murphy, dissenting:

This exclusion of "all persons of Japanese ancestry, both alien and non-alien," from the Pacific Coast area on a plea of military necessity in the absence of martial law ought not to be approved. Such exclusion goes over "the very brink of constitutional power" and falls into the ugly abyss of racism.

In dealing with matters relating to the prosecution and progress of a war, we must accord great respect and consideration to the judgments of the military authorities who are on the scene and who have full knowledge of the military facts. The scope of their discretion must, as a matter of necessity and common sense, be wide. And their judgments ought not to be overruled lightly by those whose training and duties ill-equip them to deal intelligently with matters so vital to the physical security of the nation.

At the same time, however, it is essential that there be definite limits to military discretion, especially where martial law has not been declared. Individuals must not be left impoverished of their constitutional rights on a plea of military necessity that has neither substance nor support. Thus, like other claims conflicting with the asserted constitutional rights of the individual, the military claim must subject itself to the judicial process of having its reasonableness determined and its conflicts with other interests reconciled. "What are the allowable limits of military discretion, and whether or not they have been overstepped in a particular case, are judicial questions." Sterling v. Constantin, 287 US 378, 401, 77 L ed 375, 387, 53 S Ct 190.

The judicial test of whether the Government, on a plea of military necessity, can validly deprive an individual of any of his constitutional rights is whether the deprivation is reasonably related to a public danger that is so "immediate, imminent, and impending" as not to admit of delay and not to permit the intervention or ordinary constitutional processes to alleviate the danger. United States v. Russell, 13 Wall (US) 623, 627, 628, 20 L ed 474, 475; Mitchell v. Harmony, 13 How 115, 134, 135, 14 L ed 75, 83, 84; Raymond v. Thomas, 91 US 712, 716, 23 L ed 434, 435. Civilan Exclusion Order No. 34, banishing from a prescribed area of the Pacific Coast "all persons of Japanese ancestry, both alien and non-alien," clearly does not meet that test. Being an obvious racial discrimination, the order deprives all those within its scope of the equal protection of the laws as guaranteed by the Fifth Amendment. It further deprives these individuals of their constitutional rights to live and work where they will, to establish a home where they choose and to move about freely. In excommunicating them without benefit of hearing, this order also deprives them of all their constitutional rights to procedural due process. Yet no reasonable relation to an "immediate, imminent, and impending" public danger is evident to support this racial restriction which is one of the most sweeping and complete deprivations of constitutional rights in the history of the nation in the absence of martial law.

It must be conceded that the military and naval situation in the spring of 1942 was such as to generate a very real fear of invasion of the Pacific Coast, accompanied by fears of sabotage and espionage in that area. The military command was therefore justified in adopting all reasonable means necessary to combat these dangers. In adjudging the military action taken in light of the then apparent dangers, we must not erect too high or too meticulous standards; it is necessary only that the action have some reasonable relation to the removal of the dangers of invasion, sabotage and espionage. But the exclusion, either temporarily or permanently, of all persons with Japanese blood in their veins has no such reasonable relation. And that relation is lacking because the exclusion order necessarily must rely for its reasonableness upon the assumption that *all* persons of Japanese ancestry may have a dangerous tendency to commit sabotage and espionage and to aid our Japanese enemy in other ways. It is difficult to believe that reason, logic or experience could be marshalled in support of such an assumption. . . .

I dissent, therefore, from this legalization of racism. Racial discrimination in any form and in any degree has no justifiable part whatever in our democratic way of life. It is unattractive in any setting but it is utterly revolting among a free people who have embraced the principles set forth in the Constitution of the United States. All residents of this nation are kin in some way by blood or culture to a foreign land. Yet they are primarily and necessarily a part of the new and distinct civilization of the United States. They must accordingly be treated at all times as the heirs of the American experiment and as entitled to all the rights and freedoms guaranteed by the Constitution.

[EXCERPT FROM DISSENTING OPINION OF MR. JUSTICE JACKSON]

Mr. Justice Jackson, dissenting:

Korematsu was born on our soil, of parents born in Japan. The Constitution makes him a citizen of the United States by nativity and a citizen of California by residence. No claim is made that he is not loyal to this country. There is no suggestion that apart from the matter involved here he is not law-abiding and well disposed. Korematsu, however, has been convicted of an act not commonly a crime. It consists merely of being present in the state whereof he is a citizen, near the place where he was born, and where all his life he has lived.

Even more unusual is the series of military orders which made this conduct a crime. They forbid such a one to remain, and they also forbid him to leave. They were so drawn that the only way Korematsu could avoid violation was to give himself up to the military authority. This meant submission to custody, examination, and transportation out of the territory, to be followed by indeterminate confinement in detention camps.

A citizen's presence in the locality, however, was made a crime only if his parents were of Japanese birth. Had Korematsu been one of four—the others being, say, a German alien enemy, an Italian alien enemy, and a citizen of American-born ancestors, convicted of treason but out on parole—only Korematsu's presence would have violated the order. The difference between their innocence and his crime would result, not from anything he did, said, or thought, different than they, but only in that he was born of different racial stock.

Now, if any fundamental assumption underlies our system, it is that guilt is personal and not inheritable. Even if all of one's antecedents had been convicted of treason, the Constitution forbids its penalties to be visited upon him, for it provides that "no attainder of treason shall work corruption of blood, or forfeiture except during the life of the person attainted." But here is an attempt to make an otherwise innocent act a crime merely because this prisoner is the son of parents as to whom he had no choice, and belongs to a race from which there is no way to resign. If Congress in peace-time legislation should enact such a criminal law, I should suppose this Court would refuse to enforce it.

But the "law" which this prisoner is convicted of disregarding is not found in an act of Congress, but in a military order. Neither the Act of Congress nor the Executive Order of the President, nor both together, would afford a basis for this conviction. It rests on the orders of General DeWitt. And it is said that if the military commander had reasonable military grounds for promulgating the orders, they are constitutional and become law, and the Court is required to enforce them. There are several reasons why I cannot subscribe to this doctrine.

It would be impracticable and dangerous idealism to expect or insist that each specific military command in an area of probable operations will conform to conventional tests of constitutionality. When an area is so beset that it must be put under military control at all, the paramount consideration is that its measures be successful, rather than legal. The armed services must protect a society, not merely its Constitution. The very essence of the military job is to marshal physical force, to remove every obstacle to its effectiveness, to give it every strategic advantage. Defense measures will not, and often should not, be held within the limits that bind civil authority in peace. No court can require such a commander in such circumstances to act as a reasonable man; he may be unreasonably cautious and exacting. Perhaps he should be. But a commander in temporarily focusing the life of a community on defense is carrying out a military program; he is not making law in the sense the courts know the term. He issues orders, and they may have a certain authority as military commands, although they may be very bad as constitutional law.

But if we cannot confine military expedients by the Constitution, neither would I distort the Constitution to approve all that the military may deem expedient. That is what the Court appears to be doing, whether consciously or not. I cannot say, from any evidence before me, that the orders of General De-Witt were not reasonably expedient military precautions, nor could I say that they were. But even if they were permissible military procedures, I deny that it follows that they are constitutional. If, as the Court holds, it does follow, then we may as well say that any military order will be constitutional and have done with it.

The limitation under which courts always will labor in examining the necessity for a military order are illustrated by this case. How does the Court know that these orders have a reasonable basis in necessity? No evidence whatever on that subject has been taken by this or any other court. There is sharp controversy as to the credibility of the DeWitt report. So the Court, having no real evidence before it, has no choice but to accept General DeWitt's own unsworn, self-serving statement, untested by any cross-examination, that what he did was reasonable. And thus it will always be when courts try to look into the reasonableness of a military order.

In the very nature of things military decisions are not susceptible of intelligent judicial appraisal. They do not pretend to rest on evidence, but are made on information that often would not be admissible and on assumptions that could not be proved. Information in support of an order could not be disclosed to courts without danger that it would reach the enemy. Neither can courts act on communications made in confidence. Hence courts can never have any real alternative to accepting the mere declaration of the authority that issued the order that it was reasonably necessary from a military viewpoint.

Much is said of the danger to liberty from the Army program for deporting and detaining these citizens of Japanese extraction. But a judicial construction of the due process clause that will sustain this order is a far more subtle blow to liberty than the promulgation of the order itself. A military order, however unconstitutional, is not apt to last longer than the military emergency. Even during that period a succeeding commander may revoke it all. But once a judicial opinion rationalizes such an order to show that it conforms to the Constitution, or rather rationalizes the Constitution to show that the Constitution sanctions such an order, the Court for all time has validated the principle of racial discrimination in criminal procedure and of transplanting American citizens. The principle then lies about like a loaded weapon ready for the hand of any authority that can bring forward a plausible claim of an urgent need. Every repetition imbeds that principle more deeply in our law and thinking and expands it to new purposes. All who observe the work of courts are familiar with what Judge Cardozo described as "the tendency of a principle to expand itself to the limit of its logic." A military commander may overstep the bounds of constitutionality, and it is an incident. But if we review and approve, that passing incident becomes the doctrine of the Constitution. There it has a generative power of its own, and all that it creates will be in its own image. Nothing better illustrates this danger than does the Court's opinion in this case. . . .

This section puts emphasis upon the war crimes concept in the setting of the American involvement in the Vietnam War.

The first three selections consider the question as to whether the United States is an aggressor in relation to that war. The first selection is taken from an official U.S. Government argument in defense of its policies and the other two selections are critical of the contention that the United States is validly exercising the right of collective self-defense in South Vietnam. Such an inquiry is central to the determination as to whether the United States is responsible for committing "the supreme crime" of aggressive war by its role in the Vietnam War.

LEGAL MEMORANDUM ON VIETNAM WAR OF U. S. STATE DEPARTMENT, 1966

[Excerpt]

1. The United States and South Viet-Nam have the right under international law to participate in the collective defense of South Viet-Nam against armed attack

In response to requests from the Government of South Viet-Nam, the United States has been assisting that country in defending itself against armed attack from the Communist North. This attack has taken the forms of externally supported subversion, clandestine supply of arms, infiltration of armed personnel, and most recently the sending of regular units of the North Vietnamese army into the South.

International law has long recognized the right of individual and collective self-defense against armed attack. South Viet-Nam and the United States are engaging in such collective defense consistently with international law and with United States obligations under the United Nations Charter.

A. South Viet-Nam Is Being Subjected to Armed Attack by Communist North Viet-Nam

The Geneva accords of 1954 established a demarcation line between North Viet-Nam and South Viet-Nam. They provided for withdrawals of military forces into the respective zones north and south of this line. The accords prohibited the use of either zone for the resumption of hostilities or to "further an aggressive policy."

During the 5 years following the Geneva conference of 1954, the Hanoi regime developed a covert political-military organization in South Viet-Nam based on Communist cadres it had ordered to stay in the South, contrary to the provisions of the Geneva accords. The activities of this covert organization were directed toward the kidnaping and assassination of civilian officials—acts of terrorism that were perpetrated in increasing numbers.

In the 3-year period from 1959 to 1961, the North Viet-Nam regime infiltrated an estimated 10,000 men into the South. It is estimated that 13,000 additional personnel were infiltrated in 1962, and, by the end of 1964, North Viet-Nam may well have moved over 40,000 armed and unarmed guerrillas into South Viet-Nam.

The International Control Commission reported in 1962 the findings of its Legal Committee:

. . . there is evidence to show that arms, armed and unarmed personnel, munitions and other supplies have been sent from the Zone in the North to the Zone in the South with the objective of supporting, organizing and carrying out hostile activities, including armed attacks, directed against the Armed Forces and Administration of the Zone in the South.

. . . there is evidence that the PAVN [People's Army of Viet-Nam] has allowed the Zone in the North to be used for inciting, encouraging and supporting hostile activities in the Zone in the South, aimed at the overthrow of the Administration in the South.

Beginning in 1964, the Communists apparently exhausted their reservoir of Southerners who had gone North. Since then the greater number of men infiltrated into the South have been native-born North Vietnamese. Most recently, Hanoi has begun to infiltrate elements of the North Vietnamese army in increasingly larger numbers. Today, there is evidence that nine regiments of regular North Vietnamese forces are fighting in organized units in the South.

In the guerrilla war of Viet-Nam, the external aggression from the North is the critical military element of the insurgency, although it is unacknowledged by North Viet-Nam. In these circumstances, an "armed attack" is not as easily fixed by date and hour as in the case of traditional warfare. However, the infiltration of thousands of armed men clearly constitutes an "armed attack" under any reasonable definition. There may be some question as to the exact date at which North Viet-Nam's aggression grew into an "armed attack," but there can be no doubt that it had occurred before February 1965.

B. International Law Recognizes the Right of Individual and Collective Self-Defense Against Armed Attack

International law has traditionally recognized the right of self-defense against armed attack. This proposition has been asserted by writers on international law through the several centuries in which the modern law of nations has developed. The proposition has been acted on numerous times by governments throughout modern history. Today the principle of self-defense against armed attack is universally recognized and accepted.*

The Charter of the United Nations, concluded at the end of World War II, imposed an important limitation on the use of force by United Nations members. Article 2, paragraph 4, provides:

> All Members shall refrain in their international relations from the threat or use of force against the territorial integrity or political independence of any state, or in any other manner inconsistent with the Purposes of the United Nations.

---

* See *e.g.*, Jessup, *A Modern Law of Nations*, 163 ff. (1948) ; Oppenheim, *International Law*, 297 ff. (8th ed., Lauterpacht, 1955) . And see, generally, Bowett, *Self-Defense in International Law* (1958) . [Footnote in original.]

In addition, the charter embodied a system of international peacekeeping through the organs of the United Nations. Article 24 summarizes these structural arrangements in stating that the United Nations members:

> . . . confer on the Security Council primary responsibility for the maintenance of international peace and security, and agree that in carrying out its duties under this responsibility the Security Council acts on their behalf.

However, the charter expressly states in article 51 that the remaining provisions of the charter—including the limitation of article 2, paragraph 4, and the creation of United Nations machinery to keep the peace—in no way diminish the inherent right of self-defense against armed attack. Article 51 provides:

> Nothing in the present Charter shall impair the inherent right of individual or collective self-defense if an armed attack occurs against a Member of the United Nations, until the Security Council has taken the measures necessary to maintain international peace and security. Measures taken by Members in the exercise of this right of self-defense shall be immediately reported to the Security Council and shall not in any way affect the authority and responsibility of the Security Council under the present Charter to take at any time such action as it deems necessary in order to maintain or restore international peace and security.

Thus, article 51 restates and preserves, for member states in the situations covered by the article, a long-recognized principle of international law. The article is a "saving clause" designed to make clear that no other provision in the charter shall be interpreted to impair the inherent right of self-defense referred to in article 51.

Three principal objections have been raised against the availability of the right of individual and collective self-defense in the case of Viet-Nam: (1) that this right applies only in the case of an armed attack on a United Nations member; (2) that it does not apply in the case of South Viet-Nam because the latter is not an independent sovereign state; and

(3) that collective self-defense may be undertaken only by a regional organization operating under chapter VIII of the United Nations Charter. These objections will now be considered in turn.

C. The Right of Individual and Collective Self-Defense Applies in the Case of South Viet-Nam Whether or Not That Country Is a Member of the United Nations

1. South Viet-Nam enjoys the right of self-defense

The argument that the right of self-defense is available only to members of the United Nations mistakes the nature of the right of self-defense and the relationship of the United Nations Charter to international law in this respect. As already shown, the right of self-defense against armed attack is an inherent right under international law. The right is not conferred by the charter, and, indeed, article 51 expressly recognizes that the right is inherent.

The charter nowhere contains any provision designed to deprive nonmembers of the right of self-defense against armed attack.* Article 2, paragraph 6, does charge the United Nations with responsibility for insuring that nonmember states act in accordance with United Nations "Principles so far as may be necessary for the maintenance of international peace and security." Protection against aggression and self-defense against armed attack are important elements in the whole charter scheme for the maintenance of international peace and security. To deprive nonmembers of their inherent right of self-defense would not accord with the principles of the organization, but would instead be prejudicial to the mainte-

---

* While nonmembers, such as South Viet-Nam, have not formally undertaken the obligations of the United Nations Charter as their own treaty obligations, it should be recognized that much of the substantive law of the charter has become part of the general law of nations through a very wide acceptance by nations the world over. This is particularly true of the charter provisions bearing on the use of force. Moreover, in the case of South Viet-Nam, the South Vietnamese Government has expressed its ability and willingness to abide by the charter, in applying for United Nations membership. Thus it seems entirely appropriate to appraise the actions of South Viet-Nam in relation to the legal standards set forth in the United Nations Charter. [Footnote in original.]

nance of peace. Thus article 2, paragraph 6—and, indeed, the rest of the charter—should certainly not be construed to nullify or diminish the inherent defensive rights of nonmembers.

2. *The United States has the right to assist in the defense of South Viet-Nam although the latter is not a United Nations member*

The cooperation of two or more international entities in the defense of one or both against armed attack is generally referred to as collective self-defense. United States participation in the defense of South Viet-Nam at the latter's request is an example of collective self-defense.

The United States is entitled to exercise the right of individual or collective self-defense against armed attack, as that right exists in international law, subject only to treaty limitations and obligations undertaken by this country.

It has been urged that the United States has no right to participate in the collective defense of South Viet-Nam because article 51 of the United Nations Charter speaks only of the situation "if an armed attack occurs *against a Member of the United Nations.*" This argument is without substance.

In the first place, article 51 does not impose restrictions or cut down the otherwise available rights of United Nations members. By its own terms, the article preserves an inherent right. It is, therefore, necessary to look elsewhere in the charter for any obligation of members restricting their participation in collective defense of an entity that is not a United Nations member.

Article 2, paragraph 4, is the principal provision of the charter imposing limitations on the use of force by members. It states that they:

> . . . shall refrain in their international relations from the threat or use of force against the territorial integrity or political independence of any state, or in any other manner inconsistent with the Purposes of the United Nations.

Action taken in defense against armed attack cannot be characterized as falling within this proscription. The record of the

San Francisco conference makes clear that article 2, paragraph 4, was not intended to restrict the right of self-defense against armed attack.*

One will search in vain for any other provision in the charter that would preclude United States participation in the collective defense of a nonmember. The fact that article 51 refers only to armed attack "against a Member of the United Nations" implies no intention to preclude members from participating in the defense of nonmembers. Any such result would have seriously detrimental consequences for international peace and security and would be inconsistent with the purposes of the United Nations as they are set forth in article 1 of the charter.† The right of members to participate in the defense of nonmembers is upheld by leading authorities on international law.‡

LEGAL ASPECTS OF THE VIETNAM SITUATION
Quincy Wright

Even if the cease-fire line remained legally effective, North Viet-Nam could not be accused of "aggression" against South Viet-Nam unless it had launched an unjustifiable "armed attack" upon the latter prior to the United States bombing raids across that line in February, 1965. The basic American argument to justify these raids was that they were acts of "collective self-defense," permitted by Article 51 of the United Nations

---

* See 6 UNCIO Documents 459. [Footnote in original.]
† In particular, the statement of the first purpose:
To maintain international peace and security, and to that end: to take effective collective measures for the prevention and removal of threats to the peace, and for the suppression of acts of aggression or other breaches of the peace, and to bring about by peaceful means, and in conformity with the principles of justice and international law, adjustment or settlement of international disputes or situations which might lead to a breach of the peace. . . . [Footnote in original.]
‡ Bowett, *Self-Defense in International Law*, 193–195 (1958); Goodhart, "The North Atlantic Treaty of 1949," 79 Recueil Des Cours, 183, 202–204 (1951, vol. II), quoted in 5 *Whiteman's Digest of International Law*, 1067–1068 (1965); Kelsen, *The Law of the United Nations*, 793 (1950); see Stone, *Aggression and World Order*, 44 (1958). [Footnote in original.]

Charter. The meaning of this article has been controversial.

It is true that traditional international law permitted military action in self-defense if there were an "instant and overwhelming necessity permitting no moment for deliberation," i.e., if hostile forces were about to attack. It seems clear, however, that the San Francisco Conference, by limiting self-defense to cases of "armed attack," intended to eliminate all preventive or pre-emptive action in order to maintain to the utmost the basic obligation of Members of the United Nations to "refrain in their international relations from the threat or use of force."

Furthermore it is clear that "armed attack" implies military action. Consequently military defensive action is not permissible under the Charter in response to economic, psychological, or other forms of subversion or intervention not involving military coercion. There can be no doubt but that bodies of armed "volunteers" crossing a frontier or cease-fire line, such as the Chinese in the Korean hostilities of 1950, or ostensibly private "military expeditions" or "armed bands" leaving one country for the purpose of attacking another, as the Cuban refugees in the Bay of Pigs affair of 1961, constitute, if of considerable magnitude, an "armed attack."

Finally an "armed attack" which constitutes a legitimate act of self-defense against an illegal "armed attack" cannot justify subsequent attacks by the aggressor.

According to the International Control Commission there were frequent violations of the Cease-Fire Agreement after 1957. In that and subsequent years it noted violations by the Southern Zone by permitting the establishment of United States military personnel and aircraft in its area and by entering into a *de facto* military alliance with SEATO and the United States. The United States legal memorandum sought to justify these actions by asserting that "from the very beginning, the North Vietnamese violated the 1954 Geneva accords" by leaving Communist military forces and supplies in the South and infiltrating Communist guerrillas from the North to the South. The Control Commission's report of June, 1955, however, indicated that both sides were satisfied with the manner in which withdrawals and transfers required by the agreement were effected. The United States brief asserted that 23,-000 men were infiltrated from the North to the South from 1957 to 1962, and the Control Commission noted charges of such infiltration during this period, but not until 1962 did it assess the allegations and the evidence to support them. On that date it submitted a Special Report which called attention to the "rapid deterioration of the situation," and quoted a report of its legal committee, with the Polish member dissenting:

> . . . in specific instances there is evidence to show that armed and unarmed personnel, arms, munitions and other supplies have been sent from the Zone in the North to the Zone in the South with the objective of supporting, organizing and carrying out hostile activities, including armed attacks, directed against the Armed Forces and administration of the Zone in the South. These acts are in violation of Articles 10, 19, 24, and 27 of the Agreement on the Cessation of Hostilities in Vietnam. . . . there is evidence to show that the PAVN (People's Army of Viet-Nam) has allowed the Zone in the North to be used for inciting, encouraging, and supporting hostile activities in the Zone in the South, aimed at the overthrow of the Administration in the South. The use of the Zone in the North for such activities is in violation of Articles 19, 24, and 27 of the Agreement on the Cessation of Hostilities in Vietnam.

In the same report the Control Commission concluded that South Viet-Nam had violated Articles 16 and 17 of the Geneva Agreement by receiving military aid from the United States and Article 19 by making a *de facto* military alliance with that country.

In a Special Report of 1965 the Control Commission noted a joint communiqué of February 7, 1965, from the acting Premier of South Viet-Nam and the United States Ambassador announcing military action against military installations in North Viet-Nam in response to aggression by North Viet-Nam

forces against Pleiku and Tuy Hoa; and also a communiqué
of February 8, 1965, from the North Vietnamese mission protesting the bombing in North Viet-Nam on February 7 by air
forces of "the United States imperialists." The Commission
commented without concurrence of the Canadian member:
"These documents point to the seriousness of the situation
and indicate violations of the Geneva Agreement."

There seems to be no evidence that organized contingents of
the North Vietnamese army crossed the cease-fire line until
after the United States bombing attacks began in February,
1965. Whether infiltrations before that date were of sufficient
magnitude to constitute "armed attacks" and whether they
could be justified as defense measures against the military activities of South Viet-Nam and the United States in violation
of the Geneva agreements is controversial. The Department of
State's legal brief of March 4, 1966, says:

> In these circumstances an "armed attack" is not as easily
> fixed by date and hour as in the case of traditional war-
> fare. However, the infiltration of thousands of armed men
> clearly constitutes an "armed attack" under any reasona-
> ble definition. There may be some question as to the exact
> date at which North Viet-Nam's aggression grew into an
> "armed attack," but there can be no doubt that it had oc-
> curred before February, 1965.

The reports of the Control Commission indicating gradual
increase in violations of the Geneva cease-fire by both sides
after 1958 do not permit of a clear judgment on which side
began "armed attacks." The problem is in any case irrelevant
if the cease-fire line had become ineffective because of the frustration of the elections and United States intervention, as suggested above. There is no evidence of any action by North
Viet-Nam which could be regarded as an armed attack upon
the South prior to 1958, after Ho Chi Minh had engaged in
four years of fruitless effort to carry out the resolutions of the
Geneva Conference. In these circumstances Ho Chi Minh's
action in support of the Viet-Cong did not constitute aggression or armed attack in international relations but civil strife

within the domestic jurisdiction of Viet-Nam, similar to the action of the North against the South in the American Civil War. Whether called "intervention," "reprisals" or "collective defense," the United States response by bombings in North Viet-Nam, which began in February, 1965, violated international law, the United Nations Charter, and the Geneva Agreement, if the latter were in effect.

Reprisals in traditional international law were permitted only to remedy an injury resulting from violation by another state of its obligations under international law, after the injured state had made formal complaint and demanded reparation, and had unsuccessfully sought to obtain a remedy by all peaceful means available, and provided the measures of reprisal did not exceed in severity the injury complained of. The United States "reprisals" in the Bay of Tonkin incident of August, 1964, seem to have conformed to none of these conditions, and the same was true of the Pleiku incident of February, 1965. There were no clear proof that an injury had been received because of a violation of international law by North Viet-Nam, no formal complaint to the North Viet-Nam government, no effort to obtain a remedy by peaceful means, and the response was far in excess of any alleged injury. Furthermore, the United Nations Charter abolished the traditional right of reprisals, as declared by the Security Council in April, 1964, by requiring the Members to settle their international disputes by peaceful means and to refrain from the use or threat of force in international relations except in defense against armed attack or under authority of the United Nations.

The United States relied on the obsolete doctrine of reprisals in this case rather than on the right of self-defense against armed attack. It alleged that a United States naval destroyer had been attacked by North Vietnamese torpedo boats while patrolling beyond territorial waters on August 2 and 4, 1964, in the Bay of Tonkin. North Viet-Nam contended that the destroyers were within its territorial waters, which it had extended to twelve miles, and that surveillance of these waters was necessitated because of a South Vietnamese naval attack on its installations on July 31. The United States destroyers seem not to have been injured but the United States reprisals destroyed several North Vietnamese torpedo boats and the installations in five North Vietnamese ports. Congress endorsed this reprehensible "shooting from the hip" by passing a resolution almost unanimously on August 7 authorizing the President to take similar action in the future.

By this resolution Congress:
Approves and supports the determination of the President, as Commander in Chief, to take all necessary measures to repel armed attack against the forces of the United States and to prevent further aggression. . . . the United States is, therefore, prepared, as the President determines, to take all necessary steps, including the use of armed force, to assist any member or protocol state of the Southeast Asia Collective Defense Treaty requesting assistance in defense of its freedom.

The President has cited this resolution as justification for his extensive escalation of the hostilities in Viet-Nam, but it has been contended by some Senators that the action taken requires a declaration of war under the Constitution, and others have asserted that in voting for it they had in mind only limited actions such as that in the Bay of Tonkin. The text, however, goes much further. The issue seems unimportant in view of the broad Constitutional powers of the President to use armed force without Congressional support or declaration of war.

Practice and Supreme Court decisions make it clear that the President as Commander-in-Chief and under general legislation has extensive power to use the armed forces when he deems it necessary to defend American territory or citizens or to meet treaty obligations, but not as an instrument of policy. The major limitation upon such action appears to be the Congressional power to withhold appropriations. In the Vietnamese situation Congress not only voted the funds requested by the President but authorized him to use armed force to assist SEATO states and states mentioned in the Protocol.

The United States has asserted that the SEATO Treaty and correspondence of President Eisenhower with Diem created a binding obligation to defend South Viet-Nam from armed attack. The correspondence does not seem to have involved a legal commitment to use armed force in defense of South Viet-Nam, but rather a United States policy of giving economic and military aid to build up a South Viet-Nam capable of resistance to subversion or aggression. . . .

LEGAL MEMORANDUM ON VIETNAM WAR OF LAWYERS' COMMITTEE ON AMERICAN POLICY TOWARD VIETNAM, 1967

Shortly after the United States started overt war actions in North and South Vietnam in February 1965, the Secretary General of the United Nations, U Thant, said: "I am sure the great American people, if only they knew the true facts and the background towards the development in South Vietnam, will agree with me that further bloodshed is . . . unnecessary." (Press Conference, February 24, 1965.)

A brief historical background of events follows:

a) A separate state or nation of "South Vietnam" has never existed. Before World War II the whole of Vietnam was part of French Indochina. During World War II pro-Axis French authorities in Indochina collaborated with the Japanese invaders. However, "the people of Indochina . . . resisted their Japanese overlords fiercely . . . led . . . by Ho Chi Minh, 'the Enlightened One.' The political organization which he headed was called the Viet Minh (League for the Independence of Viet Nam) and consisted of a coalition of several parties of varying political views. . . . Because of his resistance to the Japanese, Ho won considerable popularity."

b) "When Japan collapsed in August 1945, he . . . immediately proclaimed . . . a provisional government. . . . The Emperor Bao Dai abdicated his throne and called the people of Annam to support the revolutionary government of Ho Chi Minh."

During World War II, the United States was "in the camp of the Viet Minh that was to become the Viet Cong; men like General Gallagher and Major Patti had hoisted the Stars and Stripes on the side of Ho Chi Minh and Giap [General Vo Nguyen Giap is currently Defense Minister of North Vietnam] in 1945. . . ."

c) "On March 6, 1946, a . . . convention . . . signed . . . between the French Commissioner and President Ho Chi Minh . . . recognized the Vietnam Republic [of Ho Chi Minh] as a free state."

d) Shortly thereafter, mutual accusations between the French and the Viet Minh developed into armed hostilities and eventually, into the bitter and protracted French-Indochina war (1946–1954). This "war of independence," as the Vietnamese termed it, caused heavy French casualties and approximately one million deaths among the Viet Minh. During that war the French established a rival regime, the "State of Vietnam," with former Emperor Bao Dai as its President. France officially recognized the "State of Vietnam" on September 30, 1949. This was not meant to establish the separateness of *South Vietnam,* however, for the primary issue at stake throughout the eight-year war was whether the French-Bao Dai regime or Ho Chi Minh's regime was to rule over the *whole* of Vietnam.

e) The war went badly for the French, and in 1950 the United States formally announced that it would furnish "economic aid and military equipment" to meet "the threat to the security of *Vietnam"* * not South Vietnam. Secretary of State Dean Rusk testified before the Senate Foreign Relations Committee that the amount of American "aid" during the remaining four years of the Indochina war (1950–1954) was approx-

* Unless indicated, emphasis in quotations has been added.

imately two billion dollars. To most Vietnamese such massive, if indirect, participation made the United States an ally of France, a role that further prolonged the "colonial" civil war and made it even more bloody and costly.

f) By Spring 1954 the French military situation had grown even more critical, and on March 29, 1954, Secretary of State John Foster Dulles publicly proposed "united action," while acknowledging that this "might involve serious risks." Thus the willingness to enter actively into the war was accompanied by a recognition of the fact that such action might ultimately involve a confrontation with the Soviet Union and/or mainland China. The proposal was rejected by British Foreign Secretary Anthony Eden· and by Prime Minister Winston Churchill and his Cabinet because of Britain's determination to seek an end to the war through an international conference then in preparation.

g) The Conference opened in Geneva on April 26, 1954, "in a mood of deepest American gloom [whereas] Eden felt that he had warded off disaster [namely, a possible world war] and that now there was a chance to negotiate peace."

h) Peace was negotiated, and on July 21, 1954, the Conference ended with the adoption of a "Final Declaration" which reconfirmed the independence of a single, united Vietnam. (The arrangements regarding Vietnam's temporary division into two zones for a two-year period will be discussed in a later section of this analysis.)

i) A few days before the Conference ended, France, in cooperation with the United States, installed Ngo Dinh Diem as Premier of the "State of Vietnam" that is, the Saigon regime that had been created by France with Bao Dai as President.

j) Between the latter part of 1954 and Spring 1955, the French gradually withdrew their forces from Vietnam, and the United States gradually assumed their functions, supporting the Diem regime in the South until its downfall nine years later in 1963.

k) The reunification of the two zones of North and South Vietnam, which was promised for July 1956 and guaranteed by international compact, did not take place. Instead, the United States resolutely maintained the regime of Diem and his successors, despite steady and increasing discontent and insurgency in South Vietnam.

To help a country defend its independence and self-determination may be deemed a noble undertaking. Indeed, the United States Government has attempted to persuade the American people that such "defense" against aggression justifies its presence in Vietnam. But the barest outline of facts indicates that the policy of the United States has been to *prevent* the self-determination of the Vietnamese people, to *prevent* the existence of a reunited and independent Vietnam, and to transform instead the temporary zone of South Vietnam into a separate country that is militantly hostile to North Vietnam.

This determination by the United States to maintain in opposition to the 1954 Geneva Accords a separate regime in the South [. . .] created [an] insoluble legal dilemma for the United States position. The manipulation of facts and issues appears even in the title of the State Department Memorandum, which asserts that the United States is defending "Vietnam"; and this obviously false assertion is at once contradicted in the Memorandum's opening sentence, which mentions United States assistance to the "country" of "South Vietnam."

The United States cannot and does not defend both "Vietnam" and "South Vietnam" at the same time. The United States is not defending the whole of Vietnam; from the beginning the United States has asserted that its central objective is to make the temporary division of Vietnam permanent and create a separate "country" of South Vietnam.

The arguments advanced by the State Department to defend United States policy in Vietnam are untenable in many other ways. They depend upon very questionable interpretations of fact and of law.

A. The intervention is not justified by the right of collective self-defense.

Supporters of the United States course in Vietnam contend that the right of "collective self-defense" justifies intervention and that, in effect, the United States is entitled to respond to a request for assistance from South Vietnam. This claim is asserted in the State Department Memorandum to justify United States actions in Vietnam. To begin with, this contention admits that the United States is not defending itself against an armed attack by either North Vietnam or the Vietcong. They are not our enemies. Hence, under the Charter of the United Nations and under general principles of international law, there could exist *only one possible* justification for United States intervention, namely, that the United States is exercising the right of collective self-defense. Indeed, there can be no other justification for using force.

One of the abiding Principles of the Charter of the United Nations is the obligation of its Members to eliminate the *use* of force and even the *threat* of force in international relations.

Article 2 (4) : All members shall refrain in their international relations from the threat or use of force against the territorial integrity or political independence of any state, or in any other manner inconsistent with the Purposes of the United Nations.

The State Department Memorandum (Sec. 1, B) interprets Article 2 (4) with curious superficiality. Calling this Principle "an important limitation on the use of force," the Memorandum creates a misleading impression. It is not a "limitation" but the keystone of modern international law. Threat or the use of force are not "limited"; in principle they are outlawed.

The Charter acknowledges that, for the very purpose of maintaining peace, various measures, and ultimately force, may be required. It confers the competence to use force upon the Security Council, thus making force the instrument of the world community, and not of individual states:

Article 39: The Security Council shall determine the existence of any threat to the peace, breach of the peace, or act of aggression, and shall make recommendations, or decide what measures shall be taken . . . to maintain or restore international peace and security. (Articles 42 and 44 provide that such "measures" may include military sanctions.)

The essential meaning of this rule of international law is that no country shall decide for itself whether to use force—and, especially, whether to wage war through an intervention in a foreign conflict. Clearly, the United States, as a chief architect and signatory Member of the United Nations is, in principle, bound to admit that the Security Council is the only agent authorized to determine the measures required to maintain or to restore international peace.

The Charter does recognize, however, that grave emergencies may occur when an *immediate* military reaction may be necessary to prevent disaster. For these special emergencies, the Charter creates a very narrow exception to the prohibition of unilateral force:

> Article 51: Nothing in the present Charter shall impair the inherent right of individual or collective self-defense if an armed attack occurs against a Member of the United Nations, until the Security Council has taken measures necessary to maintain international peace and security.

This rule was most carefully formulated under the guidance of Secretary of State Edward R. Stettinius and United States Senator Arthur Vandenberg at the San Francisco Conference leading to the establishment of the United Nations. Article 51 constitutes, as has been emphasized by many international lawyers, the single *exception* to the keystone principle of the Charter and to contemporary world order—that is, the prohibition of unilateral use or threat of force. It is an accepted canon of construction that if a treaty grants an exception to a basic rule, such exception must be interpreted restrictively.

The State Department centers its argument on the existence of this exceptional right of individual and collective self-defense. In justifying the use of force by the United States, the State Department Memorandum overlooks the relevance of a universal abhorrence of war, and the various steps that have, as a consequence, been taken to prohibit war as an instrument of national policy. Since the Kellogg-Briand Pact of 1928 the prohibition of war has formed a part of international law and has been accepted by the United States as governing the conduct of international relations. Seizing upon the reference in the United Nations Charter to the right of self-defense as "inherent" (that is, allegedly existing outside and independent of the Charter), the State Department argues in favor of a doctrine of self-defense that did not exist even before the Charter and which, if accepted, would establish a unilateral right of military intervention and confer a competence upon nation-states to wage wars that might have the gravest consequences for the world.

B. The Charter permits collective self-defense only in case of an "armed attack." The existence of an "armed attack" is not established by the Memorandum.

The right of self-defense under the Charter arises only if an "armed attack" has occurred. The language of Article 51 is unequivocal on this point.

The term "armed attack" has an established meaning in international law. It was deliberately employed in the Charter to reduce drastically the discretion of states to determine for themselves the scope of permissible self-defense both with regard to claims of individual and collective self-defense.

Individual self-defense and, *a fortiori,* collective self-defense is not a lawful response to the commission of action unilaterally described as "indirect aggression," but only in the event that the victim state experiences an "armed attack," that is, if military forces cross an international boundary in visible, massive and sustained form. The objective of Article 51 was to confine the discretion of a state to claim self-defense to those instances "when the necessity for action" is "instant, overwhelming, and leaving no choice of means, and no moment for deliberation." In explaining Article 51, legal authorities usually invoke the classical definition of self-defense given by

Secretary of State Daniel Webster in *The Caroline*. Mr. Webster's description of the permissible basis for self-defense was relied upon in the Nuremberg Judgment in the case against major German war criminals. This judgment was, of course, based upon *pre*-United Nations law and, in turn, was affirmed unanimously by the United Nations General Assembly at its first Session (Res. 95 (I)).

There can be no disagreement with the assertion that "the principle of self-defense against armed attack is universally recognized and accepted" (State Department Memorandum, Sec. I, B). The real issue is whether the State Department's interpretation of what constitutes "an armed attack" has ever been recognized and accepted; or whether, in Mr. Webster's generally accepted words, the right of self-defense is restricted to instances "when the necessity for action" is "instant, overwhelming, and leaving no choice of means, and no moment for deliberation." The Memorandum relies upon legal authorities who themselves accept Webster's narrow conception of the permissible scope of self-defense, despite the obvious inconsistency between this conception and the allegation by the State Department that an "armed attack" upon South Vietnam has taken place.

The correct delimitation of the concept of self-defense is not a "legalistic" question. The statesmen responsible for their nation's fate insist upon this differentiation between "armed attack" and other forms of hostile behavior; in fact, they insist upon safeguards to prevent unauthorized outside intervention in their affairs even in the event of an "armed attack." For example, the distinction exists in the Charter of the Organization of American States (1948) which in Article 25 differentiates unequivocally between an "armed attack" and other forms of aggression. The distinction is also found in Articles 3 and 6 of the Inter-American Treaty of Reciprocal Assistance (Rio Treaty) of 1947, in the North Atlantic (NATO) Treaty of 1949, in the Warsaw Treaty of 1955 and in the United States–Japanese Treaty of Mutual Cooperation and Security of 1960—all four of these treaty instruments refer only to "armed attack" and make specific reference to Article 51 of the United Nations Charter. In particular, Article 2 of the Southeast Asia Collective Defense Treaty (SEATO) carefully distinguishes between "armed attack" and "subversive activities directed from without"; Article 4 (1) of the SEATO Treaty covers "aggression by means of armed attack"; while Article 4 (2) covers threats "in any way *other* than by armed attack" or ". . . by any *other* fact or situation which might endanger the peace of the area." This distinction is a crucial one. The question of life and death of many innocent victims of war may be contingent upon it—and perhaps, ultimately, the very survival of mankind. It therefore warrants the closest attention. The entire case of the State Department is based upon the premise that an "armed attack" by the North against the South has taken place in Vietnam. The Memorandum acknowledges that an "armed attack" must precede the exercise of self-defense and that indirect aggression does not satisfy this prerequisite. Astonishingly, however, the Memorandum neglects to document its conclusion that the alleged aggression amounts to an "armed attack." It merely alleges the occurrence of an armed attack by North Vietnam "before February 1965," but fails to offer any evidence that such an "armed attack" occurred.

The State Department Memorandum quotes selectively from reports of the International Control Commission (ICC), created at Geneva to supervise the 1954 arrangements, to support its claim of subversion and infiltrations by North Vietnam. It fails, however, to acknowledge or to take account of the numerous passages in the ICC reports that criticize the forbidden, and progressively increasing, military build-up by the United States in South Vietnam that started almost immediately after agreement was reached at Geneva in 1954. It is in the context of this gradually increasing military build-up by the United States that one must assess the State Department's contentions regarding the infiltration of 40,000 North Vietnamese into South Vietnam over the eleven-year period between 1954 and 1965.

These allegations, even if taken as true—in fact, they are partially contradicted by many independent sources, including the Mansfield Report—indicate some intervention by North Vietnam in the civil strife or "insurgency" in South Vietnam, but they do not establish an armed attack within the accepted meaning of Article 51 of the Charter.

Contrary to the position taken by the State Department, externally supported subversion, clandestine supply of arms and infiltration of armed personnel were well known before World War II, and the statesmen at the San Francisco Conference were well aware of the history of long debates on the definition of different forms of aggression. But the Committee chaired by Senator Arthur Vandenberg, which discussed Article 51 at length, purposely restricted the right of self-defense to a situation of *armed attack* because only these situations require *immediate* military reaction to avoid disaster. The rationale is persuasive: other forms of aggression, especially "indirect aggression," are so difficult to define and to ascertain, that too many situations might occur in which states, in good faith or bad, would claim the right of self-defense and thereby expand and intensify warfare. Any local strife could thus become internationalized by outside intervention. Evidently neither the Soviet Union nor the United States—to mention only these two participants at San Francisco—intended to allow a less precise definition of "collective self-defense" to grant each other the right to take unilateral military action whenever either state might claim to act as a collective "protector" of some government beleaguered by civil strife.

The occurrence of an "armed attack" as the essential precondition for the use of force in "self-defense" is underscored by leading authorities on international law. For example, Hans Kelsen writes:

> It is of importance to note that Article 51 does not use the term "aggression" but the much narrower concept of "armed attack" which means that . . . any act of aggression which has not the character of an armed attack in-

volving the use of armed force does not justify resort to force.

Kelsen examines a situation of the Vietnam type: State B "arming or otherwise assisting the revolutionary group" in a civil war in State A. States C and D construe this as "armed attack" by State B against State A and take war action against State B, in "collective self-defense" of State A. Then "it is very probable that [State B] will deny to be guilty of an 'armed attack' . . . and might declare this action [by States C and D] as an illegal attack, against which it considers itself entitled to exercise self-defense."

It is to prevent such developments that Judge Jessup argues against interference by outside powers in such situations:

> It would be disastrous to agree that every State may decide itself which of the two contestants is in the right and may govern its conduct according to its own decision. The ensuing conflict . . . would be destructive to the ordered world community which the Charter and any modern law of nations must seek to preserve. State C would be shipping . . . war supplies to A, while State D would be assisting State B . . . and it would not be long before C and D would be enmeshed in the struggle out of "self-defense."

Judge Jessup instead urges an "impartial blockade against both parties to the fighting." The 1954 Geneva Accords intended, as a precaution, something similar by prohibiting foreign armaments and personnel and military alliance and bases in Vietnam. The United States adopted an analogous stand-off policy, for example, during the India-Pakistan conflict in 1965 when each side charged an armed attack by the other.

Derek Bowett considers that restraint is legally *required:*

> . . . the only proper course for states which are not themselves placed in the necessity of self-defense, is . . . to abstain from intervention . . . until such time as a competent organ of the United Nations has determined what

measures are necessary for the maintenance of international peace and security, and what part those states shall take in these measures.

Mr. Bowett quotes the *Resolution on the Duties of States in the Case of Outbreak of Hostilities* (Res. 378[V] adopted by the United Nations General Assembly on November 17, 1950) which calls upon states engaged in hostilities to "take all steps practicable in the circumstances . . . to *bring the armed conflict to an end at the earliest possible moment.*" Mr. Bowett adds, "It is difficult to see how intervention by states generally could prove consistent with this end."

The State Department Memorandum supplies most of the refutation to its own contention that an "armed attack" has occurred. Its description of the long-smouldering conditions of unrest, subversion and infiltration establishes a situation that is the very opposite of an emergency demanding immediate response, one "leaving no choice of means, and no moment of deliberation." The Government's argument, therefore, appears not only to be inconsistent with Article 51 but to deny altogether the letter and spirit of the Charter, which demands that states seek peaceful solutions wherever possible. This duty is expressed in Article 2 and elaborated in Article 33 (1):

> The parties to any dispute, the continuance of which is likely to endanger the maintenance of international peace and security, shall *first of all* seek a solution by negotiation, enquiry, mediation, conciliation, arbitration, judicial settlement, resort to regional agencies or arrangement, or other peaceful means of their own choice. (Emphasis added.)

The United States had ten years within which to seek a solution without resort to force, and South Vietnam was also bound by this same obligation. The reports of the ICC are full of complaints about South Vietnam's deliberate and systematic sabotage of the machinery created by the Geneva Accords. In addition, the State Department does not sustain the charge of external aggression by infiltration. It *"estimates"* that "by the end of 1964 North Vietnam may well have moved over 40,000 armed and unarmed guerrillas into South Vietnam." Even if this admittedly uncertain and unproved allegation that these men came under *orders* from North Vietnam is accepted, the figure is not meaningful. Why should an unarmed Vietnamese who moves from one zone to another zone in his own country be classified as "guerrilla" and "infiltrator," and provide the material basis for an accusation of "armed attack"? Above all, the State Department Memorandum conveys the unwarranted impression that 40,000 outside guerrillas had *accumulated* by 1965. The Memorandum fails to deduct all those who during a period of ten or eleven years died, became incapacitated, were taken prisoners, deserted, or simply withdrew from or never participated in the insurgency.

Furthermore, the Mansfield Report shows that before 1965, infiltration from the North "was confined primarily to political cadres and military leadership," and also notes that by 1962 "United States military advisors and service forces in South Vietnam totaled approximately 10,000 men." The Report makes plain that a significant number of armed personnel were introduced from the North only *after* the United States had intervened at a time when the "total collapse of the Saigon government's authority appeared imminent in the early months of 1965":

> U.S. combat troops in strength arrived at that point in response to the appeal of the Saigon authorities. The Vietcong counter-response was to increase their military activity with forces strengthened by intensified local recruitment and infiltration of regular North Vietnamese troops. With the change in the composition of the opposing forces, the character of the war also changed sharply.

Senator Mike Mansfield, in his Commencement address at Yeshiva University on June 16, 1966, declared:

> When the sharp increase in the American military effort

began in early 1965, it was estimated that only about 400 North Vietnamese soldiers were among the enemy forces in the South which totalled 140,000 at that time.

To summarize this essential point—outside military intervention (collective self-defense) is permissible only in cases of a *particularly grave, immediate emergency,* namely "an armed attack." The kind of force allegedly employed by North Vietnam against South Vietnam cannot appropriately be regarded as "an armed attack" as specified in Article 51 of the United Nations Charter. Thus the claim of collective self-defense is unavailable to South Vietnam and, *a fortiori,* unavailable also to the United States. . . .

The next selections illustrate the effort by American citizens to rely upon international law to avoid participation in what they allege to be an illegal and criminal war. The decisions by American courts are important indicators of the limited extent to which a government will allow international law to be applied against itself.

UNITED STATES V. MITCHELL, 1965

[Excerpt]

Timbers, Chief Judge.

Defendant David Henry Mitchell, III, after a three-day trial, was convicted by a jury of willful failure to report for induction in the armed forces of the United States, in violation of Section 12 (a) of the Universal Military Training and Service Act, 50 U.S.C. App. § 462 (a). He was sentenced, under 18 U.S.C. § 4208 (a) (1), to not less than 18 months and not more than 5 years in prison and was fined $5,000.* His post-conviction motion for a judgment of acquittal or a new trial, supported on one issue by the New Haven Civil Liberties Council, was denied. He has appealed, pursuant to a notice of appeal filed by his court-appointed counsel, and has been enlarged on bail pending appeal. . . .

Opinion

I.

Issues Raised on Motion to Dismiss Indictment

(A) *Constitutionality of Draft Law As Applied*

[6] Defendant claimed that with respect to the war in Viet Nam the Universal Military Training and Service Act is being unconstitutionally applied because Congress has not declared war; that the executive in effect has declared war; and that the

* The Court recommended at time of sentencing that defendant's application for parole after 18 months of imprisonment be considered by the Board of Parole only on the condition that defendant shall unequivocally agree to report for induction in the armed forces of the United States. Cf. Selective Service Regulations, § 1642.33, 32 C.F.R. 1642.33.

intervention of the United States in Viet Nam is in contravention of various treaties and international conventions to which the United States is a party.

These contentions are wholly without merit and have been repeatedly and consistently rejected by the courts of the United States.

[7] Congress has the power to conscript for service in the land, naval and air forces of the United States in time of war and in time of peace. During the Korean war a similar contention was squarely rejected by the Court of Appeals for this Circuit in United States v. Bolton, supra, 192 F.2d at 806; cf. United States v. Herling, supra. This Court, in denying defendant's motion to dismiss the indictment, rejected defendant's contention with respect to the Viet Nam war, upon the authority of Bolton and Herling, and that ruling is here specifically confirmed.

[8] Section 6 of the United Nations Participation Act of 1945, 22 U.S.C. § 287d, authorizes the President, pursuant to a Congressionally approved agreement with the United Nations, to send men abroad to fight without a specific mandate from Congress. While Congress has not formally declared war with respect to the military action in Viet Nam, nor did it in Korea, it has given its wholehearted approval to the action of the President by appropriations and other implementing legislation. The President, as Commander-in-Chief, has always exercised the power to begin hostilities; viewed realistically, most of our wars have been in full course before Congress has gotten around to a formal declaration. Prize Cases, The Brig Amy Warwick, 67 U.S. (2 Black) 635, 665–671, 17 L.Ed. 459 (1862). Unquestionably the President can start the gun at home or abroad to meet force with force; he is not only authorized but bound to do so. Id. at 668. And under our established concept of international dependence and foreign commitments, this power must extend to repelling attacks upon our allies which threaten our own security.

[9] To read into the provision of the Constitution empow-

ering Congress to raise and support armies, U.S.Const. art. I,
§ 8, cl. 12, a limitation forbidding conscription in time of
peace, or in time of cold war or at any time short of a formal
declaration of war, would render Congress helpless to prepare
in advance against the danger of war. See Hamilton v. Regents
of University of Cal., supra, 293 U.S. at 262–263, 55 S.Ct. at
204; United States v. Herling, supra. This firmly established
principle of constitutional law has been well summarized by
Judge Phillips (construing the Selective Service Act of 1948)
in Warren v. United States, supra, 177 F.2d at 599:

"Congress has power to raise armies by conscription in
time of peace as well as in time of war. The power to do
so is essential to the national security. We must accept as
true the recitals of Congress in the Act. Moreover, we can
take judicial notice that when the Act was passed, the
balance between peace and war was so delicate that no
one could forecast the future with certainty and that our
national security required the maintenance of adequate
military, air, and naval establishments and that, without
such establishments, our survival as a nation of free and
independent people would be in jeopardy. Congress has
power to prepare against an enemy, actual or potential.
It is not required to postpone that preparation until a
time when it would be too late."

[10] Finally, defendant lacks standing to claim that the Act
is being unconstitutionally applied in drafting him to go to
Viet Nam to fight an "undeclared war." He stands guilty of
the felony of refusing to report for induction. Had he been
inducted, he might never have been sent abroad, much less to
Viet Nam. Until inducted and ordered to Viet Nam, his claim
of unconstitutional application of the Act is premature.
United States v. Bolton, supra, 192 F.2d at 806.

(B) *Defendant's Political or Philosophical Views*

[11, 12] In support of his motion to dismiss the indictment,
defendant asserted that the individual must disassociate himself from the war crimes of his government; that the United

States is committing crimes against peace; that United States authorities and their agents are committing war crimes and crimes against humanity; and that the United States violates treaties regarding war and self-determination.

Leaving aside the sickening spectacle of a 22-year-old citizen of the United States seizing the sanctuary of a nation dedicated to freedom of speech to assert such tommyrot, and leaving aside also the transparency of his motives for doing so, the decisive point is that such political or philosophical views, even if sincerely entertained, are utterly irrelevant as a defense to the charge of willful refusal to report for induction in the armed forces of the United States and as a basis for challenging an indictment so charging. . . .

MORA V. MCNAMARA, 1967

November 6, 1967. Petition for writ of certiorari to the United States Court of Appeals for the District of Columbia Circuit denied. Dissenting opinion by Mr. Justice Stewart with whom Mr. Justice Douglas joins. Dissenting opinion by Mr. Justice Douglas with whom Mr. Justice Stewart concurs. Mr. Justice Marshall took no part in the consideration or decision of this petition.

Mr. Justice Stewart, with whom Mr. Justice Douglas joins, dissenting.

The petitioners were drafted into the United States Army in late 1965, and six months later were ordered to a West Coast replacement station for shipment to Vietnam. They brought this suit to prevent the Secretary of Defense and the Secretary of the Army from carrying out those orders, and requested a declaratory judgment that the present United States military activity in Vietnam is "illegal." The District Court dismissed the suit, and the Court of Appeals affirmed.

There exist in this case questions of great magnitude. Some are akin to those referred to by Mr. Justice Douglas in Mitchell v United States, 386 US 972, 18 L ed 2d 132, 87 S Ct 1162. But there are others:

I. Is the present United States military activity in Vietnam a "war" within the meaning of Article I, Section 8, Clause 11 of the Constitution?

II. If so, may the Executive constitutionally order the petitioners to participate in that military activity, when no war has been declared by the Congress?

III. Of what relevance to Question II are the present treaty obligations of the United States?

IV. Of what relevance to Question II is the Joint Congressional ("Tonkin Bay") Resolution of August 10, 1964?

(a) Do present United States military operations fall within the terms of the Joint Resolution?

(b) If the Joint Resolution purports to give the Chief Executive authority to commit United States forces to armed conflict limited in scope only by his own absolute discretion, is the Resolution a constitutionally impermissible delegation of all or part of Congress' power to declare war?

These are large and deeply troubling questions. Whether the Court would ultimately reach them depends, of course, upon the resolution of serious preliminary issues of justiciability. We cannot make these problems go away simply by refusing to hear the case of three obscure Army privates. I intimate not even tentative views upon any of these matters, but I think the Court should squarely face them by granting certiorari and setting this case for oral argument.

Mr. Justice Douglas, with whom Mr. Justice Stewart concurs, dissenting.

The questions posed by Mr. Justice Stewart cover the wide range of problems which the Senate Committee on Foreign Relations recently explored, in connection with the SEATO Treaty of February 19, 1955, and the Tonkin Gulf Resolution.

Mr. Katzenbach, representing the Administration, testified that he did not regard the Tonkin Gulf Resolution to be "a declaration of war" and that while the Resolution was not "constitutionally necessary" it was "politically, from an international viewpoint and from a domestic viewpoint, extremely important." He added:

"The use of the phrase 'to declare war' as it was used in the Constitution of the United States had a particular meaning in terms of the events and the practices which existed at the time it was adopted. . . .

"[I]t was recognized by the Founding Fathers that the President might have to take emergency action to protect the security of the United States, but that if there was going to be another use of the armed forces of the United States, that was a decision which Congress should check the Executive on, which Congress should support. It was for that reason that the phrase was inserted in the Constitution.

"Now, over a long period of time, . . . there have been many uses of the military forces of the United States for a variety of purposes without a congressional declaration of war. But it would be fair to say that most of these were relatively minor uses of force. . . .

"A declaration of war would not, I think, correctly reflect the very limited objectives of the United States with respect to Vietnam. It would not correctly reflect our efforts there, what we are trying to do, the reasons why we are there, to use an outmoded phraseology, to declare war."

The view that Congress was intended to play a more active role in the initiation and conduct of war than the above statements might suggest has been espoused by Senator Fulbright (Cong Rec Oct. 11, 1967, p. 14683–14690), quoting Thomas Jefferson who said: *

---

* 15 Papers of Jefferson 397 (Boyd ed., Princeton 1955). In *The Federalist* No. 69, at 465 (Cooke ed., 1961), Hamilton stated:

"The President is to be Commander in Chief of the army and navy of the United States. In this respect his authority would be nominally the same with that of the King of Great Britain, but in substance much inferior to it. It would amount to nothing more than the supreme command and direction of the military and naval forces, as first General and Admiral of the Confederacy; while that of the British King extends to the *declaring* of war and to the *raising* and *regulating* of fleets and armies; all which by the Constitution under consideration would appertain to the Legislature."

"We have already given in example one effectual check to the Dog of war by transferring the power of letting him loose from the Executive to the Legislative body, from those who are to spend to those who are to pay."

These opposed views are reflected in the Prize Cases, 2 Black 635, 17 L ed 459, a five-to-four decision rendered in 1863. Mr. Justice Grier, writing for the majority, emphasized the arguments for strong presidential powers. Justice Nelson, writing for the minority of four, read the Constitution more strictly, emphasizing that what is war in actuality may not constitute war in the constitutional sense. During all subsequent periods in our history—through the Spanish-American War, the Boxer Rebellion, two World Wars, Korea, and now Vietnam—the two points of view urged in the Prize Cases have continued to be voiced.

A host of problems is raised. Does the President's authority to repel invasions and quiet insurrections, his powers in foreign relations and his duty to execute faithfully the laws of the United States, including its treaties, justify what has been threatened of petitioners? What is the relevancy of the Gulf of Tonkin Resolution and the yearly appropriations in support of the Vietnam effort?

The London Treaty (59 Stat 1546), the SEATO Treaty (6 UST 81, 1955), the Kellogg-Briand Pact (46 Stat 2343), and Article 39 of Chapter VII of the UN Charter deal with various aspects of wars of "aggression."

Do any of them embrace hostilities in Vietnam, or give rights to individuals affected to complain, or in other respects give rise to justiciable controversies?

There are other treaties or declarations that could be cited. Perhaps all of them are wide of the mark. There are sentences in our opinions which, detached from their context, indicate that what is happening is none of our business:

"Certainly it is not the function of the Judiciary to entertain private litigation—even by a citizen—which challenges the legality, the wisdom, or the propriety of the Commander-in-Chief in sending our armed forces abroad or to any particu-

lar region." Johnson v. Eisentrager, 339 US 763, 789, 94 L ed
1255, 1271, 70 S Ct 936.

We do not, of course, sit as a committee of oversight or supervision. What resolutions the President asks and what the
Congress provides are not our concern. With respect to the
Federal Government, we sit only to decide actual cases or controversies within judicial cognizance that arise as a result of
what the Congress or the President or a judge does or attempts
to do to a person or his property.

In Ex parte Milligan, 4 Wall 2, 18 L ed 281, the Court relieved a person of the death penalty imposed by a military tribunal, holding that only a civilian court had power to try him
for the offense charged. Speaking of the purpose of the Found-
ers in providing constitutional guarantees, the Court said:

"They knew . . . the nation they were founding, be its
existence short or long, would be involved in war; how often
or how long continued, human foresight could not tell; and
that unlimited power, wherever lodged at such a time, was
especially hazardous to freemen. For this, and other equally
weighty reasons, they secured the inheritance they had fought
to maintain, by incorporating in a written constitution the
safeguards which *time* had proved were essential to its preservation. Not one of these safeguards can the President, or Congress, or the Judiciary disturb, except the one concerning the
writ of habeas corpus." Id., 125, 18 L ed 297.

The fact that the political branches are responsible for the
threat to petitioners' liberty is not decisive. As Mr. Justice
Holmes said in Nixon v. Herndon, 273 US 536, 540, 71 L ed
759, 761, 47 S Ct 446:

"The objection that the subject matter of the suit is political is little more than a play upon words. Of course the petition concerns political action but it alleges and seeks to recover for private damage. That private damage may be caused
by such political action and may be recovered for in a suit at
law hardly has been doubted for over two hundred years, since
Ashby v. White, 2 Ld Raym 938, 3 id. 320, and has been recognized by this Court."

These petitioners should be told whether their case is beyond judicial cognizance. If it is not, we should then reach the merits of their claims, on which I intimate no views whatsoever.

The *Welsh* case decided in 1970 by a closely divided Supreme Court is the most recent judicial interpretation of conscientious objection. A claimant opposed to all wars need only demonstrate the sincerity of this belief. No religious basis for the belief need exist. It is expected that next year the Supreme Court will decide whether selective conscientious objection (i.e., objection to a particular war) is an acceptable ground for exemption from the draft. A high percentage of young Americans are selective conscientious objectors in relation to the Vietnam War.

WELSH V. UNITED STATES, 1970

MR. JUSTICE BLACK announced the judgment of the Court and delivered an opinion in which MR. JUSTICE DOUGLAS, MR. JUSTICE BRENNAN, and MR. JUSTICE MARSHALL join.

The petitioner, Elliott Ashton Welsh, II, was convicted by a United States district judge of refusing to submit to induction into the Armed Forces in violation of 50 U. S. C. App. § 462 (a), and was on June 1, 1966, sentenced to imprisonment for three years. One of petitioner's defenses to the prosecution was that § 6 (j) of the Universal Military Training and Service Act exempted him from combat and noncombat service because he was "by reason of religious training and belief . . . conscientiously opposed to participation in war in any form." After finding that there was no religious basis for petitioner's conscientious objector claim, the Court of Appeals, Judge Hamley dissenting, affirmed the conviction. 404 F. 2d 1078 (1968). We granted certiorari chiefly to review the contention that Welsh's conviction should be set aside on the basis of this Court's decision in *United States* v. *Seeger,* 380 U. S. 163 (1965). 396 U. S. 816 (1969). For the reasons to be stated, and without passing upon the constitutional arguments which have been raised, we reverse the conviction because of its fundamental inconsistency with *United States* v. *Seeger, supra.*

The controlling facts in this case are strikingly similar to those in *Seeger.* Both Seeger and Welsh were brought up in religious homes and attended church in their childhood, but in neither case was this church one which taught its members not to engage in war at any time for any reason. Neither Seeger nor Welsh continued his childhood religious ties into his young manhood, and neither belonged to any religious group or adhered to the teachings of any organized religion during the period of his involvement with the Selective Service System. At the time of their registration for the draft, neither had yet come to accept pacifist principles. Their views on war developed only in subsequent years, but when their ideas did fully mature both made application with their local draft boards for conscientious objector exemptions from military service under § 6 (j) of the Universal Military Training and Service Act. That section then provided, in part:

"Nothing contained in this title shall be construed to require any person to be subject to combatant training and service in the armed forces of the United States who, by reason of religious training and belief, is conscientiously opposed to participation in war in any form. Religious training and belief in this connection means an individual's belief in a relation to a Supreme Being involving duties superior to those arising from any human relation, but does not include essentially political, sociological, or philosophical views or a merely person [sic] moral code."

In filling out their exemption applications both Seeger and Welsh were unable to sign the statement which, as printed in the Selective Service form, stated "I am, by reason of my religious training and belief, conscientiously opposed to participation in war in any form." Seeger could sign only after striking the words "training and" and putting quotations marks around the word "religious." Welsh could sign only after striking the words "religious training and." On those same applications, neither could definitely affirm or deny that he believed in a "Supreme Being," both stating that they preferred to leave the question open. But both Seeger and Welsh affirmed on those applications that they held deep conscientious scruples against taking part in wars where people were killed. Both strongly believed that killing in war was wrong, unethical, and immoral, and their consciences forbade them to take part in such an evil practice. Their objection to participating in war in any form could not be said to come from a "still, soft voice of conscience"; rather, for them that voice was so loud and insistent that both men preferred to go to jail rather than serve in the Armed Forces. There was never any question about the sincerity and depth of Seeger's convictions as a conscientious objector, and the same is true of Welsh. In this regard the Court of Appeals noted, "[t]he government concedes that [Welsh's] beliefs are held with the strength of more traditional religious convictions." 404 F. 2d, at 1081. But in both cases the Selective Service System concluded that the beliefs of these men were in some sense insufficiently "religious" to qualify them for conscientious objector exemptions under the terms of § 6 (j). Seeger's conscientious objector claim was denied "solely because it was not based upon a 'belief in a relation to a Supreme Being' as required by § 6 (j) of the Act." *United States* v. *Seeger,* 380 U. S. 163, 167 (1965), while Welsh was denied the exemption because his Appeal Board and the Department of Justice hearing officer "could find no religious basis for the registrant's belief, opinions, and convictions." App., at 52. Both Seeger and Welsh subsequently refused to submit to induction into the military and both were convicted of that offense.

In *Seeger* the Court was confronted, first, with the problem that § 6 (j) defined "religious training and belief" in terms of a "belief in a relation to a Supreme Being . . . ," a definition which arguably gave a preference to those who believed in a conventional God as opposed to those who did not. Noting the "vast panoply of beliefs" prevalent in our country, the Court construed the congressional intent as being in "keeping with its long-established policy of not picking and choosing among religious beliefs," *id.,* at 175, and accordingly interpreted "the meaning of religious training and belief so as to embrace *all* religions. . . ." *Id.,* at 165. (Emphasis added.) But, having decided that all religious conscientious objectors were entitled to the exemption, we faced the more serious problem of determining which beliefs were "religious" within the meaning of the statute. This question was particularly difficult in the case of Seeger himself. Seeger stated that his was a "belief in and devotion to goodness and virtue for their own sakes, and a religious faith in a purely ethical creed." 380 U. S., at 166. In a letter to his draft board, he wrote:

"My decision arises from what I believe to be considerations of validity from the standpoint of the welfare of humanity and the preservation of the democratic values which we in the United States are struggling to maintain. I have concluded that war, from the practical standpoint, is futile and self-defeating, and that from the more important moral standpoint, it is unethical." 326 F. 2d 846, 848 (1964).

On the basis of these and similar assertions, the Government argued that Seeger's conscientious objection to war was not "religious" but stemmed from "essentially political, sociological, or philosophical views or a merely personal moral code."

In resolving the question whether Seeger and the other registrants in that case qualified for the exemption, the Court stated that "[the] task is to decide whether the beliefs professed by a registrant are sincerely held and whether they are, *in his own scheme of things,* religious." 380 U. S., at 185. (Emphasis added.) The reference to the registrant's "own scheme of things" was intended to indicate that the central consideration in determining whether the registrant's beliefs are religious is whether these beliefs play the role of a religion and function as a religion in the registrant's life. The Court's principal statement of its test for determining whether a conscientious objector's beliefs are religious within the meaning of § 6 (j) was as follows:

"The test might be stated in these words: A sincere and meaningful belief which occupies in the life of its possessor a place parallel to that filled by the God of those admittedly qualifying for the exemption comes within the statutory definition." 380 U. S., at 176.

The Court made it clear that these sincere and meaningful beliefs which prompt the registrant's objection to all wars need not be confined in either source or content to traditional or parochial concepts of religion. It held that § 6 (j) "does not distinguish between externally and internally derived beliefs," *id.*, at 186, and also held that "intensely personal" convictions which some might find "incomprehensible" or "incorrect" come within the meaning of "religious belief" in the Act. *Id.*, at 184–185. What is necessary under *Seeger* for a registrant's conscientious objection to all war to be "religious" within the meaning of § 6 (j) is that this opposition to war stem from the registrant's moral, ethical, or religious beliefs about what is right and wrong and that these beliefs be held with the strength of traditional religious convictions. Most of the great religions of today and of the past have embodied the idea of a Supreme Being or a Supreme Reality—a God—who communicates to man in some way a consciousness of what is right and should be done, of what is wrong and therefore should be shunned. If an individual deeply and sincerely holds beliefs which are purely ethical or moral in source and content but which nevertheless impose upon him a duty of conscience to refrain from participating in any war at any time, those beliefs certainly occupy in the life of that individual "a place parallel to that filled by . . . God" in traditionally religious persons. Because his beliefs function as a religion in his life, such an individual is as much entitled to a "religious" conscientious objector exemption under § 6 (j) as is someone who derives his conscientious opposition to war from traditional religious convictions.

Applying this standard to Seeger himself, the Court noted the "compulsion to 'goodness' " which informed his total opposition to war, the undisputed sincerity with which he held his views, and the fact that Seeger had "decried the tremendous 'spiritual' price man must pay for his willingness to destroy human life." 380 U. S., at 186–187. The Court concluded:

"We think it clear that the belief's [sic] which prompted

his objection occupy the same place in his life as the belief in a traditional deity holds in the lives of his friends, the Quakers." 380 U. S., at 187.

Accordingly, the Court found that Seeger should be granted conscientious objector status.

In the case before us the Government seeks to distinguish our holding in *Seeger* on basically two grounds, both of which were relied upon by the Court of Appeals in affirming Welsh's conviction. First, it is stressed that Welsh was far more insistent and explicit than Seeger in denying that his views were religious. For example, in filling out their conscientious objector applications, Seeger put quotation marks around the word "religious," but Welsh struck the word "religious" entirely and later characterized his beliefs as having been formed "by reading in the fields of history and sociology." App., at 22. The Court of Appeals found that Welsh had "denied that his objection to war was premised on religious belief" and concluded that "the Appeal Board was entitled to take him at his word." 404 F. 2d, at 1082. We think this attempt to distinguish *Seeger* fails for the reason that it places undue emphasis on the registrant's interpretation of his own beliefs. The Court's statement in *Seeger* that a registrant's characterization of his own belief as "religious" should carry great weight, 380 U.S., at 184, does not imply that his declaration that his views are nonreligious should be treated similarly. When a registrant states that his objections to war are "religious," that information is highly relevant to the question of the function his beliefs have in his life. But very few registrants are fully aware of the broad scope of the word "religious" as used in § 6 (j), and accordingly a registrant's statement that his beliefs are nonreligious is a highly unreliable guide for those charged with administering the exemption. Welsh himself presents a case in point. Although he originally characterized his beliefs as nonreligious, he later upon reflection wrote a long and thoughtful letter to his Appeal Board in which he declared that his beliefs were "certainly religious in the ethical sense of that word." He explained:

"I believe I mentioned taking of life as not being, for me, a religious wrong. Again, I assumed Mr. Bradley [the Department of Justice hearing officer] was using the word 'religious' in the conventional sense, and, in order to be perfectly honest, did not characterize my belief as "religious.' " App., at 44–45.

The Government also seeks to distinguish *Seeger* on the ground that Welsh's views, unlike Seeger's, were "essentially political, sociological, or philosophical or a merely personal, moral code." As previously noted, the Government made the same argument about Seeger, and not without reason, for Seeger's views had a substantial political dimension. *Supra,* at 4–5. In this case, Welsh's conscientious objection to war was undeniably based in part on his perception of world politics. In a letter to his local board, he wrote:

"I can only act according to what I am and what I see. And I see that the military complex wastes both human and material resources, that it fosters disregard for (what I consider a paramount concern) human needs and ends; I see that the means we employ to 'defend' our 'way of life' profoundly change that way of life. I see that in our failure to recognize the political, social, and economic realities of the world, we, *as a nation,* fail our responsibility *as a nation."* App., at 30.

We certainly do not think that § 6 (j)'s exclusion of those persons with "essentially political, sociological, or philosophical views or a merely personal moral code" should be read to exclude those who hold strong beliefs about our domestic and foreign affairs or even those whose conscientious objection to participation in all wars is founded to a substantial extent upon considerations of public policy. The two groups of registrants which obviously do fall within these exclusions from the exemption are those whose beliefs are not deeply held and those whose objection to war does not rest at all upon moral, ethical, or religious principle but instead rests solely upon considerations of policy, pragmatism, or expediency. In applying § 6 (j)'s exclusion of those whose views are "essentially political, etc.," it should be remembered that these exclusions are definitional and do not therefore restrict the category of persons who are conscientious objectors "by religious training and belief." Once the Selective Service System has taken the first step and determined under the standards set out here and in *Seeger* that the registrant is a "religious" conscientious objector, it follows that his views cannot be "essentially political, sociological or philosophical." Nor can they be a "merely personal moral code." See *United States* v. *Seeger*, 380 U. S., at 186.

Welsh stated that he "believe[d] the taking of life—anyone's life—to be morally wrong." App., at 44. In his original conscientious objector application he wrote the following:

> "I believe that human life is valuable in and of itself; in its living; therefore I will not injure or kill another human being. This belief (and the corresponding 'duty' to abstain from violence toward another person) is not 'superior to those arising from any human relation.' On the contrary: *it is essential to every human relation.* I cannot, therefore, conscientiously comply with the Government's insistence that I assume duties which I feel are immoral and totally repugnant." App., at 10.

Welsh elaborated his beliefs in later communications with Selective Service officials. On the basis of these beliefs and the conclusion of the Court of Appeals that he held them "with the strength of more traditional religious convictions," 404 F. 2d, at 1081, we think Welsh was clearly entitled to a conscientious objector exemption. Section 6 (j) requires no more. That section exempts from military service all those whose consciences, spurred by deeply held moral, ethical, or religious beliefs, would give them no rest or peace if they allowed themselves to become a part of an instrument of war.

The judgment is

Reversed

President Nixon's brief statement on the My Lai disclosures is included to give readers a sense of government thinking on battlefield war crimes. Are the occurrences at My Lai more properly viewed as a *deviation* from official war policies or as a *reflection* of these policies? How does pattern bombing of an inhabited and undefended Vietnamese village differ in intention and effect from the offenses charged against U.S. servicemen at My Lai?

PRESIDENT NIXON'S STATEMENT ON MY LAI, 1969

My Lai Massacre

Q. In your opinion, was what happened at My Lai a massacre, an alleged massacre, or what was it, and what do you think can be done to prevent things like this? And if it was a massacre, do you think it was justifiable on military or other grounds?

A. Well, trying to answer all of those questions, in sorting it out, I would start first with this statement: What appears was certainly a massacre, and under no circumstances was it justified. One of the goals we are fighting for in Vietnam is to keep the people from South Vietnam from having imposed upon them a government which has atrocity against civilians as one of its policies, and we cannot ever condone or use atrocities against civilians in order to accomplish that goal.

Now when you used the word "alleged," that is only proper in terms of the individuals involved. Under our system a man is not guilty until proved to be so. And there are several individuals involved here who will be tried by military courts, and consequently we should say "alleged" as far as they are concerned until they are proved guilty.

As far as this kind of activity is concerned, I believe it is an isolated incident. Certainly within this Administration we are doing everything possible to find out whether it was isolated, and so far our investigation indicates that it was. And as far as the future is concerned, I would only add this one point: Looking at the other side of the coin, we have a million, two hundred thousand Americans who have been in Vietnam. Forty thousand of them have given their lives.

Virtually all of them have helped the people of Vietnam in one way or another. They built roads and schools; they built churches and pagodas. The Marines alone this year have built over 250,000 churches, pagodas and temples for the people of Vietnam. And our soldiers in Vietnam and sailors and airmen this year alone contributed three-quarters of a million dollars to help the people of South Vietnam.

Now this record of generosity, of decency, must not be allowed to be smeared and slurred because of this kind of an incident. That's why I'm going to do everything I possibly can to see that all the facts in this incident are brought to light, and that those who are charged, if they are found guilty, are punished, because if it is isolated it is against our policy and we shall see to it that what these men did—if they did it— does not smear the decent men that have gone to Vietnam in a very, in my opinion, important cause.

My Lai Panel

Q. May I go back to Mr. Parnell's question, asked in the light of the My Lai incident. Would you prefer a civilian commission, something other than a military inquiry in this case?

A. I do not believe that a civilian commission, at this time, would be useful. I believe that the matter now is in the judicial process and that a civilian commission might be, and very properly could be used, by the defendants' attorneys as having prejudiced their rights.

Now if it should happen that the judicial process, as set up by the military under the new law passed by Congress, does not prove to be adequate in bringing this incident completely before the public, as it should be brought before the public, then I would consider a commission. But not at this time.

The next selection raises some question of the wider issues of criminal responsibility arising out of the Vietnam War. Where to draw the line; for what reasons? What is practical, desirable in relation to war criminals? Does punishment serve any useful purpose? The distinction between *moral clarification* resulting from an identification of war crimes and the accusation of specific individuals as criminals is important to maintain.

THE CIRCLE OF RESPONSIBILITY
Richard A. Falk

If certain acts in violation of treaties are crimes, they are crimes whether the United States does them or whether Germany does them, and we are not prepared to lay down a rule of criminal conduct against others which we would not be willing to have invoked against us.

—Mr. Justice Robert Jackson,
Chief Prosecutor for the United States
at the Nuremberg Tribunals

The dramatic disclosure of the Son My massacre has aroused public concern over the commission of war crimes in Vietnam by American military personnel. Such a concern, while certainly appropriate, is insufficient if limited to inquiry and prosecution of the individual servicemen who participated in the monstrous events that may have taken the lives of more than 500 civilians in the My Lai No. 4 hamlet of Son My village on March 16, 1968.

Son My stands out as a landmark atrocity in the history of warfare, and its occurrence is a moral challenge to the entire American society. This challenge was stated succinctly by Mrs. Anthony Meadlo, the mother of David Paul Meadlo, one of the killers at Son My: "I sent them a good boy, and they made him a murderer." (*The New York Times,* November 30, 1969.) Another characteristic statement about the general nature of the war was attributed to an army staff sergeant: "We are at war with the ten-year-old children. It may not be humanitarian, but that's what it's like." (*The New York Times,* December 1, 1969.) The massacre itself raises a serious basis for inquiry into the military and civilian command structure that was in charge of battlefield behavior at the time.

However, evidence now available suggests that the armed forces have tried throughout the Vietnamese War to suppress, rather than to investigate and punish, the commission of war crimes by American personnel. The evidence also suggests a failure to protest or prevent the manifest and systematic commission of war crimes by the armed forces of the Saigon regime.

Thus a proper inquiry must be conducted on a scope much broader than any single day of slaughter. The *official policies* developed for the pursuit of belligerent objectives in Vietnam appear to violate the same basic and minimum constraints on the conduct of war as were violated at Son My. The B-52 pattern raids against undefended villages and populated areas, "free bomb zones," forcible removal of civilian population, defoliation and crop destruction, and "search and destroy" missions have been sanctioned by the United States Government. Each of these tactical policies appears to violate international laws of war that are binding upon the United States by international treaties ratified by the government, with the advice and consent of the Senate. The overall American conduct of the war involves a refusal to differentiate between combatants and noncombatants and between military and nonmilitary targets. Detailed presentation of such acts of war in relation to the laws of war is contained in *In the Name of America,* published under the auspices of the Clergy and Laymen Concerned About Vietnam, in January 1968—several months before the Son My massacre took place. Ample evidence of war crimes has been presented to the public and to its leaders for some time, but it has not produced official reaction or rectifying action. A comparable description of the acts of war that were involved in the bombardment of North Vietnam by American planes and naval vessels between February 1965 and October 1968 may be found in *North Vietnam: A Documentary,* by John Gerassi.

The broad point is that the United States Government has

officially endorsed a series of battlefield activities that appear to qualify as war crimes. It would, therefore, be misleading to isolate the awful happenings at Son My from the overall conduct of the war. Certainly, the perpetrators of the massacre are, if the allegations prove correct, guilty of war crimes, but any trial pretending to justice must consider the extent to which they were executing *superior orders* or were carrying out the general line of official policy that established a *moral climate.*

The U.S. prosecutor at Nuremberg, Robert Jackson, emphasized that war crimes are war crimes no matter what country commits them. The United States more than any other sovereign state took the lead in the movement to generalize the principles underlying the Nuremberg Judgment. At its initiative, the General Assembly of the United Nations in 1945 unanimously affirmed "the principles of international law recognized by the Charter of the Nuremberg Tribunal" in Resolution 95 (I). This resolution was an official action of governments. At the direction of the UN membership, the International Law Commission, a body of international law experts from all the principal legal systems in the world, formulated the Principles of Nuremberg in 1950. These seven Principles of International Law are printed in full on pages 107–108, and indicate the basic standards of international responsibility governing the commission of war crimes.

Neither the Nuremberg Judgment nor the Nuremberg Principles fixes definite boundaries on personal responsibility. These will have to be drawn as the circumstances of alleged violations of international law are tested by competent domestic and international tribunals. However, Principle IV makes it clear that *superior orders* are no defense in a prosecution for war crimes, provided the individual accused of criminal behavior had a moral choice available to him.

The United States Supreme Court upheld in *The Matter of Yamashita* 327 U.S. 1 (1945) 1 sentence of death pronounced on General Yamashita for acts committed by troops under his command in World War II. The determination of responsibility rested upon the obligation of General Yamashita to maintain discipline among troops under his command, which discipline included enforcement of the prohibition against the commission of war crimes. Thus General Yamashita was convicted, even though he had no specific knowledge of the alleged war crimes. Commentators have criticized the conviction of General Yamashita because it was difficult to maintain discipline under the conditions of defeat that pervailed when these war crimes were committed in the Philippines, but the imposition of responsibility in this case sets a precedent for holding principal military and political officials responsible for acts committed under their command, especially when no diligent effort was made to inquire into and punish crimes, or prevent their repetition. *The Matter of Yamashita* has vivid relevance to the failure of the U.S. military command to enforce observance of the minimum rules of international law among troops serving under their command in Vietnam. The following sentences from the majority opinion of Chief Justice Stone in *The Matter of Yamashita* has a particular bearing:

> It is evident that the conduct of military operations by troops whose excesses are unrestrained by the orders or efforts of their commands would almost certainly result in violations which it is the purpose of the law of war to prevent. Its purpose to protect civilian populations and prisoners of war from brutality would largely be defeated if the commands of an invading army could with impunity neglect to take responsible measures for their protection. Hence the law of war presupposes that its violation is to be avoided through the control of the operation of war by commanders who are to some extent responsible for their subordinates. [327 U.S. 1, 15]

In fact, the effectiveness of the law of war depends, above all else, on holding those in command and in policy-making positions responsible for rank-and-file behavior on the field of battle. The reports of neuropsychiatrists, trained in combat therapy, have suggested that unrestrained troop behavior is almost always tacitly authorized by commanding officers—at least to the extent of conveying the impression that outrageous acts will not be punished. It would thus be a deception to punish the trigger men at Son My without also looking higher on the chain of command for the real source of responsibility.

The Field Manual of the Department of the Army, FM 27-10, adequately develops the principles of responsibility governing members of the armed forces. It makes clear that the "law of war is binding not only upon States as such but also upon individuals and, in particular, the members of their armed forces." The entire manual is based upon the acceptance by the United States of the obligation to conduct warfare in accordance with the international law of war. The substantive content of international law is contained in a series of international treaties that have been ratified by the United States, including principally the five Hague Conventions of 1907 and the four Geneva Conventions of 1949.

These international treaties are part of "the supreme law of the land" by virtue of Article VI of the U.S. Constitution. Customary rules of international law governing warfare are also applicable to the obligations of American citizens.

It has sometimes been maintained that the laws of war do not apply to a civil war, which is a war within a state, and some observers have argued that the war in Vietnam represents a civil war between factions contending for political control of South Vietnam. That view may accurately portray the principal basis of conflict (though the official American contention, repeated by President Nixon on November 3, is that South Vietnam, a sovereign state, has been attacked by an aggressor state, North Vietnam), but surely the extension of the combat theater to include North Vietnam, Laos, Thailand, Cambodia and Okinawa removes any doubt about the international character of the war from a military and legal point of view. But if one assumes that the war should be treated as a civil war, the laws of war are applicable to an extent great enough to cover the events at Son My and the commission of many other alleged war crimes in Vietnam. The Field Manual incorporates Article 3 of the Geneva Conventions of 1949, which establishes a minimum set of obligations for civil war situations:

> In the case of armed conflict not of an international character occurring in the territory of one of the High Contracting Parties, each Party to the conflict shall be bound to apply, as a minimum, the following provisions:
>
> (*1*) Persons taking no active part in the hostilities, including members of armed forces who have laid down their arms and those placed *hors de combat* by sickness, wounds, detention, or any other cause, shall in all circumstances be treated humanely, without any adverse distinction founded on race, color, religion or faith, sex, birth or wealth, or any other similar criteria.
>
> To this end, the following acts are and shall remain prohibited at any time and in any place whatsoever with respect to the above-mentioned persons:
>
> (*a*) violence to life and person, in particular murder of all kinds, mutilation, cruel treatment and torture;
>
> (*b*) taking of hostages;
>
> (*c*) outrages upon personal dignity, in particular, humiliating and degrading treatment;
>
> (*d*) the passing of sentences and the carrying out of executions without previous judgment pronounced by a regularly constituted court, affording all the judicial guarantees which are recognized as indispensable by civilized peoples.
>
> (2) The wounded and sick shall be collected and cared for.
>
> An impartial humanitarian body, such as the International Committee of the Red Cross, may offer its services to the Parties to the conflict.
>
> The Parties to the conflict should further endeavor to bring into force, by means of special agreements, all or part of the other provisions of the present Convention.

I have already suggested that there is evidence that many official battlefield policies relied upon by the United States in Vietnam amount to war crimes. These official policies should be investigated in light of the legal obligations of the United States. If found to be "illegal," such policies should be discontinued forthwith and those responsible for the policy and its execution should be prosecuted as war criminals by appropriate tribunals. These remarks definitely apply to the following war policies, and very likely to others: (*1*) the Phoenix Program; (*2*) aerial and naval bombardment of undefended villages; (*3*) destruction of crops and forests; (*4*) "search-and-destroy" missions; (*5*) "harassment and interdiction" fire; (*6*) forcible removal of civilian population; (*7*) reliance on a variety of weapons prohibited by treaty.

In addition, all allegations of particular war atrocities should be investigated and reported upon by impartial and responsible agencies of inquiry. These acts—committed in defiance of declared official policy—should be punished. Responsibility should be imposed upon those who inflicted the harm, upon those who gave direct orders, and upon those whose powers of command included insistence upon overall battlefield discipline and the prompt detection and punishment of war crimes committed within the scope of their authority.

Political leaders who authorized illegal battlefield practices and policies, or who had knowledge of these practices and policies and failed to act are similarly responsible for the commission of war crimes. The following paragraph from the majority judgment of the Tokyo War Crimes Tribunal is relevant:

> A member of a Cabinet which collectively, as one of the principal organs of the Government, is responsible for the care of prisoners is not absolved from responsibility if, having knowledge of the commission of the crimes in the sense already discussed, and omitting or failing to secure the taking of measures to prevent the commission of such crimes in the future, he elects to continue as a member of the Cabinet. This is the position even though the Department of which he has the charge is not directly concerned with the care of prisoners. A Cabinet member may resign. If he has knowledge of ill-treatment of prisoners, is powerless to prevent future ill-treatment, but elects to remain in the Cabinet thereby continuing to participate in its collective responsibility for protection of prisoners he willingly assumes responsibility for any ill-treatment in the future.

Army or Navy commanders can, by order, secure proper treatment of prisoners. So can Ministers of War and of the Navy. If crimes are committed against prisoners under their control, of the likely occurrence of which they had, or should have had knowledge in advance, they are responsible for those crimes. If, for example, it be shown that within the units under his command conventional war crimes have been committed of which he knew or should have known, a commander who takes no adequate steps to prevent the occurrence of such crimes in the future will be responsible for such future crimes.

The United States Government was directly associated with the development of a broad conception of criminal responsibility for the leadership of a state during war. A leader must take affirmative acts to prevent war crimes or dissociate himself from the government. If he fails to do one or the other, then by the very act of remaining in a government of a state guilty of war crimes, he becomes a war criminal.

Finally, as both the Nuremberg and the Tokyo judgments emphasize, a government official is a war criminal if he has participated in the initiation or execution of an illegal war of aggression. There are considerable grounds for regarding the United States involvement in the Vietnamese War—wholly apart from the *conduct* of the war—as involving violations of the UN Charter and other treaty obligations of the United States. (See analysis of the legality of U.S. participation in *Vietnam and International Law,* sponsored by the Lawyers' Committee on American Policy Toward Vietnam; see also R. A. Falk, editor, *The Vietnam War and International Law,* Vols. 1 and 2.) If U.S. participation in the war is found illegal, then the policy makers responsible for the war during its various stages would be subject to prosecution as alleged war criminals.

The idea of prosecuting war criminals involves using international law as a *sword* against violators in the military and civilian hierarchy of government. But the Nuremberg Principles imply a broader human responsibility to oppose *an illegal war* and *illegal methods of warfare.* There is nothing to suggest that the ordinary citizen, whether within or outside the armed forces, is potentially guilty of a war crime merely as a consequence of such a status. But there are grounds to maintain that anyone who believes or has reason to believe that a war is being waged in violation of minimal canons of law and morality has an obligation of conscience to resist participation in and support of that war effort by every means at his disposal. In that respect, the Nuremberg Principles provide guidelines for citizens' conscience and a *shield* that can be used in the domestic legal system to interpose obligations under international law between the government and members of the society. Such a doctrine of interposition has been asserted in a large number of selective service cases by individuals refusing to enter the armed forces. It has already enjoyed a limited success in the case of *U.S.* v. *Sisson,* the appeal from which decision is now before the U.S. Supreme Court.

The issue of personal conscience is raised for everyone in the United States. It is raised more directly for anyone called upon to serve in the armed forces. It is raised in a special way for parents of minor children who are conscripted into the armed forces. It is raised for all taxpayers who support the cost of the war. A major legal test of the responsiveness of our judicial system to the obligations of the country to respect international law is being mounted in a taxpayers' suit that has been organized by Pierre Noyes, a professor of physics at Stanford University. In this class action the effort is to induce the court to pronounce upon whether it is permissible to use tax revenues to pay for a war that violates the U.S. Constitution and duly ratified international treaties. The issue of responsibility is raised for all citizens who in various ways endorse the war policies of the government. The circle of responsibility is drawn around all who have or should have knowledge of the illegal and immoral character of the war. The Son My massacre puts every American on notice as to the character of the war. The imperatives of personal responsibility call upon each of us to search for effective means to bring the war to an immediate end.

And the circle of responsibility does not end at the border.

Foreign governments and their populations are pledged by the Charter of the United Nations to oppose aggression and to take steps to punish war crimes. The cause of peace is indivisible, and all those governments and people concerned with Charter obligations have a legal and moral duty to oppose the American involvement in Vietnam and to support the effort to identify, prohibit and punish war crimes. The conscience of the entire world community is implicated by *inaction,* as well as by more explicit forms of support for U.S. policy.

Some may say that war crimes have been committed by both sides in Vietnam and that, therefore, if justice is to be even-handed, North Vietnam and the Provisional Revolutionary Government of South Vietnam should be called upon to prosecute their officials guilty of war crimes. Such a contention needs to be evaluated, however, in the overall context of the war, especially in relation to the identification of which side is the victim of aggression and which side is the aggressor. But whatever grounds there may be for attempting to strike a moral balance of this sort, the allegation that the other side is also guilty does not operate as a legal defense against a war crimes indictment. That question was clearly litigated and decided at Nuremberg.

Others have argued that there can be no war crimes in Vietnam because war has never been "declared" by the U.S. Government. The failure to declare war under these circumstances raises a substantial constitutional question, but it has no bearing upon the rights and duties of the United States under international law. A declaration of war is a matter of internal law, but the existence of combat circumstances is a condition of war that brings into play the full range of obligations under international law.

Rather than encouraging a sense of futility, the Son My disclosures give Americans a genuine focus for concern and action. It now becomes possible to understand the human content of counterinsurgency warfare as waged with modern weapons and doctrines. The events at Son My suggest the need for a broad inquiry into the relationship between the civilian and military leadership of the country and into the systematic battlefield practices of our forces in Vietnam. The occasion calls not for self-appraisal by generals and government officials but at a minimum a commission of citizens drawn from all walks of life and known for their sense of scruples. We need a Presidential commission that has access to all records and witnesses, and is empowered to make public a report and recommendations for action. We also need a series of legal tests in domestic courts, initiated on behalf of such injured groups as civilian survivors of war crimes, young Americans who are in jail or exile because they have contended all along that the American effort in Vietnam violates international law, and servicemen who refuse to obey orders to fight in Vietnam, who complain of the illegality of "superior orders," or who seek to speak out and demonstrate against continuation of the war.

On a world scale, it would seem desirable for the UN to mount an investigation of allegations of war crimes, especially in relation to Vietnam and Nigeria. It would also seem appropriate for the UN to organize a world conference to reconsider the laws of wars as related to contemporary forms of warfare. The world peace conferences of 1899 and 1907 at The Hague might serve as precedents for such a conference call. Such an expression of world conscience is desperately needed at this time. We also need a new set of international treaties that will bind governments in their military conduct.

Given the perils and horrors of the contemporary world, it is time that individuals everywhere called their governments to account for indulging or ignoring the daily evidence of barbarism. We are destroying ourselves by destroying the environment that permits life to flourish, and we are destroying our polity by destroying the values of decency that might allow men eventually to live together in dignity. The obsolete pretensions of sovereign prerogative and military necessity had better be challenged soon if life on earth is to survive.

Townsend Hoopes was a prominent member of the Government during the Johnson Administration who gradually became disenchanted with the American role in Vietnam. Mr. Hoopes has described his own conversion in a book called *The Limits of Intervention,* in which he argues that it was impossible to carry out the American mission in Vietnam at an acceptable cost, not that the mission itself was misconceived. In this selection he argues the absurdity of regarding the diligent, well-intentioned public servants who have carried out our Vietnam policy as "war criminals." Must "war criminals" be demoniac individuals of the Nazi variety? Some question whether even German war criminals were not, by and large, ordinary individuals carrying out assigned roles, embodying what Hannah Arendt has called "the banality of evil" in her book on the Eichmann trial.

THE NUREMBERG SUGGESTION
Townsend Hoopes

I had an illuminating luncheon on November 21 with a young man who is the Washington reporter for *The Village Voice* and with a young woman who turned out to be his journalistic collaborator. Their names were Geoffrey Cowan and Judith Coburn. Massive black locks fell from his head onto football shoulders encased in Harris tweed; her own probable beauty was well concealed beneath a mouse-colored ensemble, including heavy brown stockings and over-sized granny glasses. Both were engaging, intelligent, well-educated, and not quite what they seemed. Indeed, they were journalists of a rather special genre, and on a part-time basis. His principal association is with the Center for Law and Social Policy, hers with the Institute for Policy Studies.

Their interest in me and the book I had written was quite evidently confined to the issue of moral responsibility for the Vietnam War. This issue contains, of course, profound and serious questions, disturbing to and yet earnestly pursued by those of all ages who believe our large-scale military intervention to have been a tragic mistake. We enjoyed a stimulating, robust, and candid exchange of views, accepting disagreement when we found it, as a natural product of healthy argument. It was, however, increasingly clear as we talked that, whereas my chief concern was with the broad question of how the entire nation had stumbled down the long slippery slope to self-delusion into the engulfing morass, they were almost solely interested in the narrow question of how to find and fix individual accountability, and then how to deal with those whom they had marked for punishment. We parted on friendly terms, they to write their piece, I to ponder with spreading disquiet their persistent and only thinly veiled advocacy of some kind of Nuremberg. When I read their published article in the December 4th issue of the *Voice,* I really grasped for the first time (a deficient perception) the full measure of the gulf that separates the outlook of those who came to maturity during the Second World War from the view of those who were not old enough to vote for John F. Kennedy.

The flavor of the Cowan-Coburn reporting may be gleaned from a few representative excerpts. Commenting that through my book I had recently become "a minor hero of the new establishment-oriented peace movement," they moved quickly to their central concern: "Early opponents of the war find it difficult to welcome former Vietnam policy-makers like Hoopes rushing to our side. . . . Is there a new morality in the land or are these men hedging their bets? Should we herald these Nellies-come-lately for breaking away and providing the force that may finally push us out of Vietnam, or should we remind them that they are, after all, still war criminals? . . . What treatment should be afforded the critic who bucks the system and comes over to the other side? . . . Trying to get a moral fix on men like Hoopes, one thinks of the host of World War II movies in which General Field Marshal Rommel (the Desert Fox) is treated as a hero for his attempt to assassinate Hitler when it became clear that the Fuehrer's war policy was suicidal. Rommel's crimes have been absolved by Hollywood, but one wonders whether the Nuremberg judges would have been so generous."

An American Nuremberg. Legal retribution for self-evident

"war crimes." These were the article's dominant themes, which wandered through the paragraphs in a fortunately vain search for an appropriate administrative vehicle. Obviously they were after the big fish; minnows like myself and cool swimmers like Max Frankel could be netted in due course. But "if Tojo can be sentenced to be executed by an American war crime tribunal for leading Japan into a 'war of aggression,' should the only punishment for an American President be that he is voted out of office, while his Secretary of Defense serves a secure term as president of the World Bank?"

I cannot say with any pretense of accuracy whether this curious piece of reporting is genuinely and broadly representative of the generation now in its late twenties. What is crystal-clear is that such views could not conceivably be held or expressed by anyone who was a young man during the Second World War or who was engaged in the mortal struggles of its aftermath—in Greece, in Germany, in Berlin, in Korea. But this suggests the generation gulf. Sensitive, clever children, outraged by flagrant and undeniable blunders in U.S. Vietnam policy, by wanton destruction and endless suffering, are far beyond Vietnam. They are, by and large, judgments unshaped by historical perspective and untempered by any first-hand experience with the unruly forces at work in this near-cyclonic century. When I told Mr. Cowan and Miss Coburn that their desire to impose a system of personal retribution against people of whom they disapprove could lead only to a new McCarthyism and to anarchy, they replied (and wrote) that the "anarchists" who frighten them most are those "who wield the big bombs, control the courts, and assume for themselves the power to declare all their enemies outlaws."

Staring across that void, one is moved to attempt the construction of a bridge, however slender and frail, however suspect it may seem at first to those who grew up only yesterday. The tragic story of Vietnam is not, in truth, a tale of malevolent men bent upon conquest for personal gain or imperial glory. It is the story of an entire generation of leaders (and an entire generation of followers) so conditioned by the tensions of the Cold War years that they were unable to perceive in 1965 (and later) that the communist adversary was no longer a monolith, but rather a fragmented ideology and apparat; that vigorous, uncongenial revolutionary movements thrusting up through the tatters of the colonial tent were essentially national in their meaning, even when they called themselves communist; and that the triumph of such movements was neither a triumph for Moscow and Peking nor a disaster for the United States.

Lyndon Johnson, though disturbingly volatile, was not in his worst moments an evil man in the Hitlerian sense. And his principal advisers were, almost uniformly, those considered when they took office to be among the ablest, the best, the most humane and liberal men that could be found for public trust. No one doubted their honest, high-minded pursuit of the best interests of their country, and indeed of the whole non-communist world, as they perceived those interests. Moreover, the war they waged was conducted entirely within the framework of the Constitution, with the express or tacit consent of a majority of the Congress and the country until at least the autumn of 1967, and without any press censorship. Set against these facts, the easy designation of individuals as deliberate or imputed "war criminals" is shockingly glib, even if one allows for the inexperience of the young. . . .

Truth about Vietnam, and about the painful choices which the President keeps pushing ahead of him, thus seeps slowly through the mass of our political body while the war goes on and Vietnamization threatens to make it permanent. The American people continue to be, in Henry Adams' phrase, "dragged through frightful bogs of learning." But should we, in this profoundly discouraging situation, establish a war-crimes tribunal (assuming that some celestial sponsor could be found for arranging its establishment) and try President Nixon and Dr. Kissinger as "war criminals"? The absurd questions answer themselves. What the country needs is not retribution, but therapy in the form of deeper understanding of our problems and of each other. If public opinion appears still unresolved on the question of how to terminate the war, our system still provides the opportunities and channels to resolve it—through intelligent, vigorous public debate based on a watchful observation of unfolding events. All of us, I believe, young and old alike, would do well to avail ourselves anew of these priceless constitutional facilities, arguing with the force and logic at our command in every available forum, yet judging with sympathy those who are now constitutionally entrusted with the final decisions; above all, avoiding the destructive and childish pleasure of branding as deliberate criminals duly elected and appointed leaders who, whatever their human failings, are struggling in good conscience to uphold the Constitution and to serve the broad national interest according to their lights.

This letter by Ashley King to the *New York Times* should be set off against President Nixon's statement on My Lai.

LESSON OF SON MY

To the Editor:

We shall never learn the lesson of Son My simply by raising the ranks of those brought to courts-martial. That is too easy a solution.

The war is the primal atrocitiy. The crime belongs to the nation. The war criminals are all of us. From President Kennedy through Johnson, Nixon, Congress, the Pentagon on down—or up—to all of us who pay taxes that have for the past six years financed the daily slaughter we wreak on that far away land. It is surely not without significance that the doves have not cried out for the heads of those who pulled the triggers at Son My. Nor even for those of their military superiors.

The criminals are all of us. The war itself is the great atrocity that spawns the lesser atrocities.   ASHLEY KING

New York, March 22, 1970

THE INTERROGATION OF CAPTAIN HOWARD TURNER AT THE TRIAL OF LIEUTENANT JAMES DUFFY, 1970

James Brian Duffy, age 22, is a typical American kid. He was the finest baseball player in his high school in Claremont, California. He wanted to be the best in college—California Polytechnical Institute—but he concentrated so hard on sports that his grades suffered. After a year and a half of college, he dropped out to enlist in the infantry.

After a stint as a private, he was accepted for Officer Candidate School. "During OCS I gave 100 per cent to the program. I knew that what I was being taught would soon be put into use on a battlefield. I would hate to know that someone was killed or wounded because I goofed off during my training," the young man said. "I worked hard to be an honor graduate but I didn't quite make it. There were six honor graduates and I was seventh in the class."

He went to Vietnam May 7, 1969. In the next eight months, he won the Bronze Star for valor, another for achievement, the Purple Heart, and seven other honorable citations, including the Good Conduct Medal.

But on January 12, 1970, the case of Lt. James Brian Duffy was referred to a general court-marital. The charge: murder and conspiracy to murder a captured South Vietnamese, who was shot between the eyes at point-blank range.

Duffy's company commander, Capt. Howard Turner, describes the policy which made the murder probable, if not inevitable, in the recording: "The extreme stress is on what we call the kill ratio—how many U.S. killed and how many of the enemy killed—or body count. And this has become the big thing. This is what your efficiency report is written on."

This ruthless game of body count is what led them down the trail to Phouc Tan Hung on the night of September 4, 1969. Lt. Duffy at the time was a platoon commander in Co. C, 2nd Battalion (Mechanized), 47th Infantry, 3rd Brigade, 9th Infantry Division, operating in the Binh Phouc district of South Vietnam.

He led his ambush patrol out of the base camp about 6 P.M. that evening and was moving along the woodlines about four or five miles from camp when, according to Pfc. Alvin S. Gibbs, "we heard voices coming from the woods. Lt. Duffy stated that there were not supposed to be any people living in this area and called for an artillery strike to clear the area.

"Upon first impact an old Vietnamese woman came to the edge of the woodline and started to talk to our Tiger Scout [a Vietnamese named Duc]. A few minutes later, about five more came to the edge of the woods—one young girl, two old Vietnamese men, and one middle-aged Vietnamese woman. These people were taken prisoner and we continued on with the patrol.

"We walked approximately one kilometer more where we came upon a hamlet," Gibbs' account continues. "Lt. Duffy selected one of the houses to use as an A/P [ambush point]. This house was located on the edge of the village with one bunker [inside] on each side. Lt. Duffy had the house surrounded and told the Tiger Scout to search the bunkers. He also had the prisoners placed in back of the house under guard.

"The Tiger Scout searched one of the bunkers, finding nothing. He then asked an old Vietnamese woman about possible VC activity in the area. Apparently there was nothing in the area because the patrol started to enter the house and relax for the night.

"About 30 minutes later, the Tiger Scout went into the other bunker and started calling something in Vietnamese. The Tiger Scout then backed away from the doorway and a young Vietnamese man came out. The Tiger Scout struck this man with his fist on the side of the head."

Another member of the patrol, Sp. 4 Ernest G. Jiminez, gives this account: "I was one of the first to enter the house. It took us about five minutes before we got in because the occupants refused us admission, so I kicked the door in. Once inside, we observed this woman with either two or three small children and an elderly man. . . . When Duc checked [the bunker] he found this young Vietnamese male hiding in the bunker and dragged him out. We asked him for his identification, at which time he produced a picture which looked like an ARVN [South Vietnamese Army] ID card. . . .

"Well, we figured this guy was a VC, so we tied him up to a tree just outside the house. . . . Tiger Scout Duc slapped him around a bit with his hand in order to obtain information from him."

Says Sp. 4 Anthony Baker: "Lt. Duffy and Sgt. Lanasa asked the man for his identification. He gave them an ID card similar to an Army ID card only yellow in color, and his wallet, which they emptied of all paperwork. The Tiger Scout told me that one of the papers was a sick slip from the hospital. Then Lt. Duffy tore all of the papers up, and called back to the CO and told him that the Vietnamese man had no identification at all.

"The man was then taken outside and tied with clothes to a post. His shirt was torn off, but short pants were left on him. Later Lt. Duffy and Sgt. Lanasa went back outside to question the man and Sgt. Lanasa slapped him a couple of times, spat on him, and asked Lt. Duffy to allow him to kill the man then instead of waiting for morning. At that time, Lt. Duffy said to wait until morning. Lanasa stated, 'I always wanted to shoot a gook between the eyes.'

"Based on the paperwork that was showed to us in the house," says Baker, "I would say that he was an AWOL ARVN soldier, and he stated he was an ARVN soldier."

Sp. 4 David G. Walstad, in his account, says: "I heard the commotion inside and heard the woman crying. I walked in and saw Tiger Scout pull this man out of the bunker. He was real scared and I noticed he had scars up and down his stomach. He was messed up pretty bad. Duffy called the medic [George Chunko] over and asked him how old some of the scars were. Chunko said the guy had recently been wounded."

According to Sgt. Joe N. Johnson: "The prisoner had some credentials in his pocketbook. I personally saw them. One sheet was half the size of an 8 x 10 sheet of paper and definitely showed the guy was ARVN." Sgt. Johnson reports he heard Sgt. Lanasa say that he wanted to kill him that night. Lanasa wanted to hang the guy and then said something about cutting his throat after the hanging. I don't know what made him change his mind."

After the man was tied up outside, Sp. 4 Henry Lee Williams reports: "Lanasa struck the guy in the jaw with his fist and knocked him unconscious and then poured water over him."

S/Sgt. William R. Russell, in his account, says: "Duffy suggested that [the prisoner] might have been an AWOL ARVN because he said they found an old ARVN ID card and an old ARVN Saigon pass in his possession. Duffy said he thought the guy might be a VC now because of the fresh bullet wounds in his back. Duffy opined that the wounds were fresh; however, as best as I could tell these were old wounds that had completely healed. I also noted the old vertical stomach scars and it was my impression that he had been cut open for the purpose of extraction or removal of bullets. . . . I argued with Duffy about this matter because he told me that we would kill the prisoner. I was most definitely against this.

"The prisoner's hands were tied behind his back. They dragged him outside and set him down in animal feces and tied him to a stake and removed his shirt. This was cruel in itself because the mosquitos were out in vast numbers that night and he was helpless to swat at them. He remained tied to the stake all that night."

During the night, discussion about killing the prisoner continued. Baker reports: "Lt. Duffy said we were going to kill the prisoner and Sgt. Lanasa asked if he could be the one to kill the prisoner. Lt. Duffy said to wait until morning." Baker also reports: "I remember after tearing up the papers, he [Duffy] said that nothing would be said about the papers. He didn't need an ID or papers anyway because he said he was going to kill him in the morning. After tearing up the papers he called the CO and said we have one Vietnamese prisoner, one VC prisoner, and there's no identification on him."

Sp. 4 Dennis J. Sullivan says: "Lt. Duffy didn't order anyone to kill the prisoner; he just asked who wanted to kill the prisoner." Sullivan says they were interrogating the young woman, "more or less trying to get some information off her about her husband. . . . The part that I remember was that Lt. Duffy told Duc to tell the mamasan that somebody had better start talking or he would be killed in the morning.

"When me and Chunko were guarding the people," Sullivan continues, "and the other people went next door, the old papasan and the young woman got down to me and Chunko and they were putting their hands together like praying, leaning down towards us and all. You know, we didn't know what they were saying but I imagine something had been said. . . . They looked like they were asking us for something. We concluded they were asking us not to do anything to the detainee."

When the morning came, according to Sgt. Russell, "one of the guys came around to where I was at and said, 'Sarge, in about five minutes you are going to hear the fatal shot.' I went around and spoke to Duffy. I asked him, in spite of all the discussion we had the night before concerning this matter, if he was still going to kill the guy. He said, 'Roger that!' "

Baker says: "The next morning, Lt. Duffy told Sgt. Lanasa to wake up because it was time to go kill the prisoner." Walstad recounts it this way: "When morning came, Duffy told Cowboy [Lanasa] to take the guy out and shoot him. Lanasa wanted me to go with him so I did. Gibbs and Wilson also came along with us. Lanasa pointed his M-16 right between the guy's eyes after we escorted him down the treeline away from the hootch.

"When Lanasa pulled the trigger, the round was either dead or the gun malfunctioned. Lanasa pulled the bolt back, placing another round into the chamber. The guy just stood there until Lanasa pulled the trigger again with the muzzle pointed at the guy's head, right between the eyes. The pressure kind of moved the guy backward some, after which he fell to the ground like a puppet. I don't know whether he fell backward or to his knees because my mind went sort of blank about that time. Lanasa's shot killed the guy instantly. Then I fired about 14 rounds after that. I suppose some of the bullets I fired did hit the guy. I really don't know for sure. Then Alabama [Wilson] fired three rounds at the guy. I don't know if any of the bullets struck the guy or not. I wasn't watching any longer."

Gibbs, who was also on the scene of the killing, says "the squad leader placed the M-16 to his, the prisoner's, head between the eyes. He then pulled the trigger and the weapon malfunctioned. The Vietnamese man fell to his knees, started crying and the squad leader chambered another round. At this time, I turned my head. I heard a burst of rounds fired and as I turned, I saw the Vietnamese man flipping into a rice paddy."

On that morning, September 5, the company commander, Capt. Turner, received a call from Lt. Duffy on the field telephone, reporting the killing of a prisoner attempting to escape.

Le Thi Dang, the dead man's wife, gave her own account in a subsequent interview, as translated into English by a Vietnamese interpreter, Trinh Van Khanh:

Q. Did American patrol come to your house?

A. Yes, about 52 days ago. They came to my house and spend overnight. Next morning, four American GI's took my husband to the woodline. After Americans left my house, I went to the woodline and found my husband's body. One bullet hole between eyes, one hole in the left of the stomach, one hole in the left side of the ass. I buried my husband the same day.

Q. Did you report this matter to anyone?

A. I don't know where I can report it.

Q. Is your husband a Vietcong?

A. My husband got drafted into the ARVN army unit at Quang Tri province away from my family. My husband ran away from the ARVN army. After my husband got wounded in the stomach and left the hospital, he got 19 days leave in

April, 1968, and came back to the family and never go back to his unit.

Q. Which hospital was your husband in for treatment?

A. My husband was treated at American Navy ship about 20 days, then was moved to ARVN hospital named Duytan in Da Nang city about one month. After he left hospital, my husband got leave to visit family.

Q. Did you hear any American soldier say they would kill him the next morning?

A. No, I don't understand English.

If Li Thi Dang didn't report the incident, neither did anyone else, and it might never have come to light except for a letter home, written by the medic, George Chunko. (One account said Chunko had given the widow a sedative after the killing.) He told the details of what had occurred. About three weeks later, Chunko was killed in another ambush patrol.

Suspecting foul play, the family forwarded the letter to its Congressman, who in turn forwarded it to the Pentagon for a report. The Army began an investigation. Its report stated that Chunko was killed when a Vietcong threw a satchel charge into his hootch. The death was attributed to the negligence of a fellow trooper who fell asleep, allowing the Vietcong to invade the hootch. The investigation concluded it was a normal military operation.

But the investigation led to a charge of murder—against James Brian Duffy, the Claremont high school baseball star. (The general court-martial has ruled out the death penalty in the case, but he faces life at hard labor and dishonorable discharge from the Army.)

The record shows that the following comments were made by Capt. Turner about Lt. Duffy:

"I was company commander for 10 months in combat. Lt. Duffy was one of the best leaders I have run into in 10 months. He was aggressive. He was knowledgeable of what his job was and how to do it. He was able to have his soldiers do what they were supposed to do and do it willingly. I trusted him implicitly. Anything I told him to do, I knew he would do it without any trouble at all.

". . . Basically, the people he had were two-year draftees and they're not career-type soldiers. Therefore, the least amount of personal danger they share, the better they feel about it—to a point. When it becomes a matter of pride, or being separated as a man from someone else, they will go ahead and expose themselves to danger. Taken as a whole, I think if they were given the choice they wouldn't want to go out—no. So this would create some resentment with Lt. Duffy because he made them do what they were supposed to do. They respected him for making them do the job but yet they really didn't want to go out and do it."

Lt. Duffy's civilian defense lawyer, Henry Rothblatt of New York, interviewed Col. Murray, chief psychiatrist, U.S. Army headquarters, Long Binh, Vietnam. Said Col. Murray: "Group pressure can cause a person to do something that he might not otherwise do. That's the essence of how you get guys to fight. You get them the feeling of brotherhood, and that the cause is a just one and that their buddies depend on them, and each of us will do almost anything to avoid loneliness, whatever that is."

Capt. Turner also had praise for Sgt. Lanasa. "He was only a two-year man, the type of man I would like to have stay in the Army with me and serve with me, very, very aggressive. He was a good point man. He was extremely alert. He seemed to be to be more mature than the average man we had in the company. As an example, he was a squad leader as a PFC. He knew his job and he wasn't afraid at all."

Capt. Turner explained the "group pressure" that befell Lt. Duffy and Sgt. Lanasa. " 'Go out and kill the gooks' is the word they use around here. This comes down from Brigade, this comes down from two field forces, the 25th Division and the whole works. There is nothing written, nothing I could point out and show you. . . . The more you kill, the more efficient you are.

"In fact, it became almost a policy not to take prisoners if you could possibly help it. By this we mean, bullet the guy—don't give him a chance. Kill him before he can surrender—mainly being, because you can't give people back here. That's the way it was. It's not like that now. You couldn't get the people back here to classify them. They were released to come back and fight you again."

In light of such testimony, is Lt. Duffy's an isolated case or is he a scapegoat? The psychiatrist, Col. Murray, put it this way: "I couldn't name others [incidents], but it seems perfectly reasonable that this is a rather common occurrence, to assume this under the circumstances, especially when the whole orientation of the group is—as any good fighting group—to kill and destroy. This is the goal, this is the purpose of the whole damn thing.

"In terms of finding a scapegoat or projecting onto this person [Lt. Duffy] blame for what we have in fact created, of course, we are impugning the whole country in this way. I don't know if the country is ready for it or if the Army will stand for it. . . . The trouble with this is that you are saying war is bad, and when you say that to a bunch of officers, that's terrible, you know."

On September 24, 1969, 19 days after the incident at Phouc Tan Hung, both Lt. Duffy and Sgt. Lanasa were wounded in an action in the same area. Sgt. Lanasa was evacuated to Japan and on October 3 was transferred to the U.S. Naval Hospital in Memphis, Tenn. Lt. Duffy was treated in Vietnam and remained there, awaiting general court-martial.

The next selection casts light on the extent to which the body-count approach to "progress" in the war encouraged line soldiers to murder prisoners in their custody.

LIEUTENANT DUFFY'S STATEMENT

[Excerpt]

. . . We never had much contact in the 6/31st Infantry. Only one day did I ever get in any firefight (we were ambushed three times that day) or actually see any VC, dead or alive. But we ran into many booby traps. My platoon found many but never set one off. The other platoons were not so good and had a few people killed and more wounded. One day a sergeant in another platoon was wounded very seriously in the head from a booby trap. He was a very good friend of mine and I really hated to see him get hurt. I do not know if he died or not. I also had a very good friend who was on his third tour over here get wounded from a booby trap. He was in the hospital and was asking for me. I went to see him and it really upset me to see him there in the hospital. He had been hit real hard, tearing up his legs and chest. He had lost one lung.

Before these two friends were hit I had sort of a lukewarm feeling against the enemy. But after seeing them hurt so bad I had a true hatred for all VC and from then on I wanted to kill as many of them as I could. This hatred was very strong while I was in the field, and I still have it to this day. I would go out on an operation just hoping to make contact so we could kill some more VC.

When I transferred to the 2/47th Infantry and got a new platoon, I started getting much more contact. Our company made contact on almost all of our two-day operations from mid-July to mid-September. The company had more kills than any other company in the battalion.

When I got my new platoon, I told them just as I did my first platoon that my primary concern was for their welfare and that I would take care of them no matter what. I figured my life depended on them just as much as their lives depended on me. This platoon was not as good as my first one. They were afraid to set up in woodlines at night; they did not know how to set up a good ambush; they were afraid to enter any woodline if it was booby trapped; they did not carry a proper load of ammunition; and once in contact they did not know how to use their weapons effectively. It took a couple weeks before I was able to teach them how to operate properly. But they learned fast because we had a lot of contact, and before long they became a very skillful and efficient fighting force. We set up many successful ambushes in which we killed all the VC before they even had a chance to fire a shot. They were always looking for contact.

I became very close to all the men in the platoon and we got along very well. I trusted them and they trusted me. More than once one of the men came up to me and told me how good it was to have a platoon leader you could be friends with, someone you knew you could talk to and he'd help you out. I would arrange cookouts for them, buy them whiskey (and help them drink it) and let them buy all the beer and sodas they wanted. They really appreciated all this; it let them know I cared for them. They tried to take care of me too. In the field they would round up hay, blankets and pillows for me to sleep on; shared their food and water with me, etc.

Most of the men in the platoon really enjoyed contact and looked forward to it. I know I did, so did Sergeant Lanasa (Cowboy) and the other squad leaders. Cowboy and I were very close friends. He was always a very hard worker, never complained, and was just great in a fight. He wasn't afraid of anything. He would charge right towards the enemy. Everybody else in his squad just followed him; they knew he would do the right thing.

There was only one thing that really upset me (and many other people in the platoon too). That was taking prisoners that we knew were VC and having them released by Brigade as innocent civilians. It's not hard to spot a VC after you've spent some time in the field. The only people who live out

there are farmers and the VC. The farmers are only women
and children and old men. They were always very friendly
toward us. We would stop in a house for lunch or dinner and
share our food with them, talk, play with the children and
really have a good time. I almost never saw any young men in
the rice paddies. Whenever we found any young men we immediately questioned them. I can think of only two young
men that I ever found in the field and they were just 15 years
old and still going to school. The only other young men I ever
found in the field were VC who were shooting at us.

Once we ambushed a sampan in the Plain of Reeds, which is
a free-fire zone and anybody who moves is fair game. This
sampan came down a canal at about 2100 hours. When we
opened up, two men were killed and two women were injured.
The women were yelling, "Don't shoot, don't shoot, we are
VC!" Sergeant Lanasa swam out and rescued the two women
and brought them back to shore. The next morning he carried
one of them three-quarters of a mile through swamps to an
area where we dusted them off for medical treatment and interrogation. We found out two days later that both women
had been released by Brigade as innocent civilians. This really
upset me and many others in the platoon. I mean we knew
they were VC. They were in a free-fire zone after dark. We
didn't have to save them from drowning (especially during
contact) or carry them most of a mile to dust them off. They
were just plain lucky to be alive. When they were released,
most of the men really wished that the women would have
been killed during the ambush. It's hard enough to find the
enemy, but to catch and just let them go is ridiculous.

After that incident I decided I was not going to take any
more prisoners. If at all possible I was not going to let the
situation arise where a prisoner might be taken. I told all my
squad leaders and my company commander of this. I told all
my men that if they were going to engage someone, not to
stop shooting until everyone was dead. I told them if they
were going to shoot at somebody, they had better kill him.
Nobody ever said anything against this policy and I think

most of the men agreed to it. My company commander felt the same way I did about it.

Shortly after this, we caught an NVA soldier in the Plain of Reeds. We beat him up trying to get him to talk but he wouldn't. We finally just pushed him away and were about to kill him when I was told that the Brigade commander wanted him. My company commander and battalion commander saw everything that happened and they never said a word or tried to stop us. The Brigade commander was the only one who wanted the soldier alive. I'm pretty sure Brigade didn't just let this prisoner go, but we would just rather have seen him dead. Then we would have known for sure that this was one NVA who wasn't going to kill any more Americans. We were a little bit upset when we weren't allowed to kill him.

I think it was shortly after that when we caught the AWOL ARVN in the bunker. After that incident we started getting a lot of contact again. Everybody's morale was real high, especially mine. I always enjoyed contacts. As long as none of us got hurt it was great, really exciting. I know I was never afraid of getting wounded in a fight. It was always luck anyway when you got hit, so there was no sense worrying about it. I'd had several close calls before and I figured I would get wounded some day but I wasn't bothered by it. I was sure going to get as many VC as I could before they got me. The night before I was wounded, I knew it was coming. I just hoped it wouldn't be fatal and went out on the operation.

Sometimes innocent civilians are killed out there, but it just can't be helped. We were always careful not to shoot towards any populated areas when we prepped a woodline, and even in a contact we would try not to shoot towards civilians if at all possible. But still you would hit a few, especially at night. Many of the farmers would be out after curfew wandering around, or going over to a friend's house.

They just sort of disregarded the curfew and we have no choice but to engage them, since anybody moving after curfew is supposed to be considered VC. When we kill a man after curfew and he has a valid ID or he is an old man, etc., you can pretty well guess that he was just an innocent civilian out after the curfew (but, of course, you never know for sure because anybody can be a VC, valid ID card or not). Many VC have been picked up who were living in a village under legal status. One night I had set an ambush up behind a hootch, right on a canal. There was a small sampan landing there and that's where I placed three men. At approximately 2100 hours, a sampan came up very suddenly right in front of the ambush and was headed right for the three men. The sampan was only about 10 feet away from them when the man in the sampan stood up and they saw he was holding something in his hands. So the three men immediately killed him with small-arms fire.

The next morning someone from across the canal came over and said we killed his brother last night. He said his brother had come across the canal to get some more booze for a party and he never came back. . . .

Whenever we did take prisoners, they were always roughed up and then questioned. When we worked with ARVN's or national police, we found that they were excellent interrogators. You could tell that they really hated the VC by the way they beat them when they caught one. They do not mess around at all. I once had a national policeman with me when we chased a VC through a house. The VC got away but the national policemen wanted to take one of the women in the house with us for questioning. That night he beat and kicked that woman for about two hours while he questioned her. When he was finished he came over and told me she was okay, not a VC, and to let her go in the morning. I went along with his decision. I always listened to my Tiger Scouts, ARVN's or national police and would do what they say. They always seem to know who is a VC and who isn't. And when they do find a VC they are merciless. They will beat him to an inch of his life. More than one MACV advisor has told me that ARVN's will kill their prisoners when they are finished questioning them in the field. I myself know of one case where some ARVN's who shot a VC, questioned him for a while, then shot him in the head. I even saw a picture of his body.

Of course, the ARVN's will not admit to doing this and you could never prove it, but it's being done anyway.

I know in my case, platoon leaders never got any guidance on treatment of prisoners. Battalion HQS never said anything about them. There was no SOP, there was never a request that we take any prisoners. The only thing we ever heard was to get more body count, kill more VC! We heard that all the time; it was really stressed. My squad leader told me that in his old unit they couldn't come in from the field unless they turned in a body count. Many units "pad" their body count so they can say they killed more than anybody else. The only way anybody judged a unit's effectiveness was by the number of body counts they had. If you had a lot of body counts, everybody would think you were really good. If you didn't have a lot of body counts, they would think you were a poor unit.

I know I was always conscious of how many body counts my platoon had. I kept a record on the wall of my room and had a record painted on the side of my APC. I was always proud of the fact that my platoon had more kills than any other platoon in the company and that our company led the battalion in kills. The men in the platoon were aware of all this, too, and they were proud of their record. They considered themselves to be the best platoon around. It kept our morale very high when we were leading everyone else for the month.

Some people might have thought it was wrong to judge a unit just by the number of kills they get. I think it *is* the only way a unit should be judged. That is really the only mission we have in the field, to kill the enemy. As far as I'm concerned that's why we were sent over here and that's what our job is. The only way to see how well a unit is performing its job is to see how many body counts they have. My platoon killed, found or captured about 50 enemy from mid-July to mid-September and I only had one man killed and only two seriously wounded. I always thought that was a pretty good record.

I'm out of the field now and I thank God I made it in one

piece. I am not sorry at all that I came over here. I didn't mind all that humping through the mud—I didn't even mind being wounded. That's all part of war; you can't do anything about it. Over-all, I have really enjoyed my tour over here in Vietnam and I'm glad I came over. I had a lot of good times in the field, made many friends and have learned an awful lot. I know now just how much we have back in America when I see how hard a life the Vietnamese people live here. Most have known war all their lives. It has killed their sons, even their women and children, and has destroyed their land. They must be very tired of this war. I am glad, though, that we are fighting over here and not in the United States.

I feel that by coming over here I have accomplished a great deal. I feel that I helped a few dozen GI's make it through their tour without being killed and that I was able to help the Vietnamese people, as well as our allied friends, in their fight against Communism. I am only sorry that more Americans back home do not support our efforts over here. I don't think they really know what it's all about, especially what a soldier has to go through in the field. They do not know what it's like to see Communism face to face. They think we can fight a "moral" war over here. It seems to me that only the bad guys are supposed to get killed, and even then they have to be killed in a nice way. It just doesn't work that way, everything is not black and white, and all the killing is not nice by any means. I always felt that I was living very close to death while I was in the field. It was something you had to get used to, seeing dead men, killing some myself and knowing I could be killed in a minute. It became so commonplace that I never worried about it really. That doesn't mean I enjoyed all killing and brutality—I just got used to it.

It's something you have to experience to understand. I think the only ones who really know what's going on in the battlefield are the soldiers who have to go out and kill the enemy to stay alive. They are the ones who know war best.

The final two selections in this section all emphasize the extent to which terror, torture, and brutality are present in South Vietnam prisons. These prisons are used for a wide variety of political prisoners. The prison system in South Vietnam is supported financially and administratively by the United States Government.

THE ULTIMATE FORM OF CORRUPTION
Robert F. Drinan, S.J.

On May 23 I and a few of the members of a U.S. Study Team on Political and Religious Freedoms in South Vietnam had an appointment in Washington with a highly placed official of the State Department. In the most positive way this official asserted that the number of political prisoners in South Vietnam had been continually decreasing. The study team had received a copy of a letter from another State Department official to a U.S. Senator stating the same thing.

I thought for a time at the meeting on May 23 of telling the State Department official that, on the basis of his assertions, I would cancel my commitment to go to Vietnam the next day. But I remained silent because I had agreed to go with a team whose trip had been financed by all the churches and synagogues of America. The State Department official, by his claims, stated by implication that the religious groups were misinformed and were attacking a non-problem.

As events turned out I am glad that I did not trust the State Department official.

On June 11 I was back in Washington and at another meeting told one of the high White House officials present at the May 23 "briefing" that a State Department official on May 23 had "lied" to us about the number of political prisoners. We had discovered in Vietnam that the number of political prisoners is increasing rather sharply, not decreasing. The White House official became flustered at this revelation and at the accusation. He urged that no one had "lied" and started a monologue about the difficulty of getting "hard" information. I pressed my point as much as courtesy permitted but received no satisfactory explanation of the discrepancy between what State Department officials were claiming to be the truth and the facts as they exist in South Vietnam.

The "hard" information about political prisoners which emerged in South Vietnam comes to this:

1. Of the 35,000 men, women and children in prison, about 60 percent wear a red tag on their prison garb indicating that they are "Communists." Many of these until recently used to be called "political prisoners" but that name was changed to "Communists" or "Vietcong sympathizers." The change in name may be the reason for the State Department's assertions that the number of political prisoners is "decreasing."

2. The number of persons imprisoned for "non-crimes" is actually rising rather rapidly. The rate of increase is impossible to discover because of the fact that up to one-third of all the persons detained have not been charged with any offense or given any sentence. One of the reasons for the increase (a rise admitted by Embassy officials in Saigon) is the U.S. pacification program which, as it moves into the hinterlands, ferrets out citizens suspected of being "disloyal" and turns them over to the "kangaroo courts" known as Provincial Security Councils or Military Field Tribunals.

3. A significant number of political prisoners, prior to their "non-trial," are tortured by South Vietnamese officials in order to get information about VC activities and plans. We told a United States adviser about the countless stories we had heard from reliable witnesses about incredible torture devices employed in pre-sentencing detention centers. This official conceded that he had talked to four persons who alleged that torture had been inflicted on them. He said, however, that he did not believe these four individuals. Pressed for his reasons for not believing them, the official fell silent. It was appalling beyond belief when the American functionary said to me later that off the record and in his personal capacity he hoped that the study team would expose the existence of torture which he suspected was widespread!

4. The imprisonment of thousands of non-Communist but

anti-Thieu citizens in South Vietnam (and the exile of thousands more in Paris) clearly inhibits the emergence of the system of two political parties, an arrangement specifically called for in the Constitution of South Vietnam.

No one at the State Department has yet admitted that the United States should do anything about these four findings. On June 8, a telegram, sent by the U.S. study team to President Nixon on June 5, was released to the press. On June 10 and 11 a 40-page report was given to several highly placed State and White House officials in Washington. No answers have been received.

When I left the handsome offices of the State Department on June 11, I was so depressed I did not talk for about 30 minutes. Still paralyzed by the atmosphere of Foggy Bottom and distressed by what I had heard, I took a cab with my associates. My encounters with the State Department over the period of May 23 to June 11 had not been happy ones. My companions, by their silence or their complaints, agreed. I did not know what to do. I ate a quick lunch and hastened off to a two o'clock appointment in a Senator's office. A few minutes later I related my unhappy encounters with the State Department to three influential members of Congress. They did not express surprise. Only chagrin. I too was chagrined.

I shall never forget those encounters. They have probably done more than any other event in my life to galvanize my determination to work for a government which will be honest in its communication with its citizens. Those encounters left me with the conviction that our students and our young people are profoundly disturbed because they see in their government a policy of telling lies or at least a policy of trying to deceive people. However benignly one may describe or view such a policy, I knew on June 11 that it is the ultimate form of corruption.

STATEMENT ON CON SON PRISON
HONORABLE AUGUSTUS F. HAWKINS,
JULY, 1970

CON SON

Con Son is a South Vietnamese National Prison located on a remote island in the South China sea. Four of us, Congressman Anderson, myself, a staff member, Tom Harkins, and an interpreter, Don Luce, made the trip. We were accompanied by the Director of Public Safety for the American program CORDS, Frank E. Walton, and other United States AID personnel. Our government furnishes a modest amount of aid for improvement of the national prison system.

On Con Son Island we were escorted through the prison facilities by the Commandant, Colonel Nguyen Van Ve.

After routinely visiting the more visible cell compounds, our group by virtue of unique and ingenuous circumstances observed certain areas of the prison known as the Tiger Cages in which are kept political prisoners who had the courage to express their belief in peace.

No one can possibly describe this compound except one who has experienced the brutal torture of these chambers. Attached to my report is a statement of persons who have. After observing the torture cells and talking to many of their occupants, I believe all that is reported by them.

The Tiger Cages are cells approximately 5 feet wide and 10 feet long. Five persons are crowded into this space surrounded by cement walls and floors on which inmates sleep. About a foot off the floor is an iron rod to which the legs of the inmates are shackled. Lying in this position for years causes a paralysis of the legs.

Occupants are fed a small portion of rice and are fed dried fish, often molded, and always an inadequate amount of water which forces the prisoners through exhaustion to drink their urine.

At the top of the cages are kept boxes of lime which is sprinkled into the cages to quiet any noise or disturbance. More often, however, those who protest against their treatment are beaten by trustees who thereby earn special privileges.

In opposition to prison officials, we used the walkway atop the cages to interview various prisoners. Among them several students, a Buddhist monk, and an elderly woman 60 years of age who was blinded from beatings. None we interviewed had criminal records but generally had been imprisoned, often without judicial trial, merely for participating in peace demonstrations. Although many were sick, medical care was practically non-existent. The only merciful thing observed was a separation of men and women.

I described Con Son in some detail because it represents the evils of a government that can only stay in power by suppressing the people and limiting their constitutional rights. .

Con Son is a symbol of how some American officials will cooperate in corruption and torture because they too want to see the war continued and the government they put in power protected.

Con Son dramatizes what war does to the countryside, the villages and hamlets that our planes and firepower have devastated and the thousands of civilians we have maimed, killed or made homeless.

Con Son is the type of "not-looking-at-our-own-faults-and atrocities" that endangers our American prisoners of war held by the Communists. By exposing and opposing torture regardless of by whom committed, I believe we can best help those Americans for whom we plead humane treatment and a safe return.

VIETNAMIZATION, PACIFICATION, AND LAND REFORM

Much of the Committee's time was devoted to exploring the question of what happens if and when the Americans withdraw. Vietnamization and the pacification programs have been upheld as assuring a safe and viable society. Land reform has been cited as a means of providing self-help among the peasants who have either been displaced or relocated.

In theory, there is not much to disagree with the objectives of these programs even though the statistics seem inflated with unwarranted optimism. Statistics on pacification indicate an increase in American casualties since December and in the number of Viet Cong terroristic attacks. These may be temporary trends of course.

In the final analysis, I agree with the venerable Thien Hoa's appraisal of these programs, that their success depends on the quality of the government that administers them.

CONTRIBUTORS

Quincy Wright was one of the most influential writers on the international law of war in the twentieth century.

Richard A. Falk is professor of international law and practice at Princeton University. His latest book is *This Endangered Planet.*

Townsend Hoopes was a member of the Johnson Administration and author of *The Limits of Intervention.*

Robert F. Drinan, S.J., was dean of Boston College and was elected to Congress in November, 1970. He is the author of *Vietnam and Armageddon.*

Congressman Augustus F. Hawkins went to Vietnam as a member of a fact-finding group conducting a congressional investigation of political conditions in South Vietnam.

The
Political Setting:
Documents

This is one of the earliest systematic accounts of the human consequences of the war, published in *Liberation,* February 1966. It is based largely on public sources.

AMERICAN ATROCITIES IN VIETNAM

Eric Norden

In the bitter controversy over our Vietnamese policies which has raged across the nation since the President's decision last February to bomb North Viet-Nam, there is only one point which supporters of U.S. policy will concede to the opposition: the sheer, mindnumbing horror of the war. Despite the barrage of official propaganda, reports in the American and European press reveal that the United States is fighting the dirtiest war of its history in Viet-Nam. The weapons in the American arsenal include torture, systematic bombing of civilian targets, the first use of poison gas since World War One, the shooting of prisoners and the general devastation of the Vietnamese countryside by napalm and white phosphorus. Not since the days of the American Indian wars has the United States waged such unrelenting warfare against an entire people.

Torture of prisoners and "suspects" by Vietnamese troops and their U.S. advisers is a matter of public record. "Anyone who has spent much time with Government units in the field," writes William Tuohy, *Newsweek's* Saigon correspondent, "has seen the heads of prisoners held under water and bayonet blades pressed against their throats. . . . In more extreme cases, victims have had bamboo slivers run under their fingernails or wires from a field telephone connected to arms, nipples or testicles." (*New York Times* Magazine, November 28, 1965.)

Donald Wise, chief foreign correspondent for the London *Sunday Mirror,* reports that such torture is condoned and even supervised by U.S. officers. "No American is in a position to tell his 'pupils' to stop torturing," Wise writes from Saigon. "They are in no mood either. . . ." Some of the standard tortures described by Wise include "dunking men head first into water tanks or slicing them up with knives. . . . Silk stockings full of sand are swung against temples and men are hooked up to the electric generators of military HQ's." (London *Sunday Mirror*, April 4, 1965.)

The "Viet-Cong" use terror also, of course, but theirs is of a more selective nature, if only to avoid estranging the peasants and villagers on whom they depend for food and shelter. They will kill and mutilate the body of a Government official, but they generally pick an unpopular and corrupt victim whose death is welcomed by the peasants. U.S. and Government troops in the countryside, on the other hand, feel themselves lost in an enemy sea and tend to strike out indiscriminately at real or imagined guerrillas. Thus, no Vietnamese is exempt from mistreatment and torture. As Wise reports, "Inevitably, innocent peasants are kneed in the groin, drowned in vats of water or die of loss of blood after interrogation. But you cannot identify VC from peasants. . . ." In fact, it is assumed that every peasant is a real or potential Viet-Cong rebel. "In a VC-controlled area the yardstick is rough: every young man of military age is assumed to be a VC soldier who has thrown away his weapon just before capture. Most areas of Viet-Nam are now VC-controlled. Therefore, most men in the countryside should be presumed to be VC soldiers or sympathizers." (*Ibid.*)

Many U.S. reporters have witnessed torture first-hand. Beverly Deepe, the New York *Herald Tribune's* correspondent in Saigon, writes:

> One of the most infamous methods of torture used by the government forces is partial electrocution—or "frying," as one U.S. adviser called it. This correspondent was present on one occasion when the torture was employed. Two wires were attached to the thumbs of a Viet-Cong prisoner. At the other end of the strings was a field generator, cranked by a Vietnamese private. The mechanism produced an electrical current that burned and shocked the prisoner. (New York *Herald Tribune*, April 25, 1965.)

Electrical torture is employed all over Viet-Nam, even on the battlefront. A small U.S. field generator used to power pack radios is often "modified" for torture purposes and is prized for its high mobility. The device generates sufficient voltage to provide strong and sometimes deadly shocks. According to Malcolm Browne, the A. P. correspondent who won a Pulitzer Prize for his reporting of the war, "The 'ding-a-ling' method of interrogation involves connection of electrodes from this generator to the temples of the subject, or other parts of the body. In the case of women prisoners, the electrodes often are attached to the nipples. The results are terrifying and painful. . . ." (*The New Face of War* by Malcolm Browne, Bobbs-Merrill Co., 1965.)

Less sophisticated methods than electrical torture are also used. According to Beverly Deepe:

> Other techniques, usually designed to force onlooking prisoners to talk, involve cutting off the fingers, ears, fingernails or sexual organs of another prisoner. Sometimes a string of ears decorates the wall of a government military installation. One American installation has a Viet-Cong ear preserved in alcohol. (*Op. cit.*)

There is apparently no attempt to disguise such atrocities, even for public relations reasons. Writes Malcolm Browne:

> Many a news correspondent has seen the hands whacked off prisoners with machetes. Prisoners are sometimes castrated or blinded. In more than one case a Viet-Cong suspect has been towed after interrogation behind an armored personnel carrier across the rice fields. This always results in death in one of its most painful forms. Vietnamese troops also take their share of enemy heads. . . . (*Op. cit.*)

U.S. Army Special Forces men pride themselves on their advanced methods of "interrogation," often patterned after Chinese models. In his first-hand account of the Special Forces in action, *The Green Berets*, Robin Moore gives a graphic description of a torture session presided over by a Special Forces officer of Finnish origin who had served with the Nazi

Army on the Russian Front in World War Two. (Because of Moore's embarrassing disclosures, his publishers, who had originally presented the book as "truthful . . . a factual account," were forced under pressure from Assistant Secretary of Defense Arthur Sylvester to label the material "fictionalized.")

Although torture of Viet-Cong suspects antedated the arrival in strength of U.S. forces, American technology has given it some interesting twists. The helicopter, introduced by the United States as a vital element in the air war, is now playing a role in the "interrogation" of prisoners. *Houston Chronicle* reporter Jonathan Kapstein reported the innovation, termed "the long step," on his return from an assignment in Viet-Nam.

> A helicopter pilot looked up from his Jack Daniels-and-Coke to relate what had happened to a captive he had been flying back from a battle area. A Vietnamese army officer yelled in the ear of the suspected guerrilla who was tied hand and foot. The man did not respond, so the officer and a Vietnamese soldier heaved him, struggling against his ropes, out of the UH-1B helicopter from 2,900 feet. Then over the roar of the engine, the officer began to interrogate another prisoner who had watched wide-eyed. The answers must have been satisfactory, the flier said, because, though kicked and roughly handled, the guerrilla was alive to be marched off when the helicopter landed. . . . (*Nation*, Dec. 21, 1964.)

A prisoner who "cooperates" after watching the exit of his comrade is not always rewarded. *Herald Tribune* Saigon correspondent Beverly Deepe reports an instance when "Two Viet-Cong prisoners were interrogated on an airplane flying toward Saigon. The first refused to answer questions and was thrown out of the airplane at 3,000 feet. The second immediately answered all the questions. But he, too, was thrown out." (New York *Herald Tribune,* April 25, 1965.) Sometimes there is not even the pretense of "questioning." Jack Langguth, Saigon correspondent for the *New York Times*, reports a case where "One American helicopter crewman returned to his base in the central highlands last week without a fierce young prisoner entrusted to him. He told friends that he had become infuriated by the youth and had pushed him out of the helicopter at about 1,000 feet." (*New York Times,* July 7, 1965.)

Even if a prisoner is lucky enough to make the full trip, half the fun isn't getting there. Jimmy Breslin, in a dispatch to the New York *Herald Tribune* from South Vietnam, wrote:

> At 12:00 o'clock, a helicopter came in and the shirtless Marine in the tent said it was going to Da Nang. . . . A young redheaded machine-gunner sat in the doorway, chewing on a chocolate cracker from a C-ration tin. He kicked a small spool of wire out of the doorway and made room.
> "We just rode Nuongs, you can tell that by the wire here," he said.
> "Why?" he was asked. Nuongs are Chinese mercenaries from Formosa. . . .
> "They always want the wire for the prisoners," the kid said. "Don't you know that? They get a VC and make him hold his hands against his cheeks. Then they take this wire and run it right through the one hand and right through his cheek and into his mouth. Then they pull the wire out through the other cheek and stick it through the other hand. They knot both ends around sticks. You never seen them with prisoners like that? Oh, you ought to see how quiet them gooks sit in a helicopter when we got them wrapped up like that. (New York *Herald Tribune,* Sept. 29, 1965.)

As the tempo of the fighting has increased, many Viet-Cong prisoners are spared the ordeal of torture—they are shot on the spot by their U.S. or Vietnamese captors. Writes *Newsweek's* Saigon correspondent, William Tuohy:

> Some Viet-Cong suspects do not survive long enough for the third degree. Earlier this year, in an operation along the central coast, a Government detachment failed to flush VC troops suspected of lurking in the area. However, several villagers were rounded up and one man was brought before the company commander. The Vietnamese officer briefly questioned the suspect, then turned to his adviser . . . and said, "I think I shoot this man. Okay?"
> "Go ahead," said the adviser.
> The officer fired a carbine round point-blank, striking the villager below the chest. The man slumped and died. The pa-

trol moved on. Later, a correspondent asked the adviser, who had seemed a decent enough fellow, why he had given his approval.

. . . "These people could have moved to a Government area. In this war they are either on our side or they are not. There is no in-between." (*New York Times* Magazine, Nov. 28, 1965.)

Houston Chronicle correspondent Jonathan Kapstein reported on his return from Viet-Nam:

In the pleasantly dim officers' club at Vinh Long, South Viet-Nam, a 25-year-old U.S. Army lieutenant described what he had seen one time when soldiers of the Vietnamese 7th Infantry Division captured prisoners. "They had four, all suspected of being Viet-Cong—the first prisoners they had taken in a long time. They lined 'em up and shot the first man. Then they questioned the second. His answers were unsatisfactory, I guess, because they shot him too. . . ." (*Nation*, December 24, 1964.)

As U.S. casualties have mounted even the pretense of preliminary interrogation has been dropped. Captured and wounded Viet-Cong are now executed summarily. Captain James Morris, a U.S. Army Special Forces man, reports the aftermath of an ambush he sprang on a small enemy contingent:

I moved from one dark shape to the other, making sure they were dead. When I moved up on the last one, he raised up, his arms extended, eyes wide. He had no weapon. Cowboy stitched him up the middle with his AR-15. He didn't even twitch. . . . (*Esquire,* August, 1965.)

Pulitzer Prize winning correspondent David Halberstam recounts the treatment accorded a group of Viet-Cong prisoners by Government forces after a "particularly bitter" battle near Bac Lieu:

The enemy were very cocky and started shouting anti-American slogans and Vietnamese curses at their captors. The Marines . . . simply lined up the seventeen guerrillas and shot them down in cold blood. . . . (*The Making of a Quagmire* by David Halberstam. Random House, 1965.)

The treatment of Viet-Cong POW's seems to vary with the severity of American losses in the action preceding their capture. After a platoon of the U.S. 1st Air Cavalry Division was almost wiped out in a battle in the Chu Prong foothills of the Ia Drang valley, Reuters reported:

> In one place nearby the Americans found three North Vietnamese wounded. One lay huddled under a tree, a smile on his face. "You won't smile any more," said one of the American soldiers, pumping bullets into his body. The other two met the same fate. (November 18, 1965.)

Chicago Daily News correspondent Raymond R. Coffey, reporting on the same battle, accompanied U.S. relief forces to a clearing littered with dead from the previous day's fighting. He writes:

> It was almost impossible to walk twenty paces without stumbling upon a body. . . . Suddenly a few yards away a wounded enemy soldier lifted one arm weakly and an American sergeant poured a long burst of M-16 rifle bullets into him. "Was he trying to give up, Sarge?" a man asked. "I'd like to find more of those bastards trying to give up," the sergeant said bitterly. No one disagreed with him. . . . (Chicago *Daily News*, November 19, 1965.)

Apart from the moral question, U.S. and South Vietnamese torture and execution of prisoners of war is, of course, in clear violation of international law. Both South Viet-Nam and the United States are signatories to the 1949 Geneva Conventions governing the treatment of prisoners. Article 17 states: "No physical or mental torture, nor any other form of coercion, may be inflicted on prisoners of war to secure from them information of any kind whatever." In a specific provision pertaining to undeclared or civil war, the Conventions prohibit, with respect to prisoners of war, "violence to life and person, in particular murder of all kinds, mutilation, cruel treatment and torture."

The International Red Cross in Geneva, to which the Conventions assigned the right to visit POW's and insure their proper treatment, has publicly protested U.S. treatment of prisoners in Viet-Nam. The *New York Times* declared on December 1, 1965, that "the International Committee of the Red Cross in Geneva . . . complained again that the United States was violating an international accord on the treatment of prisoners. . . ." An earlier dispatch reported that "The International Red Cross Committee is dissatisfied with the way the United States and South Vietnamese Governments observe their pledge to respect the Geneva Conventions protecting war victims. . . . The Committee's representative in Saigon has been unable to visit prisoners taken by American and South Vietnamese troops despite the affirmative reply of the two governments to its appeal for the observance of the conventions. The Saigon authorities were said to have given repeated assurances that they intended to allow the International Red Cross to visit the prisoners but to date have done nothing more about it." (*New York Times,* November 26, 1965.)

If the United States is not willing to observe the Geneva Conventions itself, it is quick to point an accusing finger at others. When the North Vietnamese Government threatened to try captured U.S. airmen as war criminals, the United States denounced any such move as a violation of the Geneva Conventions and appealed to the International Red Cross. Hans Henle, a former executive of the information Service of the International Committee of the Red Cross in Geneva, commented:

> The Viet-Cong fighters are as protected by the Geneva Conventions as the American G.I.s are. Dramatic protests against violations of the Geneva Conventions should have been made when the first Viet-Cong prisoners were shot, when they were tortured, when the American Army started to destroy Viet-Cong hospitals and to cut off medical supply. . . . It is utterly hypocritical to condone wholesale violations of the Red Cross principles on one side and protest reprisals against them. . . .
> (*New York Times,* International Edition only, October 14, 1965.)

Not content with the present level of inhumanity, some agencies of the United States Government are attempting to turn torture from a political liability to an asset. The Asso-

ciated Press reported on October 16, 1965, that Senator Ste-
phen Young, who had just returned from a fact-finding mission in Viet-Nam, "says he was told by a member of the
Central Intelligence Agency in Viet-Nam that the C.I.A. committed atrocities there to discredit the Viet-Cong. Young said
he was told that the C.I.A. disguised some people as Viet-Cong
and they committed atrocities. . . ." (Philadelphia *Inquirer,*
October 20, 1965.) Young's revelations landed like a bomb-
shell on official Washington. "The C.I.A. and the State Department went into an uproar," the *Herald Tribune* reported. "There was deep distress among State Department
officials who feared his reported remarks would have disastrous
repercussions abroad." (New York *Herald Tribune,* October
21, 1965.) But Young refused to back down. "The C.I.A. has
employed some South Vietnamese," he reiterated, "and they
have been instructed to claim they are Viet-Cong and to work
accordingly . . . several of these executed two village leaders
and raped some women. I know such men have been employed, and I question the wisdom of that."

So, as the war escalates, does the human agony in its wake.
The prospect is for more, not less, torture and shooting of
POW's. "There comes a time in every war," James Reston
writes from Saigon, "when men tend to become indifferent to
human suffering, even to unnecessary brutality, and we may
be reaching that point in Viet-Nam." (*New York Times,* September 5, 1965.) Frustrated and bitter, U.S. forces in Viet-
Nam have dehumanized their enemy, and anaesthetized their
own consciences. Graham Greene, struck by the ubiquitous
photographs of torture in the U.S. press, wrote recently:

> The strange new feature about the photographs of torture
> now appearing is that they have been taken with the approval
> of the torturers and published over captions that contain no
> hint of condemnation. They might have come out of a book
> on insect life. "The white ant takes certain measures against
> the red ant after a successful foray." But these, after all, are
> not ants, but men. . . . These photographs are of torturers
> belonging to an army which could not exist without American
> aid and counsel. . . . The long, slow slide into barbarism of

the Western World seems to have quickened. (The London *Daily Telegraph*, November 6, 1965.)

The New York *Herald Tribune* reported on May 23, 1965, that "Near the big coastal city of Hue, U.S. Marines set crops on fire and burned or dynamited huts. . . ." In July, 1965, U.S. Marines fought a Viet-Cong force which had landed in sampans on the island of An Hoa and attacked a Vietnamese navy post there. The two major towns on the island, Longthanh and Xuanmy, had been occupied by the guerrillas. Together the towns had about 1,500 inhabitants. After the Viet-Cong retreated, "the Marines were ordered to burn Longthanh and Xuanmy to prevent the Viet-Cong from reoccupying them. . . ." (*New York Times*, July 11, 1965.) Few Viet-Cong had been killed or captured, but two prosperous villages were razed and, according to U.S. sources, about 100 civilians died from U.S. fire. An A.P. dispatch from the island on July 11, 1965, reported that Americans had called An Hoa "Little Hawaii" because "of its rolling surf and happy people. In one day An Hoa became a little hell."

The two nearby villages of Chan Son and Camne in the Mekong Delta felt the brunt of U.S. "pacification" in August, 1965. Marine patrols near the villages had received light sniper fire from Viet-Cong guerrillas. What happened next was described by U.S. newsmen accompanying the Marines into the villages.

> A Marine shouted, "Kill them! I don't want anyone moving!" . . . The Marines burned huts they believed were the sites of sniper fire. A sergeant said orders called for this. . . . [After the firing died down] U.S. Marines found a woman and two children among 25 persons they killed. . . . The woman died of a wound in the side, perhaps from one of the 1,000 artillery shells poured into the area. A wailing child beside her had an arm injury. A grenade hurled by a Marine blasted two children to death in an air-raid shelter. (*New York Times*, August 3, 1965.)

How the Marines reacted to their "victory" was described by a U.P.I. dispatch from Chan Son:

"I got me a VC, man. I got at least two of them bastards."

The exultant cry followed a 10-second burst of automatic weapons fire yesterday, and the dull crump of a grenade exploding underground.

The Marines ordered a Vietnamese corporal to go down into the grenade-blasted hole to pull out their victims.

The victims were three children between 11 and 14—two boys and a girl. Their bodies were riddled with bullets.

Their father was still suffering from shock. A husky Marine lifted him on his shoulder and carried him off.

"Oh, my God," a young Marine exclaimed. "They're all kids."

A moment earlier, six children nearby watched their mother die. Her blood left a dark trail in the "air-raid shelter," where the family fled when the Marines attacked. A wrinkled grandmother had pulled her into a more comfortable position to let her die.

The terrified face of a 60-year-old man looked up from a hole; his wailing mingled with the crying of the village children.

In the village, a little boy displayed his sister who was no more than four. She had been shot through the arm.

The Marines had received a few sniper rounds from Chan Son village. . . .

The sniper fire was enough for the Marines to open up with everything they had: rifle fire, automatic fire and grenades. A number of women and children were caught in the fire. Five of them were killed and five others wounded.

Shortly before the Marines moved in, a helicopter had flown over the area warning the villagers to stay in their homes.
(New York *Herald Tribune,* August 3, 1965.)

Chan Son's neighboring village of Camne fared no better. Morley Safer, a CBS television correspondent accompanying the force occupying the town, reported that U.S. Marines had burned 150 houses in the hamlet, ignoring "the pleas of old men and women to delay the burnings so that belongings could be removed." Safer's report, delivered on "Evening News with Walter Cronkite," August 4, 1965, said that:

"After surrounding the village . . . the Marines poured 3.5 in. rocket fire, M–79 grenade launchers and heavy and light machine-gun fire. The Marines then moved in, proceeding first with cigarette lighters, then with flame throwers, to burn down an estimated 150 dwellings." Safer concluded by revealing that "I subsequently learned that a Marine platoon on the right flank wounded three women and killed one child in a rocket barrage. The day's operations netted about four prisoners— old men."

It was unusual for U.S. "pacification" teams to be accompanied by U.S. reporters, and Washington was evidently embarrassed by the widespread publicity given the Chan Son and Camne incidents. Charles Mohr reported from Saigon on subsequent "attempts by public information officers to de-emphasize the importance of civilian deaths and the burning of village huts at the hands of U.S. Marines." (*New York Times,* August 9, 1965.) And Secretary of the Navy Paul Nitze publicly supported the burning of villages as a "natural and inevitable adjunct" to defense of U.S. bases in their vicinity. Nitze declared that "Where neither United States nor Vietnamese forces can maintain continuous occupancy, it is necessary to destroy those facilities." (*New York Times,* August 15, 1965.) The final word was had by a U.S. military spokesman in Saigon who told reporters that "Marines do not burn houses or villages unless those houses or villages are fortified." When a U.S. correspondent commented that the great majority of Vietnamese villages were fortified in one way or another, the spokesman said simply: "I know it."

The Vietnamese peasant is caught in a vicious vise by U.S. "pacification" tactics. If he stays in his village he may die under U.S. fire; if he flees before the advancing troops he may still be rounded up, and shot on the spot as an "escaping Viet-Cong."

Murders of such terrified peasants are a daily occurrence in Viet-Nam, and American G.I.'s are bagging their share of the game. A typical instance was reported by the A.P. from the town of Hoi Vuc, scene of a Marine "search-and-destroy" operation:

"The sweat-soaked young Leatherneck stood over the torn body of a Viet Cong guerrilla with mixed emotions flitting over his face. For Cpl. Pleas David of Tuscaloosa, Alabama, it was a day he would never forget. David had just killed his first man. 'I felt kind of sorry for him as I stood there,' said David, a lanky 17-year-old. 'And he didn't even have a weapon.' . . ." The unarmed "Viet-Cong" was walking along a paddy dike when the four Marines approached him with leveled guns. The frightened Vietnamese saw the guns and threw himself on the ground. As the Marines ran towards him he jumped up and tried to escape. "I let him get 250 yards away and then dropped him with two shots from my M-1," the A.P. quotes the young Marine, adding "The man had been hit squarely in the back. No weapons were found with him. . . ." The Marine was congratulated by his buddies. "Maybe the Viet-Cong will learn some respect for marksmanship. When we see them we hit them," one boasted. Another declared that "David is a good example. . . . Don't think we are killers. We are Marines." (New York *Post,* April 30, 1965.)

It is official U.S. military policy to shoot and ask questions later. Thus, in an operation thirty-five miles outside of Saigon, U.S. troops rushed a peasant shack believed to harbor Viet-Cong. One U.S. Lieutenant hurled a grenade through the door but the inhabitants tossed it back out. According to the A.P., "Another American soldier charged the shack, pulled the pin on a grenade and gave the fuse a few seconds count-down before pitching it in. Following the explosion the G.I. leaped into the shack with his M-14 rifle blazing. Three men and a baby died. Two women were wounded. Shrapnel took off the lower half of one woman's leg." (November 16, 1965.)

Not all G.I.'s enjoy making war on women and children. Some have written agonized letters home. Marine Cpl. Ronnie Wilson, 20, of Wichita, Kansas, wrote the following letter to his mother:

Mom, I had to kill a woman and a baby. . . . We were searching the dead Cong when the wife of the one I was checking ran out of a cave. . . . I shot her and my rifle is automatic so before I knew it I had shot about six rounds. Four of them hit her and the others went into the cave and must have bounced off the rock wall and hit the baby. Mom, for the first time I felt really sick to my stomach. The baby was about two months old. I swear to God this place is worse than hell. Why must I kill women and kids? Who knows who's right? They

think they are and we think we are. Both sides are losing men.
I wish to God this was over.

But those American G.I.'s who react with shock and horror
to their bloody mission are a distinct minority. Most American
soldiers in Viet-Nam do not question the orders that lead them
to raze villages and wipe out men, women and children for
the "crime" of living in Viet-Cong-controlled or infiltrated
areas. Extermination of the (non-white) enemy is to them a
dirty but necessary job, and few grumble about it. Some have
even come to enjoy it. Warren Rogers, Chief Correspondent in
Viet-Nam for the Hearst syndicate, reports that:

> There is a new breed of Americans that most of us don't
> know about and it is time we got used to it. The 18- and 19-
> year-olds, fashionably referred to as high-school dropouts, have
> steel in their backbones and maybe too much of what prize
> fighters call the killer instinct. These kids seem to enjoy killing
> Viet-Cong. . . . (New York *Journal-American*, September 16,
> 1965.)

To many critics of the war this "new breed of Americans"
bears a disquieting resemblance to an old breed of Germans.

As the United States build-up has grown, there has been an
increasing reliance on air attack. Any village in "VC territory"
(which now comprises most of the country outside of the big
cities) is considered a "free strike" area. U.S. planes rain death
other vast areas of the countryside, killing Viet-Cong guerrillas
and innocent peasants alike. No attempt is made to discrimi-
nate between military and civilian targets. American pilots,
the Washington *Post* reported recently, "are given a square
marked on a map and told to hit every hamlet within the area.
The pilots know they sometimes are bombing women and
children." (March 13, 1965.) Supersonic jets and B-52 bombers blanket vast areas of the countryside with 1,000-pound
bombs, napalm and white phosphorus. According to *New
York Times'* Saigon Correspondent, Charles Mohr,

> This is strategic bombing in a friendly, allied country. Since
> the Viet-Cong doctrine is to insulate themselves among the
> population and the population is largely powerless to prevent

their presence, no one here seriously doubts that significant numbers of innocent civilians are dying every day in South Viet-Nam. (*New York Times,* September 5, 1965.)

The victims of such raids are always reported in the official U.S. enemy casualty lists as "dead Viet-Cong." The accuracy of such reports was revealed by Jack Langguth in a dispatch from Saigon:

> As the Communists withdrew from Quangngai last Monday, U.S. jet bombers pounded the hills into which they were headed. Many Vietnamese—one estimate was as high as 500—were killed by the strikes. The American contention is that they were Viet-Cong soldiers. But three out of four patients seeking treatment in a Vietnamese hospital afterward for burns from napalm or jellied gasoline, were village women. (*New York Times,* June 6, 1965.)

Quangngai province has been the scene of some of the heaviest fighting of the war. When U.S. and Vietnamese troops could not dislodge the Viet-Cong from their positions it was decided to destroy all villages in the province which were not garrisoned by U.S. or Vietnamese forces. The fate of Duchai, a complex of five fishing villages on the coast, is typical. Neil Sheehan told the story of Duchai in a dispatch to the *New York Times:*

> In mid-August United States and Vietnamese military officials decided the Communists were using Duchai as a base for their operations in the area and that it should be destroyed. For the next two months . . . it was periodically and ferociously bombed by Vietnamese and American planes. . . . At least 184 civilians died during Duchai's two months of agony. Some reasonable estimates run as high as 600. . . . When an American visits Duchai these days, villagers . . . tell him horror stories of how many of the 15,000 former inhabitants were killed by bombs and shells. "There," said a fisherman pointing to a bomb crater beside a ruined house, "a woman and her six children were killed in a bomb shelter when it got a direct hit." Duchai's solid brick and stucco houses, the product of generations of hard-earned savings by its fishermen, were reduced to rubble or blasted into skeletons. Five-inch naval shells tore gaping holes in walls, and bombs of 750 to 1,000 pounds

plunged through roofs, shattering interiors and scattering red rooftiles over the landscape. . . . Here and there napalm blackened the ruins. (November 30, 1965.)

Sheehan reported that at least ten other villages in the province had "been destroyed as thoroughly as the five in Duchai" and another twenty-five nearly as badly damaged. Four hundred and fifty other villages have been under intermittent attack by U.S. and Vietnamese planes. "Each month," Sheehan writes, "600 to 1,000 civilians wounded by bombs, shells, bullets and napalm are brought to the provincial hospital in Quangngai town. Officials say that about thirty percent of these cases require major surgery. A recent visitor to the hospital found several children lying on cots, their bodies horribly burned by napalm." (*Ibid.*)

An American doctor in the Quangngai hospital, J. David Kinzie, was moved to protest the horrors of the war in a letter to a U.S. magazine:

I have been in Quang Ngai for six months in general practice at a civilian provincial hospital, and I can remain silent no longer.

There comes a time in a doctor's life, no matter how hardened he has become, and perhaps in every man's life, no matter how cynical he may be, when he must protest as effectively as he can about the suffering of his fellow man. When one's own country is involved in the inhumanity, the responsibility becomes greater. Thus I add my belated voice.

The civilian hospital in our province in central Viet-Nam is good by Vietnamese standards. The patients, already diseased by tuberculosis, anemia, and malnutrition in many cases, are now entering more frequently from direct effects of the war. For example, a pregnant woman demonstrator with a bullet hole in her abdomen, whose fetus died later; a twelve-year-old boy brought in unconscious by relatives who described how artillery blasted their village the night before; a fifty-year-old woman, accused of being Viet-Cong, who had been beaten, electrically shocked, and had her hands punctured for three days to extort information; three other civilians also accused of supporting the Viet-Cong were released to the hospital after severe beatings and their innocence determined. Many of the victims' "crimes" consisted merely in living in an area the Viet-Cong had overrun the night before. . . .

Of course, war has always been described as evil, but does this mean that America must add to it? Our military advisers teach Vietnamese modern techniques of killing each other. Our weapons aid in more thorough destruction of themselves. Rather than liberating a people, it seems that these techniques and weapons result in innocent civilians, women, and children being beaten, burned and murdered. . . .

Is America to survive on the blood of Vietnamese civilians? Does this make us great? (*Progressive,* March 1965.)

Thousands of children are dying as a result of United States air strikes. Charles Mohr writes in the *New York Times:*

In [a] delta province there is a woman—who has both arms burned off by napalm and her eyelids so badly burned that she cannot close them. When it is time for her to sleep her family puts a blanket over her head. The woman had two of her children killed in the air strike which maimed her last April and she saw five other children die. She was quite dispassionate when she told an American "more children were killed because the children do not have so much experience and do not know how to lie down behind the paddy dikes." (September 5, 1965.)

Vietnamese villagers, driven to desperation, have occasionally descended *en masse* on U.S. bases to protest the bombings of their villages. Such demonstrations have been violently repressed. In early September a group of villagers marched on the U.S. air base at Danang demanding an end to air attacks on their villages. The demonstration was dispersed and five participants, selected at random, were arrested. Their punishment was swift. The Chicago *Daily News* reported from Saigon, "At Danang, three persons were executed by a South Vietnamese firing squad. The execution, held in a soccer stadium, was postponed at the last minute until midnight . . . because news photographers refused to obey an order that no pictures be taken until the final shot had been fired. The three were among five persons arrested Monday during a demonstration by about 200 persons in downtown Danang. They were protesting crop damage from artillery fire and air attacks by U.S. forces." (Chicago *Daily News,* September 23, 1965.) The fate of the other two arrested demonstrators was described in a U.P.I. dispatch from Saigon. ". . . the fourth man would be executed later, but at the moment . . . he was described as a 'singing bird.' The fifth demonstrator, a woman, was sentenced to life in prison although the demonstration had been so small that few were even aware of it." (Washington *Daily News,* October 4, 1965.)

The essence of U.S. bombing policy was expressed with unusual frankness by a U.S. officer serving with a helicopter unit in the Mekong Delta. Jack Langguth asked the officer what the answer was to Viet-Cong activity. " 'Terror,' he said pleasantly. 'The Viet-Cong have terrorized the peasants to get their cooperation, or at least to stop their opposition. We must terrorize the villagers even more, so they see that their real self-interest lies with us. . . . Terror is what it takes.' " (*New York Times* Magazine, September 19, 1965.)

But in the long run, the bombing only helps the National Liberation Front. According to Senator George McGovern: "To bomb [the Viet-Cong] is to bomb the women and children, the villages and the peasants with whom they are intermingled. Our bombing attacks turn the people against us and feed the fires of rebellion." (*Congressional Record,* June 17, 1965.) Robert Taber, an authority on guerrilla warfare, writes in his new book *The War of the Flea* [published by Lyle Stuart, 1965]: "The indiscriminate use of air power against presumed Viet-Cong targets does much to explain the alienation of the rural population from the Saigon Government. Country people whose only contact with the government comes in the form of napalm and rocket attacks can scarcely be expected to feel sympathetic to the government cause, whatever it may be. On the other hand, they have every reason to feel solidarity with the guerrillas, usually recruited from their villages, who share their peril and their hardships."

More than any other single factor, our air war in Viet-Nam is turning the rest of the world against the United States.

All war, of course, is hell. There is no such thing as a "clean war," in Viet-Nam or anywhere else. But even in warfare there are certain observable norms of decency which cannot be disregarded. These were laid down after World War Two in the Charter of the International Military Tribunal, under which the Nuremberg Trials of top Nazi civilian and military leaders were held. Our actions in Viet-Nam fall within the prohibited classifications of warfare set down at Nuremberg under Article 6 which reads:

> . . . The following acts, or any of them, are crimes coming within the jurisdiction of the Tribunal for which there shall be individual responsibility:
>
> a) Crimes against peace: namely, planning, preparation, initiation or waging of a war of aggression, or a war in violation of international treaties, agreements, or assurances, or participation in a common plan or conspiracy for the accomplishment of any of the foregoing.
>
> b) War crimes: namely, violations of the laws or customs of war . . . plunder of public property, wanton destruction of cities, towns or villages, or devastation not justified by military necessity.
>
> c) Crimes against humanity: namely, murder, extermination, enslavement, deportation, and other inhumane acts committed against any civilian population, before, or during the war. . . .

Under the provisions of Article 6 the United States is clearly guilty of "War Crimes," "Crimes against Peace" and "Crimes against Humanity," crimes for which the top German leaders were either imprisoned or executed. If we agree with Hermann Goering's defense at Nuremberg that "In a life and death struggle there is no legality," then no action can or should be taken against the government leaders responsible for the war in Viet-Nam. But if Americans still believe that there is a higher law than that of the jungle, we should call our leaders to account. Otherwise we shall have proved Albert Schweitzer correct when he wrote:

> It is clear now to everyone that the suicide of civilization is in progress. . . . Wherever there is lost the consciousness that

every man is an object of concern for us just because he is a
man, civilization and morals are shaken, and the advance to
fully developed inhumanity is only a question of time. . . .
We have talked for decades with ever increasing lightminded-
ness about war and conquest, as if these were merely operations on a chessboard; how was this possible save as the result
of a tone of mind which no longer pictured to itself the fate of
individuals, but thought of them only as figures or objects belonging to the material world? (*The Philosophy of Civilization.*)

The issue at stake in Viet-Nam is not, as President Johnson
constantly claims, what will happen if we leave. It is what will
happen to us as a people, and to our judgment in history, if
we stay.

CHEMICAL WARFARE IN VIETNAM

*Seymour Hersh**

It wasn't until December, 1965, that the American public first learned that U.S. planes were deliberately using defoliants and herbicides to destroy rice and other crops in South Vietnam. A *New York Times* dispatch, which said the programs "began last spring," reported that up to 75,000 crop-producing acres had been sprayed. "Crop destruction missions are aimed only at relatively small areas of major military importance where the guerrillas grow their own food or where the population is willingly committed to their cause." The dispatch said up to 60 to 90 per cent of the crops, once sprayed, were destroyed.

The first official confirmation that the defoliation program was aimed, at least in part, at food-producing areas came in March, 1966, when the State Department announced that about 20,000 acres in South Vietnam, about one-third of 1 percent of the land under cultivation, had been destroyed. The statement was issued in response to questions about the case of Robert B. Nichols, an architect who had written President Johnson asking why the United States would attempt to help the South Vietnamese grow more food and at the same time attempt to destroy their crops. Nichols had gone on a hunger strike when he received what he considered a less than satisfactory response from the White House. As one critic said later, it took the potential starvation of an American citizen to evoke a clarifying statement from the Johnson Administration about its anticrop program.

A *New York Times* dispatch in July, 1966, noted that the spraying of enemy crops was being stepped up and added: "The spraying, *begun in 1962* [my italics], has blighted about 130,000 acres of rice and other food plants." Another *Times* story, in September, 1966, quoted Washington officials as say-

* This summary of the use of chemical weapons in Vietnam is taken from Mr. Hersh's *Chemical and Biological Warfare: America's Hidden Arsenal* (Indianapolis: Bobbs-Merrill, 1968), pp. 151–57.

ing that there would be no relaxation of the crop-destruction program in South Vietnam despite a series of protests. The dispatch, however, reduced the number of acres treated. It said Defense Department officials disclosed that approximately 104,000 acres of food-producing land had been destroyed in South Vietnam, 26,000 less than had been reported ruined six months earlier in a stepped-up program. Also in September, the *Times* reported that the U.S. military, "pleased with the effectiveness of chemical-defoliation and crop-destruction missions," was taking steps to triple the capability of those efforts.

There is evidence that the effectiveness of the defoliation program was still a moot question at that time, although anticrop techniques were highly successful. Early in 1967, Secretary of Defense McNamara told Congress that "defoliation is still a rather primitive technique. . . . It depends for its effectiveness on the time of the year, the type of foliage and on wind and other conditions in the area." What McNamara meant was that despite all the research, it still often took more than a month to strip foliage from trees in South Vietnam. Such problems didn't exist with the anticrop devices, which stimulated plants into frenzied growth and death, sometimes within an hour. Although similar chemicals were used for both missions, the gap in effectiveness between killing a food plant and causing a leaf to fall away had not been solved by mid-1967.

Whether or not the Pentagon initially planned to have its defoliation program lead into an anticrop project really doesn't matter; the fact is that by the end of 1966 more than half of the C-123 missions were admittedly targeted for crops and it is probable that any effort at a trebling of capability in 1967 was aimed not at the jungles of South Vietnam but at its arable crop land.

A 1967 Japanese study of U.S. anticrop and defoliation methods, prepared by Yoichi Fukushima, head of the Agronomy Section of the Japan Science Council, claimed that U.S. anticrop attacks have ruined more than 3.8 million acres of arable land in South Vietnam and resulted in the deaths of nearly 1,000 peasants and more than 13,000 livestock. Fukushima said one village was attacked more than thirty times by C-123 crop dusters spraying agents even more caustic than the arsenic-laden cacodylic acid. The Japanese scientist concluded that "appalling inhumane acts are evident even within the limited admissions officially given out by U.S. Government leaders. . . ." U.S. officials have made it plain they considered such claims to be sheer propaganda.

In April, 1966, Joseph Mary Ho Hue Ba, Catholic representative of the National Liberation Front (NLF), charged that the U.S. use of defoliants and herbicides was killing newborn babies. The charges were made in a North Vietnamese press agency broadcast monitored in Singapore by Reuters, the British press agency. Its subsequent dispatch quoted the broadcast as contending that hundreds of Catholics had been seriously poisoned by the chemical destruction of crops, which was also causing widespread starvation.

The cacodylic acid and the phenoxyacetic acids used in Vietnam are described in most reference works as non-selective herbicides, i.e., they kill all vegetation present. One study of anticrop chemicals in Vietnam notes that the weed control handbook issued in 1965 by the British Weed Control Council lists 2,4-D and 2,4,5-T as having relatively short persistence in the soil with relatively low levels of toxicity to man and animals. The handbook adds that "prolonged exposure, notably to oil solutions, may cause skin or eye irritation to some individuals. Plastic gloves and light goggles should be available for personnel mixing spray materials. Also, for some types of mist spraying, a face mask is desirable to avoid prolonged breathing in of oil droplets." It further notes that agents must be handled with caution because they "can cause serious damage if spray is allowed to drift onto nearby susceptible crops" or if liquids used for cleaning the spraying equipment are "allowed to flow into running ditches, streams or ponds." The *Merck Index of Chemicals and Drugs* reports further that 2,4-D can cause eye irritation and gastrointestinal upset. Worry over the potential health hazards of herbicides has prompted the English Ministry of Health to set up four poison information centers around the country whose main function is to supply medical advice by telephone to citizens who suspect they've been inadvertently poisoned.

ONLY WE CAN PREVENT FORESTS

The Air Force's C-123's are designed to distribute their 1,000-gallon, 10,000-pound loads in four minutes over about 300 acres, roughly more than 3 gallons per acre, the maximum dosage recommended by Army manuals. The program, approved in the fall of 1962 by the White House, is known as "Operation Ranch Hand." Its lumbering, low-flying planes are said to be the most shot-at in the war. "We are the most hated outfit in Vietnam." *Flying* magazine once quoted Air Force Major Ralph Dresser, head of "Ranch Hand," as saying the group's slogan is "Only We Can Prevent Forests." A detailed newspaper account of Dresser's crew, the Aerial Spray Flight of the 309th Aerial Commando Squadron, noted that in an emergency the plane's high-pressure spray nozzles can eject the 1,000-gallon cargo in just thirty seconds. Emergencies apparently happen quite often: the newspaper account mentioned that four planes in the squadron took a total of 900 rifle and machine-gun hits during the previous eighteen months of operation. In such cases, the net result could be a massive overdose for the crop-land below. The going rate for a 1,000-gallon cargo of crop-killing chemicals is $5,000; in 1967 the Pentagon announced the purchase of nearly $60 million worth of defoliants and herbicides, enough for 12,000 plane rides over the countryside, each of which would theoretically blanket 300 acres of crop-land. If each mission was successful, 3.6 million acres, nearly half the arable land in South Vietnam, could be covered.*

---

* The heavy military purchases of commercial defoliants have vastly outstripped existing production capacity in the United States and a shortage of the chemicals is anticipated, *Business Week* magazine reported in April, 1967. The magazine said some industry sources believe the military demand for 2,4,5-T to be four times production capacity. In 1965 the

In his letter to Dr. John Edsall, the protesting Harvard biologist, Major General Davison claimed that

> great care has been taken to select [anticrop target] areas in which most harm would be done to the Viet Cong and the least harm to the local population. In some instances the local inhabitants, who have been forced to grow food for the Viet Cong, have requested that the herbicides be used. The Government of Vietnam has taken precautions to care for non-combatants whose food supplies have been affected . . . this is not chemical or biological warfare, nor is it a precedent for such. It is in actuality a relatively mild method of putting pressure on a ruthless enemy who has no compunctions about the murder of women and children, as well as men, and about the torture and mutilation of captives.

The Japanese study prepared by Fukushima painted a different picture of the American pressure. The report included testimony from Pham Duc Nam, a peasant, and Cao Van Nguyen, a doctor.

Pham Duc Nam told of a three-day chemical attack near Da Nang, from February 25 to 27, 1966. He said in part:

> Affected areas covered 120 kilometers east-west and 150 kilometers north-south. Five minutes was all that was needed to wither tapioca, sweet potato . . . and banana plants. Livestock suffered heavy injuries. Unlike men, who could keep clear of chemical-stricken things as food, animals had to eat just anything. Most of the river fish were found lying dead on the surface of mountain streams and brooks. The three days of chemical attack poisoned scores of people, took the lives of about 10 and inflicted a "natus" disease [with symptoms like a severe rash] upon 18,000 inhabitants.

Cao Van Nguyen's testimony included this description of a chemical attack near Saigon on October 3, 1964:

> A vast expanse of woods, approximately 1,000 hectares [nearly 2,500 acres] of crop-producing land, and more than 1,000 in-

---

chemical industry produced nearly seventy-seven million pounds of 2,4,5-T and 2,4-D. *Business Week* said the commercial shortage would hit ranchers, farmers, and utilities the hardest; it added that the Business and Defense Services Administration has been ordered to assure that military orders will be met in full.

habitants were affected. A large number of livestock were also poisoned and some of them died. The majority of the poisoned people did not take any food from these crops, nor drink any of the water that had been covered or mixed with the sprinkled farm chemicals. They had only breathed in the polluted air or the poison had touched their skin. At first, they felt sick and had some diarrhea; then they began to feel it hard to breathe and they had low blood pressure; some serious cases had trouble with their optic nerves and went blind. Pregnant women gave birth to still-born or premature children. Most of the affected cattle died from serious diarrhea, and river fish floated on the surface of the water belly up, soon after the chemicals were spread.

PACIFICATION IN VIETNAM

David Welsh*

Donald MacDonald, head of the biggest AID project in the history of the world, was hosting a dinner party at his Saigon home when the conversation shifted to the war. One of the guests suggested that the AID boys were fooling themselves with their pacification schemes, which had never worked and were not working. The color rose in MacDonald's face, as it tends to do, his eyes gleaming with some unmentionable zeal. His hand dropped to his middle jacket button, and after having established that it was securely fastened, climbed to stroke his chin. He looked dapper but grim in his shiny suit, like a salesman who really believes in his product, selling something nobody wants to buy.

"We can't get out," said a guest, a CIA official working for AID. "We're up to our necks in it now and we're going to stay. We're going to beat the communists at their own game, use their methods, cut off their cocks and cut up the women and children if that's what it takes, until we break the communist hold over these people. *We can stand it.* We're going to make this place as germ-free as an operating room. And we can afford to do a better job of it than the VC."

The hygiene imagery shocks the uninitiated, but one hears it continually from U.S. officials in the war zone. An area is "sanitized" when supporters of the National Liberation Front are killed, captured or relocated, and the "germs" are not only the Front troops and cadres, but their millions of sympathizers as well.

What is in fact being contemplated by the military men who run things in Saigon and their numberless military-minded colleagues in AID, CIA, USIS and the Embassy is a "final solution" to the Vietnamese problem. The first steps toward "solving" it, detailed in the following pages, have long since become implemented policy. But how far the military

* This report on terror and repression in Vietnam appeared in the October 1967 issue of *Ramparts*.

will be permitted to go is another matter. "We have until early 1968," said an AID official at MacDonald's party, "not to win the war but to show a credible beginning toward winning the war. Otherwise it's a question of how much longer they'll keep putting money into this operation." It remains to be seen what Washington will consider a "credible beginning," and whether the Saigon "hards" will be given permission to turn most of rural South Vietnam into a free kill zone. For this, in effect, is what they are demanding. It's what their new pacification program is all about.

PUTTING THE "HARDS" IN CHARGE

Few American officials in Saigon believe the war is going anything other than badly, although you'd never know it from their public statements. They have not, however, lost their sense of mission, their determination not only to prevent an NLF takeover in the South but to root out all trace of the "infestation." For the most part, their missionary zeal is based on U.S. power requirements. But the war controllers seem still to believe that the only thing keeping Vietnamese "hearts and minds" out of America's grasp is the Front's "grip of terror" over the population, and that once liberated from the scourge, the people will choose the "democratic alternative" of Nguyen Cao Ky or his civilian successors.

This persistent notion, central to the prevailing theories of pacification, must color the way our officials evaluate the facts of the war. Otherwise, they would stop to wonder why it takes an entire platoon of government troops to "control" a village, while the Front considers two or three part-time soldiers sufficient to do the same job. Or how NLF troops can time and again pull off audacious, close-in raids against U.S. installations and escape undetected—without a single neighborhood villager sounding the alarm. Or how word of U.S. military operations is commonly known in advance to the NLF, while

VC "main force" operations take place in relative secrecy. Surely the Front has something more than "terror" going for it: you just can't "terrorize" an entire population and expect them to give you that kind of support.

For years our officials have been telling us that the war could not be won on the battlefield alone, that without victory in the "other" war for the people's hearts and minds, the United States would never be able to leave Vietnam except in defeat. Today, the rhetoric is changing. "There's no such thing as an 'other' war," says Bob Wayne, an OSA (CIA) official working on pacification in Region II. "There's just one war, and pacification is one part of it. From now on, anyone who even *looks* like a VC is going to get killed or put in a camp, until the people can learn to cooperate with their government."

The rhetoric is changing because the reality has changed. The get-tough artists are no longer chafing under the restrictions of softies—now they're in charge. The formal transition began last fall, when President Johnson sent a team of high-ranking officials, including members of his cabinet, on a tour of Vietnam to reexamine U.S. objectives and strategy. They concluded, first, that withdrawal was inconceivable; second, that pacification was not working; and third, that pacification had to be made to work if the United States hoped to establish a stable, non-communist government in the South and exit honorably. Drastic steps were recommended, and the most drastic thing available was, of course, the military, itself perennially prone to take on additional authority.

In times of despair, governments tend to turn to hard-liners for solutions, and it was the "hards" who got the ear of the blue-ribbon team during their Vietnam visit. The team became persuaded that the organization and pressure techniques of the NLF had proved their effectiveness in controlling local populations, and that these should be studied and adopted by our side as well. The visitors from Washington were particularly impressed with the much-touted successes of Korean troops in pacifying areas of central Vietnam, using what was understood to be an improvised version of "VC techniques."

There it is again, the chronic delusion—that the threat of terror is the only thing keeping the mass of the Vietnamese people in the NLF camp. We have only to make our own superior capacity for terror credible enough, the theory goes, and the people's allegiance will swing to the government side. If the NLF has a political "infrastructure" at the village and hamlet level, well by God, *our* Vietnamese will have an infrastructure. If they assassinate Ky's village chiefs and collaborators, well then, we should assassinate theirs.

It is a way of seeing the revolution-repression phenomenon as a territorial fight between two rival Mafia gangs, each offering "protection" to a people who would just as soon be left alone entirely. The gang with the best arsenal, the most money and the most credible will-to-terror (ours, presumably) would, one supposes, win the territory and its people. Our side, of course, isn't really a gang at all, but is forced to adopt terror tactics, so abhorrent to us all, because the enemy employs them, and because the prosperous and democratic society we seek for the people cannot be realized until the enemy is defeated. If it sounds absurd, rest assured that to the police mentalities of Saigon, it has a compelling logic.

After much study all around, the decision was made last fall in Washington to transfer pacification to military control—a decision some people knew about before the studies even began. Last December the Office of Civil Operations (OCO) was set up to centralize the profusion of pacification programs run variously by AID, CIA, JUSPAO (Public Affairs Office) and the Embassy. OCO was a temporary measure, to prepare the military takeover which took effect in the spring.*

AID director MacDonald argued fervently for the change. It was in his office that the phrase "Total War" originated, mean-

---

* In the process OCO was transmogrified into CORDS (Civilian Operations in Revolutionary Development Support). Some of the job titles cited in this article may have since undergone a corresponding change.

ing that all American resources in Vietnam should be directed toward the single goal of winning the war, allocated according to long-term military requirements and coordinated under the military itself. From combat operations to the way local and national elections are conducted, to psychological warfare, terror programs, rural development, Food for Peace, inflation control, refugee detention, village informer nets, censorship, construction projects, police training—all are battlefronts in a Total War to defeat the NLF and at the same time prevent the Saigon government from crumbling.

The new line is adumbrated in a recent AID pamphlet on pacification, which states: "There has been a tendency to consider the people as a neutral force—somewhere between the VC and the government, but not really a part of either. The truth is, however, that the people cannot be neutral. If they are not part of the government, they are forced to support the Viet Cong." He who is not your friend is your enemy, and he who is not "part of the government" is not your friend. The pretense about winning the hearts and minds is over; those who persist in such delusions are being shunted from positions of authority. In or out of uniform, the "hards" are in charge now, and the name of the game is Total War.

HEADHUNTERS OF THE CIA

In the complex of offices known as "Office One" at the Embassy —local headquarters for the CIA—are the desks of members of the "Assassination Bureau," which finances and directs an ambitious program of torture and political liquidation. The highly paid bureaucrats who run it don't call themselves an assassination bureau; they refer to their section by a set of three initials which for security reasons are periodically changed. And they are not called upon to soil their well-manicured hands with the unpleasant details of murder. That is left to the Vietnamese and their U. S. advisor-commanders, organized into Provincial Reconnaissance Units (PRU) and operating with varying degrees of effectiveness in every province of South Vietnam.

The PRU, a refinement of the old "counter-terror" teams of the Diem era, are technically under the province chiefs. In practice they come under the control of Office One, which pays the men (handsomely by Vietnamese standards), outfits them with the best weapons and equipment, and provides "advisors," recruited from the Army or the Agency itself. In some areas, as in Kien Tuong province in the Delta near the Cambodian border, Special Forces men are detailed to the Agency to lead the teams. In areas of heavy military activity, a division G2 may be ordered to supervise PRU operations.

The mission of the PRU is to identify and destroy the NLF "infrastructure" in every village and hamlet, as well as to neutralize, intern or liquidate all citizens who cooperate in the smallest way with the Front. Periodically, an Agency man in civilian clothes shows up in the province with a briefcase full of piastres, to pay off informers, village chiefs and the PRU teams themselves, and reward the headhunters. Heads fetch different bounties, depending on the area and the importance of the quarry. In one Delta province, a free-lance headhunter can pull down 5000 piastres (about $42) for the head of a VC lieutenant, 500,000 ($4200) if he bags an NLF province chief.

In each district an attempt is made to compile comprehensive order-of-battle intelligence on civilian and military cadres of the Front. But PRU operations are by no means efficient. U.S. advisors believe payoffs are finding their way into the hands of corrupt officials, and that a sizable amount is funneled to the Front. Informers frequently provide wrong information. And periodic assassinations or abductions of government agents by the Front often reduce the PRU teams and their agent networks to diffidence and inaction.

As a result, the emphasis is shifting from terror directed against the NLF cadre to terror directed against the population at large. "That way everyone cooperates," said an Army sergeant in Binh Duong province, "and then we can flush the VC like so much quail." On one occasion in the Delta, the PRU went into the hamlet of Ap Binh Son, which was known to be cooperating with the Front, cut off the heads of four villagers—picked at random as an "example"—impaled them on lancets and placed the grisly display on a village bridge. But however much terror may enhance the government's ability to "control" a population center, occupation forces are still considered necessary, and the NLF continues to operate with relative impunity in the surrounding countryside.

The PRU is one of several CIA ventures designed to weaken the NLF by "unconventional" means. And there are other, comparable programs in which the Agency plays an advisory or operational role—among them, the Police Field Forces, Police Special Branch and certain operations of the Special Forces' Project Delta.

The National Police have never been particularly effective against the NLF, although AID is pumping a projected $37.8 million into its "public safety" program this fiscal year in an attempt to beef them up. AID's goal, in keeping with the Total War policy, is to achieve *total population control* in a super police state. It's all there, only slightly less explicit, in a recent AID brochure entitled, "The Public Safety Program— Vietnam," April 1, 1966, as amended. Their ideal, openly proclaimed in the brochure, is to have the name, photograph, fingerprints, *curriculum vitae* and political beliefs of *every Vietnamese over 14* on file at local and national police head-quarters; to regulate their movements; to "remove" from the locality anyone suspect. The brochure describes one "popula-tion control" method on page 43: "The Family Census consists of an inventory of the population by housing unit. The regis-tration form is a booklet in which are recorded pertinent data concerning each legal resident of a particular dwelling unit. These data include . . . all significant resources of the resi-dents, such as outbuildings, tools and domestic animals, and the political affiliations or tendencies of each resident, if known. A group photograph (highly prized by most families) is also included. Two copies of each booklet are made, of which one is held by the family and one by the authorities. . . . Armed with the appropriate booklets, the Police can cordon off an area and check every dwelling place within. Using this technique . . . they detect and apprehend illegal residents, draft dodgers, deserters, and . . . not infrequently VC infiltrators or suspects."

Practically every branch of police activity is being expanded accordingly—from the national identity card program (7,500,-000 cards issued since 1958; 2.5 million more this year, age 14 and up, "to hamper Viet Cong use of youth") ; to Resources Control ("regulating the illegal movement of people and supplies to achieve population control") ; to police communications (a 12,500-radio village and hamlet network by the end of the year) ; to the Special Branch, a top-level secret police body roughly equivalent to our FBI. At work training this Gestapo and streamlining its methods of operation are a coterie of retired American cops in the employ of the AID/CIA nexus. Under American aegis, the National Police have grown in strength from roughly 20,000 in 1965 to more than 72,000 by the end of this year (AID projection). That's almost three times as many cops per capita as in the United States, and does not include the numerous other, more powerful agencies of government control.

One of the agencies AID is proudest of is Police Field Forces, the most recent successor to Diem's infamous Combat Police. These *gendarmes,* to quote a report to the President by Robert Komer, the pacification *honcho,* "are targeted against marauding bands of Viet Cong propagandists, tax collectors, kidnappers and killers." But the Field Forces do considerably more than that. "They work just like the PRU boys," said Air Force Lieutenant Colonel Petrovich, the OCO psychological operations officer in Khanh Hoa province. "Their main job is to zap the in-betweeners—you know, the people who aren't all the way with the government and aren't all the way with the

VC either. They figure you zap enough in-betweeners and people will begin to get the idea." The Field Forces hope to have at least one company per province by the end of the year.

Working closely with the Field Forces is the Special Branch, which in Komer's words, "carries out an intelligence and operational role against the Viet Cong apparatus." One of their jobs is to man provincial interrogation centers in more than 30 provinces, centers that serve as concentration camps for political prisoners long after their usefulness to the Special Branch has ended.

Under the patronage of a CIA alter-ego known as OSA (Office of the Special Assistant) the detention camp program is being expanded. Most of OSA's construction budget—30 million piastres ($250,000) in the second military region alone —is tied up enlarging existing interrogation centers and building new ones. "We use cut-rate local contractors," said a construction boss at the unmarked OSA compound along the Nha Trang beachfront. "Nothing fancy, just rough camps, but the security's got to be good." As of last June, the blackboard in the bathroom-sized OSA construction office listed current work on provincial interrogation centers at Qui Nhon, Phan Thiet, Phan Rang, Tuy Hoa, Kontum, Pleiku, Ban Me Thuot, Nha Trang, Dalat, as well as two centers in Region III at Song Be and Ham Tan. Next door, at OSA Region II headquarters, an old French villa reconverted to resemble a giant safe, plans were being laid to put these camps to efficient use. The avowed aim of AID's Public Safety Office (and, of course, the covert aim of OSA) is to create a "nationwide network" of "interrogation centers" for the Special Branch.

"We're following General Giap, chapter and verse. The day we have the VC tax collector's head on a spike in the middle of every village in this God-forsaken country, then we'll have a chance to win this war." The terror strategists in Saigon, impressed with the hallowed precedents of successful "counterinsurgency" in Malaya and the Philippines (in reality the triumph of the big payoff and the big iron fist), are tantalized by their own imitation of enemy technique. They seem to ignore the historical evidence that revolutionary techniques do not tend to work in the hands of counterrevolutionaries, or not for long. The French colonels and generals took lessons from Giap, too, but their conscientious attempt to apply them in Algeria was little short of disaster.

Part of the Saigon American's comprehension problem lies in his preoccupation with method, and in his habit of dealing with men as if they were machines. Revealing, by contrast, are two recent examples of "VC terror" in which innocent people died. Last year near Dong Ha, a French Catholic priest stepped on a mine and was killed. The Front promptly assembled his bereaved parishioners, explaining that they were sorry, that it was an accident, that the killing of the priest was not intended. They also pointed out that mines were expensive and that care should be exercised not to set them off. When a bus hit an anti-tank mine recently in one of the northern provinces of South Vietnam, the NLF obliged the bus company to pay the cost of the mine. The company was further told to remind its drivers to keep to the mine-free center of the highway.

THE FÜHRER'S OWN REVOLUTIONARIES

Last winter allied troops moved into a "VC village" in the Delta and declared it "secure" for the first time in more than a decade. ARVN provided perimeter security. The National Police sent a contingent. Local security was established and the first pacification workers began puttering at whatever it is they do. And there was the usual small retinue of striding AID officials, military and CIA advisors and house journalists, accomplishing their missions, striving mightily to be self-effacing because "this is a Vietnamese operation." Within a fortnight of the "liberation" of this bewildered village, a black Citroen sedan with police escort pulled into town. It was the landowner, come to collect 15 years' back rent!

AID put out a pamphlet calling for a "full-scale social revolution" in South Vietnam. During the winter, about the time our landlord was dunning his long-lost tenants for all that rice, Premier Ky issued this statement: "We still have a great deal of corruption and social injustice, and I know well that the only way you can eliminate communism is by a social revolution." He also announced that more than a million hectares of land had been redistributed to new owners, including "peasants who toiled on the land but had to give most of the proceeds to absentee landlords." There were even pictures of Ky handing out the deeds to smiling, misty-eyed peasants. The deeds are probably decorating the walls of a lot of peasant huts, but that's the closest most of those people will get to owning the land they were promised—unless, perhaps, their villages become "insecure" and the Front takes over.

Ky's paper land reform and all the talk about social revolution sprang ultimately from the famous Ky-Johnson summit at Honolulu in February 1966. Johnson winked, and laid down the law: the only way to defeat a revolution is to make one yourself. Ky blinked, and said he would. The result was new impetus to a program of Revolutionary Development (RD), bigger and better than all the pacification programs that had preceded it, they said.

Rev Dev, as the program is colloquially known, was nursed to its present stage of maturity by the CIA, which officially relinquished control last year but still plays an operational role. OSA provides most of the financing. CIA advisors are still at work at the Vung Tau training center, and in the field.

The RD program is organized around 59-man, all-Vietnamese teams, which are sent into hamlets to root out Front cadres and to implant their own "infrastructure" in its stead. The prerequisite for its success is security. That's the password these days—security. AID official Tom Naughton put it this way: "All Revolutionary Development activity is under the military now, and the rationale is sound. Nation building can move only as fast as there is security. You can't separate killing the VC from winning the people."

"Security" covers a lot of ground. It means road security, considerably worse now than a year ago. It also means the assortment of government troops that protect an RD hamlet from attacks by the Front (if they don't run away), who steal from the peasants, rape their daughters and terrorize for thrills on a scale unheard of even in Diem's time. But security is especially used as a euphemism for the business end of pacification, as another word for murder, torture, internment.

Of the standard 59-man RD team, 34 are armed cadres, the "action element," with a mission similar to that of the PRU and Police Field Forces. "Census grievance" personnel move from house to house in the hamlet gathering information on the Front cadre and sympathizers, under the supervision of an intelligence officer assigned to the team. Finally, there are the political officer and his "motivation and propaganda" men, and maybe four or five cadres assigned, theoretically, to rural reconstruction. As AID says, "a full-scale social revolution is not likely to explode" until there is "security."

Cao Ngoc Phuong, a 29-year-old former botany teacher active in the Buddhist Struggle Movement, does not approve of the NLF practice of assassinating RD cadres. "But I do know that the 'Revolutionary Development' teams are very much detested by the people," she said in an interview. "They are nothing but spies and secret policemen. They don't do anything for the people. They have no ideal. Every Vietnamese knows that those secret police wouldn't be there without the Americans."

About 40,000 of these glorified junior G-men have been turned loose in the hamlets, although there are nowhere near that many in the field today. A 25 per cent defection rate is considered normal, and not surprising: the Front killed 218 of them in the first four months of this year alone. The RD training center at Vung Tau reminds one of descriptions of Hitler's Strength-through-Joy camps, only in a vastly different setting. Black pajama-clad trainees, most of them youngsters who joined to avoid the draft, stand in battalion formation and recite, at the barked command of an instructor, the 98 Duties, the 11-point Criteria, the 12 Phases of Action. Periodically they sing a ditty called, "New Life Hamlet Construction," which has 12 stanzas (corresponding to the 12 Phases of Action) and 98 notes (symbolizing the 98 Duties). Political instruction alternates with a heavy dose of military training.

THE CONCENTRATION CAMPS

A jeep full of Americans barrels past a forlorn-looking Vietnamese guard into the district chief's compound at Phu Cat, and pulls up beside the outbuilding housing the U.S. advisory team. Inside, an Army major is waiting to brief the new arrivals, already stabbing his swagger stick at a profusely annotated 1:25,000 map of Binh Dinh province.

"Now this area," he says seriously, jabbing at the map, "we thought we had it sanitized. Well, we did for a while, had it just as clean as a hospital floor. Then we pulled out and it deteriorated. Charles moved back in there, and now we have to resanitize it. And believe me, we're not pulling out this time, not until this place is as sterile as a surgeon's hands." Pausing only to acknowledge the ripple of forced appreciation, the major proceeds: "Now in this area the ROK Cav [Korean troops] has been taking a lot of casualties from ambushes, mines and booby traps, which brings me to the heart of the matter—security. That's Priority One. Without that we can't get on with our other programs such as infrastructure destruction, revolutionary development and so forth. . . . Security is not possible here as long as the population remains in their villages: the VC owned this province for too long. To take a leaf from Mao Tse-tung's Red Book, we've got to deprive the fish of the sea to swim in. Now, the Koreans say the only way to accomplish their mission is to go in and get the people out of there, and then go in after the hard core. We agree. And that's where you people come in, whether you're Refugee Division, Psy Ops, Rev Dev or what not. Because once the area is sanitized, most of these refugees—after the VC suspects are weeded out—many of them will be going back to their villages, hopefully, and we can start really moving on our nation-building type programs. Well, that's it for the broad brush. Are there any questions?"

The major, if it can be believed, is a fairly typical, middle-echelon official in the new military pacification program. But only one who had not seen the physical and moral carnage these officials are creating could be tempted not to take them seriously. No one who had seen the refugee camps—the rows of rectangular concrete barracks, unfurnished; the bodies mal-nourished even by Vietnamese standards; the garbage in a dry well; the women and children and old men clustering about one another in the dust, with no work and nothing to do; and often, the barbed wire and armed guards barring exit—could be indifferent to the Americans who created them.

"We're going to dig Vietnam up by the rice roots and re-plant it, if necessary, until their infrastructure is totally destroyed."

Of course, *all* the camps aren't that bad; some are quite nice. *All* the refugees aren't led to the camps at gunpoint; quite a few come voluntarily for a handout, after American bombs or Korean flamethrowers have splintered their villages and torn up their land and source of livelihood. They're not *all* con-centration camps, with concertina wire and government in-formers and torture rooms for segregated suspects; a few have none of these conveniences. At some camps internees are al-lowed to wander out during the day to fetch rice and water or look for work; many of them never come back. If fields are accessible, internees in a "liberal" camp may be allowed to work there under escort until nightfall, when guards lead them back to the camp. There are, very definitely, two sides to the refugee question.

"Remove the people from the guerrillas, turn the area into a free-fire zone and shoot anything that moves."

At least one out of every eight civilians in the rural areas is a "refugee"—1,801,000 in the three years ending in March, by official count, and that includes only those processed through the camps. Others flee to the rabbit-warren slums of the cities or find a family closer to home willing to put them up. Some estimates go as high as one "refugee" for every five rural dwellers, and by March of next year there will be half a million more. Even "resettlement" is a euphemism. A hundred thousand a year have returned to their ruined villages, 190,000 a year to hastily-erected shanty towns in "secure" areas—where they can be watched. The rest remain herded in "temporary" camps, makeshift affairs under tents or canopies, which may become "permanent" camps with the advent of concrete barracks and other amenities.

The camps are run by the Saigon government, and much of the $40 million a year the U.S. earmarks for "refugee relief" is funneled, if that's the word, through provincial authorities. "The Vietnamese provide ten piastres a day per person, about eight cents, to buy rice with, if rice is available," says Sammy Radow, OCO refugee officer in Region II. "If the market is short on rice, as it is about half the time, rice is distributed." Much of the time internees receive neither the ten piastres a day nor the rice, nor the clothing, supplies and materials for camp improvement that AID provides. Provincial officials prefer to pocket the cash and sell the goods on the inflated market. How the internees survive is their secret, and nobody's concern.

One reason for the tremendous recent influx of "refugees" is that it reflects a change in policy. Perhaps in mute recognition that the enemy is the people, our leaders have chosen to reenact Diem's savage, pitiful experiments in resettling the population. "Forcible removal of refugees," said an Army captain named Robinson, engaged in pacifying the Iron Triangle, "that's been the trend in the last year." OCO chief Wade Lathram says there is "no overall policy of creating refugees to deny the people to the enemy," although "in selected instances it has been found desirable—to resettle them by force, that is." The selected instances have been growing in frequency. A year ago during Operation Irving, Korean troops scoured the Phu Cat mountain area and evicted some 40,000 people from their homes, according to Radow. A few escaped; the rest were corraled in temporary camps. Last January a ROK operation in Phu Yen province "produced" 13,200 refugees.

The same month, in Operation Cedar Falls, more than 6000 peasants in the Iron Triangle, a Front stronghold, were hustled out and penned up in a camp like cattle. Their villages were razed and the area was declared a free kill zone. It was an orgy of killing, burning, bulldozing, resettling, mass demolition, but curiously, there was not a single major contact with the enemy. To compensate, the Americans stressed such victories as the seizure of "enough rice to feed 10,000 VC for a year." Unable to transport all that rice conveniently, they burned it. Before the Iron Triangle sweep was launched, civilians were warned, briefly, by leaflets and aerial loudspeakers, that anyone remaining in the area would be considered "VC" and shot on sight. But for one reason or another, no more than half the civilians in the 40-square-mile Triangle were evacuated—some because they hadn't heard, others because they wanted to stay, still others because they or their relatives were with the Front. I talked with a hard-looking young captain of the 173rd Airborne Brigade who took part in the operation. The captain, who asked that his name be withheld, estimated that despite the evacuation, almost half the casualties inflicted by the massive U.S. air strikes and ground fire were "simple villagers—VC sympathizers, probably, but not hard-core. You can't tell, of course, but women and kids—I don't know, I just never think of them as hard-core. . . ."

The pattern was repeated last April and May, when 15,000 residents of hamlets in and just below the demilitarized zone were ordered to resettle to the south near Cam Lo. A number of families refused to leave when the trucks came to take them away. It would soon be harvest time, and their rice fields were thick with grain. The Americans responded by hitting the offending villages with rockets and bombs, napalm and machine-gun fire. Among the "refugees" evacuated two days later were an old woman and a six-year-old girl lying in a shelter, roasted by napalm and helpless in their pain.

Given the "forcible removal" policy, it is not surprising that practically all the camps contain a large number of Front workers or sympathizers. The Americans, however, have not given up hope of "converting" the refugees and Front fighters. A recent report of the Refugee Division states: "The potential importance of refugees as a resource to the government, and as a resource denied to the VC, is not yet fully appreciated by many officials. . . . With their many contacts in VC-held areas, knowledgeable, satisfied refugees also have great potential for the Chieu Hoi program in encouraging defectors from the VC ranks." The Chieu Hoi (Open Arms) program brought in 20,000 "VC defectors" in 1966; an official working in the program estimated that fewer than five percent of these "defectors" were more than occasional combatants and practically none were "hard-core."

The "change-of-heart" of a returnee is often heralded with a ceremony, like the one the Koreans staged last spring at Phu Cat. The captive audience, conscripted from a refugee camp and a nearby village, stood impassively as the ten "returnees" filed up to the rostrum to shake the hands and receive the fulsome praise of Korean and South Vietnamese officers. One read a long, prepared recantation. Each received a small packet of money and a bag of rice, phlegmatically, with a curt nod of the head. An Air Force major in civilian clothes, pistol strapped to his belt, rushed around taking pictures for a leaflet he was preparing on the event. "We'll get a lot of mileage out of this one," he said. "Psy Ops, you know. We'll hit the hard core up in the An Lao Valley."

A few days later I went back to Phu Cat with an interpreter to talk with some of those returnees. Two of them said a district official had demanded, and received, half their money and two-thirds of their rice. My interpreter, whose family still lives in the mountains where the Front is strong, asked me simply, "What do you think of Vietnamese freedom?" There was defiance, suddenly, in his face. I recognized it. It was that Yankee-Go-Home look. You know.

Dr. Wulff worked in South Vietnam for six years in a West German Medical Mission, and this remarkable eye-witness report was presented in November, 1967, to the International War Crimes Commission in Roskilde, Denmark. It is taken from John Duffett, ed., *Against the Crime of Silence: Proceedings of the Russell International War Crimes Tribunal* (London and New York: Bertrand Russell Peace Foundation [O'Hare Books], 1968), pp. 522–29.

A DOCTOR REPORTS FROM SOUTH VIETNAM
Erich Wulff

Ladies and Gentlemen . . . I have just arrived from South Vietnam and I have had no time to draft a text. I decided to come here before this Tribunal for two main reasons. One, because in the six years I spent in Vietnam, I saw a certain number of things which revolted me; and when the opportunity occurred to come here, I seized it immediately. Secondly, because a number of my Vietnamese friends, who are rendered silent at the present time, asked me to come here and speak in their stead. It is particularly difficult now to continue after this film that you have just seen, which illustrates to you much better than I could do, what is happening at the present time in South Vietnam. I was not able to bring much photographic evidence: the export of this kind of thing from South Vietnam is difficult. I have not so much seen the actual events, as the effects that these have produced. I shall begin by giving a general and rather superficial view of South Vietnam at the present time, especially, to show you the present reality of South Vietnam. It is recognizable to everyone, without the necessity for a great intellectual effort. You have just seen the South Vietnamese landscape; you have seen the bomb craters. Everyone who flies over South Vietnam now can see that the landscape resembles a human skin that suffers from smallpox. There are eruptions everywhere caused by bomb craters which are especially close to isolated habitations, little hamlets, little valleys. Everyone who flies over the land can see it and can draw his own conclusions. In flying over the country, also, you see vast areas which are destroyed and devastated by chemical products. It is a grave landscape—a landscape of ashes. You see, especially in the coastal region, in the province of Quang Nam, close by Phou Yon, chains of villages, habitations, and rice fields, that have been abandoned—a blanket of death—a landscape of death. One need not be an expert to draw conclusions.

In the towns controlled by the Saigon administration and the Americans, you see whole artificial forests of barbed wire. The American troops, the province heads and the district heads have surrounded the house of every person who collaborates with the Americans with a hedge of barbed wire. The isolation of the Americans and the South Vietnamese officials from the population is immediately visible. There is a desolate chasm between the populated streets and the habitations of the Americans, of the American officers and the South Vietnamese civil servants. For anyone who knows how to look, this already gives a rather clear picture of what is happening in Vietnam. When one goes a little more deeply into events and into the techniques used by the Americans, one can distinguish several main ways by which the war is conducted. The most standard technique is "search and destroy" operations. That is what you have seen just now on the screen. What happens is that a number of helicopters will land in a village. The soldiers enter the houses, they take a certain number of people who live there, especially young ones and women. They arrest them on the pretext that they are suspected "Vietcong" and they take them to interrogation centers. The rest of the population has endured this ceaselessly. It is a nightmare of the thirty years' war. After a time the helicopters fly off, and the population remains, stricken with terror and fear.

Now what happens to these prisoners? I have had occasion while working at the Central Hospital of Hue to see about fifty prisoners from the neighboring prisons who were sent to the hospital in extremely serious condition, sometimes just before they died. I can testify to a certain amount of medical data on these prisoners and especially relate material from dossiers which concern their stories and the manner in which they became prisoners. Many Vietnamese medical students helped me—as much as they could—to establish these files. I shall read to you two examples from these original dossiers that I have before me. I shall not publicly name the prisoners because they are still in prison, and I don't want to risk their further suffering. But the names will be in the file I will submit to the Tribunal.

Mr. "X," a farmer of thirty years, is living in Pen Dim, in the Province of Quang Dien. He has been an orphan since childhood. He is married with two children. Condition: poor. He had been in prison three years before being sent to the hospital with a condition of beriberi. The man had been arrested in a raiding operation without any evidence of his guilt. He was suspected of being a Vietcong. He was tortured by kicks on his chest, head, his belly, and then by electric wires wound around the forefinger. After this, he preferred to sign the confession that was presented to him already written. Penalty: four years of prison. After this he was evacuated to the prison of Hue, where he was imprisoned.

The second example, a young girl of 20, living in Top Ku, in the province of Tun Tang, a farmer's daughter, unmarried, living with her parents in a large family. She had been in prison for two years. The arrest was quite identical with the first case—she had been arrested in the course of a raiding operation as a Vietcong suspect. She was tortured, beaten with sticks and given the electric torture. She was made to drink soapy water. The result was that she signed an avowal and was convicted to two years in prison. These are typical cases, and I shall submit them to the Tribunal. There are a few others. There are also, of course, some men and women who do not confess and their stories are much worse. They are tortured for a much longer time. No judgment by a court is usually pronounced, and they remain in prison or in a prisoner's camp for an indefinite time. This, in a few words, constitutes the raiding operations, the so-called "search and destroy" operations by the Americans. This is what happens to the people when they are caught up in them. I am convinced therefore— I convinced myself rather—when I spoke with these unfortunates among the poor fifty, that I could suspect that perhaps at least two or three of them had participated in the fighting. But most of them were simple peasants who lived quietly at home, and whose only wrong was of not having fled in time.

The success of these raiding operations from the American point of view has been very limited. In the last two years, the year 1967 especially, another method has been invented. This other process has as its objective to destroy all potential bases for the Liberation troops in such a way that certain areas or districts are stripped of all the inhabitants who happen to live there. This process is especially used in regions where raiding operations have had no lasting effect. In the minds of the Americans, then, the only alternate solution is to remove the entire population. To settle them elsewhere, and during this process of resettlement, to try to find the people who were collaborating with the Liberation Front and put them into prison, into so-called refugee camps which are well-controlled and distributed in groups and within which a confidence man is placed. But one cannot succeed in eliminating a whole population from an area; the people won't go of their own volition. They are attached to their rice fields, to their villages. The mass worship of ancestors plays an important role in the Vietnamese culture. Every peasant Vietnamese wants to live, to marry, to have his children, to die, in the place where he was born—in his own village. So people do not leave. To make them leave they have to be driven, they have to be forced to become refugees. To do this, the Americans use various procedures. According to a relatively recent vocabulary, all this is called to "generate refugees." This expression is used by most of the American civil service; it is, of course, not used at press conferences.

How does one generate refugees? First, one declares a certain region to be a "free fire zone," or a "free strike zone," or a "free target zone," which are the technical terms for this.

The Americans then send over planes; the planes drop leaflets in which the population is warned to go to the district headquarters or the chief town. Then because of a "military necessity," real or imaginary, on the part of the Americans, there will be napalm bombing, and machine gunning at will in such a zone which explains the official designation "free fire zone." Despite all this, only a part of the inhabitants leave. If the bombings become intensified, after a few weeks of increased bombing, two thirds of the population can no longer endure life in such a "free fire zone"; they then come to these urban centers. But some still stubbornly remain and the third procedure (the first was the invitation, the second the bombing) is forced evacuation. Forced evacuation is not possible everywhere, there are regions where the forces of liberation are too strong for the helicopters to land, but nonetheless the Americans try. Two provinces where forced evacuation has been practiced are Quong Sin and Phou Yen in central Vietnam. There more than half of the population was turned into refugees. The planes and the helicopters take these people at the point of a gun. They have no possibility of taking their possessions with them. This is a kind of punishment because they did not accept the invitation of the Americans initially. In these provinces massacres occurred. In these two provinces the South Korean divisions the Americans brought are operating. I base this testimony not on my own experience, but on the experience of an American friend, who has lived for two years in these provinces and who was a witness to all this. I cannot mention his name because he is still in Vietnam. Several times there were cases, when, in the course of a raiding operation an NLF soldier fired on a Korean and total massacre of the village was the response. There have been new "Ouradours and Lidices" in these two provinces on several occasions. To give you some figures on the extent of this technique, in the province of Binh Dinh, an American told me that in the month of February 1967, there were 173 evacuated towns, in other words, about half the population of this province. The same is true of the province of Phou Yen. In all, one can count about 2,000,000 refugees in South Vietnam, and I need no longer explain what the term refugee means. Other estimations go as high as 4,000,000. Before, 80 percent of the population lived in the country, now only 55 percent.

Now I would like to speak of some of the psychological and material effects of this process. In a rural culture, when the people leave their homes, the cohesion of village life is broken; the people no longer have their rice fields. They are settled around the great American bases; they have to be settled there, because these are the only places where at least a few of these unfortunates can find work. These unfortunates, almost all of whom had land—albeit small plots—in central Vietnam, now have to work as coolees, as boys, this for the men. And the women to work as bar hostesses, as prostitutes.

Very often the children begin careers as thieves, pick-pockets, and as procurers for their mothers and sisters. The uprooting that such a situation leads to, when it is prolonged over a period of years, is altogether obvious. The effects are obvious, but in addition, the Americans can achieve two other aims. They produce the necessary manpower for the maintenance and building of their bases, the need for which is rather great. And secondly, they can create an economic dependency which is almost entire on the part of these people. For their existence they're dependent on the American camp. The mode of life of these people has been everlastingly destroyed; how can they begin again? They are bound for their subsistence to the existence of the American bases. This of course, as the Americans see it, is not without psychological effects. There is created around the American bases the kind of *lumpen proletariat* that is anarchic, dependent, but which presents certain advantages for the Americans as compared to an integrated peasant population which is too readily revolutionary. These are these new plans which have been executed particularly since the arrival of Robert Komer who is responsible for "pacification" in South Vietnam.

But this undertaking has not really succeeded. In the province of Phou Yen, theoretically one of the most effectively "pacified" provinces by this process, after six months in the refugee camp, a new revolutionary organization has been rebuilt because the people had nothing: the promises were not kept. Because their relatives had been killed, this organization reconstituted itself and what is happening now is that the Americans have to re-raid again these so-called refugee villages. In Vietnam at the present time we have refugee villages of the second and third power, the people having had to leave the village that they had been brought to time and again.

I want to accentuate this—what was the American reaction to these successive failures? First of all, a total Americanization of the war and of the civil administration in South Vietnam. For six months, the Americans have centralized their civil services in each province, giving to these services a name which, though often changed, finally ended by practically reconstructing the French Annamite Protectorate of the old days. More and more the Americans have taken civil administration directly into their own hands. Secondly, these excessive failures and the humiliation that these failures lead to have had a psychological effect. There has been a change in attitude that can be observed in the American soldiers, generally at the end of the third or fourth month of their stay in Vietnam. When they arrive, they are very often subjectively full of good will; their brain is still fresh with sentences they have been taught. They believe they came here to "protect the Vietnamese population from Communist take-over," but at the end of the time they realize that they have no friends, that apart from a thin layer of collaborators and profiteers nobody wants them. No one has responded to this abstract love with which they came; and so the paternalism, the protectionism with which they wanted to surround the Vietnamese transforms itself into a kind of aggressive racism. By the end of this time they have become accustomed to calling each Vietnamese a "gook," or "slant." These are people with slant eyes, and are words of insult which the Americans fling at every Vietnamese without distinction. So what has happened is a kind of crumbling of the edifice of theoretical justification which the Americans had erected for themselves. This results in acts of blind fury; they shoot down in anger prisoners—as you saw on the screen. Another technique which was not on the screen but which the Americans themselves have bragged about in my presence is to throw prisoners alive from helicopters—without parachutes, of course. This is very frequently practiced by the Americans. They also practice torture; but a certain distinction must be made. The Americans, with their hygienic spirit, have an obsession with not getting their hands dirty. So they use the South Vietnamese police and the South Vietnamese so-called elite troops to carry out the tortures—you saw this in the motion pictures a moment ago. As you saw, in 80% of the cases, the tortures are executed by the South Vietnamese troops while the Americans remain to the side with the tape recorders: they record what the people say. The Americans hypocritically say, "These are cruel people. One can do nothing about Asiatic cruelty." These tapes go into calculating machines, and they give statistics: statistics are assimilable to the quiet conscience of the Americans. This was, for me, one of the most disgusting aspects of American behavior in Vietnam as was their blind bombings of villages.

I would like to relate to you an anecdote—there are a certain number of German nurses who served on the hospital boat, *Helgoland*. During the first month of their stay in Saigon they were invited by Americans to go in helicopters on a manhunt as a diversion. I have this information from a man who is now the Director of the *Helgoland*. A man who has been a witness to this type of cruelty, more and more of which is occurring.

I want to take advantage of this opportunity to speak to you of a little village in South Vietnam which is called Phu Loc which is in the province of Quang Nam near Danang. The thing of which I speak happened in the month of September, 1967. The village of Phu Loc was already a village for refugees built just a year ago. The village is close to the American logistic base a few kilometers from the great city of Danang. One day, some Liberation Front soldiers came into this village which is a Catholic village, mainly anti-Communist. They came into this village and attacked the American base with mortar fire. The Americans answered with artillery fire on the village. The next day the priest of the village went to the Americans, imploring them not to use drastic means, and he proposed to help them plan an ambush so that they could capture the ones who were guilty. The Americans refused this; the following day the same thing happened, there was an NLF mortar attack. But the next morning a company of Americans came and ordered the inhabitants of the village to leave their houses. They then leveled the entire village, thereby humiliating this priest who at the outset was anti-Communist as were the other villagers. The result was that all the inhabitants fled into the Liberated Zone which fortunately was not very far away. I have a few slides of the village of Phu Loc which I owe to a young American who also worked in Vietnam, who, knowing that I was coming here, gave them to me. They show the effects of American shelling and I will leave them with the Tribunal. In the last few years it has become obvious to almost everyone that what is happening has never been a civil war between Vietnamese, but that it is a war of invasion that the Americans are waging in Vietnam. It is not that this is a new event, but it is only that with the presence of 500,000 Americans this has become visible and undeniable for everyone. Many simple people don't think too much, but they see what is before their eyes. Especially among the young people we find a growing awareness that the Liberation Front has become the only body existing in Vietnam which has the support of the vast majority of Vietnamese. This consciousness is relatively new in this magnitude. The government of Thieu and Ky struck down the Buddhist revolt. For a long time it was hoped that the Buddhists might constitute a kind of third force between the Front and the Americans. This hope has been destroyed and no longer exists. The result therefore is that many youth, who first belonged to the Buddhist movement, became members of the Front of National Liberation. What is happening, is not only that the Americans are producing refugees, but they are producing more and more conscious Vietnamese Nationalists who are ready to fight against them.

Mr. Bertolino is a French journalist who gave this report to the November, 1967, International War Crimes Tribunal, and it is taken from John Duffett, ed., *Against the Crime of Silence,* pp. 536–50.

_____

REPORT ON AMERICAN CONDUCT OF THE WAR IN THE SOUTH

Jean Bertolino

My testimony will concern the treatment of civilian populations and the treatment of prisoners of war. On the subject of the treatment of civilian populations I will treat more particularly:

1. Raiding of villages—description of the attack on a village in the sector of Loc Tanh Trung, which was entirely destroyed.

2. Arbitrary detentions—the arrest in this village of four old men, simply because they were there.

3. Operation "scorched earth" in the Iron Triangle.

4. Deportation of the population—description of the refugee camp of Phu Cong, at the end of "Operation Cedar Falls," in the Iron Triangle. Rach Kien, where half of the city was emptied of its population in order to install an American camp there; at about 7:00 in the evening, the second half was proclaimed an "unsafe zone" and anything that moved was shot on sight.

5. Massacre of the population—from his helicopter General Dane shoots at anything that moves. In honor of General Ky, troops indiscriminately shot up the countryside without a care for those who might happen to be there.

6. Moral damage to the population and social deterioration —in Saigon, prostitution has become the best way to earn a living; corruption reigns; at the end of a day spent in the camp of Phu Cong, the young women, compelled by the need for money, sell themselves to the G.I.'s. Repercussions of segregation in the American Army.

7. On the treatment of prisoners of war—the beheading of four captured Vietcong, at Rach Kien.

IN THE DELTA; AT AN ATTACK ON A VIETNAMESE VILLAGE

It was daybreak. Below us, some apparently peaceful villages were lying in a row. The fourteen Iroquois helicopters, each carrying eight soldiers, were flying in tight formation. On either side of the cabins, helmeted machine-gunners, with fingers on the triggers of the 12-7s fixed on each side of the fuselage, scrutinized the groves of coconut and banana trees which surround Delta villages.

Suddenly, the weapons of the whole 28 machine-gunners began to crackle. I peered around to see what was the target capable of unleashing such a furious volley. On my left, I perceived a tiny village nestled in the heart of a banana grove. The captain, an American of Puerto Rican origin, some thirty years old, pointed at the fragile straw huts partly hidden by the vegetation. He said to me: "Here is our objective." The helicopters made a sharp turn, while the machine-gunners continued firing at the dwellings.

The Iroquois hovered over a rice field and hung one meter from the ground. Encumbered by my photographic equipment, stunned by the deafening roar of the shooting, I remained frozen in my place. A huge Negro, flinging himself out of the copter, took me by the arm saying: "Get out, get out."

I hit the shifting, slippery, wet earth, which enveloped me to the waist; on all sides there was shooting. I floundered awkwardly behind an embankment which separated two rice-paddies and, covered with mud, I witnessed a hallucination-like ballet. The Iroquois, having disembarked their men, climbed very high in the sky. Now, like enormous dragonflies, they charged down in closed ranks on the straw huts, firing strings of rockets fixed in pods on their fuselage. Then, regaining altitude, they plunged down again shooting at the silhouettes fleeing from the flaming houses. The helicopters disappeared and the noise of their whirring blades faded away. The Company, which was part of the 2nd Battalion of the 25th Infantry Division, found itself alone. After the infernal uproar of the attack, the few sporadic shots seemed like silence.

The straw huts seemed deserted. The G.I.'s approached them prudently suspicious of the least tree trunk, the least abnormal object, the least weed, in fear of booby-traps. But in this small village only 30 km. south of Saigon, in the district of Loc Tanh Trung, there were no traps. Each house was meticulously searched; one sensed that their inhabitants had fled in panic. Small bags and sacks full of rice were lying with their contents scattered on the tables. Almost all the hearth fires were lit; in some of them the water in the kettles was still boiling. Here and there, out of sight, in the bushes, at the foot of trees, even inside of the dwellings, were deep holes or entrances to tunnels which the villagers had dug to protect themselves as well as they could from the aerial and land bombardment. Methodically, a young blond corporal pulled the pin on a grenade and threw one in each hole that his attention was called to. He did not wait to see the result: no one else saw it. The grenades, exploding underground, made dull noises, and the holes caved in.

AT BA THU, THE CHILDREN ARE AFRAID OF WHITES

At the time, I tried to reassure myself—telling myself that there could not have been anyone hidden in the holes; we had heard no cry. Later I had proof to the contrary. Fifteen days after that operation, I left for Cambodia. Under the auspices of the Khmer authorities, I went into the province of Svay Rieng to visit the Vietnamese village of Ba Thu, situated only a few meters from the South Vietnamese border inside Cambodian territory.

On December 30, 1966, with the justification that Ba Thu served as a refuge for the "Vietcong," the Americans attacked it in the same way as that Company of the 2nd Battalion of the 25th Infantry Division attacked the village in the district of Loc Tanh Trung. All the banana trees, the bamboos, and the palm trees had been mowed down or deeply marked at the height of a man by the bullets of the machine-guns. Nothing but blackened beams remained of six straw huts burned by rockets. Arriving at Ba Thu with their guns spitting fire, the Americans found no one there to welcome them. When I arrived the whole population was outdoors: hundreds of children, women, old men. I approached a group of little girls. Screaming with fright, they ran away. The village chief, visibly disturbed, said to me: "What do you want, they take you for an American!" At my approach, a little boy hid himself weeping behind his mother's legs. A woman of some 40 years collapsed in tears when I paused in front of her. The chief, taking me by the arm, showed me the individual shelter holes in the ground.

"When the Americans arrived, they threw grenades into the shelters. That woman's two sons were hidden at the bottom; they died at one stroke. A young woman of 20 and a man of 40 were also killed in this raid. We are still without news of ten men that the Americans took away with them in helicopters."

Was Ba Thu a "Vietcong" village? Lacking proof, I can't give an opinion. I was surprised by the individual holes, the earthen bunkers, and also by the fact that, among all the villagers who were gathered aroung me, there were practically no young men, between the ages of 15 and 30. The Khmer official who accompanied me said that the village had already been under South Vietnamese attack, two years ago, and the people thought it prudent to build shelters in case of eventual repetition. As for the young men, he said they were "in the country."

FOUR OLD MEN ARRESTED

Whatever the political affiliations of this village, even if it were "Vietcong," this hardly excuses the U.S. unit responsible for the violations of the territory of a sovereign country not directly engaged in the Vietnamese conflict.

When I had been with my Company at Loc Tanh Trung, I had not felt, as at Ba Thu, the horror of the attack against that little Delta village. I had not felt it because I was on the side of the attacker. I was not conscious of the tragedies, the destruction, that we caused. As I said before, I did not really believe at the moment that human beings could be hiding in the holes. I even found the blond corporal with the grenades rather likeable at the time.

And then, hadn't the American captain assured me that this village was the refuge for a Vietcong battalion? At the beginning of the attack I believed that the engagement was going to be between soldiers: Americans on one side, Vietcong on the other. But when I saw four old men in custody of a G.I. coming out of a house, I got my first surprise. Thin, with emaciated faces, shrunken, wretched, these men had not the look of combatants. They had been hiding in the piles of hay drying in the sun in front of the straw huts.

The four old peasants were brought before the captain. Their knees were knocking—they were terribly afraid. The officer tied their hands behind their backs, then called over one of the ARVNS—Vietnamese soldiers who always accompany the American units. "Dien, interrogate them."

For more than an hour, the militiaman, speaking harshly and shaking them, questioned the four men: "Where are they hidden? Come on, talk, or you will be killed!"

The foot-soldiers, glad for the respite, settled against the embankments and hungrily devoured the tins of turkey, of chicken with noodles, or of ham and beans in their C-Rations. Finally, the captain, tired of waiting, gave the signal to depart. We had hardly made our exit from the village when a brisk steady fire met us. Right near me, I saw a machine-gunner fall, hit by a bullet in the leg. The Vietcong had hidden themselves in ambush in the two thickets on both sides of the trail.

"Stop. Everyone flat on the ground."

Seizing the microphone of one of the four "wireless" sets constantly in contact with the Command Post of Rach Kien, the commander of the company gave the co-ordinates of the two thickets. One minute later, 105mm shells and 80mm mortar rounds began to rain down less than 50 meters from us, in the rhythm of one every four seconds, on the two objectives. The artillery fire lasted more than two hours without interruption. When the officer ordered three of his sections to the assault on the enemy's positions, I was sure that the G.I.'s would find only mangled corpses lying next to their bunkers. I was amazed to hear blasts upon the jump-off of the assault wave and saw four G.I.'s fall, wounded in the hips and the legs.

The two thickets were not occupied until very late in the evening. We found only some empty bunkers, several stained with blood. But not a body, not a weapon were discovered. We left the village and all night as we marched along the dikes separating the rice fields toward our Headquarters, we were harassed by snipers. This is an exact account of what is called "pacification." Why was it carried out? Simply because during night patrols in this sector, American soldiers had met with some shots. What was the real result of the "pacification" . . . ? A village destroyed; men, women and children, dead in the individual shelters, mangled by grenades; a few American soldiers wounded, and four old men carried off without reason, this was the sum total of the effort.

OPERATION "SCORCHED EARTH" IN THE IRON TRIANGLE

During my sojourn, the Americans began "scorched earth," operations in War Zone C, around Tay Ninh, along the Cambodian border, and in the "Iron Triangle"—that area encompassing about 100 square miles, situated scarcely 50 km. from Saigon, near the cities of Lai Khe, Ben Cat, Ben Sat and Ben Suc.

During "Operation Cedar Falls," I was at the front lines with the 173rd Airborne Division of paratroops who, just after the passage of the B-52's had drawn the mission of clearing the communication routes of mines and booby traps and to prevent ambushes of heavy material convoys.

Several days earlier at a press conference Major Stuart had told us correspondents that the G.I.'s were going to attack and destroy a Vietcong position which had, until then, remained untouched. This position was, according to the major, the Headquarters of the Vietcong Command for the Saigon sector. Filled with mines, tunnels, hiding-places, hospitals, underground dwellings, the targeted zone had existed since the time of the Vietminh and had never been attacked by the French.

Immediately after the announcement, I took the helicopter for Lai Khe, headquarters of the 1st Infantry Brigade, also dubbed the "Iron Brigade." There, in the shade of a plantation, near the planter's house which today houses the commanding general of the brigade, a young lieutenant explained to me, on a blackboard, the attack plan.

"The paratroops and the Cavalry are going to enter the 'Iron Triangle' on one side and will form, so to speak, the 'beaters.' Other units, including the 1st U.S. Infantry and the 5th South Vietnamese Infantry, will wait at the edge of the forest for the Vietcong who will be driven out."

I was having trouble grasping all his words as the artillery fire was constant and deafening.

"We are teasing the V.C.'s a bit while waiting for the B-52's," the officer explained to me.

"When are they coming?"

"This evening. You will have to stop up your ears."

The day before my arrival, reconnaissance planes had flown over the villages in the zone to be "cleared" and had dropped pamphlets ordering the population to take refuge immediately in a camp set up for them 12 km. away in the city of Phu Cong. They had also dropped safe-conduct passes for the Vietcong on which were written: "With this safe-conduct, you can give yourself up to any of the allied forces."

I was stretched out on a cot when the B-52's came, and the bombs began to fall. In all my life, I have not heard such a roar. When the B-52's bombard South Vietnam, all of Indochina trembles. Cambodians have declared to me that the tremors reverberate even to Phnom Penh, and that windowpanes rattle there.

The next day, with the 2nd Company of the 173rd Airborne, I landed in the section that had just been bombed. It was like traveling through a moon-scape. On several hectares, craters 15 to 20 meters in diameter and at least 8 meters in depth were crowded one on another.

"The bombs were dropped on what we thought to be the center of the Vietcong headquarters," I was told by Sig Holtz, the Company Commander. "The ground below must be full of tunnels. There can't be many survivors among the Vietcong."

The medical-corps captain who accompanied our regiment told me that, even 30 meters from the impact area of a bomb, one has no chance of coming out of it. The concussion makes skulls explode like fireworks. From this point on, we had to watch out for these bombs, making sure that the artillery and the small arms kept up a veritable screen of fire in front of us, zeroing-in some 20 meters ahead of the column.

After ten minutes, we reached the jungle. Other regiments were operating around us and the air whistled with the blasts which were going off in all directions. A village of straw huts was attacked and set afire without anyone taking the trouble to see if there were anyone in the houses. I learned then from the paratroops that several women had been burned alive, but I did not see this in the sector where I happened to be.

Two days later, when the heavy weapons and armor had joined us, three tanks were placed at the head of the column in order to open up the way. They were followed by half of our unit, the other half escorted three bulldozers which, at the rear, finished the work of the tanks. At the head, a dog-handler held the leash of a German Shepherd trained to hunt down Vietcong. Several times, the animal stopped, pricked up his ears, then led us to a tunnel entrance.

"There are V.C. alive down there," the handler would cry. "My dog only smells out the living ones."

Two men sprayed the tunnel entrances with machine-gun fire, before going in pistol-in-hand. Several enemy corpses were thus found. Often the tunnels were veritable labyrinths, several kilometers long. The specialists could not go to the end of them without risk. They lowered strings of T.N.T. which they fixed to the walls. Covered with mud they came back out and lit the fuse. In a single day, they blew up more than 30 tunnels. In certain hiding-places, one sensed that, in their panic, the occupants had not been able to carry away all their equipment. Ponchos were scattered around on the water-soaked ground. Several small cloth sacks, closed by strings, each contained a bowl and a pair of chop-sticks. Some cardboard parcels, the size of boxes of kitchen matches, and enclosed in a water-tight plastic wrapping, were piled up in a corner. I opened one of them. It contained novocaine, a plastic vial of medicinal alcohol, another of mercurochrome, adhesive tape and pills for dysentery.

A battalion which was operating near our company discovered two underground hospitals, on three levels, and captured a nurse. I don't know what became of the woman for I was unable to track her down in the prisoner camps of Phu Cong or Lai Khe, nor did I see the hospitals or any of the patients. A Negro corporal who was there told me later: "Everything was blown up."

Near Provincial Route 14 which separates the Iron Triangle into two portions, the U.S. High Command halted the operations. Some women who had taken refuge in the camp of Phu Cong after the attack began and who were frightened by the display of American force, had asked for authorization to return to look for their husbands and children. In spite of the mortar and 105mm shells which continued to fall on the unoccupied positions despite the theoretical end of operations, they disappeared into the foliage. They were told to tell those who wanted to give themselves up that, if they approached by the road without weapons, they would be well treated.

The next day, the women returned, accompanied by 15 guerrillas in black pajamas stained with mud, most of them hardly 18 years old. The battle resumed and lasted another ten days. All was shattered, burned, and crushed under the tons of bombs, under the caterpillars of tanks and the giant shovels of the bulldozers.

THE PHU CONG REFUGEE CAMP

The Iron Triangle took a heavy reckoning, 500 dead—without counting the victims of the B-52's that one cannot see—among whom are women, children, and especially, the adolescents who serve in the ranks of the Vietcong. There were 6,500 refugees crowded together under tents and behind barbed wire, as in a concentration camp. Some had been able to bring their water buffaloes, hogs or their chickens. Others lived on only the rice distributed "for free" by the Americans twice a day. Rice which is in fact part of the some 4,000 tons gathered up from the villages in the Iron Triangle.

What will become of those who now have no home? The rice-fields, left fallow for a long time, will not be cultivated again. Without doubt, many will remain at Phu Cong and will attach themselves to a patch of land too small to support them. Some will go to the periphery of Saigon, already overcrowded, and to live will join in the mad scramble for the dollar. The young women will prostitute themselves to help their families; some of them did not wait long to do it. I have seen them sell themselves for 100 piasters to the G.I.'s who pass in front of them—no other solution for survival is available to them. The mothers and the elder daughters often have to care for eight or ten children. As for the men in the camp, there are none under the age of 50: they are dead, prisoners, or in the Resistance.

In the Iron Triangle, the peasants managed to eke out a subsistance living on products of their farms, their cattle, the ricefields. Here at Phu Cong is a world where the piaster and the dollar are king: where without money one cannot live. It is necessary, therefore, to earn this money—no matter how—otherwise one dies of hunger. I am not going to dwell on the conditions of life in these camps. They are inhuman. Others have already said so, and I can confirm it.

AT RACH KIEN, THE POPULATION WAS DRIVEN FROM HALF
THE CITY

Rach Kien, in the heart of the province of Long An, on the
banks of the Saigon River, 21 km. from the capital, is one of
the rare cities of the Delta to be permanently occupied by the
U.S. forces. The 25th Infantry Division, stationed at Cu Chi,
installed its 2nd Brigade there. To this small town the helicopters of the 1st "Air Cav," stationed at An Khe, came to look
for the Company that had theoretically annihilated the Vietcong battalion in their fortress in the Loc Tanh Trung area.
For want of anything better, as we have seen, that company
had to content itself with taking away four old men: four old
men who were taken to the local prison, a straw hut surrounded by barbed wire, to be interrogated more methodically
than could be done on the battlefield. The Americans often
send prisoners into "reeducation camps." Often as well, they
entrust them to the South Vietnamese Special Forces who have
some effective methods for "reeducation."

Rach Kien was one of the first "strategic hamlets" created
by Ngo Dinh Nhu in 1959. At the time the Diemist regime believed that a system modeled on the methods used by the English in Malaysia would bring an end to the Communist guerrilla. He made a mistake. In Malaysia the majority of the
guerrillas were Chinese while the peasants were of the Malay-
sian race. Ethnic rivalries prevented any collusion between the
farmers and the revolutionaries. Therefore the strategy of the
transformation of the villages into fortified hamlets worked.
But in Vietnam the peasant and the Vietcong are not only of
the same race but often from the same locality. And in spite of
efforts taken to isolate the rural population from the "rebels"
collaborative solidarity was inevitable. Rach Kien, because of
the participation of the population in the revolt, fell at the
end of one year: the militia of Nhu were executed.

From that time on the city with its 5,000 inhabitants was the
most important village occupied by the N.L.F. in South Vietnam. Situated at a center of communications by river or land,

it was at once utilized as a clearing-house and resting place. Rice from the Delta and smuggled weapons were warehoused here before being forwarded by junk, by elephant, even by truck, to the provinces in the central region between Danang and Hue where the bloodiest engagements took place. These same junks would bring back the sick and wounded N.L.F. fighters who—even so near Saigon—would find quiet, more wholesome and abundant food, and better equipped hospitals than in the damp and gloomy underground dispensaries of the jungle.

That the Vietcong could hold an important area so close to the capital was a permanent source of embarrassment to the American Command. As soon as a sufficient amount of men and material could be mustered they hastened to change this. Beginning in 1965, when G.I.'s disembarked in great numbers in South Vietnam, Rach Kien was for several days pounded by artillery. Then, in the same way that the Company of the 2nd Brigade attacked the village of Loc Tanh Trung, waves of helicopters came. They landed all around the city and disgorged foot-soldiers who began to surround it house-by-house. Under the violence of the fire the Vietcong retreated. In order not to risk the decimation of the children, the women and the old men by air strikes, mortar fire and 105mm shells, the "VC" disengaged and dispersed to surrounding hamlets.

The U.S. soldiers then took possession of half the town and drove the population into the other half. All around their positions a network of bunkers, protected by sandbags were loaded with weapons and surrounded by anti-personnel mines that could be triggered electrically by the guards. On the demarcation line between the two areas, a soldier in a sentry-box checks the papers of the peasants who must cross the U.S. sector in order to go to the fields. In the evening a tank comes to squat in the middle of the road with its cannon and its 50mm machine guns zeroed-in on the center of the market-place. After 7:00 P.M. the Americans shut themselves up in their camp; as soon as night falls they shoot at everything that moves in the other quarter.

A colonel who received me in the map-room said, "Who would come when it gets dark, but 'Charlie' who we have chased out and who uses the darkness to visit his family."

The entire wall was papered with maps of the area. On one was written the word "Confidential." I saw Rach Kien, circled in red.

"What does this circle mean?" I asked the Colonel.

"It designates the sector within a radius of 12 km. of the Command Post that we are at present trying to pacify. The village of the district of Loc Tanh Trung that we attacked when you were with us is here inside the circle."

"And beyond, what is there?"

"Beyond," answered the colonel, "we have not enough men to go. We have to content ourselves with working-over those zones with cannon and mortars. Later on, perhaps, we'll be able to extend our pacification perimeter."

At the Market-Place of Rach Kien, women, children, old men sell or buy a few fish caught in the rice paddies or yellowish pork fat. In vain, I searched this miserable mass of people which has lived abandoned in degrading poverty in the midst of the enormous American war-machine looking for youths of 15, of 20, or men of 30. The only adolescents I ever saw were held on a leash.

Several hours earlier in the trenches, some 100 meters from the village, these boys had been lying in wait with gun in hand for the comings and goings of the G.I.'s. Perhaps it was one of them who, on the day of my arrival, had fired a bullet full in the face of two young U.S. recruits. They had not listened to the warnings of the colonel, who had enjoined them not to leave the security perimeter.

A punitive expedition was organized. Half of the brigade and a unit of General Ky's Special Forces left to sweep the countryside. The four Vietcong, not even 20 years old, were surprised by young Vietnamese who could have been their brothers. They were led to the center of Rach Kien. No trial, no sentence. It was 7:00—the American soldiers retired into their perimeter. The South Vietnamese mercenaries, one of whom had tattooed on his chest, "I kill Vietcong and I love my country," ordered the prisoners to kneel. The population was energetically encouraged to come and witness the spectacle. The young militiamen pulled machetes from their belts and with a sharp slash they decapitated the four Vietcong. Seeing my cameras, they held the bloody heads by the hair, placed cigarettes in the mouths, and cried to me:

"Come on, take photo, take photo . . ."

I have, as you know, submitted these photos to the Tribunal as evidence.

GENERAL KY'S VISIT TO THE AUSTRALIAN CAMP OF BARIA

I followed General Ky throughout the whole of a day when he visited Baria, the headquarters camp of 4,000 Australians engaged in the Vietnam War. He arrived in his own personal helicopter, elegant in a gabardine naval uniform. A detachment saluted him, and the commander of the camp shook his hand:

"Good morning, General, we are going to visit the camp."

After a stop for lunch at the officers' mess, the tour began at the emplacements of the 81mm mortars.

"Attention, 61, 10, 12 . . . Fire!"

Then came the 105's. At this point the officers gave us some cotton to stop our ears. Finally, the tour finished up with the 175's, which exploded with puffs of smoke far off in the distance.

When, a little later, I flew over the zones which had been so abundantly bombarded by the exhibition firing, I saw small black forms running in the rice-fields.

FROM HIS HELICOPTER THE GENERAL HUNTS VIETCONG

One morning, Lieutenant Colonel Sig Holtz, commander of our group, introduced me to his immediate superior, General Dane, who was visiting his command. Dane was a man of some 50 years, with young features, and a pleasing countenance.

"Do you know," said the lieutenant-colonel, laughing, "that, from his Iroquois helicopter, he likes to hunt the Vietcong with a rifle."

Surprised, I asked the general:

"How do you know which are the Vietcong?"

"If they are there, they can't be anything else."

"But, General, if there are women among them?"

"I never fire on the women."

"How can you tell in the forest if they are not women?"

"It *is* difficult. But the Triangle is surrounded with rice fields and they stand out in relief well."

AS RETALIATION THE SOUTH KOREANS MASSACRE THE ENTIRE POPULATION OF A VILLAGE

On the subject of the Koreans to whom Sergeant Duncan just alluded in his deposition, I wish to testify that their primary mission is to assure the proper functioning of the pipe-line which connects Pleiku to Qui Nonh. It seems that they fulfilled this mission perfectly, for the simple reason that each time that there were any incidents along the pipe-line, the South Koreans went into the nearest village to massacre the population indiscriminately at one fell swoop.

I have this information from several sources: a leading Vietnamese citizen from Saigon, a Vietnamese intellectual who, since the arrival of the Americans, no longer engages in any political activity, and especially from a high-ranking American officer who, with a laugh, said to me:

"What a pity that we don't have more South Koreans in Vietnam. The situation would be quickly changed."

PROSTITUTION IN SAIGON

"If one believes the proverb 'when the foundation goes, everything goes,' " a French missionary declared to me, laughing, "then everything is coming along fine in Saigon."

It is true: the allusion is perfect; buildings spring up everywhere. At peak hours Tu Do Street—formerly Catinat Street —and all the adjacent streets hold crowds as dense as in Paris. The girls have never been more charming as they seem in their long thin garments with their conical hats screening gracious smiles, which the realities seem not to have erased.

But in cold fact, for numerous families, the best way to escape poverty is to place one of their daughters in the home of a G.I. as a temporary wife. One young Vietnamese girl informed me of the rates: 20,000 piasters a month for the officers, 10,000 for the enlisted men, 6,000 for Koreans, Filipinos and Negroes. Some girls, to augment their wages, succeeded in "marrying" two or three G.I.'s simultaneously, she told me.

Prostitution is by far the most profitable job that a young girl can find. By careful management, she can earn a salary greater than that of a cabinet minister. But what is overlooked are the sordid details which accompany this kind of thing.

I was invited to the home of the parents of a friend, in the populated quarter of Saigon; a quarter where modern sanitation is unknown, where black-bristled hogs wallow in the mud of the streets. The mother, with tears in her eyes, told me the most horrible story that I have heard in all my career as a reporter. One of her nieces was scarcely 15 years old. Her father had been blown up by a mine a month earlier. Her mother, who had generalized cancer, was bedridden. In spite of all the assistance that the close-knit family tried to bring to this household, the six brothers and sisters were reduced to beg in order to live. One day the eldest girl learned that she could earn lots of money with the G.I.'s and began walking the streets.

"You will not believe me," murmured my hostess. "Three of them took her to a hotel. The little one did not dare to say anything. They killed her, monsieur. She was too young; she had a hemorrhage. Filled with panic, the three G.I.'s enclosed her in a container which they dumped off in the night, here, just across from my house."

CORRUPTION IN SAIGON

"Except for the prostitutes, no girl will walk in this street," the waiter of a popular café declared to me, adding, "My daughter is a teacher and draws a salary of 3,000 piasters a month, hardly the wherewithal for a bit of rice and fish. By selling herself to a G.I., she could make ten times more. She will not do it because she is honest, but this situation is intolerable. Whether they rape or whether they buy our daughters, the result is the same."

The filth which fills the streets of Saigon must serve as fertilizer to the bars, for they shoot up like mushrooms. The boutiques of Catinat Street, the little restaurants, go bankrupt. They are replaced by rooms with soft lights in the middle of which are large bars bordered with high stools. Every evening the windows of the "Sexy Club," "Soho Bar," "Piccadilly," etc., protected from hand grenades by a stout wire-netting, frame the same spectacle: G.I.'s sipping whisky perched on stools, holding outrageously rouged and primped young Vietnamese girls—almost children—around the waist.

And the brothel-building continues; there is no lack of clientele. With 500,000 G.I.'s, there are none to spare. The troops earn between 250 and 1,000 dollars a month, and there is nothing in the rice fields that they can spend them on. A real gold-mine flows into the tills of the proprietors of the night-clubs and the purses of the entertainers.

Every evening young South Vietnamese functionaries or officers, with scooters bought on credit, come to the nightclub area to compete with the cycles and the taxis. With motors running, they park in front of the night clubs, while searching for a G.I.: "Little girl . . . little boy . . . Come with me, I know where you can have a good time. 100 piasters." Without too much effort they can triple their monthly pay.

The Saigonese's way to be a good citizen, to further the economic and social progress of the country, is to find himself a G.I. He or she will become a temporary wife, rent him a room, wash his dirty clothes, polish his shoes . . . anything. A Vietnamese without a G.I. is doomed to the meager bowl of rice and piece of dried fish. There are many who wish that this situation would last forever. There is no sound economy in South Vietnam, but a fabulously rich American presence on which thousands of parasites have fastened and multiplied in direct proportion as the infrastructure of the country has collapsed.

South Vietnam was formerly one of the leading rice-exporters in South East Asia. Now, she is obliged to buy thousands of tons from other countries while the harvest rots in her own bomb blasted fields. With Malaysia, she had one of the most flourishing rubber growing industries in the world. Now the plantations serve as headquarters for American or Allied Infantry units. Others have been decreed "free fire zones" as I saw at Cu Chi, and every three seconds, 24 hours a day, heavy artillery furiously shells them, shattering the tree trunks. This is systematic destruction of what was once one of the primary national revenues.

Vietnam's exports value only $6 million. Her imports, however, amount to around 398 millions of dollars. The gross national revenue has risen to $280 million, but on the order of $300 million has been pumped in from the U.S. and caused rampant inflation. If you add to this figure the astronomical sums which the U.S. soldiers spend on the spot for their pleasure, it is not surprising to see the people are more interested in cutting themselves a piece of the cake than in applying themselves to essential tasks.

I had been in Saigon less than an hour when all—and more —that a stranger can wish for had been offered to me: a room in a private home (10,000 piasters), washing and ironing of my laundry (1,000 piasters a month), a woman (20,000 piasters).

When there is no longer an infrastructure in a country, everything is permitted. From the highest to the lowest on the social ladder, everything is permitted. From the highest to the lowest on the social ladder, everyone conjugates the verb "to extort." The well-placed bureaucrats deliver phony visas in return for hard cold cash. Others sell under-the-counter to Chinese agents sacks of rice given by some International Agency for relief distribution to the population. Still others, employed by the Americans, specialize in the theft of military supplies for resale in the black market out in plain sight. No one is shocked, not even the G.I.'s. I saw the proof when I went to the P.X. to buy a battle dress and jungle boots, indispensible for reporting from the rice fields. The quartermaster told me, very seriously:

"As for the battle dress, okay, we have it; but the boots, I haven't had any for at least the last 15 days. I send my boys to buy them on the black market. Do what they do."

From U.S. Senate, Committee on the Judiciary, *Hearings: Civilian Casualty, Social Welfare, and Refugee Problems in South Vietnam.* 90:1 (Washington, D.C., 1968), pp. 66–69, 75–76, 145. This subcommittee, over which Senator Edward Kennedy has presided, has produced much information on the civilian casualty toll in the war. This hearing was held throughout 1967. Don Luce is the former director of International Voluntary Services in Vietnam.

TESTIMONY OF DON LUCE

Today the refugee is in only a few cases fleeing Communist terrorism. In most cases he is either fleeing in fear of bombing or because he is being forced out because of allied military action to prevent a food source for the Vietcong.

I believe that in trying to destroy the infrastructure of the Vietcong we are actually destroying the infrastructure of the Vietnamese village itself or of the Vietnamese community itself.

Senator Kennedy. Would you say, Mr. Luce, that in winning the allegiance of the people that this might be self-defeating?

Mr. Luce. I say that in doing this we are losing the allegiance of the people, not only of the refugees themselves, but also of large, other larger, groups of people within Vietnam, because they see this happening, and it creates feelings of anti-Americanism within other groups, within student groups, even within, well, relatives of these people, and especially within the rural population of Vietnam.

The thing which the Vietnamese are most concerned about, if you meet—well, talking with a Vietnamese refugee woman and I asked her "What do you want most?" She said to be away from the bombing, and this is a very typical comment and a very common concern in rural Vietnam.

I think that we have to recognize the great fear that Vietnamese have of the bombing and the complete lack of understanding of where the free strike zones are often. Innocent people wander into them and then get killed and then even worse the wild rumors that get spread from person to person after some of these things happen, it makes us look very, very bad as Americans in Vietnam.

The real problem that I want to speak about this morning is that I think there are just too many refugees in South Vietnam for an already paper-thin Vietnamese administrative system to take care of.

The problem begins by a lack of preparation and planning for the refugees. Specific examples in Binh Dzuong, the Cedar Falls operation for the Iron Triangle. This was because, partly because, the operation was prepared so quickly, partly, I suppose, because of security. No one knew in advance of the operation and several thousand refugees were created before the Vietnamese authorities knew that it was going to happen. The result was that when the refugees were brought out, well, one very simple thing which was lacking was drinking water, which had to be trucked in and the problems of sanitation and distribution of this, and then this went across everything. People were just not prepared for these refugees.

In Quang Ngai Province, at one point, the Korean Army brought in 6,000 refugees. The only place for the refugees was in another refugee hamlet which was established and in good working order.

The director of one of the other voluntary agencies explained this to me, that they took a great deal of pride in this hamlet because everything was going well, and suddenly they found themselves instead of having one family in a 3 by 5 refugee hut they suddenly had five and six families. They were not able to feed the large number of refugees who suddenly came in. The school had to be closed because the refugees moved into the school to live, the dispensary was closed because the refugees moved in. The animals, the buffalo and cattle, which the refugees brought in ate the gardens, the bananas, this kind of thing, so that again because it happened so fast with so many refugees, that no preparation was made to take care of them.

The second problem which comes up is that because there are more, so many refugees there are not adequate facilities or adequate personnel to take care of them.

Most of the refugee hamlets, centers, lack schools, and particularly lack teachers. A solution of building more schools is not adequate because of the great lack of teachers to teach in these schools.

The medical facilities, the health centers, the biggest problem is that there aren't people to man the health centers if they build them.

Because of such a large number, the selection of sites has been particularly bad for refugees.

For example, a city, the mayor of Danang may not want more refugees into an already overcrowded city, so they will end up on a beach where the people who were once farmers cannot carry out agriculture any more.

If, say, a U.S. military commander may need additional laborers for Cam Ranh Bay, the airbase at Bien Hoa, and they will end up near the airbase, again they must leave their traditional occupations of agriculture and become laborers.

Probably the most serious thing which has happened in selection of sites has been the use of the refugees for, let's say, military or a strategic purpose.

Two specific examples of this, one is in the district capital of Dak To, which I visited about a year and a half ago. The district chief explained that the refugees there, he had placed them around his district headquarters to provide security for the district capital. His feeling was that the Vietcong would not be as apt to mortar the district headquarters if the refugees were built right around his headquarters, and it would be much more difficult for them to enter into the district headquarters if the villagers surrounded him.

In Cai Be, in Dinh Tuoung, is another place where they spread the refugee huts along the road to, in a sense, form a protection for the road; again in both cases the consideration being not to provide a better life in situation for the refugees, but the objective being to protect the road or to protect the district headquarters.

I think there are two reasons why there are almost no men in the camp. One is the very obvious thing because the men are with one army or the other. The other reason is that if there are some men left, and the army comes to move them, all of these men will try to leave and hide because anyone who is sort of between the ages of 16 or 17 and, well say, 45, would be considered a Vietcong suspect and as such put into jail, imprisoned and questioned and can expect that things would be very difficult for him. And the Vietcong, I am sure, have made great propaganda value of this, probably told them that they will be shot or something like this. So that if there are any men they will try to hide or something like this.

The present policies of, say, refugees, our present policies concerning refugees, are leading to more refugees than we can handle, creating resentment against us.

One, about a year ago, a Vietnamese friend told me that: (a) our policies regarding—we were speaking particularly of the free strike zones and bombing, he said these were "sai," were wrong, the Vietnamese word "sai." A year later he said they were "sau," or evil, and I think this indicates a great deal of the change within the feeling of perhaps a year ago that we were on the wrong track, that we would perhaps make changes and this kind of thing.

Today, there is a very general feeling that what we have gotten to is a very, very bad thing.

Some specific things which many Vietnamese feel that we don't recognize, they feel that, they say that a farmer is going to return to his fields and harvest his rice. We have to recognize that, and yet our policy of the free strike zone means that if his rice field is in one of the free strike zones and he is seen there he will be shot, and this has created a tremendous amount of resentment among people knowing that this is going to happen. Often the Vietnamese farmers do not know, there aren't any lines, there can't be lines, and he may not know what is a free fire zone and what is not.

The second problem is, say, with fishing, is that the fishermen are going to go where the fish are biting, and sometimes this happens to be within an area that is considered off limits. Again the Vietnamese fisherman navigates by instinct rather than by instruments, and may end up in waters that are considered off limits, and his boat may get shot.

I have touched on the refugee problem, which also, the second, the rural problem which is extremely serious is the problem of the use of herbicides for defoliants. Just a very specific example which I will use, one pertaining to refugees, is that in the An Khe Valley in April of 1966, our team member there reported to the military that the major problem that the farmers were having there was that their crops were dying as a result of defoliants. The Army made an investigation and nothing more was done.

In July of 1967, a year and two months later, a team member reported the major problem in An Khe Valley is the use of defoliants as far as growing crops. It has been reported to the military again. But throughout Vietnam, one of the biggest problems is defoliants used particularly along canals and along roads to destroy the vegetation and prevent setting up ambushes.

Well, unfortunately, farmers grow their vegetables along canals and roads because this gives them the best access to the market, and so that a great deal of damage is done to these things. It results in a great deal of semikill to the banana trees, coconut trees and so on, where there can be no estimate on the amount of damage. It is just that you get fewer coconuts and smaller coconuts because of a partial killer.

The most dramatic things of problems in cities, perhaps, is very widespread prostitution, which the Vietnamese are very upset about, very concerned about. It is a problem of families being torn apart when they see the moral standards of people going down, children begging on the streets. Not only children of poor families, but often children of very rich families will see this as a very easy and interesting way to get money enough to buy some candy or to get some candy or to get a Salem cigarette, this kind of thing.

Senator Kennedy. If this continues, Mr. Luce, what do you think will be the outcome?

Mr. Luce. My feeling is that we could settle today or 5 years from now for exactly the same kind of negotiated settlement. That if it continues that the resentment will continue to get more and more bitter, that the pressures to hold this down will become stronger and stronger on the people, and that probably finally the whole thing will explode. But there are very strong pressures on Vietnamese people now by the police and by the Army to keep them from demonstrating, and this kind of thing. There are, as you see in the papers every day now, sort of demonstrations being nipped in the bud on a daily basis. Some of them are against the Government, and many are specifically anti-American.

TESTIMONY OF ROGER HILSMAN, FORMER U.S. OFFICIAL

I think it goes against—these free fire zones and interdiction bombing, unobserved shelling of suspicious movement or of suspicious installations—does go against the principle that the effective way to deal with a guerrilla war is to win the allegiance of the people. I think this is a specific instance of what I meant that military measures in a successful counterguerrilla strategic concept must be subordinated to political measures, to winning the allegiance of the people.

I think it would be a mistake to think that the refugees come toward the Government side out of sympathy. I think many of them who have been bombed and shelled and leave their ancestral homes and villages for this reason come toward the Government side simply because the Vietcong do not bomb, and that they will not at least be bombed and shelled. I have greater worries that some of the refugee camps are rest areas for the Vietcong, precisely because of this.

OVER VIETNAM: AN EYEWITNESS REPORT
*Jonathan Schell**

This book is about what is happening to South Vietnam—to
the people and the land—as a result of the American military
presence. I shall not discuss the moral ramifications of that
presence. I shall simply try to set down what I saw and heard
first-hand during several weeks I spent with our armed forces
in South Vietnam last summer. What I saw and heard had to
do mostly with the destruction that was going on in South
Vietnam, but at the same time I found that the peculiar character of this war tended to be defined for me by how the men
in our armed forces reacted to the various special conditions
of the war: the immense disparity in size and power between
the two adversaries, the fact that Americans are fighting ten
thousand miles from home, the fact that the Vietnamese are
an Asian and non-industrialized people, the fact that we are
bombing North Vietnam but the North Vietnamese are incapable of bombing the United States, the fact that our bombing in South Vietnam can be met only by small-arms fire, the
fact that it is often impossible for our men to distinguish between the enemy and friendly or neutral civilians, the anom-
alousness and the corruption of the Saigon government, the
secondary role played by the South Vietnamese Army we are
supposedly assisting, the fact that the enemy is fighting a guerrilla war while we are fighting a mechanized war, and, finally,
the overriding, fantastic fact that we are destroying, seemingly
by inadvertence, the very country we are supposedly protecting. Like many Americans, I am opposed to the American
policy in Vietnam. As I came to know the American men who
were fighting there, I could feel only sorrow at what they were
asked to do and what they did. On the other hand, I could
not forget that these men, for the most part, thought they
were doing their duty and thought they had no choice, and I
could not forget, either, that they were living under terrible

* From Jonathan Schell, *The Military Half* (New York: Alfred A.
Knopf, 1968) , pp. 3–5, 14–16, 130–38, 142–45.

stress and, like fighting men in any war, were trying to stay alive and hold on to their sanity. If our country stumbled into this war by mistake, the mistake was not theirs. If our continuing escalation of the war is wrong, the guilt is surely not theirs alone. If one disaster after another is visited upon the Vietnamese people, these disasters are the inevitable consequence of our intervention in the war, rather than of any extraordinary misconduct on the part of our troops. Thousands of Americans, of course, have lost their lives or been wounded in Vietnam, many of them in the belief that they were fighting for a just cause, and some of the men I came to know in Vietnam will lose their lives or be wounded in that same belief. Some of our men have been brutalized by the war, just as I might have been brutalized if I had been fighting beside them, and just as men on both sides of all wars have been brutalized. Yet some of them have done the job assigned to them without losing their compassion for the noncombatant Vietnamese, or even for the enemy in combat. In this article, however, I am not writing, essentially, about the men in our armed forces. I am writing about a certain, limited segment of the war— about the destruction by the American forces, as I observed it (mostly from the air), of a particular rural area of South Vietnam. All of us must share the responsibility for this war, and not only the men who bear arms. I have no wish to pass judgment on the individual Americans fighting in Vietnam. I wish merely to record what I witnessed, in the hope that it will help us all to understand better what we are doing.

As I flew over the coast of Mo Duc District, where over ninety per cent of the houses had been destroyed, I asked the pilot about the people who had lived there, and he answered, "All the personnel that were down there were pretty much V.C."

The villages had been destroyed in many ways and in a great variety of circumstances—at first by our Marines and later by our Army. In accordance with the local policy of the 3rd Marine Amphibious Force, a village could be bombed immediately and without the issuing of any warning to the villagers if American or other friendly troops or aircraft had received fire from within it. This fire might consist of a few sniper shots or of a heavy attack by the enemy. Whatever the provocation from the village, the volume of firepower brought to bear in response was so great that in almost every case the village was completely destroyed. A village could also be destroyed if intelligence reports indicated that the villagers had been supporting the Vietcong by offering them food and labor, but in such a case the official 3rd Marine Amphibious Force rules of engagement required that our Psychological Warfare Office send a plane to warn the villagers, either by dropping leaflets or by making an airborne announcement. Because it was impossible to print rapidly enough a leaflet addressed to a specific village and specifying a precise time for bombing, the Psychological Warfare people had largely abandoned leaflet drops as a method of warning, and had begun to rely almost completely on airborne announcements. There was no official ruling on when troops on the ground were permitted to burn a village, but, generally speaking, this occurred most often after fire had been received from the village, or when the province chief had given a specific order in advance for its destruction. In some cases, the villagers had been removed from an area in a big-scale operation and then the area had been systematically destroyed. By the beginning of September, there had been two large Army operations of this kind. Five thousand inhabitants of the valley of the Song Ve were made to leave their homes. In Binh Son District, along ten kilometres of coastline south of the former village of Tuyet Diem, five thousand people were "extracted." But for the most part the destruction occurred sporadically and piecemeal, without a guiding plan. Although most of the villages in the province had been destroyed, the destruction of villages in large areas was not ordinarily an objective of the military operations but was viewed as, in the words of one official, "a side effect" of hunting the enemy.

On the second day, the 1st of the 101st began to spread out into the countryside in small units; several of them met heavy resistance from the enemy and suffered casualties. That night, the FAC pilots said that the unit ground commanders had called for an unusually large number of air strikes throughout the area of operation. The pilots described the targets to each other in terms of topographical features, or by coördinates on their maps, because they did not know the names of any of the towns or rivers in the area. One FAC pilot remarked that the units involved in Operation Benton must be "really kill-hungry," for three of the companies had chosen as code designations for themselves the names Cutthroat, Marauder, and Assassin.

On the morning of the third day of Operation Benton, I flew over the 1st of the 101st's area of operation with Major Billings, whom I had flown with during Operation Hood River. I saw that, except for two or three houses, the village of Duc Tan, which had stood below the evacuated command post, had been destroyed. Some groups of houses in Duc Tan had been completely annihilated by bombs; the only traces of their former existence were their wells or back gardens. Other houses had been burned to the ground by napalm. Most of the fields around the destroyed village had been eliminated by the deep craters of delayed-fuse bombs or else had been covered with debris. More craters were scattered across other fields in the Chop Vum area and across mountainsides, and the gray squares of freshly burned individual houses dotted most of the landscape. Major Billings told me that these houses had been burned by phosphorus rockets fired from helicopter "gunship" patrols. A few minutes later, I watched a gunship cruise low over the landscape. It wheeled suddenly and fired several phosphorus rockets into a group of three houses that stood in a clump of palms. White smoke puffed up, and the houses burst into flames. The helicopter circled and then charged the houses again, firing more rockets into the fields and gardens. Several hilltops and small mountains that had been green and wooded when I saw them three days earlier were burned black by napalm. Fresh artillery craters were spattered over the fields around the landing zones. At that point, approximately twenty per cent of the houses in the Chop Vum area had been destroyed.

Major Billings had been assigned to guide a "preplanned strike," but before he could locate the target on the ground a ground commander called for an "immediate" strike, which meant a strike carried out a few hours, at most, after it was requested, whether by a ground commander or by a FAC pilot. "We picked up some sniper fire earlier this morning from a couple of hootches down below us, at about 384 297, and we'd like you to hit it for us," the ground commander said. Major Billings flew over the hundred-metre square described by the coördinates, and found that it included the two large stone churches along the road, in the village of Thanh Phuoc. The ground commander was in charge of a hilltop landing zone that was a little over half a kilometre from the churches. When he had received the sniper fire, he had apparently scanned the horizon, noticed the two church steeples, which were the only buildings that stuck up above the lines of trees, and decided that the snipers were firing from the churches. In front of one church, a white flag flew from the top of a pole as high as the church itself.

"Let's have a look and see what's down there," said Major Billings. He took our plane on a low pass over the churches. The churches were surrounded by twenty or thirty houses. About half of these had stone walls and red tile roofs. The others had clay-and-bamboo walls and thatched roofs. One thatch-roofed building was perhaps fifty feet long and thirty feet wide, and appeared to be some sort of gathering place. Flower gardens were in bloom in front of both churches. Behind both, plots of vegetables stretched back through glades of palm trees to rice fields. After climbing to fifteen hundred feet again, Major Billings got into contact with the ground commander and said, "Two of those structures seem to be structures of worship. Do you want them taken out?"

"Roger," the ground commander replied.

"There seems to be a white flag out front there," Major Billings said.

"Yeah. Beats me what it means," the ground commander replied.

An hour later, three F-4 fighter-bombers reached the target area, and the flight commander radioed to Major Billings—who had spent the time trying to spot suspicious activities—to say that they were prepared to strike with seven-hundred-and-fifty-pound bombs, rockets, and 20 mm.-cannon strafing fire.

"We can use all that good stuff," said Major Billings.

"What kind of a target is it?" asked the flight commander.

"They're military structures. You can tell by how they look that they're military structures," Major Billings answered. Just then a fleet of ten helicopters moving in tight formation arrived at the hilltop landing zone. Major Billings went on to say that he would have to wait until the helicopters left before he gave clearance to bomb.

I asked him whether he thought it was necessary to bomb the churches.

"Well, if the V.C. don't care and just go in there and use the place to fire on our troops, then we've got to wipe it out," Major Billings said. "And the V.C.—the V.C. are *the first ones to blow up a church*. They go after the churches on purpose, because the churches won't always go along with what the V.C. are doing. *They* don't care at all about blowing up a church and killing innocent civilians."

As the helicopters rose from the hilltop, Major Billings said to the flight commander, "Believe it or not, two of those big buildings down there are churches. I'll check with the ground commander again to see if he wants them taken out."

"No kidding!" said the flight commander.

"Say, do you want those two churches hit down there?" Major Billings asked the ground commander.

"That's affirmative," the ground commander replied.

"O.K., here goes," said the Major. Then, addressing the F-4 pilots, he said, "Make your passes from south to north. I'll circle over here to the west."

The Major brought the O-1 into a dive, aiming its nose at

the village, and fired a phosphorus rocket. Its white smoke rose from a patch of trees fifty yards to the south of one church. "Do you see my smoke?" he asked the flight commander.

"Yeah, I got you," the flight commander said. "I'll make a dry run and then come in with the seven-hundred-and-fifty-pounders."

A minute later, an F-4 appeared from the south, diving low over the churches in a practice run. As it pulled out of its dive, it cut eastward and began to circle back for the next pass. A second F-4 made its dive in the same way, and released its bombs. A tall cloud of brown smoke rolled up from the vegetable garden in back of one of the churches.

"That's about a hundred metres off," Major Billings said. "See if you can move it forward."

"O.K. Sorry," the flight commander said.

The third plane also sent its bombs into the vegetable garden. The first plane, on its second pass, sent its bombs into rice fields about sixty yards to one side of the churches. Three pillars of brown smoke now rose several hundred feet in the air, dwarfing the churches and the houses. On the second plane's second pass, a bomb hit the back of one church directly—the church with the white flag on the pole in front.

"Oh, that's nice, baby, real nice," Major Billings said. "You're layin' those goodies right in there!"

When the smoke cleared, the church was gone except for its façade, which stood by itself, with its cross on top. The white flag still flew from its pole. The third plane sent its bombs into the rice fields to the side. The first plane fired rockets on its third pass, and they landed in the vegetable garden behind the destroyed church, leaving it smoking with dozens of small brown puffs. Several of the rockets from the next volley hit the other church, obliterating its back half and leaving two holes the size of doors in the roof of the front half. Four or five of the houses around the church burst into flame.

"That's real fine!" said Major Billings.

"Where do you want the twenty mike-mike?" asked the

flight commander. ("Twenty mike-mike" is military slang for 20-mm.-cannon strafing fire, which fires a hundred explosive shells per second.)

"Lay it right down that line you've been hitting," Major Billings said. "Put it right down across those hootches, and we'll see if we can start a few fires." (Strafing rounds often set houses on fire, whereas bombs rarely do.)

As one of the F-4s made the first strafing run, the path of fire cut directly through the group of houses around the churches, sparkling for a fraction of a second with hundreds of brilliant flashes.

"Goody, goody! That's right down the line!" exclaimed Major Billings. "Why don't you just get those hootches by the other church, across the road, now?"

"Roger," answered the flight commander.

On the second strafing pass, the flashing path of shells cut across the group of houses on the other side of the road.

"Real fine!" Major Billings said. "Now how about getting that hootch down the road a bit?" He was referring to a tile-roofed house that stood in a field about a hundred yards to the west of one church. The path of fire from the third strafing pass—the final pass of the strike—cut directly across the house, opening several large holes in its roof.

"Right down the line!" Major Billings said. "Thanks, boys. You did a real fine job. I'm going to give you ninety-per-cent Target Coverage."

"Did I get any K.B.A.s?" the flight commander asked. (The number of killings credited to each pilot is not kept as an official statistic, but most pilots try to keep track of their K.B.A.s informally.)

Major Billings, who told me he had not seen any people in the area, either before or during the strike, answered, "I don't know—you'll have to wait until ground troops go in there sometime. But I'd say there were about four."

As the two men were talking, perhaps a dozen houses in the strafed area began to burn. First, the flames ate holes in the roofs, and then they quickly spread to the walls, turning each house into a ball of flame. Most of the houses burned to the ground within a few minutes, leaving columns of black smoke rising from the ruins.

Major Billings called Chu Lai to give his Bomb Damage Assessment Report. "There were two Permanent Military Structures Destroyed, ten Military Structures Destroyed, and five Damaged," he said.

I asked him whether he considered the houses and the churches military structures.

"Oh, that's just what we call them," he replied.

A few minutes later, the ground commander on the hilltop got in touch with Major Billings to request another immediate strike. "There's a row of bunkers down below our hill here, along a tree line, and we've seen the V.C.s down there," the ground commander said. "We see their heads poppin' in and out. We'd like to get an air strike put in down there."

Major Billings flew over the spot the ground commander had indicated, and found a line of trees about half a kilometre from the hill. The dark openings of several bunkers showed on the near side, and a row of several houses was standing on the far side.

"I've got you," Major Billings said. "Do you want us to put 'em in along that tree line down there? There are a couple of hootches down there, too."

"Affirmative. We've been getting trouble from that whole general area down there."

"O.K.," said Major Billings wearily, pronouncing the first syllable long and high, and the second low. "We'll do that as soon as the fighters come in."

Three F-4s arrived in the area twenty minutes later, and the flight commander announced that they were carrying napalm and thousand-pound bombs, which are the largest normally used in South Vietnam.

The first bombs of the strike landed about a hundred metres off target. One bomb turned an entire rice field into a crater about thirty-five feet across and six feet deep, and splashed mud over the surrounding fields. The next two bombs annihilated two houses with direct hits. Two more bombs landed next to the tree line, breaking most of the trees in half and hurling one palm tree fifty or sixty metres into a field.

"O.K., you got that tree line real good," Major Billings said. "Now let's get some of those hootches to the south of it with the napes." He directed the pilots to a group of a dozen houses that stood about forty yards from the tree line. The first canister landed beside two houses, which were instantly engulfed in napalm. When the smoke cleared, only the broken, blackened frames of the houses remained in the intense blaze, which continued after the houses were burned to the ground, because the napalm itself had not yet finished burning.

"Beautiful!" cried Major Billings. "You guys are right on target today!"

The next canister did not land directly on any of the houses, but it landed close enough to splash napalm over four of them, and these houses immediately burned down.

With the strike completed, Major Billings told the fighter-bomber pilots, "I'm giving you a hundred-per-cent Target Coverage. Thank you very much. It's been a pleasure to work with you. See you another day."

"Thank *you*," the flight commander answered.

Captain Leroy had been given the coördinates of two pre-planned strikes, and these turned out to be situated on the southern and eastern flanks of the hill that had been evacuated by the command post on the first day of the operation. The southern flank was heavily wooded, and the first air strike, which consisted of both napalm and bombs, blew several gaping holes in the trees, but no further effect was visible. The eastern flank, a broad, gently inclined slope, was terraced at its base and wooded above that, except for the summit, which was blackened and bald, having been bombed and burned during the L.Z. prep. Halfway up the eastern flank, where the terraced fields came to an end, small paths curved up to several groups of three or four houses ranged around courtyards in small clearings in the woods. Starting at the base of the hill, Captain Leroy guided the F-4s up the slope, giving instructions to the pilots to "get those hootches." Napalm splashed on two groups of houses, and they immediately began to burn, but a number of napalm canisters landed far from their mark, and Captain Leroy was displeased with the performance as a whole.

As though to set things right, he announced to me, "O.K., now it's *my* turn to get me a hootch," and brought the plane into a dive and lined up in his front windshield a group of houses that were about three hundred yards from the original target area. He fired a rocket—the only one he had left—and white smoke puffed up about twenty yards from the houses. "Damn! Missed!" he exclaimed. But about thirty seconds later the houses burst into flames. "Hey, I got it!" he said, in a surprised voice. "It must be as dry as hell down there."

Three people ran out of one house and along a narrow path toward a line of trees, where they disappeared from sight. "Look! See those people?" Captain Leroy said. "They're running for their bunkers. See the bunkers where they're running to?"

He reported to Chu Lai that six military structures had been destroyed.

A minute later, I asked him if he judged that the people who had run out of the house were members of the Vietcong.

"All the innocent civilians have had a chance to get out of here if they wanted to," he answered. "They're always warned. I saw a Psy War plane dropping leaflets."

I asked where all the civilians that had left had gone.

"Oh, they go to friends' houses—places like that," he said.

I remarked that there had been almost no people in sight on the roads since the operation began.

"They got out before the operation began," he said. "Look. Those villages are completely infested with V.C., just like rats' nests, and the only solution is to burn them out completely. That's the only way we can do it."

Captain Leroy continued to circle, watching the countryside below.

A few minutes later, a flight commander called him on the

radio. "We've got some twenty mike-mike up here left over from another strike, and we wondered if you could use it anywhere," the pilot said.

"I'll check with the ground commander," Captain Leroy answered, and he did so, whereupon the ground commander said he would check with his unit commanders. Ten minutes later, he called back and said, "They don't have any place you can use it right now, but I wondered if you could put it on top of the old command post to explode any artillery shells that are still up there, so that the V.C. can't get them."

Captain Leroy directed the fighter-bombers to the target. The 20-mm.-cannon shells sparkled briefly on the hilltop as the planes made three passes, but there were no secondary explosions.

As Captain Leroy turned back to Chu Lai, his radio picked up a conversation on the ground.

A voice from a ground unit said, "We killed four V.C. this morning, sir. We turned around and saw that these guys were following us. They saw that we had spotted them, and we fired, and they took evasive action. We got all four of them, though. They didn't have weapons, but they were wearing the short V.C.-type black-pajama uniforms, and they were definitely of military age. No question about that, sir."

On the way back to the base, I asked Captain Leroy how the FAC pilots liked their assignment in Vietnam.

"At the beginning, they'd probably prefer to be zooming around in the F-4s, but after they get the FAC assignment, they like it all right. There's no complaining," he answered.

This remarkable description of what it is like to be under American air attack is one of the very few available, and it was written for the Japanese newspaper *Asahi Shimbun*. It is taken here from the collection of Mr. Honda's dispatches, *The National Liberation Front (So-called "Viet Cong")* (Tokyo: Committee for the English Publication of "Vietnam—A Voice from the Villages," 1968), pp. 43–45.

TERROR FOR HELICOPTERS

Katsuichi Honda

The village had been attacked by gunships (armed helicopters) many times. We could clearly see the helicopter in the air through nipa palm leaves as it kept machine gunning and shooting rockets at the nearest hamlet while circling it. This didn't seem so dangerous to us because we knew what the helicopter was aiming at and we had time to take refuge. What was most terrifying was to have a helicopter attack you suddenly on a whim after you thought it was going to pass you by.

One evening at about six o'clock, I was listening to a BBC broadcast from London on the radio I had borrowed from Mr. Thieu. A helicopter was coming straight from the north in the twilight. We were not being especially careful because many helicopters came and returned overhead that day. Suddenly, we heard a blast just about our house. A rocket! Startled, we ran to the air-raid shelter. Mr. Thieu, who had been lying in a mosquito net, jumped into the shelter faster than a chased rabbit and got there before we did. Just then there was a big bang and the vibration of an explosion coming from the nipa palm thicket just behind us.

We felt relieved. It would have been too late for us to take refuge if it had hit the house. We were amused at remembering how Mr. Thieu had leaped into the shelter, but we were also greatly impressed by the remarkable rapidity of his reflex movements. The radio, left behind under the mosquito net, was broadcasting U.S. Army announcements: "About 50 Viet Cong were killed in skirmishes in the Mekong Delta, while U.S. casualties were light with four soldiers dead and . . ."

Again, many farmers would be killed.

One day, at half past six, as it was getting dark we lit metal hand lamps. A boy guerrilla and his little sisters from a farm house near-by were enjoying a visit with us. Feeling uneasy about a helicopter approaching from the northwest, I peeped out of a crack in the nipa palm wall. A signal light was rapidly drawing near, when suddenly red points began shooting out of the side of the helicopter. A machine gun sweep!

"They're firing!" I yelled in Japanese, and this time I was the first to jump into the shelter, followed by all the others. The sound of machine guns was like someone banging on galvanized iron. Bullets were splashing the water in the paddy field, and piercing the palm leaves. It was a passing event. The shelter was jammed with men like a commuter train full of passengers. The gun muzzles must have been pointed down vertically to the course when firing began, so the bullets came to the hut simultaneously with the helicopter and this happily gave us time enough to take refuge. The little sisters hurried back to their home.

About thirty minutes later, we heard a helicopter approaching from the opposite side, and Mr. Thieu went out to see it. As soon as the shape appeared over the black shadow of a palm thicket he ran back, saying, "Put the lights out!" Blowing out the lights, we ran to the entrance of our shelter. It was pitch-dark and I made a misstep and knocked my head hard against the packed dirt of the shelter. I saw stars and at the same time heard the sweep of machine guns. At that moment, I thought, "This is it!"

Passing over us, the helicopter flew away firing at random at farm houses along the canal about 500 yards from the hut. I could see the lines of fire distinctly since tracers were used.

They seemed to fire whimsically and in passing even though they were not being shot at from the ground nor could they identify the people as NLF. They did it impulsively for fun, using the farmers for targets as if in a hunting mood. They are hunting Asians. Perhaps the reason why such whimsical firing occurred around sunset was that they felt like using up remaining bullets allotted to them that day before they got back to the base. This whimsical firing would explain the reason why the surgical wards in every hospital in the towns of the Mekong Delta were full of wounded.

The next day, bombardment by gunboats on the Mekong was heavier than usual. Early in the morning, we saw about ten shells fall near the edge of the paddy fields and palm thicket about 500 yards from our hut. That evening, the guns fired continuously almost like a lot of small arms. They seemed to be firing as if beating time, seven or eight times every ten seconds. The villagers living near the Mekong were more afraid of gunboats than they were of helicopters.

This account of the Son My massacre appeared in the May 27, 1968, issue of *Viet Nam Courier*, published in Hanoi and circulated throughout the world. It understates the actual deaths, but the larger account was amplified in the U.S. press over a year later. The Vietnamese have also released voluminous documentation on similar crimes.

SON MY MOTHERS CALL FOR VENGEANCE

The Women's Committee for Liberation of Son My village, Son Tinh district, Quang Ngai province (South Viet Nam), has just denounced the massacre of 502 people, most of them women and children, perpetrated by U.S. troops on March 16.

The unheard-of savagery and magnitude of the massacre were denounced in a letter sent to the PLAF fighters calling on them to exact vengeance. The letter gave the following details:

"At 6:30 A.M. on March 16, 1968, all the enemy batteries installed around Son My started pounding the village for more than half an hour. The eleven choppers came in, strafing the locality and landing American troops whose sanguinary intention was visible on their faces. They shot at all that came in sight: men, women, children, elderly people, plants and animals, and destroyed everything: crops, fruit-trees, houses . . .

"The inhabitants, who were going about their work, setting off for market or for fishing, had hardly time to run to safety when the GIs came and fell on them.

"Vo Thi Phu, mother of a 12-month-old baby, was shot dead. She had only time to say to Tuyet, a 12-year-old girl, 'Tell my husband that my savings are hidden under the door step and he should take good care of our child.' The baby, which tried to suck at its mother's breast, cried when it found only blood instead of milk. The Yankees got angry and shouted 'Viet Cong, Viet Cong,' and heaped straw on mother and baby and set fire to it.

"Other GIs pulled Mui and Mot out of their trench, beat them, threw into the same trench and blew it up with a mine:

the two women and four children of theirs were killed.

"In another shelter, Mrs. Trinh and a child were found dead, their bodies cut into halves and horribly maimed by a mine explosion. Duc, a lad, tried to escape but was killed at the entrance of his shelter.

"Little Lien took refuge in a trench with her grandparents. When her grandma was killed, she urged her grandad to move to another shelter but received no answer: he was also dead. Panic-stricken, she ran to Mrs. Mai and Mrs. Thi's, two blind women, but found them killed together with eight other people.

"In another house, she saw Mrs. Mot sitting on the edge of a shelter, and called to her: the old woman had received a bullet in the forehead and had died. Little Lien also found the inert body of Mrs. Minh, her head leaning against the shelter wall, her eyes staring. She ran toward Mrs. Ngan: that pregnant woman died after she had been raped by the GIs. Her four children were also killed on the edge of their shelter. Then Lien rushed to Mrs. Vo Thi Mai, who had just had her baby: she was dead, and her child in an agitated state by her.

"Lien rushed from place to place, shouting at the top of her voice, but got no reply: she only saw dead bodies and burning huts. Never will she forget such horrible scenes.

"In Lang hamlet, at the foot of Hon Voi hill, the U.S. aggressors committed monstrous crimes.

"After raping to death Mrs. Sam, a sexagenarian, the aggressors made a deep slash in her body with a bayonet. Mrs. Lien, who hid in a cupboard, was brought out and killed. Her body was found 4 days later.

"Mui, 14, was raped and shut in her hut. The GIs set fire to it, guarded the door and pushed back the poor little girl who tried to run from the fire.

"Phung Thi Ly, a young mother of four, received a burst of machine-gun shots. She said to her mother, 'I'm going to die. Take care of my two children who are in the shelter.' Mustering her strength, she shouted, 'Down with U.S. imperialism!' before breathing her last, lying on her back, fist closed and hugging two of her children who died of wounds on their breasts.

"Worse still, the aggressors threw over one hundred women and children and many dozen old people into a canal dug in front of Mr. Nhieu's house and murdered them with machine-gun fire and hand grenades. The victims' corpses were disfigured beyond identification and a common grave had subsequently to be dug by the survivors for them all."

The letter concluded:

"In one day only, 502 people including over 170 children were massacred, 300 houses destroyed and over 870 head of cattle killed.

"Our coastal village so green with coconut palms, bamboos and willows is now but heaps of ashes."

THE TOMBS OF BEN SUC

Jonathan Mirsky

In the first fortnight of January, 1967, the village of Ben Suc, north of Saigon, was obliterated by bulldozers. The 3,800 Vietnamese villagers were disposed of in various ways: forty were shot when they tried to flee the encircling American forces, 100 "Vietcong suspects" were taken away to prison, the rest were bundled off in trucks and landing barges down the Saigon River to a refugee camp. All this was done to eliminate what *The New York Times* called an "embarrassing problem" for the Saigon government. Also, it was designed to provide additional room to maneuver for the First Division during Operation Cedar Falls which swept back and forth across the Iron Triangle.

During August I saw the Iron Triangle and Ben Suc, talked to the Vietnamese survivors of Cedar Falls, and interviewed some of the participating Americans. The lessons of Ben Suc are numerous and many of the protagonists have learned them very well.

The largest American base near Ben Suc is Bien Hoa, less than 20 miles from Saigon. The night before I went out to Bien Hoa to visit an American friend at Third Corps Headquarters, I had a drink with a young technician stationed in Vietnam to assist in the installation of navigation equipment at the Saigon airport. He filled me with stories of *American* ineptitude and *Vietnamese* skill (a switch from the usual anti-Vietnamese ear bending one endures in Saigon) and ended the evening by leaning forward and murmuring confidentially: "Professor, you know what? Most Americans out here are too blind stupid to see it, but all Vietnamese have written invisibly on their chests 'I am a Vietnamese. I am a human being. Please treat me as such.' "

With this admonition still in my ears I drove down to Bien Hoa with a friendly AID man who was to deliver me to my host. In his fresh cords and neat tie he could have been catching the 8:24 from White Plains—except for the pistol I spot-

ted in his attaché case. Ben Suc lay heavily on my mind and
it turned out that my companion had been in charge of the
refugees on January 8 when the operation began. My acquaint-
ance of the evening before might have been pleased by the
AID man's compassion: "Ben Suc was about the nicest, lushest
village you ever saw. There were shade trees and big houses
with tile roofs, strong cattle and hard ferry landings so the
people could bathe on the banks of the river." He asserted,
however, that the 3,800 villagers were "mostly VC families,
and had been for twenty-five years."

A great problem for those planning the operation, he said,
was that no refugee camp could be set up beforehand: to do
so would have tipped the hand of the planners. The "refugees"
(Webster says: "Refugee . . . one who flees to a place of
safety") with their animals and belongings found themselves
transported initially to shelters holding ten families, each family in 10 x 20 feet. "Several hundred people," he said, have "fil-
tered back" to the Ben Suc area, although it is now a Free Fire
Zone (anything moving is an unquestioned target) in which
they "must take their chances." Ben Suc is not a "secure area."

What then, I asked, was accomplished? He replied that an
assembly point had been "denied" to a VC battalion and that
a significant VC Headquarters may have fallen as well. He
hadn't seen the refugees since six days after the investing of
Ben Suc ("I wasn't on that job too long") but he believed
their accommodations to be better than before. Also, "the Vietnamese, unlike Europeans, are very capable refugees."

When I arrived in Bien Hoa, I discovered that my old
friend was now a very important AID man in Third Corps
(twelve provinces) operations. And he, too, had played a significant role at Ben Suc. He plunged straight into accounts of
the raid given by the *Times* and *The New Yorker* (journals
much maligned as "trouble making" by his colleagues) , which
he regarded as generally accurate. All refugee operations are
horrible, he agreed, remarking further that he might justly be
convicted as a war criminal for his role in this one. But after

all, "it was best for all concerned if the villagers were moved." Contradicting his colleague with whom I had just driven out, he insisted that any idea of Ben Suc as a prosperous village was "bullshit"; he mentioned particularly that there were no schools.

"All refugee movements are miserable, but this was the most successful in the history of the world," because the people were allowed a long time to move and could bring their animals. The AID people were forced, he said, to argue fiercely against the army's scheme for Ben Suc: to knock out all 3,800 villagers with gas sprayed from the air, and let them wake up after they had been carted unconscious to a "secure" site. My friend told me he insisted during the operational planning that this would create 3,800 "instant Vietcong," and persuaded the top echelon to allow a peaceful move over an "extended period." Naturally, some people in Ben Suc were VC and tried to escape, which explains the shootings and imprisonments. But it was not true, he continued, that the village was VC; it was basically "friendly—with a VC infrastructure of course." The army spread the story of Ben Suc being a Vietcong village in order to make its destruction more acceptable in America.

I announced that I wished to visit the Ben Suc area to see what remained. My friend, who had already offered me every facility including a personal helicopter, replied that Ben Suc was now a "hotly contested area, a Free Fire Zone," and that if I landed I wouldn't last fifteen seconds.

What, I wanted to know, was gained by the removal of the 3,800 people eight months before? "They were saved from the cross fire of war."

An hour later I was flying—or rather swooping—over the Iron Triangle. Under normal circumstances a three-man helicopter must be man's most marvelous form of locomotion, diving and soaring, hovering and banking high and low. It offered me a horribly perfect and perfectly horrible view. The term Iron Triangle is journalese. Far from being a Maginot Line-like area, it is—or rather was—many square miles of flat, delta farming country, full of trees, paddies, ponds, streams, dikes and—once—villages and people. Colors of brilliant green and earth brown predominated.

All is changed. The Americans have, as my pilot said, "lowered the vegetation." Thousands of trees have been knocked over to afford vast "fields of fire." The paddies, now rusty metallic colors, were sprayed to prevent further rice planting, and are full of gigantic B-52 bomb craters, shell holes from the constant cannonading, and dive-bomb holes. Operation Cedar Falls, begun more than eight months ago, has settled into day after day of constant pounding from artillery and air, turning the whole once fertile shimmering farmland into a moonscape, in which the only human remains are the stone tombs of the Vietnamese which used to surround the villages.

The irony is that the First Division still hardly dares venture into the area. My helicopter scooted through a steady barrage, saved from a shell below or a bomb above because the pilot constantly alerted Forward Observers about our course. Somehow, miraculously, magically, despite the hourly battering that must make their teeth rattle, the Vietcong lurk in their holes, caves and tunnels, eating and drinking God knows what, but prepared to shoot anyone who ventures into what is clearly acknowledged to be their terrain. That explains why I was told not to land at Ben Suc.

Everything, I suppose, is relative. As we flew over this lunatic wasteland my pilot said: "One year ago this was strictly Victor Charlie. Now, it's calmed down considerably." About thirty seconds later he added: "Chances are if we have to make a forced landing it would be quite a while before the VC got to us. Plenty of time for a rescue."

Then we were over Ben Suc. All the reports are right. There is nothing there. Great brown bulldozer swirls replace the village. The pilot spoke in my ear: "I walked down there—there used to be a street—and saw the people sitting in front of their houses." We hovered, moved slightly, hovered again. We were about 100 feet up and I had to battle a sudden urge to leap from the helicopter onto the bulldozer scars as a—useless—apology to the 3,800.

Before I could unbuckle myself we were shooting back the way we came. The pilot continued, ever helpful and instructive: "We bomb the paddies by day to deny food to the VC . . . as a matter of fact we destroy pretty much anything that might be useful. Those B-52 raids are something. You never know when they're coming. They can't be heard. Too high. Sometimes we bomb at night, so Charlie's out harvesting and suddenly the whole world falls in around his ears."

As we flew across the Saigon River and over "friendly" territory, the contrast was startling. It was the "before" part of the picture: neatly articulated rice paddies, canals, the normal colors of nature, plenty of trees, and amongst the trees—*people,* in hamlets and villages, densely strung together. "Lowering the vegetation" entails more than knocking down coconut palms.

But the refugee settlement at Lai Chu is not like a Vietnamese village in any respect, whether in environment, arrangement of houses or population make-up. Villages in this part of Vietnam are typically somewhat random in layout, interspersed with trees, bushes, gardens, ponds and grass. The gridlike pattern of Lai Chu in its grassless, treeless, waterless, red-brown setting deceives the airborne observer into thinking he is looking down on an army camp. Five hundred and eighteen families live here in cement-block, aluminum-roofed, one-room "dwellings" (the official word), each backed by a small garden.

The two Americans in charge are fully dedicated to the welfare of the refugees—they must be to live in this bare and unpleasant place, housed in trailers and living on tinned PX food. I was taken round by one of the Americans, a recent junior college graduate and Navy veteran of Vietnam, now married to a Vietnamese. He is employed by the International Rescue Committee.

The people of Lai Chu built their own houses with American-supplied materials. For their labor they were paid in American cooking oil, which they exchanged in the neighboring village for other goods. Why, I asked, were they not paid in cash? "There isn't any. Besides, this way the oil gets onto the market and everybody's happy." (I used to hear the same explanation in Taiwan for why U.S. AID powdered milk was allowed to be sold—it "got into the economy.")

Each family in Lai Chu had received a plot of land from the government. To the surprise of the Americans, only 100 of the 518 families have claimed their deeds. "They don't seem enthusiastic about farming." I soon learned that more than half the families are without menfolk; many are in jail, the NLF, the ARVN or dead. Furthermore, there is little water at Lai Chu and these people are rice farmers. The Americans want them to cultivate peanuts and sweet potatoes, which meets with little response although the tools and seeds are waiting.

The young American seemed genuinely troubled that the people of Lai Chu do not claim or work their land. A good deal of international concern arose over Ben Suc and dozens of visitors arrive to see what has become of the villagers. The camp is supposed to be a model, a "showcase." I said that I saw no reason why the refugees should trust the Americans or do anything they suggest, since it is we who destroyed their homes and uprooted their lives. He looked hurt. "But we tell them we don't work for the U.S., or for Saigon. We just want to help them."

During our conversation two American enlisted men who have formed an attachment to Lai Chu showed up with a truckload of scrap lumber. All of the visible men—about four, none of whom was young—scrambled onto the truck, and began dropping the enormous boards onto the ground while a crowd of women and children watched, standing carefully in the meager shade of their houses to avoid the sun's glare. The boards would be used to improve the interiors of their houses. I stood with the people and asked them questions about their lives.

Were they getting enough rice? No, they weren't. Back at Bien Hoa I had been warned not to believe this "inevitable" story, it was only a "gripe" . . . except that the young American agreed with them. They were *"supposed* to be getting it from the Province; but someone is sitting on it—I've heard rumors about the Vietnamese refugee administration selling the rice." (It later developed that the Vietnamese official in charge was "away" and his storehouse locked.)

I asked other questions as they crowded around, old ladies with betel-stained toothless mouths, young matrons, dozens of children. Obviously, they thought I had come to do something for them; this made me feel helpless because I certainly couldn't help them at all. I could only pry further into their miserable lives.

Why didn't they farm their plots? "We are rice farmers. We have no water. We know nothing about peanuts." What did they want most? "Rice to eat, rice to plant, a school, a pagoda, a medical center . . . ." The interpreter added, sadly: "They want everything."

Remembering that my friend had said there had been no school in Ben Suc, I asked if their children had been to school there. Yes, yes. But they had stopped sending the children for some time because, afraid of the constant bombing, they preferred to keep them at home. (Back at Bien Hoa this was greeted with disbelief. The bombing was going on *near,* not *in* Ben Suc, so why not send the children to school? The villagers had in fact good reason to be afraid: Ben Suc had been bombed in 1965.)

If the war were over, would they stay in their new, clean village, or return to Ben Suc which they knew no longer existed?

"We would return. We are rice farmers, and there is water there and our family graves."

What if the Vietcong were there? (In Vietnam it is always important to treat the Vietcong as separate, and in no way connected with anyone present.)

"Oh, no! We would stay here!"

This delighted the American who was listening. Looking at me triumphantly, he said it proved that, although the villagers found life hard here, they wanted nothing to do with Victor Charlie. I persisted. Why, if the war were over, would they prefer to stay away from Ben Suc with the VC in it?

They all began speaking at once. The interpreter said: "They are afraid. If they return to Ben Suc and the Vietcong are there, the Americans will come back and destroy the village again."

Later, sitting in the trailer of the second AID man I found yet another veteran of the Ben Suc operation, an army colonel, one of whose peripheral jobs was keeping an eye on Lai Chu. After telling me how regularly the refugees received their rice (I think he believed it) and hearing the opposite from me, he told me with great seriousness of his difficulties in getting the Vietnamese authorities to cooperate in administering this kind of help.

I pointed out that since *we* had taken total responsibility for wiping out Ben Suc, we also had ultimate responsibility for the survivors, particularly in the light of our infinite resources. The colonel agreed. Turning to the AID man, I asked him to say frankly how he would feel if the refugees went back to Ben Suc as they said they would in the event of peace. He replied he would be "very disappointed" because he "honestly" felt that he could provide a better life for them in Lai Chu than they could find at Ben Suc.

Back in January, this same colonel had been reported as being full of enthusiasm for the Ben Suc operation. As he rose to leave, I asked him if he would recommend more Ben Sucs elsewhere. He looked at me silently and suddenly said: "No. The Brass are after me to go after a much bigger place. I've been fighting them for five months. It's not a good idea. We can't deal with this kind of problem. To tell you the truth, I don't think we can afford any more Ben Sucs."

In May–June, 1969, a study team, comprised mainly of religious leaders, visited South Vietnam and issued a report on civil and religious freedom in areas the Saigon regime controls. The following extract is taken from U.S. Senate, Committee on the Judiciary, *Hearings: Civilian Casualty, Social Welfare and Refugee Problems in South Vietnam.* 91:1, June 24–25, 1969 (Washington, D.C., 1969), Pt. 1, pp. 99–105.

REPRESSION IN SOUTH VIETNAM

The large majority of those imprisoned in South Vietnam are held because they oppose the government; they are "political prisoners." Undoubtedly, a great many of these are, as the government classifies them, "Viet Cong." Legally speaking, they are properly prisoners of war—although they are kept in a separate category from military prisoners. Others are "civilians related to Communist activities"; i.e., V.C. agents, and are accurately classified as such. Still others, many of them detained without hearing or trial, should be classified differently. Some of these have been picked up in "search and destroy" sweeps and are innocent of anything save being present in an area of military operations. Others are clearly political prisoners. They are nationalists and not Communists, but are seen by the government as inimical to its continuing control. In the official statistics very few "detainees" and "political prisoners" are so classified. The government places the vast majority of prisoners in either the "Communist" or the "criminal" category.

The classification of prisoners in 41 Correctional Centers as given by Col. Nguyen Psu Sanh, Director of Correctional Institutions, is:

	Percent
Criminals	16.98
Communists	64.25
Civilians related to Communist activities	4.16
Military	11.91

Political activities harmful to national interest 0.21
War prisoners temporarily in correctional centers 2.49

Colonel Sanh said that there are 35,000 prisoners in these Correctional Centers. The senior American advisor to Col. Sanh, Mr. Don Bordenkercher, estimated that, in addition, there are 10,000 held in interrogation centers. He reported that the number had gone up gradually since the Tet offensive of 1968 when the jump was precipitate. Ambassador Colby, General Abrams' Deputy for Pacification, said that the number of prisoners had gone up and will continue to go up as the pacification program (Civil Operations and Revolutionary Development Support) develops.

The national police in Saigon and in the provinces are the official organ for making arrests. In addition, there appear to be many other arrests and detention agencies. It is clear that those arrested are taken to a variety of detention centers for interrogation and that many are held in these centers for periods of time up to two years. According to the U.S. Mission, American advisors are involved only with cases of Viet Cong sympathizers and with persons apprehended during military operations; e.g., "Operation Phoenix," the 18-month-old program which pools information from half a dozen U.S. and South Vietnamese intelligence and security agencies with the purpose of identifying and capturing Viet Cong political agents.

Doubtless the total number of political prisoners in South Vietnam—including those held as prisoners of war by intelligence agencies and in military prisons, as well as those in the correctional institutions and those held by various other arresting agencies—far exceeds the official statistics and estimates. Due to the wide range of arresting and detention agencies, and the inadequacy of statistical methods, no accurate count of prisoners can be made.

In addition to the provincial Correctional Centers, there are four large prisons for essentially civilian prisoners. These are Chi Hoa in Saigon, Phu Nu in Thu Duc (for female prisoners),

Tan Tiep near Bien Hoa, and Con Son on an island off the southeastern coast. Team members were enabled by the Ministry of the Interior to visit Chi Hoa, Thu Duc, and Con Son Island Prison. They were also shown through the interrogation center at National Police Headquarters.

The following statistics, provided by prison officials, further illustrate the government's desire to de-emphasize the so-called "political prisoner" category.

Warden Pham Van Lien of Chi Hoa prison reported to Team members on June 3, 1969, this prisoner classification:

	Percent
Criminals	45.0
Communists	40.0
Civilians condemned by military court	4.0
Military	10.0
Political—non-Communist	.6

Prison Governor Minh, of Thu Duc Prison, classified the 1,126 prisoners held by him on June 3, 1969, as:

Criminal offenders	265
Communists	843
Civilians condemned by military courts	15
Military prisoners	3
Political prisoners	0
Prisoners of war	0

The Warden of Con Son Island prison reported that there were 7,021 men and boys in Con Son, of whom:

Were soldiers who committed political offenses (helped or sympathized with the V.C.)	984
Were civilians who had worked directly with the V.C.	2,700
Were soldiers who committed criminal offenses	769
Were civilians who committed criminal offenses	252
Were detainees, never tried or sentenced	2,316

(Note that only the Warden of Con Son Island prison separately identified unsentenced detainees in his statistics. The rest of the breakdowns presumably distribute the detainees among the classifications according to file, or dossier, information.)

There are no figures available on the religious affiliation of prisoners. Warden Lien reported that there were about 120 Buddhist monks in Chi Hoa prison on June 3 when Team members visited.

THU DUC (WOMEN'S PRISON)

Members of the Study Team spent several hours at the Women's Prison, where the staff, headed by Prison Governor Minh, explained the prison's operation and enabled members to see what they requested. The administration of the prison seemed commendable in many respects. The dispensary was reasonably clean. There were two large rooms filled with power sewing machines where the inmates made military uniforms. There were sewing classes, classes in English and other educational opportunities provided.

The cells and large prison rooms were overcrowded. This was especially hard on nursing mothers and those with small children. Fifty women, some with babies, lived in a crude building 40' by 30'. Sanitation was primitive and inadequate. There was evidence that some prisoners had not received needed medical attention.

Team members were especially concerned about the large number of prisoners who had not been sentenced after many months of detention, the looseness and inaccuracy of prisoner classification, the inhumanity of some sentences (one slight old woman who, according to her dossier, had passed V.C. letters, had served ten years of a fifteen-year sentence), and the extreme youthfulness of many of the inmates. Governor Minh told the Team that there were fifty children from birth to 13 years of age in prison (the very youngest, of course, belonged to the women prisoners), and forty young offenders from 13 to 17 years.

To judge from both interviews and official explanations, the circumstances of many classified as "Communist" did not justify this classification. Two students who were called "Communist" were found by the Team members to be unsentenced detainees. Their dossiers said that they were being held because they had exhibited "leftist tendencies" and had written for a Saigon University paper which was later suspended. In another building twenty percent of the women said they had not been tried or sentenced. It seemed obvious that prisoners who had been accused of "leftist tendencies" or who had not yet been tried could not justly be categorized as "Communist." Yet they were and were forced to live with persons who were considered "hard core Communists."

CHI HOA

Chi Hoa is often referred to as the "showcase prison." *Since 1963 American funds have been available for the improvement of facilities, and American advisors have helped set up rehabilitation programs.* The Team was given an attractive brochure with pictures of prisoners in classes, at worship, and enjoying recreational activities. The brochure states that "the present Vietnamese system of corrections is . . . based on the principles of humanity, charity and equality."

The Warden said that there were about 5,500 men and boys now in prison of whom 40 percent were "Communist" and only .6 percent were "non-Communist political" prisoners. Each prisoner wore a colored badge indicating his classification. The Warden estimated that 40 percent of the inmates had not yet been tried or sentenced. He said someone from the Ministry checked the lists every month and an effort was made to have those prisoners who had been in longer than six months brought to trial and sentenced.

The Team members were taken on a tour of the prison. Wherever they went, they found the halls and cells clean. They were shown the vocational classes in which about 300 prisoners were enrolled and met daily over a six-month period.

Team members saw the Catholic Chapel, a Buddhist shrine

and a Buddhist pagoda. In the pagoda, they talked with several monks who are in prison for resisting the draft. These monks were the only prisoners in any of the institutions who did not stand at rigid attention. Sometimes prisoners shouted ear-splitting anti-Communist slogans when Team members stopped to see them.

The Warden estimated that there were 200 children from 10 to 14 years of age and 200 from 14 to 18 in the prison not yet sentenced. All children, he said, were in a separate section and given education. Team members asked to see the children's section and were shown to cells. In one room, about 40′ by 25′, there were 47 children *under 8 years of age*. One child, 4 years old, said he was in prison because he had been caught stealing a necklace. The children were squatting in one end of the room eating when the Team members entered. They live in a bare room, with sanitary facilities at one end. No materials for play or study were in evidence. The food was rice with vegetables and fish. It looked adequate. The children seemed to be well physically. When the Team entered, the children left their bowls of food and assembled in lines without any order from the adult in the room or from the Warden. All, even the 4-year-old, stood at attention and did not move or speak; only their eyes followed the visitors' moves. In the next cell, similar in size, there were 67 children slightly older but under 10 years. The situation was the same in all respects.

The Team members saw three cells in the men's section, the same size as the cells for children. There were about 50 men in each of the rooms viewed. Some of the men were preparing over tiny burners various kinds of food which had been brought by friends or relatives. None of the men in these three cells had been sentenced.

Upon asking to see the disciplinary cells, the Team members were shown a room with iron rings for shackling prisoners, which, we were told, were seldom used. The iron looked rusty. Team members did not get to see any of the 100 prisoners who the Warden said were in solitary.

The prison is in the form of a hexagon, four stories high

facing inside. The wedge-shaped area in front of each of the six sections contains water tanks for bathing and washing clothes and an open space. The Warden said that after 5 P.M. the inmates are allowed here for sports and bathing. Since there is an average of about 1000 inmates in each section, it is obvious that only a very small proportion of the inmates could play soccer, volley ball, bathe or wash clothes at one time.

CON SON ISLAND PRISON

Con Son Island Prison, an escape-proof prison about 50 miles off the southeast coast, is said by officials to contain 7,021 prisoners, most of them "political." In many of the barracks, the majority of the prisoners were "political" prisoners who had been "tried" before a Military Field Court, usually without legal representation. They wore red tags which identified them as either V.C. or V.C. sympathizers. Those with yellow badges (detainees) presented another kind of problem. A show of hands taken in a number of barracks revealed that many detainees had been imprisoned as long as a year and a half with little hope of being released unless, conceivably, a place was required for new prisoners. It was explained that frequently the means or records necessary to determine whether charges should be brought were unavailable. There was a failure to observe even a minimum amount of due process in the overwhelming majority of cases. The same circumstances were recited over and over by the prisoners; they were either being held on charges of sympathizing with or aiding the enemy, or they had been rounded up after a military action in their village and were held. Others were students who had indicated their support for peace.

The tour had been carefully arranged by prison officials. The only time the Team members deviated from the prepared pattern, successfully demanding to see Camp No. 4 instead of the camp that the prison authorities had scheduled, they saw something of significance. There were large dark dormitory cells (three out of about ten such cells were inspected) in which there were from 70 to 90 prisoners each, all of whom (as determined by a show of hands) were condemned to life in prison. None had had lawyers or any trial other than a judgment by a military tribunal.

The prison authorities denied the existence of "tiger cages," reputed small barred cells in which prisoners being disciplined were chained to the floor in a prone position. Although recently released prisoners referred to this practice from actual experience, the Team members were unable to elicit any more from the prison officials than that the "tiger cages" were no longer in existence. (At first any knowledge of such things was denied.) One prisoner, however, speaking surreptitiously to the Team members said, in answer to a question, "Yes, the 'tiger cages' are here, behind Camp No. 2 and Camp No. 3. You looked in the wrong place." The Team members had looked behind Camp No. 4.

Taking into consideration the conditions under which such a prison had to operate, it seemed that an attempt was being made by the prison officials to conduct as clean and sanitary an operation as they could. There was a 1.3-million-dollar expansion underway (funded and supervised by the U.S.A.) which would provide 72 additional barracks.

Pursuing further the question of how prisoners were disciplined, the Team members were told that only 10 out of the 7,021 prisoners were under discipline. On request, the visitors were shown two of these ten. They had been in solitary for six months because of their refusal to salute the flag. One said he would never salute it. His legs were deeply marked, the Colonel in charge explained this was the result of a past disease. Questioned directly, the prisoner said it was the result of a long period in leg irons.

Although Team members observed no brutality, they felt that to have no disciplinary barracks other than a small number of maximum security cells was highly unusual. The Team members noted the fearful reaction of the inmates whenever prison officials appeared, surmising that there must exist a high degree of punitive regimentation.

A disturbing aspect of the prison situation in Vietnam is physical abuse of prisoners. U.S. officials (there are American advisors at every level of Vietnamese bureaucracy) agree that there is torture, but insist that it does not take place in the correctional centers but in the interrogation and detention centers where the prisoners are taken first. Accounts by ex-prisoners verified the fact that torture in detention and inter-rogation centers is general procedure.

Frequently, the interrogation center at the National Police Headquarters in Saigon was mentioned as a scene of torture. However, many informants said that the types and extent of torture administered in some of the detention centers in the provinces were far worse than in the National Police Interroga-tion Center in Saigon.

Although Team members were allowed to visit the National Police Headquarters in Saigon, it was an arranged visit. There was no evidence of the forms of torture here described. Colonel Mau said that modern interrogation techniques ruled out the need for physical violence. Team members saw the interroga-tion rooms but no prisoners were being questioned. The Team's evidence for the tortures described come from inter-views with ex-prisoners testifying to what they had endured and seen, together with the statements of doctors and others who had treated the victims. While the testimony of prison officials and the appearances of the National Police Head-quarters cannot be lightly dismissed, the sheer weight of wit-nesses' statements seemed overwhelming and conclusive to Team members.

All prisoners are oppressed by conditions of overcrowding. Sometimes, however, many prisoners are stuffed into small cells which do not allow for lying down or, sometimes, even for sitting; and this, when it is steaming hot, when excrement accumulates, and when the prisoners are seldom released for exercise, is torture indeed.

Beating is the most common form of abuse. Intellectuals appear to receive "favored" treatment and seldom are sub-jected to torture other than beating. This is done with wooden sticks and clubs. ("Metal" was mentioned by one observer.) The blows are applied to the back and to the bony parts of the legs, to the hands, and, in a particularly painful form, to the elevated soles of the feet when the body is in a prone position. Beating of the genitals also occurs. A number of commentators also described the immersion of prisoners into tanks of water which are then beaten with a stick on the outside. The pain is said to be particularly intense and the resultant injuries are internal.

Another type of water torture in which a soaked cloth is placed over the nose and mouth of a prisoner tied back-down to a bench is said to be very common. The cloth is removed at the last moment before the victim chokes to death, and then in reapplied. In a related form, water is pumped into the nose.

The most common procedure is said to be the elevation of the victim on a rope bound to his hands which are crossed behind his back. One witness described a "bicycle torture" used in this center. For about a week the prisoner is forced to maintain a squat position with an iron bar locking his wrists to his ankles; "afterwards he cannot walk or even straighten up," it was said.

An intellectual who was arrested in 1966 and spent the first six months of his two and one-half years term in an interrogation center described what he called the "typical case" of a woman law student in a nearby cell. She had been in the interrogation center for six months when he arrived and stayed for the next six months during his own imprisonment there. Throughout this year, she was tortured mostly by beating. When she was finally called before a tribunal to hear the charges, she had to be carried by two fellow prisoners. The tribunal, apparently because of her status, heard her case carefully and determined that it was a case of misidentification. Someone in Zone D had reported a V.C. returnee or spy who looked like her.

The same informant said, as a number of others did, that sexual torture was common. Though apparently it was not used on this woman student, it is used on many women.

Frequently coke and beer bottles were prodded into the vagina. Also, there were a number of accounts of electrical wires applied to the genitals of males and females, as well as to other sensitive parts of the body. Another informant told of the torture by electricity of an eight-year old girl for the purpose of finding her father: "She said her father was dead and they just kept torturing her. . . . They tortured her mother too." This was said to have occurred in the National Police Interrogation Center (Saigon) during 1968. Several ex-prisoners testified that it is not unusual to torture family members, including children, before the eyes of the prisoner. "Then," explained a woman teacher who had been imprisoned twice, "the prisoner will tell anything."

A respected physician told Team members that recently police brought a dead girl from an interrogation center to a city hospital and asked the Doctor there to certify to death from natural causes. On examination of the cadaver, the Doctor found signs of beating and sexual violation. He refused to so certify. Pressure was brought on the head of the hospital to issue the certificate. Such incidents are not unusual.

LEGAL STANDARDS AND PROCEDURES

The heart of the problem of assessing the conditions of political imprisonment in South Vietnam lies in the matters of standards and procedures. The key questions are: who is subject to arrest and imprisonment; and, how in each case is this determination made? If either the standards for determining who is subject to arrest, or the procedures for making the determination is loose, then enormous potential for official capriciousness exists and the freedoms of those subject to such caprice are ephemeral.

The Study Team found both the standards and the procedures to be loose by any measure, even by the most generous measure of allowance for the exigencies of civil and guerrilla warfare. The evidence is more than adequate to sustain the conviction of the Study Team that this looseness is used deliberately to suppress political dissent and to oppress some religious groups. In particular, loyal nationalists who are in basic disagreement with the government fear with good reason retaliation for expressing their views.

Naturally, the particular kind of war being waged in South Vietnam bears upon the judgments of the Team. Government of Vietnam officials quite properly see an analogy between the civilians arrested for guerrilla war activities—sabotage, espionage and the organization and support of National Liberation Front military cadres—and soldiers taken as prisoners in more conventional war. The validity of the analogy should be granted. We cannot class as suppression of political freedoms the imprisonment of those actively engaged in conducting war against the government. Moreover, the need for procedures to permit speedy imprisonment without exposing the government to the risk of further war-like activity on the part of the arrested persons must be conceded.

It is humbling for Americans to be reminded that their own history is replete with invasions of individual rights made in the name of wartime emergency: the suspension of the writ of habeas corpus during the Civil War, for instance, and the evacuation of persons of Japanese ancestry from the West Coast during World War II. An American cannot presume to sit with clean hands in judgment upon the Government of South Vietnam. But both the principles of justice to which their constitutions commit the United States and the Republic of Vietnam, and the pragmatic concern for winning popular support for democratic principles compel this Team to confine the restrictions on freedom made in the name of wartime exigency to those actually necessitated by war.

Loose and inadequate standards and procedures do not represent concessions to those wartime exigencies. Minimization of risk of war-like activities against the government is not achieved by the imprisonment, for instance, of loyal nationalists who advocate forming a coalition government with N.L.F. representatives. Nor does minimization of such risks require imprisonment of powerless people who scurry to avoid exposure to the demands of both N.L.F. and government forces, in so-called "insecure" areas, and are arrested on suspicion with the expectation that brutal interrogation may yield a "confession" which will warrant detention.

In fact, imprisonments of this kind create the unnecessary risk of alienating loyalties; a hazard made doubly severe by the highly political character of a war in Vietnam. The seriousness of this hazard is underscored by the statement to the Team of one young man, a resident of a rural province, that probably a majority of the men his age who reside in "secure" areas (under Government of South Vietnam control) of that province have experienced arrest and detention at least once during their lives. The evidence available to the Team suggests that the number of such arrests is steadily and continuously increasing.

The limits of the "war exigencies" justification are well illustrated by Article 29 of the Republic of Vietnam Constitution which clearly contemplates the existence of exceptional circumstances such as war. It provides:

"Any restriction upon the basic rights of the citizens must be prescribed by law and the time and place within which such a restriction is in force must be clearly specified. In any event the essence of all basic freedoms cannot be violated."

STANDARDS

Authority for imprisonment of non-conventional criminals is found in the State of War Law, Law No. 10/68, adopted by the National Assembly and promulgated by the President on November 5, 1968. It amends the State of War Decree promulgated prior to the present Constitution, on June 24, 1965, and as amended authorizes, among other things:

"The search of private houses, both by day and night;

"Fixing the place of residence of those elements judged dangerous to national security;

"Prohibition of all demonstrations or gatherings harmful to public security and order;

"Prohibition of the distribution of all printed matter harmful to national security;

"Control and restriction of communications and travel, consonant with security requirements; . . ."

In particular, the euphemistic language of the second paragraph quoted requires elaboration. Under it, numbers of persons are "assigned residence" in one or another of the provincial or national prisons by action of a Provincial Security Committee for specified but renewable terms, not exceeding two years, because they are "judged" to be "elements . . . dangerous to national security." Such a standard patently abdicates to the judging body the determination of who is to be subject to such imprisonments, with little, if any, legislative guidance or control. In fact, it was determined that students with nothing more than the notation in their files that they exhibited "left-wing tendencies" were being incarcerated in national prisons whose administrator classified them in his census as "Communists"; i.e., in the same category with individuals found to have assumed leadership roles in organizing war-like activity for the N.L.F. Others claimed to the Team that they had been detained for no other reason than that local officials responsible for their arrests expected to extort bribes as conditions for their release.

Under the heading of "prohibition of . . . gatherings," the Team learned of a Saigon political leader who was sentenced by a military field court to imprisonment for one year because he called a press conference without proper advance clearance from Republic of Vietnam authorities. (In this man's case, a known requirement appeared to have been deliberately violated, but the sentence suggests that the State of War Law is being used for more than minimization of military risks to national security.)

The standards just quoted should be read in conjunction with Article 4 of the Constitution which provides:

"Article 4.

(1) The Republic of Vietnam opposes Communism in any form.

(2) Every activity designed to publicize or carry out Communism is prohibited."

The looseness of the prohibition against activity designed to "publicize or carry out" Communism parallels that inherent in the other standards we have discussed. Under it, President Thieu, in an interview he generously afforded the members of the Team, justified the detention of Truong Dinh Dzu as a "political prisoner" on the ground that he had allegedly advocated the formation of a coalition government in which the N.L.F. would participate. This would violate Article 4, President Thieu reasoned, since such advocacy is *ipso facto* prohibited by that article. It may be unnecessary to point out, in response to this reasoning, that the Constitution also provides machinery for its own amendment, a process hardly likely to be completed without someone having first advocated a result barred by the language of the provisions being amended.

ANTI-VIETCONG CORDON DISRUPTS LIFE OF A VILLAGE

*Terence Smith**

Phuhoadong, South Vietnam, Sept. 23—For eight days this dusty farming village northwest of Saigon has been surrounded by a tight cordon of American and South Vietnamese soldiers.

The central market and all the shops have been shuttered and the fertile rice fields left untended while the soldiers have combed the village house by house in search of Vietcong. Traffic to and from the village has been completely cut off.

The cordon was drawn because the village is thought to be a command center and key supply point for local guerrilla units. By every military measure the operation has been a thorough success.

Seven hundred soldiers quietly encircled the village in a few hours on the night of Sept. 15. The surprise was apparently complete. As far as is known no Vietcong slipped through the net, though several tried to shoot their way out. Twenty-two were killed, 17 have been taken prisoner and 13 surrendered, and 23 suspects were arrested. In addition, 11 draft-dodgers have been picked up.

The military men who planned and executed the cordon are pleased so far. Lieut. Col. Ronald Ochis, commander of the joint American-South Vietnamese force, told a visitor today that the local Vietcong network has been "knocked for a loop." He added: "It will be months before they recover from this one."

The villagers of Phuhoadong are not so sure that the operation has been a success. They had seen four cordon operations in the last 15 months, including one that lasted 13 days. The Vietcong are everywhere, they say, and will be back when the Americans leave.

The villagers have also seen another side of the operation, one that Col. Ochis failed to mention in his briefing. Twenty

---

* This dispatch is one of many which frequently appear in the daily press. It was in the *New York Times*, September 24, 1969.

houses were destroyed and five persons were badly burned when canisters from allied illuminating shells dropped onto thatched roofs and set them on fire.

The Americans are replacing the houses, but it will be at least a month before the work is finished.

All commerce in Phuhoadong has come to a standstill and only military traffic is on the streets. The food of the villagers is running out.

REPEATED INTERROGATION

Each day all men and women aged 18 to 45 have been herded into the compound that surrounds the village school. There they have been detained and repeatedly interrogated on the whereabouts and identification of guerrillas.

Each evening the villagers have been sent home with the warning not to venture beyond their houses after 7 P.M. Then the darkness has been pierced by powerful searchlights and illuminating flares and anything that has moved after nightfall has been shot, or at least shot at.

The people taken to the school have been receiving a meal at noon. For the first three days it was Army rations, but now it is rice and fish, which are more popular.

Tran Van Hieu, a woodcutter with nine children, would have bought food at the market had he been able, but he had no money. Squatting in a shaded corner of the school compound today waiting his turn for interrogation, Mr. Hieu explained that he supported his family by cutting timber in the jungle and selling it in the market for fresh fish and salt and rice.

"I have not worked for eight days," he said through an interpreter. "When I don't work, my children have no food. For the last three days they have been eating soup made from rice and water."

For reasons like the case of Mr. Hieu, Le Minh Hoang, a Government employee in the district office, thinks the cordons do more harm than good.

"It's hard for people when they can't work," he said. "The VC make them pay taxes, but never as much as they would make in eight days. I thing it is very good propaganda for the VC."

Mr. Hoang also said that some villagers had lost jobs as day laborers and houseboys in the nearby town of Chuchi.

Not all the Americans involved think the operation has been a success. A junior officer at the district headquarters looked at the deserted central market and shook his head.

"They say this village is 80 per cent VC supporters," he remarked. "By the time we finish this it will be 95 percent."

Saburo Kugai is director of the Institute of American Studies in Japan and has twice visited North Vietnam. This account is based on his interviews there during late 1969.

THE BALANG AN MASSACRE

Saburo Kugai

Balang An may not sound familiar to American newspaper readers, but the fact remains that it is situated only five miles south of Chu Lai, one of the five major American footholds in Vietnam,* and 4.5 miles from Son My. In their desperate efforts to defend these five and other major footholds, the U.S. forces are carrying on what they call Accelerated Pacification Operations to establish a no-man's-land in the environs up to between 7–8 miles and 12–13 miles from the footholds. Living space is not to be left for inhabitants or their houses, nor even for animals and plants. The massacres at Son My, Balang An and Thanh Binh were all perpetrated in the course of genocidal operations carried out by U.S. forces to establish a no-man's-land around the base at Chu Lai to ensure it security.

I heard the following in Hanoi from Mr. Duc Son (42 years of age), who narrowly survived the Balang An massacre. I hope that his testimony will be compared with the *New York Times* account of November 15, 1969.†

* Saigon, Bien Hoa, Da Nang, Hue and Chu Lai.

† "The task of the investigators is complicated by the fact that last January, most of the inhabitants of the peninsula were forcibly evacuated by American and South Vietnamese troops in the course of a drive to clear the area of Vietcong. More than 12,000 persons were removed from Balangan Peninsula by helicopters and taken to a processing camp near this provincial capital. Heavy American bombing and artillery and naval shelling had destroyed many of the houses and forced them to live in caves and bunkers for many months before evacuation . . . An elaborate interrogation and screening procedure, in which American intelligence agents were said to have taken an important part, yielded only a hundred or so active Vietcong suspects. Most of the people were sent to a newly established refugee camp. . . . Despite the extensive movement of the population and the military operation, the Vietcong remain active in the area."

DUC SON'S TESTIMONY

When the Accelerated Pacification Operations started, Balang An had already been subject to bombing raids by aircraft, including the B-52's, and a massive spraying of defoliants. At 5 A.M. on January 13, 1969, ten Seventh Fleet warships opened fire, with 60 guns pounding away at Balang An to destroy the three hamlets there. Soon ground fire joined the shelling. Ten armored vehicles and several bulldozers arrived from the city of Quang Ngai, and destroyed all the fields, houses, granaries and bunkers. An LH-19 helicopter arrived overhead, shouting orders for all villagers to gather at an appointed field. Well aware of the fate that would be in store for them if they assembled, the villagers refused to obey. Some 8,000 American soldiers surrounded the village and moved in closer, tightening the circle till they were about five meters from each other, to drive the villagers to one point. In so doing, the Americans deprived the villagers of all their living conditions by destroying every well, killing all water buffaloes and burning all rice stocks. Many men, most likely targets of suspicion and liable to be drafted into the army, took shelter in bunkers, leaving mostly old men, and women and children to be rounded up, packed into helicopters and carried to a camp surrounded by barbed wire. Quite a few were killed, as they resisted when forced to board helicopters.

The Americans checked every remaining bunker, and attacked them with gas and machine-guns. They checked every bunker more than once, making such a careful search that many of the survivors were hunted out. The Accelerated Pacification Operations lasted for one month, and by the end of the month, more than 600 had been murdered. Balang An district was reduced to barren red earth.

But some villagers managed to escape to the liberated areas, and some others ingeniously dodged the roundup, so that just about half the population of Balang An, 11,000 persons, were carried to the camp at Son Phu village by helicopters. A 10-year-old boy, wearing pants and naked from the waist up, is said to have walked 40 miles to a liberated area.

The Americans at the camp picked out 1,200 "Vietcong" suspects, including women and children. In mid-March, the 1,200 suspects were put into jute rice bags, each in one, with many bags containing two children, and dumped into a number of small fishing boats linked up, while American soldiers in a motorboat then trailed behind them at high speed. The motorboat was then banked at full speed, turning the fishing boats upside down. Jute bags that remained on the surface were strafed. The following day, a countless number of the drowned began drifting ashore in Quang Ngai and Quang Nam provinces.

Two companies of lackeys,* who accompanied the 8,000 American troops, were yelling in Vietnamese: "We've done this in Balang An to sound a warning!"

What I have set out above is the gist of what I heard Duc Son tell in Hanoi about the mass slaughter at Balang An. While listening I asked him some questions. I asked: "What is going on with the survivors now detained in the camp at Son Phu?"

The Accelerated Pacification Operations were carried out at Balang An by the worst and the most atrocious of all American soldiers, Son said, but an attack on Son Phu by the Liberation Armed Forces † forced them to move the detainees to nearby Binh Chau. The movement was preceded by the arrival at Binh Chau of some American and puppet troops, who carried out an atrocious mopping-up operation, with bulldozers destroying all houses and bunkers, and helicopters carrying barbed wire to sent up a camp. The puppet head of Binh Chau village and his police chief friend take shelter at night at the U.S. military bases in fear of possible assaults by the detainees and the NFL, as they are continuing their strug-

---

* Susan Sontag in her account, *Trip to Hanoi,* 1968, writes that there is no better word than "lackeys" to describe them. I quite agree with her.

† A general term for the three categories of armed forces: the regular army of the National Front for Liberation, provincial combat units and the militia.

gle within the camp and are in contact with the Liberation Armed Forces, Son said.

"In Balang An district, there are six strongholds, four for the Americans and two for their puppets, but they are still unable to assert their administrative authority in the district. The Americans built a new seven-kilometer road linking National Highway No. 1 (Hanoi-Saigon) to the coast, with barbed wire fences set up 100 meters from the road on both sides, and with guards posted here and there to defend it. But the Liberation Forces have attacked the road and put it out of order. Three armed helicopters (one of them with flare bombs) are always overhead on a round-the-clock watch. But the rigorous living conditions have never made the inhabitants forsake their land, because they are living up to the principle of 'lying flat on the ground' in a People's War."

Son went on to say: "Balang An is five miles south of Chu Lai, and four miles from ill-fated Son My (Pinkville). Up until a few years ago, it was a safety-zone for the U.S. But now that it is liberated, Balang An poses a serious threat to the U.S. forces in Chu Lai. When they refer to Balang An as a 'warning,' they imply that Balang An is but a model of many other areas affected throughout South Vietnam as a result of the spreading war by the people who have offered all-out resistance to the American aggressors. If this were not so, their 'warning' could have no significance, and there would have been no need for it."

"The U.S. forces, however, have been unable to make the killing of 1,750 people, young and old, men, women and children at Balang An a 'warning.' The Americans have never been able to move more than 200 meters from their four strongholds. Mines laid by the Americans outside the barbed-wire entanglements surrounding their strongholds, were dug out for the NFL forces to blow up American tanks and armored vehicles, instead. Since camps were built to detain villagers, so far as I know, more than 20 of them have fled to the liberated districts with the help of some puppet soldiers sympathetic to them."

THE FACE OF WAR, DECEMBER, 1969 *

A brief word about how Vietnam looks. Flying over and driving through the Delta, our general impression was that the area looks relatively untouched and prosperous. There are no stretches of deserted or razed villages, and we saw only some evidence of past defoliation. Still the war is ever present. The sound of mortar fire is sporadic during the day but almost continuous at night. And when we drove out to the village of Cho Gau, fifteen miles or so outside My Tho, late in the afternoon with some young CORDS officers with whom we were spending the night, they were noticeably nervous when we found ourselves waiting unduly long for a ferry that was to take us across a river that stood between the hamlet and the road back to My Tho.

The view of I Corps from the air is quiet different. Along the coast in the vicinity of Route 1, the "street without joy," there are large stretches of desolated country with abandoned and burned out villages and long reaches of defoliated trees and underbrush stretching along canal and river banks.

Perhaps the Vietnamese can best describe their own country. The quotation below is from a pamphlet used at the Vietnamese training center at Vungtau where Revolutionary Development cadre, village and hamlet officials, Peoples Self-Defense Force personnel and others are trained.

Rural Vietnam today is desolate, bleak and in many areas deserted. Gardens are plowed by either bombs and shells or by men digging not furrows for seed but shelters and trenches. Houses appear in irregular patterns, some curiously unscathed by the ravages of war, but many are destroyed or knocked askew and lean drunkenly, adding to the mournful loneliness which is the hallmark of abandoned areas. Previously lush rice fields are overgrown with weeds, the silence unbroken by the

* From U. S. Senate, Committee on Foreign Relations, *Vietnam: December 1969*, 91: 2, February 2, 1970 (Washington, D.C., 1970) , p. 15. This report was prepared by two staff consultants who went to South Vietnam at the end of 1969.

peasant's songs passed from generation to generation, the abandoned land devoid of even the herds of cattle and buffalo that formerly roamed. Many villages have become ghost towns, their inhabitants having fled to the cities as war refugees or to the mountains or forests to escape ever-impending death.

LETTER TO HIS PARENTS
CAPTAIN WILLIAM H. MILLER
printed in the Bridgeport Post, February 17, 1970

Editor's note: The following letter was written by Captain William H. Miller, Company Commander attached to the 25th U.S. Army Infantry Division, in Vietnam. Captain Miller sent the letter to his parents, who live in the Bridgeport area, and asked them to submit it to the *Post* for publication. The letter reads as follows:

Dear Mom and Dad,

I am writing to you today because I am terribly upset over the charges that have been made against Lt. William Calley. Nothing I can say will save that young man. He has been fed to the world—a goat, so to speak. What I want to say is difficult, for I have neither the command nor the knowledge of the English to express what I feel. Mylai is a village in Quang Nai province, in the north of South Vietnam. I have participated in many Mylai-type operations, where a lot of innocent civilians were killed. I feel guilty, certainly, but I can tell you without reservation that Mylai will continue to occur as long as our government continues to pursue the course of action that it has over the past 25 years. It is not the Lt. Calleys that are at fault. It is our people—our people. They sent us out to fight a war, and when we fight it, they criticize us for the way we fight that war. I am a veteran of four wars—Korea, Lebanon, Dominican Republic, and Vietnam, so I can speak with some authority on the subject of war. Together with the fact that I have some education in the processes of American politics, I am able to make some very pointed observations. War and domestic politics are as different as day and night. Let the military fight the wars, and let the politicans run the government, and ask not the butcher how he kills the pig, for he too has an unpleasant task. We in the military carry out orders for the President, who in turn takes his orders from the people. If you do not want any more Mylais, then get the troops out of Vietnam. If you want to secure this poor but humble country, then leave us here to kill, slaughter, brutalize, and mutilate the people. That is our job, and don't ever forget it.

Now I ask, if you and the people of the United States did not want us to do that, why do you provide us with weapons of mass destruction? Logically it follows that you want us to kill, slaughter, brutalize, and mutilate the people. The citizens of the United States are paying about 2 billion dollars per month for that. Isn't it ridiculous?

Let me get to the core of the problem: Never has a war been so reported, photographed, publicized, philosophized, analyzed, and misunderstood. Never have Americans been so sorely misused. We are involved in a war that will never end. We are, in fact, on the verge of losing all our international prestige. We must, as Americans, pursue a course of action that will lead to isolationism. It has been said that isolationism cannot be tolerated. Well, when that was said, we had oceans between us and the world. Today, transportation and communication systems are such that this is not true any more. Let us disinvolve ourselves of all conflicts that do not have a direct impact on our health, wealth, or comfort. In other words, stay home and protect our people. I think that I understand this war. What Calley did is reprehensible, but not without justification. Don't blame him. Blame our people for putting him and others in a position where these things can happen. War is hell, it has been said. Amen.

All my love,
Bill

Mr. Gott is a British journalist who visited North Vietnam. This report appeared in the *Manchester Guardian Weekly*, February 28, 1970, p. 13.

PRECISION BOMBING NOT VERY PRECISE
Richard Gott

The Fourth Zone of North Vietnam—the four provinces south of the 19th Parallel that the Americans call "the pan handle" —has had more bombs dropped on it than any other area in the history of the world. It looks like it; though today, rather more than a year since the bombing stopped, lush vegetation is beginning to hide some of the worst scars.

But even if the inhabitants, about 20 per cent of North Vietnam's population of 20 million, wished to forget the war, the pounding by American bombers of the mountainous areas of neighbouring Laos—which reverberates daily through the Fourth Zone—is a constant reminder that the war is not over. Vietnam's problem is not solely one of reconstruction.

During a five-week visit to North Vietnam I have been able to drive as far South as the 18th Parallel and to spend some days in the province of Hatinh. This area, where the bombing redoubled its intensity of 1968, is still a shattering sight. Some times, bouncing along in an old Russian jeep, I would look out and see a perfectly normal landscape of women planting rice and boys on the backs of buffaloes. This place, I would mentally note, has been left alone; I must be careful not to exaggerate.

Then, round the next corner would come a broken bridge, a burnt-out house, a cratered rice field or a string of twisted railway trucks. Some valleys are almost showpieces of destruction, the hillsides deeply scored and floor barren and deserted. Only an occasional small ridge indicates where once was a rice field.

Much of the bombing north of Vinh concentrated on the areas where road and railway ran in harness. With a bridge as well, all havoc was let loose. In underdeveloped countries people like to live near roads and rivers and railways. Inevitably they concentrate near bridges. We shall never know how many people were killed, but the authorities appear to have been tireless in organising the evacuation and probably most of the houses by bridges were empty when the bombs fell.

One village I visited near a main road had moved the inhabitants out of the hamlets nearest the road and billeted them on those farther away. But the bombing was normally very wide of the mark—even on the best days an error of 400 yards seems to have been regarded by the Americans as a good average. Sheer tonnage, however, told in the end. Every major bridge, except that at Ham Rong, was destroyed. And they are big affairs, often huge girder bridges swung from five or six stone pillars.

I counted more than twenty large ones on my 200-miles journey south for Hanoi; the small ones were too many to count. The Ham Rong bridge, a battered wrecked piece of engineering which some how managed to hold together, apparently accounted for the loss of 99 American planes. It has become, for the Vietnamese, their symbol of successful resistance.

On the road south from Hanoi one passes first through the town of Phuly. Harrison Salisbury of the *New York Times* saw its remains early in 1967. It has been bombed repeatedly since. Largely built after 1954, its misfortune was to have the river on one side, the railway on the other and Route No. 1 running through the middle. A tempting target. Formerly a town of more than 10,000, it has been levelled, obliterated, razed to the ground. My interpreter knew these phrases, and when he used them in conversation in Hanoi, I hadn't really believed that he understood their literal meaning. But his English was exact.

At Phuly the railway turns south-east to the textile town of Nam Dinh, North Vietnam's fourth largest urban centre. Here fifty workers were killed at a weaving factory while changing shifts. At least half the town has been destroyed. Three and four storey houses have been swept away, their size only indicated by the neat piles of brick recovered from the rubble, and the occasional shell left standing. Here there is a church with a hole knocked in its side and an intact madonna surveying the desolate scene, as in the famous photograph of Dresden.

Farther south again, at Ninh Binh, where the railway rejoins the road, the scenes of destruction are the same, though on a smaller scale. At Thanh Hoa, an engineering plant, a fertiliser factory, a power station, and a rice mill proved irresistible to the bombers, smashing not only the basis of an industry geared principally to agricultural development, but also the houses of the workers, in a town which once held 60,000.

The list is endless. Vinh, a major industrial city and port—the third largest town in North Vietnam after Hanoi and Haiphong—wholly destroyed. Or the small town of Hatinh, which once housed 12,000. To judge from a few remaining facades, it was once a rather pretty colonial town.

It had paved streets, and more unusual, paved pavements. A church, a pagoda, a new hospital with 200 beds, an agricultural implements workshop, a small power station for the needs of the town and to assist the rural electrification programme. All gone. These were not towns I was specially taken to see. They just happened to be on the road South.

They did take me, at my request, to the Dong Loc crossroads, one of the principal areas where the Americans concentrated their bombs after March, 1968, and destined to become famous in the annals of aerial bombardment. During the four years' bombing, over 40,000 bombs were dropped here, and the figure is easy to believe. More incredible still is that 50 per cent of all the bombs dropped on this area fell during the limited bombing period in 1968.

Perhaps more extraordinary than anything is that in spite of all this destruction, the roads to the South were kept open. "Infiltration" actually increased. Heavy bombardment could not prevent the small quantity of supplies needed by the South from getting through. Nor did it affect the determination of the Vietnamese to continue the war. "What did you feel when the bombing finally stopped?" I asked the man responsible for keeping the roads open in one of the Fourth Zone provinces.

He replied quite simply, without a propaganda flourish, "I knew we had to do two things: to try to supply more men and goods to our Southern people, and to rebuild the roads and bridges."

The result of the bombing in this southern area of North Vietnam must throw serious doubts on the advantages of air superiority, and by implication on the effectiveness of the continuing air war in the South and in Laos. From what I have seen, there is clearly no such thing as precision bombing. Even against very lightly defended targets, a vast quantity of bombs had to be dropped over a very wide area.

This is not to deny that the bombing of the North has done very great damage. Vietnam has not been bombed back into the Stone Age, but a promising underdeveloped country that was pushing its way through the middle of the nineteenth century, has been forcibly smashed back into the eighteenth. The only result of this unpleasant experiment has been to prove the very definite limitations in warfare of air superiority. They were known already.

This dispatch in the *Guardian* (London and Manchester), January 30, 1970, raises fundamental questions about the accuracy of official U.S. and Saigon data on casualties, and reinforces the more critical accounts published here.

SAIGON "FALSIFYING" CASUALTY FIGURES

The former director of a Canadian Government medical mission to Vietnam yesterday accused the Saigon Government of falsifying for three years the scale of war casualties, malnutrition, and plague in South Vietnam.

Dr. Alje Vennema said in London that plague victims in one provincial hospital at Quang Ngai—where the alleged Pinkville massacre took place—were 10 times greater than the South Vietnam Ministry of Health's official figure for the whole country over the same period.

His records, compiled as mission director at Quang Ngai hospital from 1965–67, are the first substantial challenge to Saigon's figures, on which journalists and the World Health Organisation rely. WHO has already designated it as having in recent years the world's worst prevalence of pneumonic and bubonic plague epidemics.

PLAGUE CASES

Dr. Vennema, aged 37, a Dutchman who resigned his post in August, 1968, to do postgraduate research in tropical medicine at Sully hospital, has consolidated his Quang Ngai records into a paper.

He told a press conference: "Between 1965 and 1967 we treated some 2,500 plague cases at Quang Ngai alone, in comparison with the Health Ministry's figure of altogether 250 for the whole country."

In the three years they treated 12,000 civilian war casualties, most suffering from artillery wounds received in a zone under fire from the Americans. Thirty per cent of wounded were women and 40 per cent children under 16. The death rate was 15–20 per cent.

Considering that large parts of the province were too far from the hospital to send wounded, he estimated that from 1965–7 40,000 people in Quang Ngai (population about 700,000) might have been injured by artillery, bullets, or napalm. Burns accounted for 10 per cent of his cases.

Last November during a United States Senate Committee hearing, he said, the Saigon Health Ministry put total civilian casualties at "no more than 30,000 a year."

CONFUSE

"They have under-reported plague, never reported malnutrition, and they have under-reported war casualties," Dr. Vennema went on. By 1967, malnutrition accounted for more than a third of child deaths in Quang Ngai. Infant mortality rates were 32½ per cent of children under one, half the children under five, and a third of the under-15s.

Dr. Vennema was guest speaker at a press conference to announce the Medical Aid for Vietnam campaign's biggest contribution so far to consignments of medical supplies for North Vietnam and the Vietcong. It is giving £6,500 towards a £13,000 consignment of drugs and surgical instruments. The rest was subscribed by British and American Quakers.

WAR CRIMES AND THE NATURE OF
THE VIETNAM WAR

Gabriel Kolko

There are no census takers of the barbarism of the twentieth century, and there has been far too much of it to measure. The executioners are not willing, and the victims are rarely able, to provide exact details. What is certain in Vietnam, save to those who have neither the will nor the interest to confront truth, is the general magnitude and quality of the United States's combat against the Vietnamese. This relationship necessarily has a logic and structure which leads to war crimes as the inevitable consequence of a war that is intrinsically criminal. More important, the war is the outcome of post-World War II American policy toward the world and its effort to resolve the U.S.'s greatest dilemma in the second half of this century: to relate its industrial power to the political and ideological realities of popular revolutionary movements in the Third World.

After the Second World War the United States pursued its diplomacy on the traditional postulate of military power ultimately being based on physical plant, economic capacity, and the ability to destroy it. This assumption was also a definition of the nature of the world conflict, which after 1945 designated the Soviet Union as the primary threat to American security and interests. Such a premise, which not so much discounted as ignored the mobilizing potential of ideology and the capability of Third World guerrilla and liberation movements, gave the United States supreme confidence in the efficacy and strategic doctrines of its own military. This armed force was designed essentially to operate against a centralized, industrial society, a reinforcing proposition Washington thought the military and diplomatic facts, as well as its own economic priorities, warranted. Every strategy has a price tag, and strategic bombing has a predictable and relatively low cost, but it also necessitated a vulnerable industrial enemy.

The Korean war shattered a half-century of conventional wisdom and raised a critical dilemma. It immediately proved the limits of existing military strategy and technology against decentralized, nonindustrial nations. Apart from political or humanitarian considerations, there were no decisive targets against which to employ the atomic military technology on which the U.S. had pinned the bulk of its hopes and money.

After weakening its power everywhere else in the world, and embarking on what was to become the second most expensive war in its history, the United States waged the Korean war with "conventional" arms intended for combat between industrial nations. Fought against comparatively poorly armed peasants, it was a war unlike any in modern history, and the Korean precedent reveals the principles and tactics to emerge in Vietnam in a more intensive form. Within three months the U.S. destroyed all usual strategic targets in North Korea and over the last two years of the war it dropped about six times the tonnage used during the first year. Half the South Korean population was homeless or refugees by early 1951, 2.5 million were refugees at war's end, twice that number were on relief, over 1 million South Korean civilians died, and estimates of North Korea's losses are greater yet. As Major General Emmett O'Donnell, Jr., head of the Far Eastern Bomber Command, reported to the Senate in mid-1951: "I would say that the entire, almost the entire Korean Peninsula is just a terrible mess. Everything is destroyed. There is nothing standing worthy of the name." The Korean war, in brief, became a war against an entire nation, civilians, and soldiers, Communists and anti-Communists alike, with everything regarded as a legitimate target for attack.

For the Koreans, the war's magnitude led to vast human suffering, but the United States learned that it was unable to translate its immense firepower into military or political victory for itself or its allies. There was, in brief, no conceivable relationship between the expenditure of arms and the political or military results obtained. As the official Army history relates, utilizing high mobility, decentralization, and tunnel defenses, the North Korean and Chinese armies greatly improved their equipment and logistics and ended the war "a formidable foe who bore little resemblance to the feeble nation of World War II." Massive firepower had resulted in enormous civilian casualties and barbarism, but inhumanity was not victory.

The implications of Korea to the United States's future were monumental, conjuring up the prospect of political and military defeat in Asia and vividly revealing the limits of its power. Massive land armies were both very expensive and of dubious utility, and it was in this context that John Foster Dulles attempted to break through the enigma with his "massive retaliation" debate—never satisfactorily translating it into a coherent and relevant strategy. Not only did Soviet nuclear power rule out attacking Russia with impunity, but even Washington in the spring of 1954 doubted whether Vietnamese peasants could be made to stop fighting if Moscow were destroyed, and the debate over employing atomic bombs at Dien Bien Phu only revealed that in close combat and mixed battle lines, atomic bombs indiscriminately destroy friend and foe alike.

The dilemma of relating American technology to agrarian and decentralized societies was not resolved by the time President Kennedy came to office. Without delving into the "counterinsurgency" planning and assumptions which the President immediately authorized General Maxwell Taylor to coordinate and study, it is sufficient to observe not only that the U.S. began making its commitments in Vietnam keenly aware of the failures of the past, but it was still encumbered with the same limitations which might only repeat the Korean precedent of mass firepower, wholesale destruction of populations, and political-military failure. Nor is it necessary to review the familiar history of how the Kennedy and Johnson administrations intensified their involvement in Vietnam. More relevant is the distinctive character of that war, and the assumptions and manner in which the United States has employed its military might. I propose to outline the political and environmental structure of the war and to show why the United States consciously employs a technology that is quantitatively far greater than that used in Korea but inevitably requires the same outcome in Vietnam: the destruction of untold masses of people and their society, and the concomitant moral immunization of the American civilians and soldiers called upon to sustain and implement the Government's grand strategy.

A WAR WITHOUT FRONTS

One of the most significant realities of the war in Vietnam, a fact which makes "legal" combat impossible and necessitates endless crimes against civilians and combatants alike, is the absence of conventional military fronts and areas of uncontested American control. The Tet Offensive proved once again that combat can occur anywhere and that the military initiative rests with the NLF. American forces, in reality, form enclaves in a sea of hostility and instablity, able temporarily to contest NLF physical control over large regions but incapable of substituting Saigon's political infrastructure to establish durable control by winning the political and ideological loyalties of the large majority of the people. Perhaps most ironically, the NLF has been able to transform this American presence, which it has not been able to remove physically, into a symbiotic relationship from which they extract maximum possible assets in what is intrinsically an intolerable and undesired situation. For this reason as well, they are able to endure the war the longest, prevail, and win at the end, even should they lose a great number of military encounters.

The Pentagon's statements notwithstanding, there now exists more than sufficient documentation proving that the U.S. claims to "control" 67 percent of the South Vietnamese population, as before Tet 1968, or 92 percent as of late 1969, bear no relationship to reality. Suffice it to say, the Pentagon also maintains private figures, data that simply reinforces the inescapable conclusions of a logical analysis of its own releases, that a very substantial majority of the South Vietnamese are not under the physical "control" of either the Saigon regime or U.S. forces. Apart from political loyalty, which claims on hamlet control ignore, the supreme irony of the war in Vietnam is that hamlets labeled "secure" for public purposes, such as Son My, are often the hardest hit by American arms. The reason is fundamental: areas, villages, and large population concentrations the NLF operationally control frequently cooperate in Saigon-sponsored surveys and projects to spare themselves unnecessary conflict with U.S. and Saigon forces. To lie about the presence of the NLF to a visiting pacification officer is a small matter in comparison to the certain military consequences the truth will invite. What the Pentagon describes as the "secure" area in Vietnam is often a staging and economic base as secure and vital to the NLF as its explicitly identified liberated zones.

Therefore we read innumerable accounts of trade and movement between Saigon-"controlled" areas and those of the NLF, and of "friendly" villagers and Saigon's Popular Forces (only one-eighth of whom are trusted with arms) who fail to report NLF combat units and infrastructures. Hence, too, the existence of at least 5,000 NLF political workers in the greater Saigon area, to use minimal American figures, and the undoubted accuracy of the NLF claim to have parallel governments in all the major cities and towns. American admissions that three-quarters of the NLF budget in 1968 was raised from taxes collected from one-half the Vietnamese population, that Saigon's eight largest corporations paid an average of $100,000 each in taxes to the NLF, or that it puchases vast quantities of supplies from "secure" towns, is much more to the point. To some critical measure, "secure" areas are both a part of, and vital to, the NLF. And to be "secure" is not to be a continuous free-fire zone. The question is not who claims "control" but who really possesses it. For the most part, such control as the U.S. may have is temporary and ultimately is based on its ability and willingness to apply firepower, and certainly is not a consequence of any popular support for its financed and universally corrupt regimes in Saigon.

The refugee camps and program are good examples of the NLF's ability to turn what the U.S. intends as adversity into a dual-edged institution from which they may gain as much as a repressive situation allows—so long as it retains the respect and political loyalties of the people. These camps were both the inevitable by-product of America's massive firepower applied to all Vietnam and its explicit desire to reconcentrate the population so as to better control it. "You have to be able to separate the sheep from the goats," to quote one Pentagon-sponsored analyst in 1966. "The way to do it is harsh. You would have to put all military-age males in the army or in camps as you pacify the country. Anyone not in the army or in camp is a target. He's either a Viet Cong or is helping them."

By May, 1969, the war had produced 3,153,000 refugees since 1965, 612,000 still remaining in camps and with only a tiny fraction having been resettled in their original villages. The large majority of the refugees were seeking to escape the free-fire zones and rain of fire the Americans were showering on them. Their political loyalties were anti-Saigon in the large majority of cases, and the intense squalor, degradation, and corruption in the camps undoubtedly mitigates such small sympathy for the anti-NLF cause as may exist. No less significant about the camps is the very high percentage of old men, women, and children in them—that is, noncombatants. In this sense, by entering the American camps, refugees escape the American bombs, while the younger men generally remain in the combat areas. Roger Hilsman put it another way in 1967: "I think it would be a mistake to think that the refugees come toward the Government side out of sympathy . . . . [They] come toward the Government side simply because the Vietcong do not bomb, and that they will not at least be bombed and shelled. I have greater worries that some of the refugee camps are rest areas for the Vietcong, precisely because of this."

Refugee camps therefore become incubators of opposition as well as potential shelters for it, just as many reported NLF defectors, very few of whom are regular combatants, are now suspected of returning to NLF ranks after a period of recuperation. Such integration of the institutional structure of "secure" areas with that which the NLF dominates, this profound lack of clear lines and commitments among the Vietnamese, attains its ultimate danger for the Americans when it is revealed that the Vietnamese support for the NLF extends to parts of the highest levels of the Saigon regime. We know little of the process by which Vu Ngoc Nha, Huynh Van Trong, and their thirty-nine associates penetrated the intimate circle of the Thieu regime and became privy to its secrets, but it is certain that many officers, soldiers, and administrators of the Saigon regime are secretly committed to the NLF cause, and it is no less certain that most other Saigon leaders are deeply dedicated to enriching themselves, even via trade with the NLF regions, and are totally unreliable for the U.S.'s ultimate purposes. Such an army of unwilling conscripts, corrupt officers, and politically unreliable elements in their midsts is a dubious asset to the U.S. and alone scarcely an unmanageable threat to the NLF. Hence the chimera of "Vietnamization." The various administrations have known all this, and much more.

It is one of the lessons of twentieth-century history that repression and social disintegration generate forces of opposition that otherwise would not have existed, and Vietnam is no exception. No one can comprehend the development and success of the NLF without appreciating this fact. Vietnamese forced out of their villages by air and artillery strikes and into decrepit and unsanitary camps know full well that the Americans are responsible. The army of prostitutes are aware of the source of their degradation. The peasant whose crops are defoliated knows who to blame. Apart from its attractive political program and land reform policy, the NLF has successfully capitalized on the near universal Vietnamese hatred of foreign invaders, a fact that has made its political infrastructure and loyalties of the people to it increasingly durable even as growing firepower is inflicted upon them. "They say this village is 80 percent VC supporters," one American officer commented last September as his men combed a village. "By the time we finish this it will be 95 percent." Such insight is scarcely atypical, but appears to be universal in the available documents on this aspect of the war.

The realism of repression intensifying resistance, as well as every other phase of the struggle in Vietnam I have mentioned, sets the indispensable context in which the U.S. applies its military power, for it long ago abandoned operating within the acknowledged political limits of South Vietnam. More precisely, by employing sheer physical might, the U.S. has sought to compensate for and transcend its unavoidable political weaknesses in its Vietnam adventure. The various men in the White House and Pentagon know better than any of us that the lines are indeed everywhere, and that the Vietnamese people are overwhelmingly real and potential enemies. And since the Vietnamese long ceased to be promising ideological targets, tractable to successive corrupt regimes, they have virtually all become physical targets everywhere. Quite apart from the results—for the United States is slowly learning that its efforts have become both militarily insufficient and politically self-defeating—the necessary logic of American military strategy in Vietnam is to wage war against the entire Vietnamese people, men, women, and children alike, wherever they may be found. So long as it remains in Vietnam, it cannot fight another kind of war with any more hope of success.

MACHINES AGAINST PEOPLE: AMERICAN MILITARY PREMISES

The original theory of counterinsurgency in White House circles in 1961 was that a limited number of men, wise in the ways of guerrilla ideology and tactics, could enter the jungles with conventional small arms and win. Given the political, military and ideological realities, this premise by 1964 was utterly discredited, and there followed a major scramble to develop new "miracle" weapons intended to overcome the NLF's clear military superiority. The problem, however, is that it requires five to seven years to translate a sophisticated weapons concept into adequate field deployment, and in 1965 weapons ideas already in progress were designed overwhelmingly for a war in Europe. A mass of exotic crash research proposals proved, on the whole, to be expensive miscarriages, and it was already-commissioned projects in helicopters and gunships that were most readily transferable to the Vietnam context. The helicopter's distinctive value pointed to the defining objective condition of the military phase of the Vietnam war: decentralization and a lack of military targets. Without the mobility the helicopter provided, General Westmoreland has estimated, one million more troops would have been required to fight the same war on the ground.

While the United States has sought to discover and procure weapons uniquely designed for the decentralized agrarian and jungle environment, it has also attempted to utilize existing weapons first designed for such concentrated strategic targets as industry and air-missile bases. This, by necessity, has required employing weapons, such as the B-52, originally constructed for intensive, nuclear warfare against stationary targets. It has adjusted for decentralized mobile targets simply by dropping much greater quantities of explosives of immense yield on vast regions with very few permanent military installations. Militarily, the United States has therefore fought the war with whatever decentralized-style weapons it could develop as well as the sheer quantity of firepower which "conventional" weapons employ. The preeminent characteristic of both these approaches is that they are intrinsically utterly indiscriminate in that they strike entire populations. And while such strategy violates all international law regarding warfare, and is inherently genocidal, it also adjusts to the political reality in South Vietnam that the NLF is and can be anywhere and that virtually the entire people is Washington's enemy.

I am not contriving something the Pentagon does not already know. "The unparalleled, lavish use of firepower as a substitute for manpower," writes one of its analysts in an official publication, "is an outstanding characteristic of U.S. military tactics in the Vietnam war." From 315,000 tons of air ordnance dropped in Southeast Asia in 1965, the quantity inflicted on the region in the year 1969 reached 1,388,000 tons. Over that period, 4,580,000 tons were dropped on Southeast Asia, or six and one-half times that employed in Korea. To this we must add ground munitions, which rose from 577,000 tons in 1966 to 1,374,000 tons in the entire year of 1969. And to these intensive-destruction weapons applied extensively we must also add the wide-impact decentralized weapons that are employed in ever greater quantities alone or in conjunction with traditional explosives. For the family of cluster bomb weapons and flechette rockets, which the Air Force rates as "highly successful," I have no procurement data. Suffice it to say, these are exclusively antipersonnel weapons covering much wider areas than bombs. CS (a type of advanced tear gas) procurement is one example: from 1965 to 1969 the amount purchased went up twenty-four times. Procurement for defoliants and anticrop chemicals is erratic because of in-ventory and production problems, though the Air Force's far-too-conservative data on acreage sprayed have risen quite consistently from less than 100,000 acres in 1964 to an adjusted annual rate of fifteen times that in 1969. Procurement in 1964 was $1.7 million and $15.9 million in 1970, with an inventory in 1970 almost equal to new purchases.

Translated into human terms, the U.S. has made South Vietnam a sea of fire as a matter of policy, turning an entire nation into a target. This is not accidental but intentional and intrinsic to the U.S.'s strategic and political premises in the Vietnam War. By necessity it destroys villages, slaughters all who are in the way, uproots families, and shatters a whole society. There is a mountain of illustrations, but let me take only one here—that of the B-52—which reveals how totally conscious this strategy is.

The B-52 costs about $850 million to operate in Southeast Asia in fiscal 1970, and they drop about 43,000 tons a month. On what? The one official survey of actual hits that I have been able to locate states that "enemy camps," often villages full of civilians, "were where intelligence said they would be" in only one-half the cases. In "the other half, intelligence was faulty, and the camps were either not there or the VC had not been in the target area when the bombs fell." Then on whom did the bombs fall? On Vietnamese peasants in both cases, on thousands of Son Mys.

Stated another way, in 1968 and 1969 the U.S. used about 7,700 to 7,800 tons of ground and air ordnance during an average day. At the time of the 1968 Tet offensive, the Pentagon estimates, NLF forces were consuming a peak of 27 tons of ammunition a day, and half that amount during an average day in April, 1969. Roughly, this is a ratio of 250 or 500 to one. Inequalities of similar magnitude appear when one compares overall supply, including food, which for all NLF and DRV forces in the south was 7,500 tons per month at the end of 1968. At the beginning of 1968 American fuel needs alone were 14 million tons a month. Out of this staggering ratio of conspicuous consumption has come only conspicuous failure for the U.S., but also a level of firepower that so far exceeds distinctions between combatants and noncombatants as to be necessarily aimed at all Vietnamese.

In an air and mechanical war against an entire people, in which no fixed lines exist and high mobility and decentralization give the NLF a decisive military advantage, barbarism can be the only consequence of the U.S.'s sledgehammer tactics. During Tet 1968, when the U.S. learned that the "secure" areas can become part of the front when the NLF so chooses, U.S. air and artillery strikes destroyed half of Mytho, with a population of 70,000, four-fifths of Hue's inner city, more than one-third of Chaudoc, killed over 1,000 civilians in Ben Tre, 2,000 in Hue—to cite only the better known of many examples. But what is more significant to the ultimate outcome of the war is that such barbarism is also accompanied by an ineffectuality—entirely aside from the question of politics and economics—which makes the U.S.'s failure in Vietnam certain.

Indiscriminate firepower is likely to hit civilian targets simply because there are many more of them, and directly and indirectly that serves the U.S.'s purposes as all administrations define them. But we know enough about mass firepower and strategic bombing to know not merely that it is counterproductive politically but also an immense waste militarily. As a land war, the Vietnam campaign for the U.S. has been a mixture of men and mobility via helicopters, with the NLF generally free to fight at terms, places, and times of its own choosing. And because of ideology and allegiance, the NLF always fills the critical organizational vacuum the Americans and their sponsored Saigon regime leave behind. But even when in the field, the U.S. soldier lacks both motivation and a concept of the ideological and political nature of the war, which makes him tend toward terror and poor combat at one and the same time. Had he and his officers the will and knowledge to win—which, I must add, would scarcely suffice to attain victory—the American army would not be repeating the tale of Son My over and over again. For Son My is simply the foot soldier's direct expression of the axiom of fire and terror that his superiors in Washington devise and command from behind desks. No one should expect the infantryman to comprehend the truths about the self-defeating consequences of terror and repression that have escaped the generals and politicians. The real war criminals in history never fire guns, never suffer discomfort. The fact is, as the military discussions now reveal, that morale and motivation are low among troops, not merely toward the end of tours of duty, or when combat follows no pattern and "morale goes down and down," to quote one Pentagon analyst, but also because an unwilling foreign conscript army has not and cannot in the twentieth century win a colonial intervention.

We can scarcely comprehend the war in Vietnam by concentrating on specific weapons and incidents, on Son My, B-52s, or defoliants. What is illegal and immoral, a crime against the Vietnamese and against civilization as we think it should be, is the entire war and its intrinsic character. Mass bombing, the uprooting of populations, "search and destroy"—all this and far more is endemic to a war that can never be "legal" or moral so long as it is fought. For what is truly exceptional and unintended in Vietnam, from the Government's viewpoint, are the B-52 missions, defoliants, and artillery attacks that do not ravage villages and fields. Specific weapons and incidents are deplorable, but we must see them as effects and not causes. The major undesired, accidental aspect of the entire Vietnam experience, as three administrations planned it, was that the Vietnamese resistance, with its unshakable roots everywhere in that tortured nation, would survive and ultimately prevail rather than be destroyed by the most intense rain of fire ever inflicted on men and women. For the history of America's role in Vietnam is not one of accident but rather of the failure of policy.

Given what is so purposeful and necessary to the United States' war in Vietnam, and the impossibility and the undesirability of America relating to that nation by other than military means, there is only one way to terminate the endless war crimes systematically and daily committed there—to end the intrinsically criminal war now, to withdraw all American forces immediately. And while the Vietnamese succor and heal their wounds, Americans must attempt to cure their own moribund social illness so that this nation will never again commit such folly and profound evil.

CONTRIBUTORS

Eric Norden is a free-lance writer who lives in New York.

Seymour Hersh is a journalist who has covered the Pentagon for UPI. In 1970 he won the Pulitzer Prize for his account of the My Lai massacre.

David Welsh is a free-lance writer and former editor of *Ramparts*.

Dr. Erich Wulff worked in South Vietnam for six years as a member of a West German Medical Mission.

Jean Bertolino is a French journalist who reported from Vietnam.

Jonathan Schell is a specialist in Far Eastern history and a journalist.

The
Psychological and Ethical
Context

I have put together here in slightly modified form two statements of testimony—the first given before a Senate Subcommittee on Veterans' Affairs, chaired by Senator Alan Cranston,
and the second at a Congressional Conference on War and
National Responsibility held in Washington, D.C., both delivered in 1970. In both statements I sought to contain my
sense of ethical outrage within a genuine "psychohistorical"
analysis, one that connects larger political and military policies
with the individual-psychological state of GIs that leads to
atrocity.

VICTIMS AND EXECUTIONERS
Robert Jay Lifton, M.D.

I have done psychiatric work at a number of Veterans' hospitals and out-patient clinics, and at the Walter Reed Army
Institute of Research. During the Korean War I served as an
Air Force Psychiatrist in Korea and Japan. I have spent almost seven years living and working in the Far East, and made
visits to Vietnam in 1954 and in 1967.

I have done research on such "extreme situations" as the
psychological aspects of Chinese thought reform (or "brainwashing") , and the psychological effects of the atomic bomb
in Hiroshima. I have been greatly concerned with the application of psychological methods to the study of historical
events, and with the general psychology of the *survivor*.

I would like to comment upon the psychological predicament of the Vietnam veteran, both from the standpoint of war
in general and of the nature of this particular war.

For veterans of any war there is a difficult transition from
the "extreme situation" of the war environment to the more
ordinary civilian world. This was noted after World War I,
World War II, and the Korean War, but only recently have
we begun to appreciate the problem from the standpoint of
the psychology of the survivor. The combat veteran of any war
has survived the deaths of specific buddies, as well as the
deaths of anonymous soldiers on his and on the enemy's side.
He survives the general war environment, within which he

was taught that killing was not only legitimate but proper and necessary.

Upon returning to civilian life the war veteran faces several important psychological tasks in relationship to the deaths he has witnessed. He must, first of all, struggle with anxiety he continues to feel, often in association with the indelible images of death, dying and suffering that constitute the survivor's "death imprint." He must also struggle with feelings of guilt and shame resulting directly from the war experience. These guilt feelings can relate simply to the fact that he survived while so many others died, or they may focus upon the specific death of one particular buddy who in some way, he feels, was sacrificed, so that he, the veteran, could go on living. His sense of guilt may also relate to his having killed enemy soldiers, or having done various other things in order to stay alive. But his overall psychological task is that of finding meaning and justification in having survived, and in having fought and killed. That is, as a survivor he must, consciously or unconsciously, give some form to the extreme experience of war, in order to be able to find meaning in all else he does afterwards in civilian life.

These psychological tasks are never perfectly managed, and as a result the veteran may experience anything from a mild readjustment problem to disabling forms of psychiatric impairment. Typically, the returning veteran manifests a certain amount of withdrawal from civilian life, a measure of distrust of the civilian environment—a feeling that what it offers him may well be counterfeit—and some confusion and uncertainty about the meaning of his wartime experience and of his future life. His overall adjustment is greatly influenced by the extent to which he can become inwardly convinced that *his* war, and *his* participation in that war, had purpose and significance.

All of this is true for the Vietnam veteran. But in addition his psychological experience is influenced by certain characteristics of the war in Vietnam. The average Vietnam GI is thrust into a strange, far-away, and very alien place. The Vietnamese people and their culture are equally alien to him. Finding himself in the middle of a guerrilla war in which the guerrillas have intimate contact with ordinary people, the environment to him is not only dangerous and unpredictable but devoid of landmarks that might warn of danger or help him to identify the enemy. He experiences a combination of profound inner confusion, helplessness, and terror.

Then he sees his buddies killed and mutilated. He may experience the soldier-survivor's impulse toward revenge, toward overcoming his own emotional conflicts and giving meaning to his buddies' sacrifices by getting back at the enemy. And in an ordinary war there is a structure and ritual for doing just that—battle lines and established methods for contacting the enemy and carrying out individual and group battle tasks with aggressiveness and courage. But in Vietnam there is none of that—the enemy is everyone and no one, never still, rarely visible, and usually indistinguishable from the ordinary peasant. The GI is therefore denied the minimal psychological satisfactions of war, and, as a result, his fear, rage, and frustration mount.

(The "pep talk" by the company commander just prior to My Lai was actually part of a funeral ceremony for a fallen sergeant. GIs remember being told to "kill every man, woman, and child in the village" so that "nothing would be walking, growing, or crawling" when the company left. They recall also to have been urged to "let it out, let it go." Which they did.)

At the same time he notices that the South Vietnamese fight poorly or not at all; and rather than ask himself why this is so, he tends to associate them with the general corruption and deterioration he sees all about him. Any previous potential for racism is mobilized and he comes to look upon Vietnamese as inferior people or even nonhuman creatures.

This dehumanization of the Vietnamese by the individual GI is furthered by his participation in such everyday actions as the saturation of villages with bombs and artillery fire, and the burning of entire hamlets. Observing the death and injuries of Vietnamese civilians on such a massive scale, and the even more massive disruptions of village life and forced relocations, he cannot but feel that the Vietnamese have become more or less expendable.

That is why Vietnam veterans I have talked to were not really surprised by the recent disclosures of atrocities committed by American troops at My Lai and elsewhere. Virtually all of them had either witnessed or heard of similar incidents, if on a somewhat smaller scale. Hence Paul Meadlo's public statement that what he and others did at My Lai "seemed like it was the natural thing to do at the time." Another former infantryman, Terry Reed, who described a similar incident elsewhere, made a public statement of even greater psychological significance. He said: "To me the war was being ambushed every three to five days, being left with scores of wounded GIs. Then come right back at the enemy by going into an innocent village, destroying and killing the people." What these words suggest is hcw, under the extraordinary stress of an impossible situation, GIs come to see all Vietnamese, whatever their age or sex or affiliation, as interchangeable with the enemy, so that killing any Vietnamese can become a way of "coming right back" at those responsible for wounding or killing their own buddies.

Meadlo went on to say that immediately after killing a number of Vietnamese civilians he "felt good" and that "I was getting relieved from what I had seen earlier over there." Applicable here is an established psychological principle that killing can relieve fear of being killed. But there is something more operating in connection with these massacres: the momentary illusion on the part of GIs that, by gunning down these figures now equated with the enemy—even little babies and women and old men—they were finally involved in a genuine "military action," their elusive adversaries had finally been located, made to stand still, and annihilated—an illusion, in other words, that they had finally put their world back in order.

Other veterans have reported witnessing or participating in

killings of civilians without even the need for such an illusion. Sometimes these killings have been performed with the spirit of the hunter or the indiscriminate executioner—pot shots at random Vietnamese taken from helicopters, heavy fire directed at populated villages for no more reason than a commanding officer's feeling that he "didn't like their looks." In addition there have been many accounts of such things as the shoving of suspects out of helicopters, the beheadings of Vietcong or Vietcong suspects, and of various forms of dismembering the bodies of dead Vietnamese. The American infantry company responsible for My Lai, upon first entering a combat zone, had a kind of visual initiation into such brutalization in the form of a weapons carrier they encountered with its radio aerial strung with Vietnamese ears.

Actions such as these require an advanced state of what I have called psychic numbing—the loss of the capacity to feel—and of general brutalization. Where such actions are committed in a direct face-to-face fashion—without even the psychological protection of distance that is available to those who drop bombs from the sky or direct long-range artillery fire—the psychological aberration and the moral disintegration are very advanced indeed. For while there is little ethical difference between killing someone far away whom one cannot see, and looking directly into the victim's eyes from five or ten feet away while pulling the trigger, there is a considerable psychological difference between the two acts.

The Vietnam GI also is profoundly affected by atrocities committed by the Vietcong, by South Vietnamese soldiers, and by South Korean forces. All of these contribute both to his numbing and his brutalization. But it is one's own atrocities that haunt one most. And no one can emerge from that environment without profound inner questions concerning the American mission in Vietnam and the ostensibly democratic nature of our allies there—even if, as is often the case, the GI resists these questions and keeps them from his own consciousness.

Whatever kind of adjustment the returning Vietnam veteran appears to be making, he must continue to carry images of these experiences inside of him. Survivors of a special kind of war, these men constitute a special kind of veterans' group. Murray Polner, a historian who has now interviewed more than two hundred Vietnam veterans as part of an investigation of their experiences, has found that none of the men he talked to—not one of them—was entirely free from doubt about the nature of the American involvement in Vietnam. This does not mean that all of them actively oppose the war, but rather that as a group they have grave difficulty finding inner justification for what they have experienced and what they have done.

That is exactly what former Army Captain Max Cleland, a triple-amputee, meant when he told this Subcommittee last month: "To the devastating psychological effect of getting maimed, paralyzed, or in some way unable to reenter American life as you left it, is the added psychological weight that it may not have been worth it; that the war may have been a cruel hoax, an American tragedy, that left a small minority of young American males holding the bag." It is also what a nineteen-year-old marine who had lost part of his leg and was awaiting medical discharge meant when he told Polner (as quoted in trans-*action* magazine. November, 1968) : "I think any other war would have been worth my foot. But not this one. One day, someone has got to explain to me why I was there." This inability to find significance or meaning in their extreme experience leaves many Vietnam veterans with a terrible burden of survivor guilt. And this sense of guilt can become associated with deep distrust of the society that sent them to their ordeal in Vietnam. They then retain a strong and deeply disturbing feeling of having been victimized and betrayed by their own country.

As a result many continue to be numbed as civilians, the numbing now taking the form of a refusal to talk or think about the war. Some become almost phobic toward television broadcasts or newspaper reports having anything to do with the war. A number of those I spoke to could only take jobs permitting them to remain isolated from most of their fellow Americans, often night jobs. One Vietnam veteran told me, "I worked at night because I couldn't stand looking at those nine-to-five people who sent me to Vietnam." Yet these men are also affected by the deep ambivalence of the general American population about the war in general, an ambivalence which extends to those who have fought it. It is difficult for most Americans to make into heroes the men who have fought in this filthy, ambiguous war, and if they try to do so with a particular veteran there is likely to be a great deal of conflict and embarrassment all around. There is in fact an unspoken feeling on the part of many Americans that returning veterans carry some of the taint of that dirty and unsuccessful war.

From work that I and a number of others have done on related forms of war experience and survival, we can expect various kinds of psychological disturbance to appear in Vietnam veterans, ranging from mild withdrawal to periodic depression to severe psychosomatic disorder to disabling psychosis. Some are likely to seek continuing outlets for a pattern of violence to which they have become habituated, whether by indulging in antisocial or criminal behavior, or by, almost in the fashion of mercenaries, offering their services to the highest bidder. Similarly, many will hold onto a related habituation to racism and the need to victimize others. Any of these patterns may appear very quickly in some, but in others lie dormant for a period of months or even years and then emerge in response to various internal or external pressures.

What I have been saying is that we cannot separate the larger historical contradictions surrounding the American involvement in Vietnam from the individual psychological responses of our soldiers. Indeed the Vietnam veteran serves as a psychological crucible of the entire country's doubts and misgivings about the war. He has been the agent and victim of that confusion—of on the one hand our general desensitization to indiscriminate killing, and on the other our accumulating guilt and deep suspicion concerning our own actions. We sent him as an intruder in a revolution taking place in a small Asian society, and he returns as a tainted intruder in our own society. Albert Camus urged that men be neither victims nor executioners. In Vietnam we have made our young men into both.

Of course Vietnam veterans need and deserve improved medical and psychiatric facilities, as well as better opportunities for education and employment. But if we are really concerned about the psychological and spiritual health of America's young men—and indeed, about our own as well—we shall cease victimizing and brutalizing them in this war.

MY LAI AND THE MALIGNANT SPIRAL

The war in Vietnam has involved Americans in a malignant spiral of self-deception, brutalization, and numbing. Contradictions surrounding our intervention contribute directly to the brutalization of our troops; their indiscriminate killing of Vietnamese not only decimates that society and its people but reverberates back to the mother country and throughout the world; our leaders in turn are required to move more deeply into illusion and encourage similar illusion on the part of the American people; and *our* entire society undergoes a form of disintegration from which it may take decades to recover, if it is to recover at all. I would like to say something about each of these turns of the spiral.

Our policy in Vietnam is based upon three myths. The first of these concerns the nature of the war, and converts a forty-five-year-old anticolonial revolution into an "outside invasion" of the South by the North. The second myth concerns the nature of the government we support, and converts a despotic military regime without standing among its own people into a "democratic ally." The third myth holds that we can "Vietnamize" the war (leave and still keep the present government in power in the South) by turning it over to a regime that lacks legitimacy and an army that has shown little will to fight—by a program that is American rather than Vietnamese, and one that few if any Vietnamese really want to implement.

The massacre at My Lai is a product of our self-deception.

Turning to the rest of the American population and its response to My Lai, we can identify at least three psychological mechanisms called forth to avoid facing such unpleasant truths: denial (The massacres didn't really happen, or have been exaggerated) ; rationalization (All war is hell) ; and the mobilization of self-righteous anger (Stop picking on our boys. They [the Vietnamese] had it coming to them. *You* [the bearer of the news] ought to be sent to Vietnam to fight) . We know something about the ways in which groups, and even nations, distance themselves from—refuse to feel—their own atrocities; we have the experience of Nazi Germany for that. But I would stress that in so doing, in refusing to feel not only My Lai but the entire Vietnam War, we partake precisely in the psychic numbing and brutalization experienced by GIs, even if indirectly and in less extreme form.

Our numbing and brutalization are furthered and hardened by the insistence on the part of our leaders that My Lai is no more than an isolated incident in a war that will be solved, at least for us, by Vietnamization.

The paradox here is that many of these same leaders would like to take us out of Vietnam but are prevented from doing so by the self-deceptions contained within their worldview. They are bound by a cosmology that contrasts absolute American purity with absolute Communist depravity. Also contained in this cosmology is a dangerous form of technicism that leads Americans to view Vietnam (or Vietnamization) as no more than "a job to be done" through the application of "American know-how"—and to ignore psychological and historical forces surrounding the long-standing Vietnamese struggle against Western invaders.

The cost of this American self-deception to the Vietnamese people has become grotesquely clear. But there is no way of measuring its mounting cost to our own society. What we can say is that Americans as a national group have become participants in, and survivors of, a sustained pattern of killing and dying which we inwardly sense to be not only brutal but ultimately absurd. That is, the larger American population shares the experience of Vietnam combat veterans in being unable to find the inner significance that any survivor requires in relationship to his death immersion. Our own justifications for our actions convince us incompletely if at all, and we are left with the numbing and brutalization required to protect those justifications and fend off a sense of guilt. We are already experiencing the consequences of this general process, and our psychological scars are likely to be extensive and permanent.

It is no secret that a very large percentage of our most gifted young people feel betrayed and victimized—by the war, by our political leaders, by the older generation, and by our society in general. What we are now learning is that large numbers of Vietnam veterans bring back into that society a similar but more painfully concrete sense of betrayal and victimization, of having been used badly, sacrificed without purpose, by their country. Again these emotions extend throughout the American population: everyone feels in some way betrayed and victimized—either by the war and its advocates, or by those who oppose the war and raise the specter of defeat.

Even without the war it is quite possible that the general dislocations and antagonisms in our society would have eventually led to considerable violence. But desperate emotions in response to the war escalate the possibilities for violence from all sides: from returning GIs who can neither absorb their experience nor rid themselves of the habit of killing; from the young who are enraged by their country's demand that they participate in evil forms of killing and dying; from blacks who associate this war against a nonwhite race with their own sense of racial oppression; and most dangerous of all, from backlash-prone groups throughout American society who cling nostalgically to their cosmology and feel not only betrayed and victimized by protesters but duped by leaders who promised them a brief and glorious victory.

Self-deception, moreover, tends to expand to other realms, and this expansion could be accelerated by the need to deny its existence in regard to Vietnam. Hence the danger of other Vietnams occurring in Southeast Asia, Latin America, or elsewhere. And the apocalyptic prospect of similarly spreading self-deception in the Faustian area of nuclear weapons systems. In that area a little numbing and a little self-deception, even in the absence of brutalization, could mean the extinction of virtually everyone.

Clearly, our task is to break out of this malignant spiral. We cannot do so through detached psychological—or for that matter economic or political—analysis. Rather we must commit ourselves to precisely what our leaders are failing to do: We must confront events like My Lai by reporting them as accurately as we can and interpreting them with whatever wisdom we possess. We must convey the full story of what has been going on in Vietnam, not by simply inundating the American people with grotesque details and thereby mobilizing their resistance to the truth, but by giving *form* to these details and events within the larger context of the Vietnam War and its causes. We must also take actions both forceful and wise, that express our absolute opposition to the national policies and directions which have brought us to this point. Finally, we must evolve and act upon a new worldview—a very different cosmology—that reaches beyond My Lai and Vietnam, and beyond our present political and military policies and structures.

As a citizen, and as a psychiatrist working in the field of psychohistory, I fear for my country. We are in the midst of a national crisis of unique historical and psychological dimensions. My Lai is no more than the tip of the iceberg—or to return to my original image, it is just one turn of the spiral. But we had better face My Lai if we are going to unwind that malignant spiral, cease our destruction of Vietnamese and American societies, and apply ourselves to the larger problem of human survival.

There is no more apt expression of protest than a mock-prayer, no more apt protester than a West Point graduate, and no one more equipped to protest humanely than the rare physician who takes seriously his Hippocratic Oath. Gordon S. Livingston brings all of these elements together—first in a "prayer," then an explanation of it, and finally some observations on trying to be a healer in a situation of anti-healing.

HEALING IN VIETNAM
Gordon S. Livingston, M.D.

THE BLACKHORSE PRAYER

(Composed by Dr. Livingston and distributed by him at ceremonies for Colonel George S. Patton III)

God, our heavenly Father, hear our prayer. We acknowledge our shortcomings and ask thy help in being better soldiers for thee. Grant us, O Lord, those things we need to do thy work more effectively. Give us this day a gun that will fire 10,000 rounds a second, a napalm which will burn for a week. Help us to bring death and destruction wherever we go, for we do it in thy name and therefore it is meet and just. We thank thee for this war fully mindful that while it is not the best of all wars, it is better than no war at all. We remember that Christ said, "I came not to send peace, but a sword," and we pledge ourselves on all our works to be like Him. Forget not the least of thy children as they hide from us in the jungles; bring them under our merciful hand that we may end their suffering. In all things, O God, assist us, for we do our noble work in the knowledge that only with thy help can we avoid the catastrophe of peace which threatens us ever. All of which we ask in the name of thy son, George Patton. Amen.

LETTER FROM A VIETNAM VETERAN

Sir:
Public disaffection with the war in Vietnam is now general, and as a result the American agony there may be near an end.

But several of the fundamental reasons for our failure there are not widely acknowledged. Thirty thousand dead Americans and countless dead Vietnamese require some sort of an accounting.

A few autobiographical notes by way of background. I am a graduate of the U.S. Military Academy. I had decided while still a cadet that I wished to become a physician. At that time, the Army would allow qualified USMA graduates to attend medical school with the understanding that they would make military medicine their career. First, however, it was necessary to spend two years as an officer with one of the "combat arms." Accordingly, after becoming qualified as a Ranger and a parachutist, I served as an infantry lieutenant with the Eighty-Second Airborne Division at Fort Bragg, North Carolina. After two years, I applied for a five-year leave of absence and was accepted at Johns Hopkins School of Medicine from which I graduated in 1967. I interned at Walter Reed General Hospital, and in 1968 volunteered for Vietnam.

Before leaving, I managed to get permission to attend a course given by the Foreign Services Institute, a State Department subsidiary, which included six weeks of study on the politics, religions, culture, and history of Vietnam as well as on our military and civil operations there. An additional five weeks were devoted to intensive language training from which I emerged considerably short of fluency, but with some limited ability to communicate. This course is one normally presented to prospective CORDS (civil affairs) personnel being assigned to Vietnam. Following this, I spent five weeks at Fort Rucker, Alabama, undergoing training as an Army flight surgeon.

I arrived in Vietnam in November, 1968, with the rank of major and was assigned as regimental surgeon (the latter word is without surgical connotation; all Army doctors are called surgeons) to the Eleventh Armored Cavalry Regiment ("Blackhorse"). This is a 5,000-man unit operating generally north of Bien Hoa in the III Corps area. When I joined it, the regiment was commanded by Colonel George S. Patton III, the son of the Second World War general. In the months to follow I was to come to know Patton quite well. As a member of the regimental staff, I ate at his table and attended his nightly briefings. To a significant degree he symbolized the actions and attitudes that are a source of our alienation from the Vietnamese and our consequent politico-military defeat in the war.

It is difficult to summarize the experiences that led to my expression of disaffection with our effort. In the end what I objected to was not so much individual atrocities, for these can be found in any war; war itself is the atrocity. What compelled my stand was the evident fact that at an operational level most Americans simply do not care about the Vietnamese. In spite of our national protestations about self-determination, revolutionary development, and the like, the attitude of our people on the ground, military and civilian, is one of nearly universal contempt.

This arrogant feeling is manifested in a variety of ways, from indiscriminate destruction of lives and property to the demeaning handouts that pass for civic action. The Vietnamese, a sensitive and intelligent people, are well aware of our general lack of regard and generally reward our efforts with the indifference or hostility that they deserve. We in turn attempt to create the illusion of progress by generating meaningless statistics to support predictions of success which have proved invariably incorrect. And the dying goes on.

Specific examples of our disregard for the Vietnamese are legion. At one point the corps commander issued a document entitled "U.S.–Vietnamese Relations" detailing many of these instances. It represented official acknowledgment of the problem, but its exhortation to "avoid creating embarrassing incidents" was an exercise in futility. Numerous examples are available from my own experience including the running down and killing of two Vietnamese women on bicycles with a *helicopter* (the pilot was exonerated) ; driving tracked vehicles through rice paddies; throwing C-ration cans at children from moving vehicles; running truck convoys through villages at high speeds on dirt roads (if the people are eating rice at the time it has to be thrown away because of the dust).

In the area of medical civic action, it was the policy to give no more than a two-day supply of medicine to any patient lest the excess fall into Vietcong hands. Since visits to any given village are generally infrequent, this meant that the illusion of medical care was just that.

Another example of the dehumanization of our relationships with the Vietnamese is evident when a civilian is admitted to one of our military hospitals. He is given a new name. In the place of a perfectly adequate, pronounceable Vietnamese name, he is given an appellation that is easier for Americans to remember. The nature of some of the designations chosen reveals their impact and intent—"Bubbles," "Ohio," and "Cyclops" for a soldier who had lost an eye.

Finally, one need only listen to a conversation between Americans concerning Vietnamese to appreciate the general lack of regard. The universal designation for the people of Vietnam, friend or enemy, is "gook" (also "slope" and "dink"). On the whole, this has no conscious pejorative connotation as used casually, but it does say something about our underlying attitude toward those for whose sake we are ostensibly fighting. How we can presume to influence a struggle for the political loyalties of a people for whom we manifest such uniform disdain is to me the great unanswered, indeed unanswerable, question of this war.

The analogy is depressingly clear between our failure to relate successfully to the Vietnamese and to the black people who comprise an "underdeveloped nation" within our own society. In both cases our behavior is racist in the true sense of opposing the overwhelming forces generated by a people's search for pride and identity. The price of our lack of perception is defeat abroad, and, if not corrected, may be the dissolution of society at home.

And then there is the military. General David Shoup has spoken on this issue more convincingly than I ever could. Vietnam provides a case study of how inimical to the goals of the nation can be the individual self-interest of its soldiers. Colonel Patton may be a case in point. He received numerous decorations while pursuing unrelentingly the one major criterion by which a commander's performance is judged: the body count. He was able to make the appropriate public noises about the importance of civic action, but he was never more honest than the night he told his staff that "the present ratio of 90 percent killing to 10 percent pacification is just about right." In my experience, Patton was neither the best nor the worst of the military there. He is simply the product of the misbegotten and misguided idea that a single-minded dedication to destruction is to be highly rewarded. That he was unable to grasp the essentially political nature of the war is not surprising. What is surprising is that our society should expect its soldiers to function in a political role and believe them when they say they can.

My work with the Eleventh ACR was mainly in the area of medical civic action. Using the eight general medical officers and 200 enlisted medics assigned to the unit, we attempted to establish regular, frequent, medical visits to a limited number of rural villages. We also tried to provide evacuation of those people requiring surgery or hospitalization. In addition, attempts were made to attack some of the public health problems (personal hygiene, waste disposal) that were at the root of much of the disease we saw. Finally, efforts were made to involve Vietnamese health officials in immunization programs, dispensary building, and the like so that something would remain after we had gone. Success in all these areas was very modest. Some necessary surgery was done, many acute illnesses benefited from antibiotic therapy, and a start was made on long-term treatment of the numerous cases of tuberculosis we encountered. When I left, one dispensary was being built, which the government of Vietnam had promised to staff. Important to me was the *idea* our efforts represented and to which the Vietnamese responded: namely, that people from different cultures can relate successfully on the basis of mutual regard; that by offering our technical expertise the Vietnamese could help themselves. There is nothing original about this concept; ostensibly it underlies all U.S. "pacification" efforts. In reality, however, the idea is diluted in its application by the pervasive myth of American superiority, and the result is that civic action in the majority of instances I observed represented little more than patronizing handouts.

Meanwhile the war ground on. My views were well known in the unit. I felt, however, that my ability to influence events by individual persuasion was insignificant when the self-interest of everyone lay in the direction of more war, more death. Even the regimental chaplain endorsed the standing order of the unit when he prayed for "wisdom to find the bastards and the strength to pile on."

I finally felt I must protest. The occasion presented itself on Easter Sunday at the change of command ceremony for Colonel Patton, which was attended by General Abrams and some twenty other general officers. It was a true dance of death, with Patton recounting his successes and Abrams awarding him the Legion of Merit as "one of my finest young commanders." As the ceremony concluded with the chaplain's benediction, I passed among the guests handing out copies of the enclosed prayer, about two hundred in all.

There was some initial concern among the guests at the ceremony that the prayer might be genuine. Those who knew Colonel Patton well recalled that the previous Christmas he had sent out cards featuring a color photograph of dismembered enemy bodies and bearing the greeting, "Peace on Earth, Colonel and Mrs. George S. Patton." One reporter rushed up to the Chaplain and asked him if he had written "that prayer." The Chaplain, thinking the newsman was referring to the benediction read at the ceremony, replied, "Of course." A trip to Saigon by the Regimental Public Information Officer was required to straighten out the misunderstanding and kill the story.

But the official reaction came quickly. I was relieved of my duties and confined to my trailer for forty-eight hours. I then received a psychiatric evaluation (a routine preliminary to judicial action), and a formal investigation was performed.

It was elected not to initiate court martial proceedings; instead I received a letter of reprimand and was transferred to the Ninety-Third Evacuation Hospital at Long Binh. I worked there in the emergency room for one month until the decision was made by the USARV commander to send me back to the U.S. as an "embarrassment to the command." A request from me that I be allowed to complete my tour at the Ninety-Third Evac was refused. I returned to the States on May 17. An amusingly ironic footnote to my expulsion was provided when, shortly before my departure, I was awarded (privately) the Bronze Star for an action that had occurred four months previously.

Upon my arrival in the U.S., I submitted my resignation stating my intent to speak out publicly—in or out of the military. Even though I had some four-and-a-half years of obligated service remaining, the Department of the Army elected to accept the resignation and I received a general discharge on July 17.

That in essence is my story. I tell it both in sorrow and with hope. I believe that this nation and its institutions are capable of better direction given better information. Mine was a limited view as is that of any one person; I make no claim to the whole truth, but this is what I saw.

JUST KEEP HIM ALIVE FOR A FEW MINUTES

> The regimen I adopt shall be for the benefit of my patients according to my ability and judgment, and not for their hurt or for any wrong.
>
> Hippocratic Oath

"Just keep him alive for a few minutes so we can question him. After that he can die. It doesn't matter to me." This order from my commanding officer in Vietnam concerned a badly wounded Viet Cong soldier I was treating. In a way that no abstraction could, that statement brought me face to face with my sense of ethical priorities; to me the situation epitomized the moral quandary confronting a medical officer in that war.

Most doctors go to Vietnam as draftees, unenthusiastic

about either the military or the war. It is not too difficult to rationalize the mission of the Medical Corps ("To conserve the fighting strength") with the more traditional obligation of the physician to treat patients one at a time. Until, that is, something happens to reveal the incompatibility of one's medical and military responsibilities in the context of what this nation is doing in Vietnam. In my case it was the first wounded enemy soldier to come under my hand with the requirement that I argue and barter with his interrogators to secure his evacuation.

The majority of military doctors are not confronted with this directly. Those wounded VC and North Vietnamese who survive to be evacuated are taken to special hospitals, inferior in every respect to the facilities available to American wounded. The latter go to air-conditioned, well-equipped installations; the enemy is treated in facilities which have last priority on supplies and personnel. These hospitals are staffed (understaffed might be a better word) largely by physicians with little or no surgical training, while Americans are uniformly treated by well-qualified surgeons. When I was in Vietnam the chief medical officer at the VC hospital at Long Binh, the only such facility in the entire III Corps area, was an obstetrician.

So much for the medical care provided the enemy. What about the efforts directed toward the people of Vietnam, for whose sake, as we all know, this war is being fought? Let me describe for you the way one of our most supposedly generous and effective "pacification" efforts is administered—the Medical Civic Action Program, or MEDCAP. There are, of course, differences in kind and effectiveness of these programs from unit to unit and place to place in Vietnam. I describe my own experience based on a rather broad observation of the activities in central III Corps in 1968–69. I believe them to be representative of conditions elsewhere especially in attitude.

The concept is simple enough: U.S. medical personnel go out to a local village, set up shop, and provide treatment for whomever needs it. The Vietnamese, of course, respond enthusiastically to this opportunity to receive the benefits of modern medical science and flock to be treated. Unfortunately, treatment is limited by several circumstances:

First, diagnosis is complicated by the difficulty of getting symptoms through an interpreter; diagnostic tools available include the stethescope and the doctor's clinical acumen. More important, however, is the doctor's complete inability to treat adequately any but the most superficial problems. Any given village is unlikely to be visited more often than every two months, if that, and official policy is to restrict distribution of medicines to a two-day supply lest excess fall to the Viet Cong. Facilities are not generally available for evacuation of those cases needing hospitalization. The result of all this is a parody of medical care unsatisfying to both patients and physicians, most of whom feel quite cynical about their role in this charade. One cannot long treat obvious cases of tuberculosis with cough medicine and still retain a feeling of professional competence. Such a purely symbolic exercise, however, produces multitudes of pictures for home consumption of Americans looking concerned about Vietnamese; it also generates some of those statistics which are the indices of "progress" cited by those who decide how much dying it takes till we finally reach that light at the end of the tunnel.

The medical evacuation helicopter pilots in Vietnam are widely respected for their willingness to fly extremely dangerous missions to evacuate wounded. When a life is at stake they will spare no risk—as long as it is an American life. Two incidents demonstrate this vividly. I spent a night in a village in I Corps in which six Vietnamese women were wounded by a grenade. I felt it doubtful that one of them would survive without prompt evacuation and so stated in my radioed request for a helicopter. The request was refused, although, based on my experience in circumstances of similar risk, I was convinced the mission would have been flown for a wounded American.

The second incident involved a nineteen-year-old U.S. soldier, a chaplain's assistant, who was shot one night in a village adjacent to a U.S. encampment. The radio message was mistransmitted so that the helicopter pilot understood the wounded man to be a Viet Cong. He declined to come into a landing zone close to the soldier, and while the latter was being transported overland to a safer area, he died—a case, one might say, of mistaken identity.

It seemed only slightly surprising to me, then, when one day a suggestion was made to me by the Chief Army Anesthesiologist in Vietnam that we might use succinyl choline in interrogating prisoners to paralyze the muscles of respiration and induce them to talk. He offered to administer the drug.

Nonmedical examples of the dehumanizing effects of the war—on both us and the Vietnamese—are well documented elsewhere in this book, as they are in my own experience. What I am attempting to illustrate with the above examples is that a medical officer in Vietnam is required to function in a uniquely inhumane environment. Even if he does not participate directly in this inhumanity, the military physician is lending his sanction to it by his membership in the organization responsible (as in a less immediate sense is every American). This point is obscured by the rationalization that the doctor's work is *constructive* ("Someone has to treat the wounded"). But what of our role in facilitating the functioning of a military machine which has dead and maimed human beings as its end product? The thought often struck me that what I was seeing in operation in Vietnam might be called the "General Motors of Death." The technology, middle-management philosophy of many of the participants, and penchant for statistics are all suggestive of a large industrial organization. It is only as one watches the "finished product" coming off the medevac helicopters or lying in the fields and villages that it is borne in beyond rational denial that the business we are in is death.

Physicians are supported in their work by a view of themselves not just as competent technicians for hire, but as decent, thinking human beings. The most cynical among us take some pride in membership in a profession, the values of which are a centuries-old expression of our humane obligations to other men, an affirmation of our common humanity. Violence is being done these values in our name, and in the name of our country. Our participation is both solicited and compelled. There must be some among us who can yet remember that the most eloquent word in the language, the loudest moral expletive, the final refuge of a besieged conscience is still . . . No.

Americans are not unique in seeking to wish away their atrocities. The Germans did it too. Opton and Duckles made use of survey techniques to study the kinds of psychological defenses people call forth to avoid accepting the unacceptable.

IT DIDN'T HAPPEN AND BESIDES, THEY DESERVED IT
Edward M. Opton, Jr., and Robert Duckles

A fictional German psychiatrist, the creation of satirist Art Hoppe, tells his American patient who is troubled by My Lai to repeat three times a day: "I didn't know what was going on. These things happen in war. I was only following orders as a good American. Our soldiers are good American boys. The war is to save the world from Communism. Our leaders were wrong. The unfortunate victims were members of an inferior race." With a single exception, Hoppe's compilation of German clichés after the "Final Solution" accurately summarizes American reactions to My Lai, as they emerged in a survey we and our colleagues at The Wright Institute in Berkeley, California, made last December.

Our sample was not large—most of our data come from 42 long interviews with randomly selected telephone subscribers in Oakland, California, plus four in-person interviews—but the results are consistent with larger, less intensive surveys by the *Wall Street Journal, Minneapolis Tribune,* and *Time. Time* reported that 65 percent of its sample of 1608 individuals denied being upset by the news of the alleged massacre at My Lai. Americans have reacted like Germans to reports of atrocities. During one interview, an airline hostess was asked to inspect the *Life* magazine photographs of My Lai. As she viewed the mangled bodies and the contorted faces of those about to die she trembled, her chin dropped to her chest, her eyes closed to shut the pictures out. For several seconds she seemed unable to move. But she recovered quickly, for we then asked, "You said before that you weren't surprised. Do you have any other reactions besides that?" she responded: "No, I don't . . . It . . . when people are taught to hate it doesn't surprise me how they react, particularly when they are given a weapon; it just seems to be one of the outcomes of war . . ." Another said: "I can't take the responsibility of the world on my shoulders too strongly myself . . . it upsets me. I'm having my problems and can't take this stuff too seriously, since it causes me worries and problems."

In 1946 Moses Moskowitz reported on a survey of German opinion: "The most striking overall impression is the absence in the German of any emotional reaction toward Jews, be it positive or negative. It was shocking at times to listen to people decrying the evils of Nazism, reciting the horrors of concentration camps . . . without one word of sympathy for the victims."

One would expect S/Sgt. David Mitchell, one of the accused in the My Lai case, to say: ". . . I can recall no such case where I know of anyone being hurt. . . . it is my opinion that what they say happened did not happen." And one might expect the same response from George Wallace: "I can't believe an American serviceman would purposely shoot any civilian . . . any atrocities in this war were caused by the Communists." But total denial is by no means confined to those implicated in the alleged massacre, or to superpatriots. A man who felt that the U.S. should, but cannot, get out of Vietnam, told us: "Our boys wouldn't do this. Something else is behind it." Another complete denial came from a woman, who at one moment advocated withdrawal by the end of 1970 but also endorsed the idea of escalating and winning the war, no matter what the consequences, *but* without killing innocent people. As for My Lai: "It's too unbelievable that they would do something like that." Another, asked if he believed the massacre really happened, said: "I can't really and truly. No, I don't. I think it could have been a prefabricated story by a bunch of losers."

Strong doubts serve the same purpose as complete denial. "Anything could happen. How do we know what's going on?" asked a man who wanted the war escalated. One of several individuals who felt so threatened by the subject that they cut off the interview in the middle, said: "No, sometimes I don't [believe that the massacre happened]. Sometimes I think that our newspapermen get a little bit wild."

One of the principal justifications our respondents offered was the idea that orders must be followed. Even some of the more dovish respondents gave statements like this: "What would their punishment have been if they had disobeyed? Do they get shot if they don't shoot someone else?" And from another "moderate" dove: "They were given an order to do something. They will shoot you if you don't. They had no choice."

Only a few recalled that some of the GIs *had* refused to shoot. One of those few was asked what the men should have done. He said: "What a lot of them did, refuse. Quite a few of them refused. Fact is, I even read where one of them shot himself in the foot so he would be evacuated, so he wouldn't have any part of it." When asked what they personally would have done if ordered to line up people and kill them, 74 percent of women said they would have refused, but only 27 percent of men. Those over 36 more often favored putting the enlisted men who did the shooting on trial than did those under 36, and slightly more of the older group expressly said that the men should have disobeyed orders to kill civilians.

The idea that whatever happened was justified by orders received implies a projection of guilt to somewhere higher up, and a number of our respondents made this explicit. Germans, similarly, tended to blame the German war crimes on Hitler, their leaders, the National Socialist party, the SS, or on military fanatics. But the idea that Germans, as individuals, might have been responsible for selection and toleration of their leaders was steadfastly rejected. While the question of responsibility was not specifically asked of our predominantly dovish sample, *no one extended the scope of responsibility to himself in particular or the American people in general.*

Another popular justification was the idea that the alleged victims were not really civilians, but enemies: "Now had these

civilians, had these women set booby traps for these people?"
Another man who felt he was a "dove" ("I'd hate to say I'm
a hawk"), yet who wanted the U.S. to "let out the stops," said:
"These little bastards are devious," implying in context that
the women and children were not really innocent bystanders.

None of those interviewed said that My Lai was justified as
revenge for NLF actions, but many seemed to *think* so: "I
understand that the Vietcong, from the start, have bombed
school yards, schoolhouses, movie theaters, restaurants . . .
just worthless bombing and it's killing innocent people by
the score. And these are their own people."

There was, however, one justification reportedly used by
post-war Germans which we did not hear. Our respondents,
with one exception, did *not* tell us that, as Art Hoppe put it,
"the unfortunate victims were members of an inferior race."
Both hawk and dove respondents often said that GIs tend to
look on Vietnamese civilians as subhumans, as "gooks,"
"slopes," "dinks." But with the one exception ("I think it's
true"), every subject coupled this awareness of racial prejudice
in others with an abstention from publicly subscribing to it
himself.

The various ways of defusing the emotional potential of
My Lai were used by hawks and doves alike, though not in
equal proportions. Hawks, more than others, tended to justify
the alleged massacre. Both hawks and doves argued in one way
or another that no massacre happened. The doves tended to
comfort themselves with the thought that My Lai occurred in
every war, hence they need not be upset. Whether it is Vietnamese peasants or one's next-door neighbor, emotional
detachment makes it possible to keep one's attention and concern focused on Number One. No evil intent is necessary for
men to tolerate, or even reluctantly to applaud war crimes, all
that is required is self-centeredness.

Perhaps it is an old American story for the draftee to be more at war with the regular army than with his designated "enemy." But when one is fighting an atrocity-prone war, there is something particularly poignant and tragic about what Sterba calls "the kids who pulled the triggers for the old men who ran this war in 1969," kids who Sterba thinks have a great deal in common with the kids on the other side. It would be too simple to view the entire Vietnam War as an expression of the older generation's filicidal (son-murdering) impulses, as I have heard a psychoanalytic colleague do; but this article lends some support for that kind of thesis. It also makes clear that the battle between the new youth culture and its older antagonists is nowhere fought with greater intensity than in Vietnam, where the former is represented by the "grunts" and the latter by the "lifers" or regulars.

COVER YOUR ASS

James P. Sterba

SAIGON.

When we were fighting up north, we got ambushed by a whole battalion of N.V.A. [the North Vietnamese Army] and there was so much stuff flying you couldn't tell if you killed anyone or not. But another time, I was on a patrol with a buddy and we stopped at this fork in the trail and we started smoking cigarettes and joking, and two gooks walked right down the trail at us. It was like time stood still. We looked at them and they looked at us and then we blew their — away. You walk up and see them dead, that you just killed them, and you say, "Goddamn, I just killed that man." But then you think, "Well, Jesus Christ," and you look at his gun and you know he'd have done the same thing to you if he'd had the chance. Before I came over here, I thought to myself, "Damn, could I kill a man?" Well, you learn fast in Vietnam.
    —Specialist 4 Herbert McHenry, twenty-one years old, from Akron, Ohio—a grunt. (Grunt: G.I. slang for a frontline soldier, Army or Marine.)

If you hung around enough at the muddy firebases and in the jungles with the kids who pulled the triggers for the old men who ran this war in 1969, you sometimes got the feeling between the hours of boredom and the seconds of terror and the daily entrances by jet and nightly exits by aluminum box, that the kids could work things out with the kids on the other side. That if the wires from the Pentagon to the South Vietnam command nerve centers and from Hanoi to the Cambodian caves had all of a sudden fallen still, the kids sent here to kill each other might have all stood up in the sun, dropped the guns and started picking flowers and crying—like a scene out of "Elvira Madigan."

Of course, that didn't happen in 1969, or in the opening days of 1970, and it would undoubtedly never happen in a modern war. But in 1969, Vietnam seemed like that kind of a war. It was not a war of national hate, but a hated, dreary struggle. All the early romance and idealism were gone. Their flickering lights were snuffed on June 8, when President Nixon announced withdrawal in a statement at Midway that must stick in the minds of every mother and father whose son has since left home for his year of war.

The touted air cavalries had gotten their big headlines years ago, swarming like locusts up the Anlao, the Iadrang and a hundred other valleys. The Marines had made their amphibi-ous assaults and had fought their Khesans. The airborne paratroopers had already saved both Hamburger Hill and the American Embassy, and the thought of saving them again was somewhat distasteful. The big medals had been distributed too often already and nobody came to the ceremonies any more to take pictures. The colonels who had begged to come here in 1965 to get their stars had already got them or been washed out.

Now, the tactical operations centers and headquarters were air-conditioned and computerized and filled with middle-aged career men who occasionally caught colds and wrote memos suggesting the cooling systems be turned down. The sergeants pushing booze at base bars were making more money than the American generals pushing the war—but less money than some South Vietnamese generals pushing anything they could get their hands on. The war was still costing more than $500 a second. University extension courses were being taught

in classrooms on huge, paved and sometimes lawned rear
bases, where old sergeants were getting tougher and tougher
about unshined boots.

At these big bases, jogging was on the increase, along with
sunbathing and softball tournaments. At Tansonnhut in
November, the Army announced the formation of "Armed
Forces Theater Vietnam, a touring military production group"
that kicked off the 1969–70 theatrical season with "You're a
Good Man, Charlie Brown."

Worlds away from all this, however, amid the mud and the
dust and the mosquitoes and the blood and the dead and the
dying, the grunts—it was a proud name they had chosen (from
the grunting sounds made by foot soldiers under heavy field
packs) —were still getting their legs blown off. But in 1969
they were not the same grunts as before—the ones who filled
the all-volunteer units a couple of years ago, not the gung-ho
enlistees and toughened three-war sergeants whom information
officers cited in 1969 as evidence of the professionalism of the
American military machine. These grunts did not come from
the ranks of the post-World War II silent, or Jack Kerouac's
fifties, or the concerned early sixties, or even the committed
mid-sixties. All those had come and gone back and joined the
American Legion or the real silent majority—the one that
keeps the florists in money on Decoration Day. Some of the
men of early Vietnam, the "lifers," were back for their fifth and
sixth tours, but only a relative few—the most compassionate
and the most restless—saw jungle rot and blood instead of
charts and cables.

No, these grunts were somehow unlike those others. These
grunts were the class of 1968—they had come out of that
America some of their commanders had seen only from the
windows of the Pentagon. They were graduates of an American nightmare in 1968 that stemmed mostly from the war they
had now come to fight—the year of riots and dissension, of
assassinations and Chicago, the year America's ulcer burst.

If they had not been in Chicago, they had certainly heard
about it or watched it on television. If they hadn't fought the

draft, they were aware that it was being fought. If they hadn't demonstrated against the war, they knew people who had. If they were too young, or too busy, or too far removed from the vocal and violent disputes over the war, they were at least aware of them. Many of them, probably the majority, had not physically committed themselves to either polarized side in the division, but even those in high school were well aware of the sides—as those before them had not been.

But before they knew it, both high-school football and college restlessness were over, and the process of unnatural selection that would determine who fixed helicopters and filed papers in the rear and who "humped the boonies" (or "beat the bush" looking for Vietcong) had begun. If they were high-school graduates and naive, or high-school dropouts and innocent, or if they were college students very much concerned and anti-war, they wouldn't enlist; the high-schoolers would mostly just put off their decisions about the military, thinking of college or a job. The collegians would think that since they were against the war and the military-industrial complex anyway, but didn't quite have the conviction for jail or exile, it was best to let the "green machine" swallow them up. One couldn't possibly volunteer to be a part of it. One had to be consistent, so you let the military take you.

What many of them didn't know was what the Army would do with them as draftees. It would make most of them (including most of the college men, regardless of what it had said about giving the collegians jobs to fit their abilities) grunts. And the arithmetic was there on what happened to grunts as they entered basic training: 15,000 dead and 45,000 wounded in 1968. The dead and wounded were not file clerks or grease monkeys or radio repairmen. The dead and wounded were grunts, overwhelmingly.

The members of the class of 1968 went through advanced infantry training at places like Fort Polk, Louisiana, or the "Shake and Bake" school for instant noncommissioned officers at Fort Benning, Georgia. Their M.O.S. (Military Occupational Specialty) would be stamped on their records: 11B, which meant infantry rifleman. But most of them would have no real idea of what it meant to be an "11 bush," even after they stepped off the troop planes at Bienhoa and Camranh Bay and the data-processing machines were matching them with units. Many were scared when they were trucked or flown to their new units' headquarters, but they didn't pay much attention when, during those first days of "in-country processing," the re-enlistment sergeants gave their spiels about not having to stay "out there" very long if they would only sign up for another three years. If they signed, then after only eight months in the Army, four or five of which had already been spent in training in the States, they could go home for a month and then come back and finish their year in Vietnam as a file clerk or a security guard.

It wouldn't be long, however, before many of them would be trying to remember what the re-enlistment sergeant had said.

One of their first tasks was learning grunt language. As replacements, they weren't new members of the unit, they were "cherries." They learned that grunts never die, they get "greased." They never said yes, they said "That's a Roge," or "Roger that." Their opponents were not the enemy, they were "gooks" or "dinks." In fact, to many grunts any Vietnamese was a "gook." Grunts would not put on their equipment, they would "saddle up." They didn't stage ambushes, they "blew bushes." They "humped the boonies" or "busted bush." Some of them never looked for the enemy, they went "Chuck-hunting." (Vietcong = "Victor Charley" = "Charley" = "Charles" = "Chuck.")

"My second day out, we blew a bush and four gooks were entirely wiped out. First dead ones I saw. You get a little sick. I ain't never shot one. Most of the time, you don't know who killed them 'cause everybody's just firing and you can't see them anyway. We went into a base camp once and this gook in a bunker shot up two guys in my platoon and our medic. Just killed them like that and he got away. Funny feeling. Just like that, they were dead. It's hard to say how you feel except scared. You don't really get mad. You just think it could be you."

Sgt. Nicholas Francic was twenty-one years old and had spent the first eleven months of 1969 on the line with the First Infantry near Dautieng as a draftee from Pittsburgh. With two weeks left in Vietnam, he was thinking about going home to "the world."

"I don't think I'll talk about it when I get back to the world because it would just be so hard to believe. Before I came over here, guys would tell war stories and I'd say, 'Bull— just war stories.' But now I'd believe anything anybody ever told me about it over here. I don't think anybody could believe half the stuff that's going on here. I'm glad I'm gettin' out. I don't know what I'd do if I was just gettin' here now.

"When I first got here, I didn't see a base camp for like four months. Just jungle. Sleeping on the ground every night. Once you got jungle rot and ringworm and rashes, you couldn't get rid of them 'cause you were in the same conditions every day. They try and give you clean clothes—like socks—but you just put them on and five minutes later you're back in the mud again. If anybody had told me three years ago I'd be doing this stuff, seeing all this stuff—the dead guys and all—I'd have told them they were crazy. I didn't think I could ever do it. But, you'd be surprised what you can do out here."

Pfc. M. A. Dirr, a twenty-one-year-old Marine from Cincinnati, lay on a bed in a ward room on the U.S.S. *Repose,* a hospital ship, off the coast of Danang in September. The drugs made him feel "weird," he said.

"I don't know whether it was an R.P.G. [rifle-propelled grenade] or one of our tanks. It was dark and some other guys [Marines] were about 50 meters away and they didn't know it was us and they opened up on us."

Was it worth it?

"Boy, after that, I don't see any sense in fighting over here," he said. Dirr wouldn't fight any more. At the end of his bed where his feet were supposed to be, there was only one lump in the sheet—his contribution to peace with honor having been one foot.

The officers' club bar next to the handball building at the Americal Division headquarters in Chulai is a thatched-roof structure that looks as though it had been franchised by Trader Vic's. Its open-air porch overlooks the jagged, rock-and-sand shore of the South China Sea, panning a postcard view. At one end of this view, across a gully, is a helicopter landing pad with a large red cross painted in the middle of it. Occasionally, between sips on rum and Cokes or gin and tonics, a bar visitor would see a helicopter settle down on the pad and five or six young men in bluish-green shirts jump out to it and pull off a stretcher holding a young wounded soldier and take him into the adjoining surgical ward. From the bar, however, it was out of focus and looked like some sort of dance or ritual.

On some nights during the movies at the bar, the officers would have to pull their chairs closer to the speakers because the helicopters coming in across the gully were making so much noise.

"You don't want to ride in that one," said a young radioman in a makeshift air-control tower at Landing Zone Baldy southwest of Danang in August, nodding to a helicopter as he popped the top on a Pepsi and petted Whore, his dog.

"That's the dead-guy run."

Maybe it was true that there were no real fronts in Vietnam, but there were definite levels of safety. From America, it was all just Vietnam, that tiny strip of Southeast Asia that had swallowed up so much money, life and will. If you were a soldier, just coming tc Vietnam was bad enough—where in Vietnam seemed irrelevant, until you got here.

The thirty-six-square-mile Army headquarters at Longbinh, for example, was safe, really safe, even though it was hit by rockets occasionally and somebody was killed or wounded. The 50,000 men who spent their year at Longbinh were known to the grunts as "R.E.M.F.'s" (rear-echelon mother—). R.E.M.F.'s, the grunts said, were the ones who would go home being for the war and telling war stories, 99 per cent of which would be baloney. The biggest battles at Longbinh were fought between the M.P.'s and drunken soldiers, and there were far more casualties from accidents there than from rockets.

Division headquarters was also the very rear. It caught rockets, too, but the handball courts, charcoal pits, swimming pools, bars, striptease dancers, mattresses, slot machines, refrigerators and hot and cold running water made up for them. If the war was anything at these places, it was boring.

There were many more soldiers at these big bases than anywhere else in Vietnam, and most of them were career officers and noncommissioned officers and enlisted men with special training. You had to look for draftees at these places, and when you found them, chances were it was because they had extended their time in Vietnam (a choice rewarded by a shorter term in the Army), because they had a "critical skill" (like churning out Army press releases), because they had some medical defect or because they had re-enlisted. There were many young dissidents in the rear in 1969, and although a few were outspoken publicly, they had to be extremely careful because the threat was always there that they would be jerked out of their relative security and transfered into the jungles, enlistees or not. In 1969, the career Army ruled the rear.

But as you went toward the battlefields—from the division to the brigade to the battalion to the company—the proportions reversed. At the company level in 1969, enlistees were rare, black faces were much more numerous, and draftees were everywhere. It was a rather neat dichotomy: between the men in the military and the kids in the war; the majority in the rear and the minority in the front; the comfortably bored and the miserably scared; the soldiers who had heeded their country's call and had become one of the military's "own" (the Army protects its own, they said), and the soldiers who had pretended not to heed it; the living and the dying. Although the Army claims ignorance on the matter, grunts in several line companies estimated that 80 to 90 per cent of the soldiers in their ranks were draftees and that from 20 to 40 per cent of them had had some college.

"That's all they seem to do any more with college guys is make them 11 bushes," said Specialist 4 Joseph Whalen, a platoon leader and graduate of Boston College with a degree in political science.

Once you got down there on the ground in the boonies among the lowest form of military might—the 11 bushes—it was amazing how much your values changed. Despite what all the philosophers and politicians and social scientists said, you were an animal with one basic instinct dominating all others: survival. The grunts have a phrase for it: "Cover your ass." Live. And it is equally amazing how difficult it was to think or talk about politics, philosophy, the Old—let alone New— Mobe, when you were bothered with staying alive. It didn't matter whether you were from Harvard, Columbia, North- eastern, Oklahoma State, A & M or P.S. 23, you still had to stay alive for 365 days and New Left Notes and the old col- legiate concern weren't worth a damn. Dry socks, hot meals, mosquito repellent and a clean M-16 rifle were far more im- portant.

It would take a book—perhaps less by a gifted writer—to describe the dehumanizing experience of being shot at. The barricades and billyclubs and tear gas at Columbia and Chicago seem so cheap after that first shot zings over your head. Absolutely everything becomes at once irrelevant except survival. If there was ever an event that "blew your mind," being shot at was it. After it, you were not the same person. Those who had been through the experience would warn others away from it, but somehow think less of those who had not had the experience.

"I don't really have anything against demonstrators, or blame people for not coming here," said Lieut. James Fried- man, twenty-one, of Burlington, Iowa, during Christmas dinner at Landing Zone Professional west of Chulai. "But after you get in the Army and are sort of jerked over here and have been through some bad stuff, it's almost like being older than those people."

To live, if you were a grunt, you had to shoot back. You had to become a killer, or at least a potential killer in the most immediate sense. Thus, you could still find a lot of tough guys out there in 1969. And if you stuck a microphone in their faces, they'd say, "Bomb Hanoi" or "Invade the North" or "Nuke the gooks." And why not? When your life was on the line, you were for everything that helped preserve it right at that instant. Many of the concerned grunts, before they got here, had serious qualms about the use of napalm. But, now, in the middle of combat, they would tell you there was absolutely nothing in the world more beautiful than the sight of those silver canisters tumbling end over end from a jet bomber and exploding in a huge ball of red flames and black smoke right where the gooks were shooting from. They felt like cheering, and sometimes they did.

Some grunts would even say that they liked to kill. "I've killed eighteen myself," said Sgt. Eddie Allen, a twenty-three-year-old 75th Infantry ranger from Muncie, Indiana. "I don't talk about it much, but I don't mind it. In fact, I sort of enjoy it."

Shy, quiet and friendly S.Sgt. Patrick Tadina, twenty-seven, from Honolulu, had spent forty-four months in Vietnam in 1970, mainly, he said, because he didn't know what else he could do. He had become one of the most decorated enlisted men of the war: two Silver Stars, two Vietnamese Crosses of Gallantry, five Bronze Stars all with "V" for valor, and three Purple Hearts. Tadina said he didn't particularly like killing people, just outsmarting them. His personal body count was 109.

It was during the times when death was close—when an arm or a leg had to be lifted by a crying friend out of the dirt and placed on a litter next to a young soldier yelling, "Jesus Christ, oh, my God, it hurts," and the Medevac chopper is still five minutes away as the medic's stained fingers fumble with the needle and the morphine bottle—that they all looked twelve years old.

It happened daily in 1969. Toward the end of the year, an average of fourteen were killed and 100 wounded per day.

Pfc. Dennis Storey, the platoon humorist, had been the point man that day in November just east of the Dongnai River when his platoon, of the First Battalion, 28th Infantry, First Infantry Division, was ambushed. The VC had thrown a switch detonating a Claymore mine as the platoon walked by it. It was so quick. Bang, and two guys didn't have any legs any more, and all the rest put their heads in the dirt and put their M-16's up over their helmets and pulled the triggers until they heard the VC's AK-47's stop cracking. Then silence, some yelling, a radio call for a Medevac. Storey had been lucky. He had walked past the mine before it exploded.

"Wasn't scared a bit," he said later. "You see, I know I'm gonna die before my year is up."

Sometimes the silliest things would happen out there in the boonies where the war was supposed to be such serious business. The battalion officers would spend hours in front of their maps, charting the next day's operation. The communications codes were set, the various coordinates were plotted, the strategy unveiled in sessions that reminded one of the pregame locker room. These meetings would end and the officers would all emerge into the sun and say nothing about the plan. It was all on a "need-to-know basis." It was so hush-hush at times that you felt they must all work for the C.I.A.

The next morning, as the countdown grew short, the plotters would appear nervous as they briefed the company officers. But when the company officer spread word to the grunts to "saddle up," the grunts would mope along, scowling and muttering about playing another "damned lifer game," the kind they'd been through dozens of times before, the kind they were still dirty and tired from doing a few days ago.

But for the planners, these productions were exhilarating, intricate affairs, in which the power of the huge American military might was most visible—all that fire power, that "air-mobility."

Then the grunts would move out, perhaps on foot, or by truck, or by the greatest kind of John Wayne moveout the Army had, the "combat assault" or "eagle flight." And the battalion commanders and majors would climb into their "Charley bird" (command and control helicopter), and the artillery support would be poised, the Cobra gunships ready to scramble.

As the grunts neared the scene of their secret search for "Charley," the colonels would be hovering above in the cool morning air, hoping for a "good contact." Then the grunts, if on an eagle flight, would be dropped in and quickly fan out as the radio networks were checked and everyone waited to see whether or not the "L.Z. [landing zone] was hot." It usually wasn't. And so after about thirty minutes, the majors and the colonels would fly back to their firebases and tend to other business, while closely monitoring the radios to see if the grunts made "contact." ("War is hell, but contact's a mother—," the grunts said.)

"None of my guys are gung ho," said First Lieut. Bodie Delaney, leader of the Third Platoon, Alpha Company, First Battalion, 501st Brigade, 101st Airborne Division in Thua-thien Province west of Hue. "Out of twenty-eight guys, I have six college graduates, one with a master's in zoology, ten guys with some college and all but one with high-school diplomas. All but four of them were drafted. Everybody falls into the same category. All of them are reduced to the same level—cover your ass for a year.

"All of them hate this war. There's a lot of superstition even among the college grads. I carried a church key. It became the platoon church key, but one day it was missing and I knew I must have left it back on a hill where we spent the night, about a mile away. Well, they all moaned and gave me all sorts of hell and then got a squad together and went all the way back there—there were gooks around there—to get that church key.

"Funny what happens to you out there. I thought for a long time about what would happen the first time I saw a gook. Could I kill him? When you see a dead one, it's a barbarous-type feeling, I guess. You really feel proud. There he is laying there in the dirt with his head blown off."

Specialist 4 Gregory Chizmadia sat in the recovery ward of a medical company in Dautieng in November, hoping his foot (from which a plantar wart had just been removed) wouldn't heal too fast so that he wouldn't have to go "back out there." He was nineteen and had quit school in Detroit to enlist and study radio and telephone repair. But, he said, "I didn't get it. They made me an 11 bush. Said they needed them bad."

Chizmadia didn't want to talk about his experiences since arriving in Vietnam on May 6, but after two hours of chatter about the Jets, Detroit, girls and his sore foot, the conversation began drifting:

"I tell you, you're scared as hell when the stuff starts flying. At first I was scared all the time. *Beaucoup* ambushed. In June, June 11 it was, we walked into that damn base camp and I was gonna re-up [re-enlist to get out of the field] right away. We had ten guys re-up after that. It was really bad. Lots of dead people. We had a C.O. who was really gung ho, a lifer. He wanted that body count. And after that fight, the dead gooks were laying there, already dead, and he went out and shot each one in the head with his sixteen.

"Sometimes it was real bad and we was in really thick jungle and it was hard and our C.O. said once that we couldn't have any food and water till we got a gook. Finally, he was with another platoon, so we pretended that we got one. We all started shootin' and yellin' and he came over and we said we saw some and hit one but they got away. There wasn't no blood or nothing, but the C.O. believed it and he brought us some water in.

"Boy, I don't want to go out there again. I ain't never seen a gook yet that was alive. I'm glad to say I haven't killed anyone over here. I hated every day of it out there."

He was asked about the war.

"It doesn't seem right, all those lifers back there in the Pentagon makin' us come out here and fight this thing. Just doesn't. I haven't seen hardly anybody here who says they are for it unless they're back in the rear."

On a sizzlingly hot day in August, it was less than ironic, then, when a helicopter touched down on Landing Zone Center, on a hill above the Hiepduc Valley northwest of Chulai, and dropped off a re-enlistment sergeant.

That was the day that a ragged, demoralized, exhausted company—Alpha, Third Battalion, 21st Infantry, American Division—trudged up the hill from a week of hell in the valley below with only half the men it had started with. World-famous Company A, the one that had refused, for an hour, to go to war, was being given the opportunity by the United States Army to re-enlist, to serve for three more years, but not "out there." By the end of the day, the re-enlistment sergeant's results, remarked one officer, had been "out-standing."

Jerome Frank describes the increasing blurring of rules and therefore of criteria for atrocity, by the changing technology of war. He sees these trends as having malignant psychological impact upon returning veterans as well as upon American society at large.

THE CHANGING CLIMATE OF ATROCITY
Jerome D. Frank, M.D.

As long as wars were fought primarily by organized, uniformed soldiers, it was possible to maintain a distinction between legitimate killing and war crimes. A soldier could justifiably try to kill his enemy counterpart who was trying to kill him, but it would be a criminal act wantonly to attack a member of the enemy population whose fate was irrelevant to the outcome of the struggle and who did not threaten the soldier's life.

Under conditions of modern war, however, this distinction has become increasingly blurred. Since a nation's war potential now depends heavily on its industrial capacity, all productive citizens have in a sense become combatants—that is, war has become "total." Hence the use of artillery and air power to inflict massive carnage on civilians has come to be viewed as a necessary part of the struggle for victory. So this form of mass murder has been accepted as legitimate. Furthermore, wars are increasingly characterized by guerilla activities in which it is impossible to distinguish friend from foe. An enemy soldier may be dressed as a peasant; and a child, a crippled old man or a nursing mother may hurl a grenade. So the exhausted, hungry, frightened soldier, thirsting for revenge for the deaths of comrades in arms, is all too prone to attack civilians first and ask questions afterwards.

In short, whatever tidiness old-fashioned wars may have possessed has long since vanished, and with it attempts to arrive at generally agreed upon definitions of war crimes are doomed to futility. Since one cannot distinguish between acceptable and unacceptable forms of killing by the degree of suffering they inflict, an atrocity is simply a form of killing deemed illegitimate by the group that so labels it. Americans are outraged by the beheadings and disembowelings performed by the North Vietnamese, while they in turn describe napalming and crop-poisoning as "the most cruel and barbaric means of annihilating people." Both are right.

What are the psychological effects on young men of performing acts which, even though carried out in the heat of battle, violate the codes of conduct in which they have been reared? In every society the killing of children, women, the elderly and infirm is condemned; and guilt for this act is not necessarily washed away by the fact that the victim might have been about to kill oneself.

To be sure, humans are remarkably ingenious in finding ways of exculpating themselves, and one method, especially available to the military, is to claim to have acted under orders. Obedience to superiors is a cornerstone of all organized societies. An experimental study surprisingly revealed that about two-thirds of normal American adults will deliver powerful electric shocks they believe to be potentially lethal if told to do so by a person perceived as possessing legitimate authority. Soldiers are trained to be unquestioningly obedient at all times; so for them it must be very easy to transfer to their commander any guilt they might feel for committing atrocities.

It may well be that most returning combat soldiers will, as in the past, have few residual scars of their war experiences and will doff their aggressiveness and their guilt with their uniforms. However, it is a disquieting thought that even in stable societies with high morale whose armies are returning victorious, there is typically a rise in crimes of violence after each war.

American society today is in conflict about its aims and values, its institutions are under attack, and groups within it are becoming ever more polarized. This polarization along racial, age, economic and other dimensions will aggravate the bitterness and resentment felt by returning soldiers who failed to achieve victory in a particularly unpleasant war. The search for scapegoats, a prime means of discharging pent-up rage, will not lack for targets. Some veterans will blame those opposed to the war for having cheated them of victory by stabbing them in the back; others will feel that those who supported the war did so to enrich themselves at the expense of the fighting man. Schooled in killing and with their inhibitions weakened and moral sensibilities blunted by their war experiences, some veterans could readily choose violent means to express their frustrations. As a result, whatever the final outcome on the battlefield, in the end the chief loser of the Indochina war may well be the United States.

Peter Bourne is unique among American psychiatrists in having had the opportunity to investigate the basic-training as well as the combat experience. The special nature of both, he tells us, contribute directly to My Lai.

FROM BOOT CAMP TO MY LAI

Peter G. Bourne, M.D.

"American boys would never do something like that," was the response of many people in the United States to the first reports of the My Lai massacre. Obsessed with the inviolate image of the all-American boy, the notion of wholesale wanton murder of women and children posed an irreconcilable contradiction that was intolerable for many people. This cognitive dissonance was dealt with in a variety of well-recognized and by now all too familiar mental maneuvers. One segment of the population denied the validity of the reports, saying that there was no real evidence that the massacre had taken place, although clearly there was. Others argued that it was best to ignore any such incidents because publicizing them only provided comfort to the enemy. A variation on this theme was to respond to accounts of American atrocities by talking only of Viet Cong atrocities, as though this both explained and justified acts by Americans. A further group sought to reidentify or relabel the victims in such a way as to make their slaughter more acceptable. They were really Viet Cong; women and children in the village had previously thrown grenades and shot at GIs, or constant enemy attacks had been mounted from this village—all were statements without foundation that were used to justify what had occurred. Perhaps the most bizarre rationalization of all is that some of the men at My Lai had smoked pot the night before the massacre, and that this was responsible for their acts.

Some members of the peace movement have also been guilty of not facing the real issue. In completely absolving the individuals actually involved and in placing the blame exclusively on the policymakers and field commanders, they have ignored the question of how the individual soldier can end up committing these acts.

What we have to face is that these men did in fact murder in cold blood a large number of women and children who were not combatants and who were not threatening or endangering their lives. What we should ask is how the past experience of these men both in the United States and in Vietnam permitted them or even preconditioned them to commit such acts. Two events play a clearly contributory role in preparing GIs psychologically for events such as My Lai. One of these is the initial militarization process as experienced in Basic Training, and the other is the socialization to war itself and specifically to killing, which occurs once the individual arrives in Vietnam.

The unique psychological processes which the individual undergoes in Basic Training have been well identified. During the first four weeks of training the recruit is subjected to a systematic stripping process in which many elements of his civilian identity and self-image are deliberately denuded from him. The recruit brings with him to Basic Training a set of values, beliefs, and expectations about his rights as an individual member of society. He has taken for granted a whole framework of supporting cultural factors, a conception of himself and his achievements which reflects the status he has been accorded in his past social environment, and a set of defensive maneuvers which have served him well in dealing with conflicts, failures, and other personal adversity. The early weeks of training are characterized by physical and verbal abuse, humiliation, and a constant discounting and discrediting of everything in which the recruit believes and everything which serves to characterize him as an individual. His head is shaved, his ability to think independently is scorned, and every moment of his day is minutely programmed and scheduled. Even his accustomed language pattern must be renounced, and college graduates are reduced under the taunts of sarcastic drill sergeants to a vocabulary of monosyllabic conformity interspersed with obscenities adopted from their mentors. More recently drill sergeants with Vietnam experiance have been noted for boasting to recruits about the way they have tortured prisoners and committed other atrocities. It is primarily a way of mocking the humanitarian beliefs that the recruit brings with him from civilian life, but it is also effective in persuading many individuals that to be accepted and to survive in the military system they must adopt or at least pay lip service to the same values as these clearly very powerful sergeants.

Above all, expressive signs of respect for superiors and for the Army are coercively and continuously demanded as a way of constantly reinforcing recognition of the recruit's subservient and stigmatized role.

Around the fourth week of training a sudden change occurs when the recruits are taken to the firing range and learn to handle a weapon. At the end of that week they are tested on their proficiency with the rifle, and they fire for scores that will go on their permanent record. It is the first time the Army has given the recruit any recognition for an attribute or skill, and even the fact that he is being tested on his ability to fire a rifle implies that he must have acquired some degree of proficiency with it. For the first time since the recruit arrived in Basic Training the Army allows the man to be accepted in his new role as a "soldier." During the rest of Basic Training the recruit receives recognition for learning one skill after another and is increasingly accepted and rewarded by the Army, but only for the attributes he acquired in training, and not for anything he brought from his previous environment.

The whole of Basic Training has evolved in the guise of a masculine initiation rite that often has particular appeal to the late adolescent struggling to establish a masculine identity for himself in society. The second half of Basic Training carries with it the clear implication that the trainee is acquiring manly status as he learns each new military skill.

Military training and particularly Basic Training embody the concrete realization of attitudes and activities that are diametrically opposed to the practice and spirit of democracy.

Obedience, the keystone of military order, is incompatible with the candid expression of opinion and the right to question and critically examine courses of action, prerogatives that are inherent in the role of the mature citizens in a democracy. Obedience instilled in Basic Training leads effectively to dependence with a reliance upon and acceptance of the will of others. Responsibility for one's own welfare and for the consequence of one's acts is relinquished and remains habitually in the hands of superiors.

Basic Training accomplishes three specific objectives which are maintained by subsequent existence in the military environment. First, the recruit must reject his preexisting identity and envelop himself instead in the institutional identity of the military organization. Second, he must accept his impotence in the face of military discipline and recognize the crushing recrimination it can inflict if he should seek to challenge it. And third, he must be convinced of the legitimacy and righteousness of the system.

While on the surface the use of a rifle and training in other forms of violence may seem to be the predominant features of Basic Training, they are often hollow mechanistic acts divorced from any recognition of their real consequences. When the soldier arrives in Vietnam he has yet to undergo the brutalizing psychological experiences that have allowed atrocities to become commonplace occurrences there. The GI arriving for the first time in Vietnam differs from the draftee originally entering the military more in the degree to which he has become acculturated to the military system than to any specific propensity for killing.

On his arrival in Vietnam the GI is immediately thrust into an environment where killing and the struggle for survival are a daily fact of life. To stay alive by any means possible for the next twenty-four hours becomes the motivating force, and to do so the GI has little choice but to fall back on the training and resources the Army has provided him. The Army has already taught him to relinquish personal initiative, and the more hazardous and frightening the environment the more he is willing to be dependent upon the orders of superiors, even at the expense of abandoning previous values, beliefs, and independence.

A sense of general frustration exists among the military command in Vietnam. Despite the overwhelming military strength of the United States, it has been held to a stand-off for ten years by a disgruntled peasant population and a second-rate military power. Commanders make little secret of their frustrations, which then seep down to the lowliest GI. Often there is an implied message to the soldier in the field that anything he does to relieve the sense of stalemate will be condoned if not praised by his superiors. This leads not only to the counting of civilian casualties as Viet Cong to inflate body counts, but also to a feeling that when there is any question about a person's identity it is better to shoot first and ask questions later. I witnessed an old woman and an eighteen-month-old child being shot by indiscriminate firing into a village. It was readily agreed that they should be counted at Viet Cong casualties because it was known to be a Viet Cong-controlled village and because the colonel commanding the outfit had expressed the expectation that the attack would result in many enemy casualties.

Overriding all other issues is a strong racist flavor that pervades the attitude of the military toward all Vietnamese and which enjoys tacit endorsement by many senior officers. At the headquarters of General William Westmoreland, for instance, separate toilet facilities were built for Americans and Vietnamese. When it is so hard to distinguish those who have allegiance to the Viet Cong, it becomes much easier for the GI in his frustration to lump all Vietnamese together as "slopes," "gooks," or "dinks," because at least he can identify that category.

An essential element in most massacres or atrocities is a preceding psychological step in which the victims are relabeled and identified as being different, inferior or even subhuman, which then allows one to commit acts that would be unthinkable if the victims were viewed as human beings like ourselves. This essential element was clearly present with the Jews in Nazi Germany and with Negroes in the South. The Army has contributed significantly to allowing all Vietnamese to be viewed in a stigmatized and inferior role, and therefore to making them vulnerable to a variety of mistreatment by American troops. The usual rationalization is of course made that life is cheap to Asians, and therefore killing them is justifiable.

Any reader of the accounts of the My Lai massacre will be struck by the fact that it was not a single isolated event, but the culmination of lesser acts which had gradually escalated in their scope and brutality over many months. A major part of the blame for atrocities in Vietnam must lie with a command attitude that has consistently turned a blind eye to minor war crimes and to isolated atrocities, thereby condoning such acts in the eyes of the GIs.

Those who have never been in combat frequently say in regard to atrocities, "I could never do something like that." Unfortunately, however civilized we may regard ourselves to be, we probably all have the potential for such acts, and the veneer of civilization is far thinner than many of us would like to believe. There is a thrill in killing that lies latent in most of us, but which can readily surface under the right circumstances. Military training encourages the individual to relinquish all responsibility for his acts and to submit himself entirely to the control of superiors. There is then a tendency for the individual not to place the same internal censorship on his behavior because he has become accustomed to the military as an outside force setting those limits for him. When it does not, as has been the case with atrocities in Vietnam, he still feels absolved from taking that responsibility himself.

Military service, and particularly military service in a combat zone, asks the individual soldier to completely reverse much of his usual value system. Killing, the destruction of property, and a variety of other acts which are condemned in civilian life are suddenly in a complete reversal given a positive connotation and are rewarded by praise, medals, and the implication that they reflect manliness. Unfortunately this reversal of values, while it is intended to be highly restricted and limited to certain well-circumscribed areas, rarely remains so and there is considerable spill over into other values and behaviors. Black marketeering, which many soldiers would never consider in a civilian setting, is readily acceptable in a combat zone, and sexual promiscuity which would be condemned by many GIs in the United States becomes an accepted part of their life in Vietnam. Values do not exist isolated in a vacuum but are part of an intricately entwined belief system, and it is hard to reverse a single element without reversing an entire constellation of values. There can be little doubt that in the combat situation it becomes often meaningless to ask the soldier to make the fine discriminations that distinguish a "legitimate" act of war from a war crime.

Acts of barbarism and indiscriminate slaughter of innocent people does not occur exclusively in the military context. There are many civilian instances where atrocities have been committed. The danger of the military lies in its ability to systematically inculcate through its training and socialization process a high potential for committing atrocities in otherwise normal individuals in whom such tendencies would remain largely controlled.

This sequence of Daniel Berrigan's poems and commentary on his visit to Hanoi—from children to new model privy to bombed hospitals—says a great deal about the suffering, industry, and industrial level, of our "enemies." And when Father Berrigan tells us that, when witnessing films of our bombings, "I felt like a Nazi watching films of Dachau," he tells us something of the profoundly disturbing, and yet potentially liberating, possibilities of American conscience. After having been a fugitive from justice for four months, Father Berrigan is now imprisoned at the Federal Correctional Institution at Danbury, Connecticut.

THE GIFT

Daniel Berrigan

At one point of our interview we were interrupted by an air warning. We walked immediately to the shelter in the backyard; and I saw there, as I rounded a corner underground, three beautiful children, like a frieze against the wall in the half darkness, come to life, the children eating in supreme calm their dishes of rice, the oldest girl feeding the smallest child, her brother.

Children in the Shelter

Imagine; three of them.

As though survival
were a rat's word,
and a rat's end
waited there at the end

and I must have
in the century's boneyard
heft of flesh and bone in my arms

I picked up the littlest
a boy, his face
breaded with rice (his sister calmly feeding him
as we climbed down)

> In my arms fathered
> in a moment's grace, the messiah
> of all my tears. I bore, reborn
>
> a Hiroshima child from hell. . . .

There was talk first of an improved privy, of which a model sat in solitary splendor on the table before us. The genius of the method, as anyone could realize who has visited or worked in developing countries, consisted in breaking the immemorial disease cycle between human elimination and the crops and fruit trees nourished by human faeces spread upon the fields. According to the new plan, after every use of the privy, ashes were sprinkled over the faeces and all dampness and germs removed. Eventually, when the manure was spread upon the fields, it was odorless and germless.

They presented the model privy to Zinn and myself.

The gift moved me, poetically speaking.

Progress in Rural Develoment: A
Lecture on Privies, and a Gift to
Our Countrymen

> In the municipal hospital, in the bone-chilling cold
> the dispassionate voices, Viet and English, unfolded
> an invincible case for improvement of village privies.
>
> Doubters, we sniffed with our senses the odorless faeces
> achieved by new methods of drying. We stood.
> The photographer readies. Passed to the doctor's hands
>
> and to ours, and on through ten thousand miles
> into marveling America (and carefully constructed
> as a boat in a bottle, as a model of Model T)
> that gift, that two-seated wonder.

A new kind of village well had also been contrived; wells free of disease and diseased water were now in use in most villages; a well for every four or five families.

(There followed a series of movies in which a succession of horrors committed against medical facilities was repeated, one after another, with a kind of enervating sameness. The details are of no great moment, except as they would assure us that the attacks upon medical facilities lie beyond the scope of explanation based upon error and chance. Some 248 attacks have destroyed some 127 major medical installations. This includes 24 major hospitals, 39 district hospitals, and 54 other sanitary installations. Every attack seemed to have a single-minded plan. The planes always separate over an urban area; one group attacks the city itself, another concentrates upon a hospital area. The visiting team from the International Crimes Commission declared that they had never seen such destruction as has been wreaked upon the medical facilities of the North.)

I am quoting what follows from my notes, scrawled in the changing light of a film in progress, in a hand shaking with emotion and shame. As I wrote I felt like a Nazi watching films of Dachau. On and on, a record of perfidy and extermination. Leprosarium, TB hospitals, lying-in hospitals, general hospitals, medical stations. Destroyed, destroyed. A hospital in the vicinity of Hanoi destroyed by cluster bombs, some three hundred beds in complete ruins. Only five provincial hospitals remain untouched. It must be stressed that most of the hospitals are far from any other population centers. The only conceivable purpose of the attacks is to maim and kill the patients, and to induce terror in the medical workers, in order that the entire society might be intimidated.

The Childrens' Hospital on the outskirts of Hanoi is in ruins.

The attacks on the hospitals usually follow a general pattern. The first wave drops the larger explosives. A second wave sprays the survivors with fragmentation bombs. The purpose seems to be to ensure that North Vietnam will never again have sufficient medical facilities for a civilized future.

The first bombing of the largest leprosarium of the country was in December of 1965. The 2,600-bed hospital has now, after two years of repeated bombings, been destroyed and is in complete ruin.

The hospital destruction has included shelling by the Seventh Fleet, the use of explosives and CBU bombs, and phosphorus bombs; all have resulted in the wide-spread killing of patients and medical workers.

The air war has induced a profound change in the medical structure in the North. Now former hospitals are broken up into smaller medial units. Children are born, patients are operated upon, the victims of bombing are treated medically, all in smaller underground shelters.

There followed a hearbreaking summary of four "classical" cases of wounding of civilians by CBU bombs. The director of the surgical hospital conducted this surgical experiment, upon us. We were allowed to see in some detail, in the medical explanation, the X-rays of four victims of "antipersonnel warfare": a child of ten years, a young woman twenty-three years old (a teacher), a girl of twelve, and an older woman about fifty-five. It would be to no profit to give medical details here. These were exemplary cases of those who, in schools or streets or backyards or homes, had been wounded in the course of massive antipersonnel bombings. The teacher had some two hundred pellet wounds on her body. The boy had suffered the death of his younger brother and his father. The teacher and pupil had been wounded in the course of an ordinary day of school.

We can testify that these patients exist as described; we went from the X-ray lecture immediately to visit them, where they had been brought to one room in order to be viewed. We returned to the room for another cup of scalding tea; the hospital was murderous cold.

Arthur Miller here raises the problem of Americans' failing to draw the proper conclusions from their televised war-viewing—even concerning such simple questions as, who is doing the burning? and Why?

THE AGE OF ABDICATION

Arthur Miller

Man's capacity for deluding himself has always been cited as one of the chief causes of war, but the reporting from Vietnam is making even a little honest self-delusion hard to come by. On television the other night they showed how another fifteen thousand Vietnamese peasants were forced out of their villages by Americans who then proceeded to burn down their thatched houses to deny shelter to the Viet Cong.

Watching this short piece of film, I thought once again how ineptly this era has been characterized. Nearly every play and novel is about the lack of human communication, the unreality of contemporary life, but here was the kind of incident visible to the whole world which in former wars would have been a state secret for fifty years after the war was over. Watching it, I thought that it was not a lack of communication we suffer from, but some sort of sincerity so breathtaking that it has knocked us morally silly.

The peasants involved here, the reporting disclosed, had not wanted to have their homes burned; our people had no land to give them to replace what they were being forced to vacate; and some of them had had to leave so quickly that they left their working tools behind.

Horrible as the whole spectacle was, I could not help feeling for a few moments afterward that despite its clarity and completeness, something remained unspoken in it. And soon the question formed itself which, I think, now goes to the heart of the matter. How is it that we never see Vietnamese peasants burning down their own houses?

NO SCORCHED EARTH

This is not as ridiculous as it sounds when we recall the Yugo-slavs, the Russians, and if a dim memory is not mistaken, the Americans during the Revolution who destroyed buildings to deny them to the enemy. Even the Nazis scorched the German earth before the advancing Russian armies. I am certain that where I live more than one citizen would feel no pain as he fired his house to keep it from an invader, if we ever faced a war here.

Frankly, I am amazed that our Psywar people haven't thought of this. Here we are, pumping blood and money into a fight to help these people retain their freedom, and we can't even find a native pyromaniac, let alone a patriot, to fire his own roof. Instead there is always the same old Zippo torch, the GI's standing around looking rather uneasy, and the villagers looking on with Oriental resignation.

Imagine the effect if for once we could see villagers lighting the flames and maybe even a few shaking their fists toward the jungle where the wily Viet Cong must be biting their nails in futile anger at shelter lost. It would be enough to get Senator Fulbright to stop trying to drag Secretary Rusk before a Senate Foreign Affairs Committee hearing, for in one stroke we would have understood why we're in Vietnam.

What we have come to, it seems to me, is the level of belief we accord most advertising. We know perfectly well our teeth well never be white again but we go on buying teeth-whitening dentifrices; we really don't believe that any good will come out of this war, but most of us go right on paying for it and will as likely as not vote back into power the men who escalated it to its present size.

But there is no secret about any of this, and no lack of communication either. Since it is we and not the Vietnamese who are burning down their houses, it can only mean that they don't share our urgency and would much rather live where they always lived and work the land they have always worked, Viet Cong or no Viet Cong. In short, it is our war against

Hanoi and not the war of the people of Vietnam against the Viet Cong.

THIS AGE—AND HISTORY

So what's the moral? For one thing we might think seriously about changing the name of the age. It is not the Age of Anxiety, not any more; nor the Age of the Credibility Gap, not with the mountain of facts available about this war. We see, we hear, and from Bishop Sheen to U Thant to General Ridgway we are given an understanding of the futility and the moral insanity of what we are doing.

But we do not affirm or deny what is given us, we simply abdicate. Ours is the Age of Abdication. I'm speaking of the great majority, of course. The protestors, in and out of the Senate, merely prove the rule, and there is nothing at present in their favor but history.

As Karl Jaspers weaves his way skillfully through the varieties of experiencing—and avoiding—Nazi-linked guilt, the parallels impress themselves still further, and more disquietingly, upon the American reader. Nor is it especially reassuring to recognize that we are dealing with common denominators of all large-scale atrocity.

GERMAN GUILT

Karl Jaspers

MORAL GUILT

Every German asks himself: how am I guilty?

The question of the guilt of the individual analyzing himself is what we call the moral one. Here we Germans are divided by the greatest differences.

While the decision in self-judgment is up to the individual alone, we are free to talk with one another, insofar as we are in communication, and morally to help each other achieve clarity. The moral sentence on the other is suspended, however—neither the criminal nor the political one.

The moral guilt exists for all those who give room to conscience and repentance. The morally guilty are those who are capable of penance, the ones who knew, or could know, and yet walked in ways which self-analysis reveals to them as culpable error—whether conveniently closing their eyes to events, or permitting themselves to be intoxicated.

Our duty to the fatherland goes far beneath blind obedience to its rulers of the day. The fatherland ceases to be a fatherland when its soul is destroyed. The power of the state is not an end in itself; rather, it is pernicious if this state destroys the German character. Therefore, duty to the fatherland did not by any means lead consistently to obedience to Hitler and to the assumption that even as a Hitler state Germany must, of course, win the war at all costs. Herein lies the false conscience. It is no simple guilt. It is at the same time a tragic confusion, notably of a large part of our unwitting youth. To do one's duty to the fatherland means to commit one's whole person to the highest demands made on us by the best of our ancestors, not by the idols of a false tradition.

It was amazing to see the complete self-identification with army and state, in spite of all evil. For this unconditionality of a blind nationalism—only conceivable as the last crumbling ground in a world about to lose all faith—was moral guilt.

Each one of us is guilty insofar as he remained inactive. The guilt of passivity is different. Impotence excuses; no moral law demands a spectacular death. Plato already deemed it a matter of course to go into hiding in desperate times of calamity, and to survive. But passivity knows itself morally guilty of every failure, every neglect to act whenever possible, to shield the imperiled, to relieve wrong, to countervail. Impotent submission always left a margin of activity which, though not without risk, could still be cautiously effective. Its anxious omission weighs upon the individual as moral guilt. Blindness for the misfortune of others, lack of imagination of the heart, inner indifference toward the witnessed evil—that is moral guilt.

The moral guilt of outward compliance, of *running with the pack,* is shared to some extent by a great many of us. To maintain his existence, to keep his job, to protect his chances a man would join the Party and carry out other nominal acts of conformism.

Nobody will find an absolute excuse for doing so—notably in view of the many Germans who, in fact, did not conform, and bore the disadvantages.

Yet we must remember what the situation looked like in, say, 1936 or '37. The Party was the state. Conditions seemed incalculably permanent. Nothing short of a war could upset the régime. All the powers were appeasing Hitler. All wanted peace. A German who did not want to be out of everything, lose his profession, injure his business, was obliged to go along —the younger ones in particular. It is decisive for the meaning of compliance in what connection and from what motives he acquired his membership in the Party; each year and every situation has its own mitigating and aggravating circumstances, to be distinguished only in each individual case.

Morality is always influenced by mundane purposes. I may be morally bound to risk my life, if a realization is at stake; but there is no moral obligation to sacrifice one's life in the sure knowledge that nothing will have been gained. Morally we have a duty to dare, not a duty to choose certain doom. Morally, in either case, we rather have the contrary duty, not to do what cannot serve the mundane purpose but to save ourselves for realizations in the world.

But there is within us a guilt consciousness which springs from another source. Metaphysical guilt is the lack of absolute solidarity with the human being as such—an indelible claim beyond morally meaningful duty. This solidarity is violated by my presence at a wrong or a crime. It is not enough that I risk my life to prevent it; if it happens, and if I was there, and if I survive where the other is killed, I know from a voice within myself: I am guilty of being still alive.

I quote from an address I gave in August 1945: "We ourselves have changed since 1933. It was possible for us to seek death in humiliation—in 1933 when the Constitution was torn up, the dictatorship established in sham legality and all resistance swept away in the intoxication of a large part of our people. We could seek death when the crimes of the régime became publicly apparent on June 30, 1934, or with the lootings, deportations and murders of our Jewish friends and fellow-citizens in 1938, when to our ineradicable shame and disgrace the synagogues, houses of God, went up in flames throughout Germany. We could seek death when from the start of the war the régime acted against the words of Kant, our greatest philosopher, who called it a premise of international law that nothing must occur in war which would make a later reconcilement of the belligerents impossible. Thousands in Germany sought, or at least found death in battling the régime, most of them anonymously. We survivors did not seek it. We did not go into the streets when our Jewish friends were led away; we did not scream until we too were destroyed. We preferred to stay alive, on the feeble, if logical, ground that our death could not have helped anyone. We were guilty of being alive. We know before God which deeply humiliates us. What happened to us in these twelve years is like a transmutation of our being."

In November 1938, when the synagogues burned and Jews were deported for the first time, the guilt incurred was chiefly moral and political. In either sense, the guilty were those still in power. The generals stood by. In every town the commander could act against crime, for the soldier is there to protect all, if crime occurs on such a scale that the police cannot or fail to stop it. They did nothing. At that moment they forsook the once glorious ethical tradition of the German Army. It was not their business. They had dissociated themselves from the soul of the German people, in favor of an absolute military machine that was a law unto itself and took orders.

True, among our people many were outraged and many deeply moved by a horror containing a presentiment of coming calamity. But even more went right on with their activities, undisturbed in their social life and amusements, as if nothing had happened. That is moral guilt.

But the ones who in utter impotence, outraged and despairing, were unable to prevent the crimes took another step in their metamorphosis by a growing consciousness of metaphysical guilt.

INDIVIDUAL AWARENESS OF COLLECTIVE GUILT

We feel something like a co-responsibility for the acts of members of our families. This co-responsibility cannot be objectivized. We should reject any manner of tribal liability. And yet, because of our consanguinity we are inclined to feel concerned whenever wrong is done by someone in the family— and also inclined, therefore, depending on the type and circumstances of the wrong and its victims, to make it up to them even if we are not morally and legally accountable.

Thus the German—that is, the German-speaking individual —feels concerned by everything growing from German roots.

It is not the liability of a national but the concern of one who shares the life of the German spirit and soul—who is of one tongue, one stock, one fate with all the others—which here comes to cause, not as tangible guilt, but somehow analogous to co-responsibility.

We further feel that we not only share in what is done at present—thus being co-responsible for the deeds of our contemporaries—but in the links of tradition. We have to bear the guilt of our fathers. That the spiritual conditions of German life provided an opportunity for such a régime is a fact for which all of us are co-responsible. Of course this does not mean that we must acknowledge "the world of German ideas" or "German thought of the past" in general as the sources of the National-Socialist misdeeds. But it does mean that our national tradition contains something, mighty and threatening, which is our moral ruin.

We feel ourselves not only as individuals but as Germans. Every one, in his real being, is the German people. Who does not remember moments in his life when he said to himself, in opposition and in despair of his nation, "I am Germany"—or, in jubilant harmony with it, "I, too, am Germany!" The German character has no other form than these individuals. Hence the demands of transmutation, of rebirth, of rejection of evil are made of the nation in the form of demands from each individual.

Because in my innermost soul I cannot help feeling collectively, being German is to me—is to everyone—not a condition but a task. This is altogether different from making the nation absolute. I am a human being first of all; in particular I am a Frisian, a professor, a German, linked closely enough for a fusion of souls with other collective groups, and more or less closely with all groups I have come in touch with. For moments this proximity enables me to feel almost like a Jew or Dutchman or Englishman. Throughout it, however, the fact of my being German—that is, essentially, of life in the mother tongue—is so emphatic that in a way which is rationally not conceivable, which is even rationally refutable, I feel co-responsible for what Germans do and have done.

I feel closer to those Germans who feel likewise—without becoming melodramatic about it—and farther from the ones whose soul seems to deny this link. And this proximity means, above all, a common inspiring task—of not being German as we happen to be, but becoming German as we are not yet but ought to be, and as we hear it in the call of our ancestors rather than in the history of national idols.

By our feeling of collective guilt we feel the entire task of renewing human existence from its origin—the task which is given to all men on earth but which appears more urgently, more perceptibly, as decisively as all existence, when its own guilt brings a people face to face with nothingness.

As a philosopher I now seem to have strayed completely into the realm of feeling and to have abandoned conception. Indeed language fails at this point, and only negatively we may recall that all our distinctions—notwithstanding the fact that we hold them to be true and are by no means rescinding them—must not become resting places. We must not use them to let matters drop and free ourselves from the pressure under which we continue on our path, and which is to ripen what we hold most precious, the eternal essence of our soul.

GUILT OF ALL?

If we hear the imperfections in the political conduct of the powers explained as universal inevitabilities of politics, we may say in reply that this is the common guilt of mankind.

For us, the recapitulation of the others' actions does not have the significance of alleviating our guilt. Rather, it is justified by the anxiety which as human beings we share with all others for mankind—mankind as a whole, which not only has become conscious of its existence today but, due to the results of technology, has developed a trend toward a common order, which may succeed or fail.

The basic fact that all of us are human justifies this anxiety of ours about human existence as a whole. There is a passionate desire in our souls, to stay related or to reestablish relations with humanity as such.

How much easier we should breathe if, instead of being as human as we are, the victors were selfless world governors! With wisdom and foresight they would direct a propitious reconstruction including effective amends. Their lives and actions would be an example demonstrating the ideal of democratic conditions, and daily making us feel it as a convincing reality. United among themselves in reasonable, frank talk without mental reservation, they would quickly and sensibly decide all arising questions. No deception and no illusion would be possible, no silent concealment and no discrepancy between public and private utterances. Our people would receive a splendid education; we should achieve the liveliest nationwide development of our thinking and appropriate the most substantial tradition. We should be dealt with sternly but justly and kindly, even charitably, if the unfortunate and misguided showed only the slightest good-will.

But the others are human as we are. And they hold the future of mankind in their hands. Since we are human, all our existence and the possibilities of our being are bound up with their doings and with the results of their actions. So, to us, to sense what they want, think and do is like our own affair.

In this anxiety we ask ourselves: could the other nations' better luck be due in part to more favorable political destinies? Could they be making the same mistakes that we made, only so far without the fatal consequences which led to our undoing?

They would reject any warnings from us wicked wretches. They would fail to understand, perhaps, and might even find it presumptuous if Germans should worry over the course of history—which is their business, not that of the Germans. And yet, we are oppressed by one nightmarish idea: if a dictatorship in Hitler's style should ever rise in America, all hope would be lost for ages. We in Germany could be freed from the outside. Once a dictatorship has been establishd, no liberation from within is possible. Should the Anglo-Saxon world be dictatorially conquered from within, as we were, there would no longer be an outside, nor a liberation. The freedom fought for and won by Western man over hundreds, thousands of years would be a thing of the past. The primitivity of despotism would reign again, but with all means of technology. True, man cannot be forever enslaved; but this comfort would then be a very distant one, on a plane with Plato's dictum that in the course of infinite time everything that is possible will here or there occur or recur as a reality. We see the feelings of moral superiority and we are frightened: he who feels absolutely safe from danger is already on the way to fall victim to it. The German fate could provide all others with experience. If only they would understand this experience! We are no inferior race. Everywhere people have similar qualities. Everywhere there are violent, criminal, vitally capable minorities apt to seize the reins if occasion offers, and to proceed with brutality.

We may well worry over the victors' self-certainty. For all decisive responsibility for the course of events will henceforth be theirs. It is up to them to prevent evil or conjure up new evil. Whatever guilt they might incur from now on would be as calamitous for us as for them. Now that the whole of mankind is at stake, their responsibility for their actions is intensified. Unless a break is made in the evil chain, the fate which overtook us will overtake the victors—and all of mankind with them. The myopia of human thinking—especially in the form of a world opinion pouring over everything at times like an irresistible tide—constitutes a huge danger. The instruments of God are not God on earth. To repay evil with evil—notably to the jailed, not merely the jailers—would make evil and bear new calamities.

In tracing our own guilt back to its source we come upon the human essence—which in its German form has fallen into a peculiar, terrible incurring of guilt but exists as a possibility in man as such.

Thus German guilt is sometimes called the guilt of all: the hidden evil everywhere is jointly guilty of the outbreak of evil in this German place.

It would, indeed, be an evasion and a false excuse if we Germans tried to exculpate ourselves by pointing to the guilt of being human. It is not relief but greater depth to which the idea can help us. The question of original sin must not become a way to dodge German guilt. Knowledge of original sin is not yet insight into German guilt. But neither must the religious confession of original sin serve as guise for a false German confession of collective guilt, with the one in dishonest haziness taking the place of the other.

We feel no desire to accuse the others; we do not want to infect them as it were, to drag them onto our path of doom. But at the distance and with the anxiety of those who stumbled onto it and now come to and reflect, we think: if only the others might not walk in such ways—if only those among us who are of good-will might be able to rely on them.

Now a new period of history has begun. From now on, responsibility for whatever happens rests with the victorious powers.

THE WAY OF PURIFICATION

Purification in action means, first of all, making amends.

Politically this means delivery, from inner affirmation, of the legally defined reparations. It means tightening our belts, so part of their destruction can be made up to the nations attacked by Hitler's Germany.

This way of purification by reparation is one we cannot dodge. Yet there is much more to purification. Even reparation is not earnestly willed and does not fulfill its moral purpose except as it ensues from our cleansing transfutation.

Clarification of guilt is at the same time clarification of our new life and its possibilities. From it spring seriousness and resolution.

Once that happens, life is no longer simply there to be

naively, gaily enjoyed. We may seize the happiness of life if it is granted to us for intermediate moments, for breathing spells—but it does not fill our existence; it appears as amiable magic before a melancholy background. Essentially, our life remains permitted only to be consumed by a task.

The result is modest resignation. In inner action before the transcendent we become aware of being humanly finite and incapable of perfection. Humility comes to be our nature.

There we are able, without will to power, to struggle with love in discussing truth, and in truth to join with each other.

Then we are capable of unaggressive silence—it is from the simplicity of silence that the clarity of the communicable will emerge.

Then nothing counts any longer but truth and activity. Without guile we are ready to bear what fate has in store for us. Whatever happens will, while we live, remain the human task that cannot be completed in the world.

Hannah Arendt demonstrates, again from the German example, the virtual impossibility of ordinary courts' getting at the fundamental truths of large-scale atrocity. Justice cannot be served, she tells us in this Introduction to a detailed journalistic account of a trial of accused Auschwitz murderers, because of "the lack of definitive yardsticks for judging crimes committed in these extraordinary and horrible conditions." Existing legal criteria are simply inadequate to the combination of evil and obfuscation perpetrated by high technology and technocratic bureaucracy.

ON RESPONSIBILITY FOR EVIL
Hannah Arendt

Of about 2,000 SS men posted at Auschwitz between 1940 and 1945 (and many must still be alive), "a handful of intolerable cases" had been selected and charged with murder, the only offense not covered by the statute of limitation in December, 1963, when the Frankfurt trial began. Investigation into the Auschwitz complex had lasted many years—documents ("not very informative," according to the court) had been collected and 1,300 witnesses questioned—and other Auschwitz trials were to follow. (Only one subsequent trial has so far taken place. This second trial began in December, 1965; one of the defendants, Gerhard Neubert, had been among those originally accused in the first trial. In contrast to the first trial, the second has been so poorly covered by the press that it took some "research" to determine whether it had occurred at all.) Yet in the words of the prosecutors in Frankfurt: *"The majority of the German people do not want to conduct any more trials against the Nazi criminals."*

Exposure for twenty months to the monstrous deeds and the grotesquely unrepentant, aggressive behavior of the defendants, who more than once almost succeeded in turning the trial into a farce, had no impact on this climate of public opinion, although the proceedings were well covered by German newspapers and radio stations. (Bernd Naumann's highly perceptive reportage, which originally appeared in the *Frankfurter*

Allgemeine Zeitung, was the most substantial.) This came to light during the heated debates in the first months of 1965—in the midst of the Auschwitz proceedings—over the proposed extension of the statute of limitation for Nazi criminals, when even Bonn's Minister of Justice, Mr. Bucher, pleaded that the "murderers among us" be left in peace. And yet, these "intolerable cases" in the "proceedings against Mulka and others," as the Auschwitz trial was officially called, were no desk murderers. Nor—with a few exceptions—were they even "regime criminals" who executed orders. Rather, they were the parasites and profiteers of a criminal system that had made mass murder, the extermination of millions, a legal duty. Among the many awful truths with which this book confronts us is the perplexing fact that German public opinion in this matter was able to survive the revelations of the Auschwitz trial.

For what the majority think and wish constitutes public opinion even though the public channels of communication—the press, radio, and television—may run counter to it. It is the familiar difference between *le pays réel* and the country's public organs; and once this difference has widened into a gap, it constitutes a sign of clear and present danger to the body politic. It was just this kind of public opinion, which can be all-pervasive and still only rarely come into the open, that the trial in Frankfurt revealed in its true strength and significance. It was manifest in the behavior of the defendants—in their laughing, smiling, smirking impertinence toward prosecution and witnesses, their lack of respect for the court, their "disdainful and threatening" glances toward the public in the rare instances when gasps of horror were heard. Only once does one hear a lonely voice shouting back, Why don't you kill him and get it over with? It was manifest in the behavior of the lawyers who kept reminding the judges that they must pay no attention to "what one will think of us in the outside world," implying over and over again that not a German desire for justice but world opinion influenced by the victims' desire for "retribution" and "vengeance" was the true cause of their clients' present trouble. Foreign correspondents, but no German reporter so far as I know, were shocked that "those of the accused who still live at home are by no means treated as outcasts by their communities." * Naumann reports an incident in which two defendants passed the uniformed guard outside the building, greeted him cordially with "Happy Holidays," and were greeted in return with "Happy Easter." Was this the *vox populi?*

It is, of course, because of this climate of public opinion that the defendants had been able to lead normal lives under their own names for many years before they were indicted. These years, according to the worst among them—Boger, the camp's specialist for "rigorous interrogations" with the help of the "Boger swing," his "talking machine" or "typewriter" —had "proved that Germans stick together, because [where he lived] everyone knew who [he] was." Most of them lived peacefully unless they had the misfortune to be recognized by a survivor and denounced either to the International Auschwitz Committee in Vienna or to the Central Office for Prosecution of National Socialist Crimes in West Germany, which late in 1958 had begun to collect material for the prosecution of Nazi criminals in local courts. But even this risk was not too great, for the local courts—with the exception of Frankfurt, where the state's attorney's office was under Dr. Fritz Bauer, a German Jew—had not been eager to prosecute, and German witnesses were notoriously unwilling to cooperate.

The information we get seems to indicate that discrepancies were a matter not only of deposition but of general attitude and behavior as well. The outstanding example of this more fundamental aspect—and perhaps the most interesting psychological phenomenon that came to light during the trial— is the case of Pery Broad, one of the youngest defendants, who wrote an excellent, entirely trustworthy description of the Auschwitz camp shortly after the end of the war for the British occupation authorities. The Broad Report—dry, objective, matter-of-fact—reads as though its author were an English-

---

* Sybille Bedford, in *The Observer* (London), January 5, 1964.

man who knows how to conceal his fury behind a façade of supreme sobriety. Yet there is no doubt that Broad—who had taken part in the Boger-swing game, was described by witnesses as "clever, intelligent, and cunning," had been known among the inmates as "death in kid gloves," and seemed "amused by all that went on in Auschwitz"—was its sole author and wrote it voluntarily. And there is even less doubt that he now greatly regrets having done so. During his pretrial examination before a police officer, he had been "communicative," admitted to having shot at least one inmate ("I am not sure that the person I shot wasn't a woman"), and said he felt "relieved" by his arrest. The judge calls him a many-faceted (*schillernade*) personality, but that says little and could just as well apply, though on an altogether different level, to the brute Kaduk, whom the patients in the West Berlin hospital where he worked as a male nurse used to call Papa Kaduk. These seemingly inexplicable differences in behavior, most striking in the case of Pery Broad—first in Auschwitz, then before the British authorities, then before the examining officer, and now back again among the old "comrades" in court—must be compared with the behavior of Nazi criminals before non-German courts. In the context of the Frankfurt proceedings there was hardly any occasion to mention non-German trials, except when statements of dead people whose depositions had incriminated the defendants were read into the record. This happened with the statement of an Auschwitz medical officer, Dr. Fritz Klein, who had been examined by British interrogators at the very moment of defeat, in May, 1945, and who before his execution had signed a confession of guilt: "I recognize that I am responsible for the slaying of thousands, particularly in Auschwitz, as are all the others, from the top down."

The point of the matter is that the defendants at Frankfurt, like almost all other Nazi criminals, not only acted out of self-protection but showed a remarkable tendency to fall in line with whoever happened to constitute their surroundings—to "coordinate" themselves, as it were, at a moment's notice. It is as though they had become sensitized not to authority and not to fear but to the general climate of opinion to which they happened to be exposed. (This atmosphere did not make itself felt in the lonely confrontation with examining officers, who, in the case of those in Frankfurt and in Ludwigsburg—where the Central Office for the Prosecution of Nazi Crimes is located and where some of the defendants had undergone their first interrogation—were clearly and openly in favor of conducting these trials.) What made Broad, who had concluded his report to the British authorities twenty years earlier with a kind of cheer for England and America, the outstanding example of this sensitization was not so much his dubious character as the simple fact that he was the most intelligent and articulate of this company.

Only one of the defendants, the physician Dr. Lucas, does not show open contempt for the court, does not laugh, insult witnesses, demand that the prosecuting attorneys apologize, and try to have fun with the others. One doesn't quite understand why he is there at all, for he seems the very opposite of an "intolerable case." He spent only a few months in Auschwitz and is praised by numerous witnesses for his kindness and desperate eagerness to help; he is also the only one who agrees to accompany the court on the trip to Auschwitz, and who sounds entirely convincing when he mentions in his closing statement that he "will never recover" from his experiences in concentration and extermination camps, that he sought, as many witnesses testified, "to save the lives of as many Jewish prisoners as possible," and that "today as then, [he is] torn by the question: And what about the others?" His codefendants show by their behavior what only Baretzki, whose chief claim to notoriety in the camp was his ability to kill inmates with one blow of his hand, is stupid enough to say openly: *"If today I were to talk, who knows, if everything should change tomorrow I could be shot."*

II

It would be quite unfair to blame the "majority of the German people" for their lack of enthusiasm for legal proceedings against Nazi criminals without mentioning the facts of life during the Adenauer era. It is a secret to nobody that the West German administration on all levels is shot through with former Nazis. The name of Hans Globke, noted first for his infamous commentary on the Nuremberg Laws and then as close adviser to Adenauer himself, has become a symbol for a state of affairs that has done more harm to the reputation and authority of the Federal Republic than anything else. The facts of this situation—not the official statements or the public organs of communication—have created the climate of opinion in the *pays réel,* and it is not surprising under the circumstances that public opinion says: *The small fish are caught, while the big fish continue their careers. . . .*

The defense, curiously inconsistent even apart from the "hollow oratory," based its little-man theory on two arguments: first, that the defendants had been *forced* to do what they did and were in no position to know that it was criminally wrong. But if they had not considered it wrong (and it turned out that most had never given this question a second thought), why had it been necessary to force them? The defense's second argument was that the selections of able-bodied people on the ramp had in effect been a rescue operation because otherwise "all those coming in would have been exterminated." But leaving aside the spurious nature of this argument, had not the selections also taken place upon orders from above? And how could the accused be *credited* with obeying orders when this same obedience constituted their main, and actually, their only possible, excuse?

Still, given the conditions of public life in the Federal Republic, the little-man theory is not without merit. The brute Kaduk sums it up: "The issue is not what we have done, but the men who led us into misfortune. Most of them still are at liberty. Like Globke. That hurts." And on another occasion:

"Now we are being made responsible for everything. The last ones get it in the neck, right?" The same theme is sounded by Hofmann, who had been convicted two years before the Auschwitz trial started for two murders in Dachau (two life sentences at hard labor) and who, according to Höss, "wielded real power in the camp," although according to his own testimony, he hadn't done a thing except "set up the children's playground, with sandboxes for the little ones." Hofmann shouts: "But where are the gentlemen who stood on top? They were the guilty ones, the ones who sat at their desks and telephoned." And he mentions names—not Hitler or Himmler or Heydrich or Eichmann, but the higher-ups in Auschwitz, Höss and Aumeier (the officer in charge before him) and Schwarz. The answer to his question is simple: They are all dead, which means to one of his mentality that they have left the "little man" in the lurch, that, like cowards, they have evaded their responsibility for him by allowing themselves to be hanged or by committing suicide.

The matter is not that easily settled, however—especially not at Frankfurt, where the court had called as witnesses former department chiefs of the *Reichssicherheitshauptamt* (the SS Head Office for Reich Security), in charge, among other things, of the organization of the "final solution of the Jewish question," to be executed in Auschwitz. In terms of the military equivalents of their former SS ranks, these gentlemen ranked high above the accused; they were colonels and generals rather than captains or lieutenants or noncoms. Bernd Naumann, who very wisely refrains almost completely from analysis and comment to confront the reader all the more directly with the great drama of court proceedings in the original form of dialogue, considered this little-man issue important enough to add one of his infrequent asides. Faced with these witnesses, he finds, the defendants "have plenty of reason to think how easily, how smoothly, many an 'exalted gentleman' whom they had served either willingly or under some duress has succeeded, without any psychic scruples, in returning from the far-away world of Germanic heroics to today's bourgeois respectability," how "the big man of the past who, as far as the Auschwitz personnel was concerned, had resided in the SS Olympus, leaves the courtroom head held high, with measured steps." And what is a defendant—or, for that matter, anybody else—supposed to think when he reads in the *Süddeutsche Zeitung,* one of the best daily German newspapers, that a former prosecutor at one of the Nazis' "special courts," a man who in 1941 had published a legal commentary that, in the newspaper's opinion, was frankly "totalitarian and anti-Semitic," now "earns his living as a judge of the federal constitutional court at Karlsruhe"? . . .

All postwar trials of Nazi criminals, from the Trial of Major War Criminals in Nuremberg to the Eichmann trial in Jerusalem and the Auschwitz trial in Frankfurt, have been plagued by legal and moral difficulties in establishing responsibilities and determining the extent of criminal guilt. Public and legal opinion from the beginning has tended to hold that the desk murderers—whose chief instruments were typewriters, telephones, and teletypes—were guiltier than those who actually operated the extermination machinery, threw the gas pellets into the chambers, manned the machine guns for the massacre of civilians, or were busy with the cremation of mountains of corpses. In the trial of Adolf Eichmann, desk murderer *par excellence,* the court declared that "the degree of responsibility increases as we draw further away from the man who uses the fatal instruments with his own hands." Having followed the proceedings in Jerusalem, one was more than inclined to agree with this opinion. The Frankfurt trial, which in many respects reads like a much-needed supplement to the Jerusalem trial, will cause many to doubt what they had thought was almost self-evident. What stands revealed in these trials is not only the complicated issue of personal responsibility but naked criminal guilt; and the faces of those who did their best, or rather their worst, to obey criminal orders are still very different from those who within a legally criminal system did not so much obey orders as do with their doomed victims as they pleased. The defendants admitted this occasionally in their primitive way—"those on top had it easy . . . issuing orders that prisoners were not to be beaten"—but the defense lawyers to a man conducted the case as though they were dealing here, too, with desk murderers or with "soldiers" who had obeyed their superiors. This was the big lie in their presentation of the cases. The prosecution had indicted for "murder and complicity in murder of *individuals*," together with "mass murder and complicity in mass murder"—that is, for two altogether different offenses.

III

Only at the end of this book, when on the 182d day of the proceedings Judge Hofmeyer pronounces the sentences and reads the opinion of the court, does one realize how much damage to justice was done—and inevitably done—because the distinctive line between these two different offenses had become blurred. The court, it was said, was concerned not with Auschwitz as an institution but only with "the proceedings against Mulka and others," with the guilt or innocence of the accused men. "The search for truth lay at the heart of the trial," but since the court's considerations were limited by the categories of criminal deeds as they had been known and defined in the German penal code of 1871, it was almost a matter of course that, in the words of Bernd Naumann, "neither the judges nor the jury found the truth—in any event, not the whole truth." For, in the nearly hundred-year-old code, there was no article that covered organized murder as a governmental institution, none that dealt with the extermination of whole peoples as part of demographic policies, with the "régime criminal," or with the everyday conditions under a criminal government (the *Verbrecherstaat*, as Karl Jaspers has termed it) —let alone with the circumstances in an extermination camp where everybody who arrived was doomed to die, either immediately by being gassed or in a few months by being worked to death. The Broad Report states that "at most 10–15 per cent of a given transport were classified as able-bodied and permitted to live," and the life expectancy of these selected men and women was about three months. What is most difficult to imagine in retrospect is the ever-present atmosphere of violent death; not even on the battlefield is death such a certainty and life so completely dependent on the miraculous. (Nor could the lower ranks among the guards ever be entirely free from fear; they thought it entirely possible, as Broad put it, "that to preserve secrecy they might also be marched off to the gas chambers. Nobody seemed to doubt that Himmler possessed the requisite callousness and brutality." Broad only forgot to mention that they must still have reckoned this danger less formidable than what they might face on the Eastern Front, for hardly any doubt remains that many of them could have voluntarily transferred from the camp to front-line duty.)

Hence, what the old penal code had utterly failed to take into account was nothing less than the everyday reality of Nazi Germany in general and of Auschwitz in particular. In so far as the prosecution had indicted for mass murder, the assumption of the court that this could be an "ordinary trial regardless of its background" simply did not square with the facts. Compared with ordinary proceedings, everything here could only be topsy-turvy: For example, a man who had caused the death of thousands because he was one of the few whose job it was to throw the gas pellets into the chambers could be criminally less guilty than another man who had killed "only" hundreds, but upon his own initiative and according to his perverted fantasies. The background here was administrative massacres on a gigantic scale committed with the means of mass production—the mass production of corpses. "Mass murder and complicity in mass murder" was a charge that could and should be leveled against every single SS man who had ever done duty in any of the extermination camps and against many who had never set foot into one. From this viewpoint, and it was the viewpoint of the indictment, the witness Dr. Heinrich Dürmayer, a lawyer and state councilor from Vienna, was quite right when he implied the need for a reversal of ordinary courtroom procedure—that the defendants under these circumstances should be assumed guilty unless they could prove otherwise: *"I was fully convinced that these people would have to prove their innocence."* And by the same token, people who had "only" participated in the routine operations of extermination couldn't possibly be included among a "handful of intolerable cases." Within the setting of Auschwitz, there was indeed "no one who was not guilty," as the witness said, which for the purposes of the trial clearly meant that "intolerable" guilt was to be measured by rather unusual yardsticks not to be found in any penal code.

All such arguments were countered by the court thus: "National Socialism was also subject to the rule of law." It would seem that the court wanted to remind us that the Nazis had never bothered to rewrite the penal code, just as they had never bothered to abolish the Weimar Constitution. But the carelessness was in appearance only; for the totalitarian ruler realizes early that all laws, including those he gives himself, will impose certain limitations on his otherwise boundless power. In Nazi Germany, then, the Führer's *will* was the *source* of law, and the Führer's order was valid law. What could be more limitless than a man's will, and more arbitrary than an order justified by nothing but the "I will"? In Frankfurt, at any rate, the unhappy result of the court's unrealistic assumptions was that the chief argument of the defense—"a state cannot possibly punish that which it ordered in another phase of its history"—gained considerably in plausibility since the court, too, agreed to the underlying thesis of a "continuity of identity" of the German state from Bismarck's Reich to the Bonn Government.

The lack of definitive yardsticks for judging crimes committed in these extraordinary and horrible conditions becomes painfully conspicuous in the court's verdict against Dr. Franz Lucas. Three years and three months of hard labor—the minimum punishment—for the man who had always been "ostracized by his comrades" and who is now openly attacked by the defendants, who as a rule are very careful to avoid mutual incrimination (only once do they contradict each other, and they retract in court the incriminating remarks made in their pretrial examinations) : "If he now claims to have helped people, he may have done so in 1945, when he tried to buy a return ticket." The point is, of course, that this is doubly untrue: Dr. Lucas had helped people from beginning to end; and not only did he not pose as a "savior"—very much in contrast to most of the other defendants—he consistently refused to recognize the witnesses who testified in his favor and to remember the incidents recounted by them. He had discussed sanitary conditions with his colleagues among the inmates, addressing them by their proper titles; he had even stolen in the SS pharmacy "for the prisoners, bought food with his own money," and shared his rations; "he was the only doctor who treated us humanely," who "did not look on us as unacceptable people," who gave advice to the physicians among the inmates on how to "save some fellow prisoners from the gas chambers." To sum up: "We were quite desperate after Dr. Lucas was gone. When Dr. Lucas was with us we were so gay. Really, we learned how to laugh again." And Dr. Lucas says: "I did not know the name of the witness until now." To be sure, none of the acquitted defendants, none of the lawyers for the defense, none of the "exalted gentlemen" who had gone scot-free and had come to testify could hold a candle to Dr. Franz Lucas. But the court, bound by its legal assumptions, could not help but mete out the minimum punishment to this man, although the judges knew quite well that in the words of a witness, he "didn't belong there at all. He was too good." Even the prosecution did not want "to lump him together with the others." It is true, Dr. Lucas had been on the ramp to select the able-bodied, but he had been sent there because he was suspected of "favoring prisoners," and he had been told that he would be "arrested on the spot" if he refused to obey the order. Hence, the charge of "mass murder or complicity in mass murder." When Dr. Lucas had first been confronted with his camp duties, he had sought advice: His bishop had told him that "immoral orders must not be obeyed, but that did not mean that one had to risk one's own life"; a high-ranking jurist justified the horrors because of the war. Neither was very helpful. But let us suppose he had asked the inmates what he ought to do. Wouldn't they have begged him to stay and pay the price of participation in the selections on the ramp—which were an everyday occurrence, a routine horror, as it were—in order to save them from the feeble-minded, Satanic ingenuity of all the others?

IV

Reading the trial proceedings, one must always keep in mind that Auschwitz had been established for *administrative* massacres that were to be executed according to the strictest rules and regulations. These rules and regulations had been laid down by the desk murderers, and they seemed to exclude—probably they were meant to exclude—all individual initiative either for better or for worse. The extermination of millions was planned to function like a machine; the arrivals from all over Europe; the selections on the ramp, and the subsequent selections among those who had been able-bodied on arrival; the division into categories (all old people, children, and mothers with children were to be gassed immediately); the human experiments; the system of "trustee prisoners," the capos, and the prisoner-commandos, who manned the extermination facilities and held privileged positions. Everything seemed foreseen and hence predictable—day after day, month after month, year after year. And yet, what came out of the bureaucratic calculations was the exact opposite of predictability. It was complete arbitrariness. In the words of Dr. Wolken—a former inmate, now a physician in Vienna, and the first and one of the best of the witnesses: *"Everything changed almost from day to day. It depended on the officer in charge, on the roll-call leader, on the block leader, and on their moods"*—most of all, it turns out, on their moods. "Things could happen one day that were completely out of the question two days later. . . . One and the same work detail could be either a death detail . . . or it could be a fairly pleasant affair." Thus, one day the medical officer was in a cheerful mood and had the idea of establishing a block for convalescents; two months later, all the convalescents were rounded up and sent into the gas. What the desk murderers had overlooked, *horrible dictu,* was the human factor. And what makes this so horrible is precisely the fact that these monsters were by no means sadists in a clinical sense, which is amply proved by their behavior under normal circumstances, and they had not been chosen for their monstrous duties on such a basis at all. The reason they came to Auschwitz or similar camps was simply that they were, for one reason or another, not fit for military service.

One could be tempted to indulge in sweeping statements about the evil nature of the human race, about original sin, about innate human "aggressiveness," etc., in general—and about the German "national character" in particular. It is easy and dangerous to overlook the not too numerous instances in which the court was told how "occasionally a 'human being' came into the camp" and after one short glance left in a hurry: "No, this is no place for my mother's child." Contrary to the view generally held prior to these trials, it was relatively simple for SS men to escape under one pretext or another—that is, unless one had the bad luck to fall into the hands of someone like Dr. Emil Finnberg, who even today thinks that it was perfectly all right to demand penalties ranging "from prison to death" for the "crime" of physical inability to shoot women and children. It was by far less dangerous to claim "bad nerves" than to stay in the camp, help the inmates, and risk the much greater charge of "favoring the prisoners." Hence those who stayed year in and year out, and did not belong to the select few who became heroes in the process, represented something of an automatic selection of the worst elements in the population. We do not know and are not likely ever to learn anything about percentages in these matters, but if we think of these overt acts of sadism as having been committed by perfectly normal people who in normal life had never come into conflict with the law on such counts, we begin to wonder about the dream world of many an average citizen who may lack not much more than the opportunity.

In any event, one thing is sure, and this one had not dared to believe any more—namely, "that everyone could decide for himself to be either good or evil in Auschwitz." (Isn't it grotesque that German courts of justice today should be unable to render justice to the good as well as the bad?) And this decision depended in no way on being a Jew or a Pole or a German; nor did it even depend upon being a member of the SS. For in the midst of this horror, there was Oberscharführer Flacke, who had established an "island of peace" and didn't want to believe that, as a prisoner said to him, in the end "we'll all be murdered. No witnesses will be allowed to survive." "I hope," he answered, "there'll be enough among us to prevent that."

v

Had the judge been wise as Solomon and the court in possession of the "definitive yardstick" that could put the unprecedented crime of our century into categories and paragraphs to help achieve the little that human justice is capable of, it still would be more than doubtful that "the truth, the whole truth," which Bernd Naumann demanded, could have appeared. No generality—and what is truth if it is not general?—can as yet dam up the chaotic flood of senseless atrocities into which one must submerge oneself in order to realize what happens when men say that "everything is possible," and not merely that everything is permitted.

Instead of *the* truth, however, there are *moments of truth,* and these moments are actually the only means of articulating this chaos of viciousness and evil. The moments arise unexpectedly like oases out of the desert. They are anecdotes, and they tell in utter brevity what it was all about.

There is the boy who knows he will die, and so writes with his blood on the barrack walls: "Andreas Rapaport—lived sixteen years."

There is the nine-year-old who knows he knows "a lot," but "won't learn any more."

There is the defendant Boger, who finds a child eating an apple, grabs him by the legs, smashes his head against the wall, and calmly picks up the apple to eat it an hour later.

There is the son of an SS man on duty who comes to the camp to visit his father. But a child is a child, and the rule of this particular place is that all children must die. Thus he must wear a sign around his neck "so they wouldn't grab him, and into the gas oven with him."

There is the prisoner who holds the selectees to be killed by the "medical orderly" Klehr with phenol injections. The door opens and in comes the prisoner's father. When all is over: "I cried and had to carry out my father myself." The next day, Klehr asks him why he had cried, and Klehr, on being told, "would have let him live." Why hadn't the prisoner told him? Could it be that he was afraid of him, Klehr? What a mistake. Klehr was in such a good mood.

Finally, there is the woman witness who had come to Frankfurt from Miami because she had read the papers and seen the name of Dr. Lucas: "the man who murdered my mother and family, interests me." She tells how it happened. She had arrived from Hungary in May, 1944. "I held a baby in my arms. They said that mothers could stay with their children, and therefore my mother gave me the baby and dressed me so as to make me look older. [The mother held a third child by the hand.] When Dr. Lucas saw me he probably realized that the baby was not mine. He took it from me and threw it to my mother." The court immediately knows the truth. "Did you perhaps have the courage to save the witness?" Lucas, after a pause, denies everything. And the woman, apparently still ignorant of the rules of Auschwitz—where all mothers with children were gassed upon arrival—leaves the courtroom, unaware that she who had sought out the murderer of her family had faced the savior of her own life. This is what happens when men decide to stand the world on its head.

In a section frequently overlooked because of the many riches in his recent study of Gandhi, Erik Erikson relates massacre— what we are calling atrocity—to a combination of the "policing mind" and the possession of technological weaponry. In contrast we have Gandhi's "instrument" of Satyagraha or "truth force," with its magnificent, tenuous, almost absurd—and still highly illuminating—structuring of events to achieve justice while avoiding not only physical but spiritual violence.

GANDHI VERSUS THE POLICING MIND
Erik H. Erikson

On April 13, 1919, General Dyer had forbidden the citizens of Amritsar, the Sikh holy city in the Punjab, to gather in public assembly. A few thousand, many without knowledge of the ordinance, had gathered unarmed, as previously planned, in the ruins of a public garden named Jallianwalla Bagh, which was surrounded by high walls permitting access and exit only through a few narrow gates. The general had ordered his men to fire on "the mob." All of this is well known as the "Massacre of Jallianwalla Bagh." But the word *massacre* suggests the hot carnage of a multitude by a rampant soldiery or mob. It does not convey the cold-bloodedness of this event, which was rather in the nature of mechanized slaughter. The soldiers stood on somewhat higher ground only 150 yards from the first row of an entirely unarmed mass of over 10,000 people crowded into one corner of the walled-in grounds. Twenty-five of the general's soldiers were equipped with rifles; the general ordered them to start shooting without warning, and the men fired 1,600 shots in ten minutes, killing 379 persons and wounding 1,137. Thus, they wasted less than one tenth of their shots in this shooting gallery.

I present these well-known details because one must try to envisage what has become of man as a military, or maybe one should say a *policing mind,* in the possession of mechanized weapons. Not that one could entertain the idea of a society altogether without police or should indulge in treating policemen as a separate species, like henchmen. They are only the willing puppets serving an overwhelming propensity of human nature, namely, brutal righteousness. I cannot make this point any stronger than by reminding the reader that, in my open letter to the Mahatma, I had reason to accuse him, too, of implicit violence in his policing and sentencing of the bathing children in South Africa. For we all have become obedient to the policing mind; and once we have learned to reduce "the other"—*any* living human being in the wrong place, the wrong category, or the wrong uniform—to a dirty speck in our moral vision, and potentially a mere target in the sight of our (or our soldiery's) gun, we are on the way to violating man's essence, if not his very life.

What, then, could the Bombay police chief have meant by the "instinct" of the masses? And what kind of instinctual aberration explains the policing mind that massacres with righteousness as well as with accuracy? That we must discuss in the conclusion of this book. In the meantime, we may say that to have faced mankind with nonviolence as the alternative to these aberrations marks the Mahatma's deed in 1919. In a period when proud statesmen could speak of a "war to end war"; when the superpolicemen of Versailles could bathe in the glory of a peace that would make "the world safe for democracy"; when the revolutionaries in Russia could entertain the belief that terror could initiate an eventual "withering away of the State"—during that same period, one man in India confronted the world with the strong suggestion that a new political instrument, endowed with a new kind of religious fervor, may yet provide man with a choice.

THE INSTRUMENT

Tactics We have reported Gandhi's saying that God appears to you not in person but in action. But this also means that the full measure of a man—and that includes his unconscious motivation—can never be comprehended in isolation from his most creative action. What, then, is the essence of the social tools which Gandhi created?

Here I will roughly follow Joan Bondurant's indispensable treatment in her *Conquest of Violence,* which analyzes six Satyagraha campaigns in a fashion both scholarly and compassionate. If I do not fully accept either her discourse or her conclusions, it is, I believe, because she writes as a political scientist, whereas I must come to some psychological conclusions. Neither of us (she would agree) can hope to do more than approximate the meaning which Satyagraha had for its originator, his first followers, and the Indian masses. And both of us must restate these meanings in the terms of our disciplines and our days in the West: the truth (Gandhi would tell either of us) can only be revealed in the kind of appraisal which is *our* action. Satyagraha purports to be a strategy which depends, every minute, on the unmistakable experience of something as evasive as "the truth." I have tried to trace what truth had come to mean to Gandhi, throughout his development, in order to fathom what it may have meant to him in a given action; and even then the interpretation of his meaning was bound by our own imagery and terminology. If this seems too elusive even to attempt to formulate, I will ask the reader in how many connotations he has used the term "reality" throughout his life, or "virtue," or "health," not to speak of "identity"—all terms which serve to characterize the essence of a man's being and action.

Sat, we are told, means "it is." We can come closer to "what 'is' " only by asking further: in comparison with what, where, and when? In comparison with what might have been or what should be, or with what only seems to be or is only felt to be? Thus "what is" is obviously relative to any era's world-image, and to the methodologies which determine what questions are considered important and are asked relevantly. Yet, for each individual, "what is" will also depend on his personal way of facing being in all its relativity—relative to an absolute Being who alone is truth, or relative to non-being, or relative to becoming. Gandhi commits himself only to "the relative truth as I have conceived it," but he also clings firmly to the dictum that only insofar as we can commit ourselves on selected oc-

casions "to the death" to the test of such truth in action—only
to that extent can we be true to ourselves and to others, that
is, to a joint humanity. This seems to call for an altogether
rare mixture of detachment and commitment, and for an almost mystical conflux of inner voice and historical actuality.
And in spite of the fact that it opens up wide every opportunity for self-deceit and the misuse of others, Gandhi, "in all
modesty," considered it his mission to lead his contemporaries
into "experimental" action. As he wrote to C. F. Andrews:

> I have taken up things as they have come to me and always in
> trembling and fear. I did not work out the possibilities in
> Champaran, Kheda or Ahmedabad nor yet when I made an un-
> conditional offer of service in 1914. I fancy that I followed His
> will and no other and He will lead me "amid the encircling
> gloom."

Yet there is no reason to question the fact that the sudden conviction that the moment of truth *had* arrived always came
upon him as if from a voice which had spoken before he had
quite listened. Gandhi often spoke of his inner voice, which
would speak unexpectedly in the preparedness of silence—but
then with irreversible firmness and an irresistible demand for
commitment. And, indeed, even Nietzsche, certainly the Mahatma's philosophical opposite, claimed that truth always approached "on the feet of doves." That is, the moment of truth
is suddenly there—unannounced and pervasive in its stillness.
But it comes only to him who has lived with facts and figures
in such a way that he is always ready for a sudden synthesis
and will not, from sheer surprise and fear, startle truth away.
But acting upon the inner voice means to involve others on
the assumption that they, too, are ready—and when Gandhi
listened to his inner voice, he often thought he heard what
the masses were ready to listen to. That, of course, is the secret
of all charismatic leadership, but how could he know it was
"the truth"? Gandhi's answer would be: Only the readiness
to suffer would tell.

Truthful action, for Gandhi, was governed by the readiness

to get hurt and yet not to hurt—action governed by the principle of *ahimsa*. According to Bondurant "the only dogma in
the Gandhian philosophy centers here: that the only test of
truth is action based on the refusal to do harm." With all respect for the traditional translation of *ahimsa*, I think Gandhi
implied in it, besides a refusal not to do physical harm, a determination not to violate another person's essence. For even
where one may not be able to avoid harming or hurting, forc-
ing or demeaning another whenever one must coerce him, one
should try even in doing so, not to violate his essence, for such
violence can only evoke counter-violence, which may end in a
kind of truce, but not in truth. For *ahimsa* as acted upon by
Gandhi not only means not to hurt another, it means to respect the truth in him. Gandhi reminds us that, since we can
not possibly know the absolute truth, we are "therefore not
competent to punish"—a most essential reminder, since man
when tempted to violence always parades as another's policeman, convincing himself that whatever he is doing to another,
that other "has it coming to him." Whoever acts on such
righteousness, however, implicates himself in a mixture of
pride and guilt which undermines his position psychologically
and ethically. Against this typical cycle, Gandhi claimed that
only the voluntary acceptance of self-suffering can reveal the
truth latent in a conflict—and in the opponent.

A few years ago I had occasion to talk on medical ethics to a
graduating class of young doctors and found myself trying to
reinterpret the Golden Rule in the light of what we have
learned in clinical work, that is, in the encounter of two individuals as "unequal" as a therapist and a patient.

I suggested that (ethically speaking) a man should act in
such a way that he actualizes both in himself and in the other
such forces as are ready for a heightened mutuality. Nothing
I have read or heard since has dissuaded me from the conviction that one may interpret Gandhi's truth in these terms. In
fact, Gandhi made a similar assumption when he viewed
Satyagraha as a bridge between the ethics of family life and
that of communities and nations.

Bondurant concludes that the "effect" of Gandhi's formulation was "to transform the absolute truth of the philosophical *Sat* to the relative truth of ethic principle capable of being tested by a means combining non-violent action with self-suffering." The truth in any given encounter is linked with the developmental stage of the individual and the historical situation of his group: together, they help to determine the *actuality*, i.e., the potential for unifying action at a given moment. What Bondurant calls "veracity," then, must have actuality as well as reality in it, that is, it depends on acting passionately as well as on thinking straight; and acting passionately would include acting upon and being guided by what is most genuine in the other. Truth in Gandhi's sense points to the next step in man's realization of man as one all-human species, and thus to our only chance to transcend what we are.

All this, then, depended on stringent conditions which Bondurant summarizes under *rules*, a *code of conduct*, and certain orderly *steps*. Here I must select a few combinations.

The essential preliminary steps in any of Gandhi's campaigns were an objective investigation of facts, followed by a sincere attempt at *arbitration*. Satyagraha must appear to be a last resort in an unbearable situation which allows for no other solution and is representative enough to merit a commitment of unlimited self-suffering. It, therefore, calls for a thorough *preparation* of all would-be participants, so that they may know the grievances as factually true and join in the conclusion that the agreed-upon goal is both just and attainable. But they must also be sure of being on the side of a truth which transcends all facts and is the true rationale for Satyagraha. Gandhi's helpers had to be convinced of all the basic propositions, and sufficiently so that they could promise to abide by the nonviolent code. In Ahmedabad, Gandhi was sure that not only the local mill workers, but workers anywhere in the world should refuse to accept conditions such as were then acute, even as he was sure that a man in Ambalal's position should not be permitted (because he should not permit himself) to insist on the defeat of the workers. But he also "picked" Ambalal because, in all his intransigence, Ambalal knew that Gandhi was right, and he respected his sister for standing up for reform—against him, her brother.

But to continue in a more general vein: in any campaign the widest *publicity* or (if one wishes) agitation was necessary in order to induce the public either to intervene in advance, or to provide public pressure in support of the action to be taken. That action, in fact, had to be *announced* in all detail in advance, with a clear *ultimatum* binding to all, and yet permitting the resumption of arbitration at any stage of the enfolding action—an arbitration, that is, conducive to face-saving all around. Therefore, an *action committee* created for this purpose would select such *forms of non-cooperation*— strike, boycott, civil disobedience—as would seem fitting as the *minimum force necessary to reach a defined goal:* no quick triumph would be permitted to spread the issue beyond this goal, nor any defeat to narrow it. The quality of such fitness, however, would vastly transcend the question of mere feasibility: for it would encompass *issues* which were at the same time central to the *practical* life of the community and *symbolic* for its future—as was for example, the land around a peasant's homestead in Champaran, or the right of Untouchables in a given locality to pass over a temple road on the way to work, or the right of all Indians to take from their sea, without paying taxes to a colonial government, the salt necessary to make their food palatable and their bodies resistant in the heat of their subcontinent.

We can see from this once-revolutionary list how the choice of issues in Gandhi's India has changed the legal conscience of mankind in regard to grievances and rights now taken for granted in many parts of the world. As to the rules for the resisters, they must *rely on themselves,* for both their suffering and their triumph must be their own; for this reason Gandhiji forbade his striking workers to accept outside support. The movement must *keep the initiative,* which includes the willingness to atone for miscalculations as well as the readiness to adapt to changes in the opponent, and to readjust both the strategy and (as far as they were negotiable) the goals of the campaign. And in all of this, the resister must be consistently *willing to persuade* and to enlighten, even as he remains ready *to be persuaded* and enlightened. He will, then, not insist on obsolete precedent or rigid principle, but will be guided by what under changing conditions will continue or come to feel true to him and his comrades, that is, will become *truer through action.*

Such truth, however, could not depend on individual impressions and decisions. It could reveal itself only as long as the resisters' actions remained co-ordinated and were guided by a code which was as firm as it was flexible enough to perceive changes—and to obey changing commands. The leader would have to be able to count on a discipline based on the Satyagrahi's commitment to suffer the opponent's anger without getting angry and yet also without ever submitting to any violent coercion by anyone; to remain so attuned to the opponent's position that he would be ready, on the leader's command, even to come to the opponent's help in any unforeseen situation which might rob him of his freedom to remain a counterplayer on the terms agreed upon; and to remain, in principle, so law-abiding that he would refuse co-operation with the law or law-enforcing agencies *only* in the chosen and defined issues. Within these limits, he would accept and even demand those penalties which by his chosen action he had willingly invoked against himself.

And then, there is the leader's self-chosen suffering, which is strictly "his business," as Gandhi would say with his mild-mannered rudeness. For there must be a leader, and, in fact, a predetermined succession of leaders, so that the leader himself can be free to invite on himself any suffering, including death, rather than hide behind the pretext that he was not expendable. As we saw, in the first national Satyagraha, Gandhi's arrest turned out to be *the* critical factor, even as the Ahmedabad Satyagraha floundered over the critical issue of Gandhi's decision to fast. For once the leader decides on a "true" course, he must have the freedom to restrain as well as to command, to withdraw as well as to lead and, if this freedom should be denied him by his followers, to declare a Satyagraha against them. If such singular power produces a shudder in the reader of today—indoctrinated as he is against "dictators"—it must not be forgotten that we are now speaking of the post-First World War years when a new kind of charismatic leadership would emerge, in nation after nation, filling the void left by collapsing monarchies, feudalisms, and patriarchies, with the mystic unity of the Leader and the Masses. And such was the interplay of the private and the public, the neurotic and the charismatic, during the period when these sons of the people assumed such a mystic authority, that we must recognize even that most personal of Gandhi's decisions, namely, his *fast*, as part of an "Indian leadership Indian style."

Fasting, we may consider in passing, is an age-old ritual act which can serve so many motivations and exigencies that it can be as corrupt as it can be sublime. As recently as January 1967, Pyarelal found it necessary to reassert in the Indian press the rules Gandhi had laid down for public fasting in a public issue. And Pyarelal concludes that fasting

> cannot be resorted to against those who regard us as their enemy, or on whose love we have not established a claim by dint of selfless service; it cannot be resorted to by a person who has not identified himself with, or worked for the cause he is fasting for; it cannot be used for gaining a material selfish end, or to change the honestly held opinion of another or in support of an issue that is not clear, feasible and demonstrably just. . . . To be legitimate, a fast should be capable of response.

Gandhi, at one time, urged any individual or authority that was "fasted against" and which considered the fast to be blackmail "to refuse to yield to it, even though the refusal may result in the death of the fasting person." Obviously, only such an attitude would do honor to him who thus offers his own life. On the other hand, Gandhi insisted that the fasting person must be prepared to the end to discover or to be convinced of a flaw in his position. The Indian writer Raja Rao told me on a walk how a friend of his had written to Gandhi that he was going to fast in order to underline certain demands. Gandhi wrote back suggesting that the friend write down ten demands worthy of a fast and Gandhi would initial the list without reading it. The friend pondered the matter and thought of other ways to protest!

Everything that has been said here, however, should make us very cautious in referring to the outcome of a sincere fast or to any part of a genuine Satyagraha campaign as a "failure." For as we saw in the national *hartal* of 1919, the choice of withdrawal or suspension may be the only way in which the leader can keep the spiritual initiative and thus save the instrument—dented but not broken—for another day. In this sense, the Ahmedabad mill owners' yielding was not a "capitulation"; for in an ideal Satyagraha campaign both sides will have had a chance to make the outcome a mutually beneficial one—as was the case even with the Bania deal in Ahmedabad. And, of course, new principles far beyond any circumscribed "success" or "failure" are being forced on the imagination of a wider audience in any Satyagraha worthy of the name. At any rate, even today, the surviving mill owners are far from registering a sense of having given in. *"We* forced him to fast," one said; and another: "We were ready to grant that much, anyway"; while all agree that the Event radically changed labor relations in Ahmedabad and in India.

This brings us to a final item in the inventory of Satyagraha which, at least locally, is most far-reaching: it is what in Gandhian terminology is called the "constructive program." In Champaran, the failure most keenly felt by Gandhi (and this, I believe, *was* a failure in the sense of a lack of essential completion) was the absence of any lasting impact on the everyday lives of the people of Bihar. In Ahmedabad Gandhi insisted, in the very days of the strike, on consolidating the gains of labor initiated by Anasuya and subsequently sustained in many significant ways by Ambalal and the other mill owners— gains in the general concept of work as a dignifying activity in itself; in the solidarity of all the laborers, in factory conditions, and in the welfare of the worker population.

In his World War II diary, *The Warriors,* a subterranean classic now beginning to surface, Glenn Gray takes us to the spiritual heart of combat. We find that war itself—with its demand for numbing, its distortions of death and guilt—places one always on the verge of atrocity. But we note also that Gray's war—World War II—when compared to Vietnam, still had contours and a suggestion of rules.

ON KILLING

J. Glenn Gray

The enemy was cruel, it was clear, yet this did not trouble me as deeply as did our own cruelty. Indeed, their brutality made fighting the Germans much easier, whereas ours weakened the will and confused the intellect. Though the scales were not at all equal in this contest, I felt responsibility for ours much more than for theirs. And the effect was cumulative. . . . Because of its peculiar character, one other episode haunts my mind and may be briefly set down. It happened in southern France shortly after our invasion. One day an attractive French girl appeared at our temporary headquarters and confessed that she had worked for a time with the local Gestapo and now feared the revenge of the Maquis. The French security officer with whom I was working interrogated her calmly at some length and soon found out that she had been in love with the Gestapo captain in charge of this district and had been persuaded to aid him on occasion in his repressive measures against the Resistance. Since our unit had to move on almost at once, the French officer wrote a report of his interrogation for the civil authorities of the liberated city— and closed it with his recommendation that the girl be shot! On the way to the city jail with the girl, he picked up some pictures of his wife and children, which he had had developed in a local photography shop during our brief stay. After showing them to me for my comment and approval, he carried them to the girl in the car ahead. Ignorant of the fate he had decreed for her (and which would almost certainly be carried out at once under conditions at that time), the girl admired the family snapshots and the two of them laughed and joked for many minutes. Passers-by might easily have mistaken them for lovers.

There was little savagery or blood lust in this French officer. He did not hate the girl, so far as I could tell, though he hated her deeds. He would, in fact, have been quite willing to sleep with her the night before ordering her execution. When I remonstrated with him about such callousness, he made clear to me that he regarded himself as an army officer in a quite different way from himself as a human being. The two personalities could succeed each other with lightning rapidity, as I was to see on numerous occasions. As a human being, he was capable of kindness, even gentleness, and within limits he was just and honest. In his capacity of functionary, he could be brutal beyond measure without ever losing his outward amiability and poise. I observed precisely the same qualities in the Fascist and Nazi politicians and police with whom it was my fate to deal.

After months of this sort of experience, I began to detect with a kind of horror that I was becoming inured to cruelty and not above practicing it myself on occasion. . . .

> The man I interrogated and took to Army proved to be a spy. . . . I went to Army two days later, after he had been "broken" by endless interrogation and considerable beating. . . . It recalled the memory of Scarpelini in Italy, whom I also apprehended and turned over. . . . One thing contents me, that these were not innocent soldiers. They knew what they were facing. The German had been an idealistic Nazi for fifteen years. . . . Am I responsible for their deaths? Both might well have escaped had it not been for me. . . . Certainly they had blood on their hands, and desired to have more. Is their blood on mine? But I am more fortunate than many soldiers who must kill more innocent men. Perhaps the hardest thing of all is that I feel no guilt. (War journal, November 4, 1944)

The fighting man is disinclined to repent his deeds of violence. Men who in private life are scrupulous about conventional justice and right are able to destroy the lives and happiness of others in war without compunction. At least to other eyes they seem to have no regrets. It is understandable, of course, why soldiers in combat would not suffer pangs of conscience when they battle for their lives against others who are trying to kill them. And if the enemy is regarded as a beast or a devil, guilt feelings are not likely to arise if he is slain by your hand. But modern wars are notorious for the destruction of nonparticipants and the razing of properties in lands that are accidentally in the path of combat armies and air forces. In World War II the number of civilians who lost their lives exceeded the number of soldiers killed in combat. At all events, the possibilities of the individual involving himself in guilt are immeasurably wider than specific deeds that he might commit against the armed foe. In the thousand chances of warfare, nearly every combat soldier has failed to support his comrades at a critical moment; through sins of omission or commission, he has been responsible for the death of those he did not intend to kill. Through folly or fear, nearly every officer has exposed his own men to needless destruction at one time or another. Add to this the unnumbered acts of injustice so omnipresent in war, which may not result in death but inevitably bring pain and grief, and the impartial observer may wonder how the participants in such deeds could ever smile again and be free of care.

The sober fact appears to be that the great majority of veterans, not to speak of those who helped to put the weapons and ammunitions in their hands, are able to free themselves of responsibility with ease after the event, and frequently while they are performing it. Many a pilot or artilleryman who has destroyed untold numbers of terrified noncombatants has never felt any need for repentance or regret. Many a general who has won his laurels at a terrible cost in human life and suffering among friend and foe can endure the review of his career with great inner satisfaction. So are we made, we human creatures! Frequently, we are shocked to discover how little our former enemies regret their deeds and repent their errors. Americans in Germany after World War II, for instance, feel aggrieved that the German populace does not feel more responsibility for having visited Hitler upon the world. The Germans, for their part, resent the fact that few Americans appear to regret the bombing of German cities into rubble and the burning and crushing of helpless women and children. It appears to be symptomatic of a certain modern mentality to marvel at the absence of guilt consciousness in others while accepting its own innocence as a matter of course.

No doubt there are compelling historical reasons why soldiers in earlier times have felt comparatively little regret for their deeds and why modern soldiers in particular are able to evade responsibility so easily. It is wise to assume, I believe, that the soldiers who fight twentieth-century wars are morally little better or worse than their grandfathers or great-grand-fathers in previous wars. Nevertheless, there are some novel factors in our time that, taken together with the traditional ways of escape, make it easier for the majority of soldiers to carry the guilt for the destruction of the innocent in contemporary conflicts. These novel factors lie both in our contemporary interpretation of guilt and in the nature of recent combat.

Our age seems peculiarly confused about the meaning of guilt, as well as its value. With the rise of modern psychology and the predominance of naturalistic philosophers, guilt has come to be understood exclusively in a moral sense. Its older religious and metaphysical dimensions have been increasingly forgotten. Moreover, these naturalistic psychologists have tended to view guilt feelings as a hindrance to the free development of personality and the achievement of a life-affirming outlook. They like to trace guilt to the darker, subconscious levels of the soul and emphasize its backward-looking character as opposed to the future-directed impulses of the natural man. Hence guilt, when reduced to moral terms, has more and more been branded as immoral. To some, it is associated with a species of illness, which must be cured by psychiatric treatment. Though these modern doctors of the soul realize that the uninhibited man is not an attainable ideal, they still strive for the goal of acceptance of oneself and one's nature for what they are. The individual is released as far as possible from regret for past deeds and from the hard duty to improve his character.

Even if these doctrines get modified in actual practice and are seldom read in their deeper meanings, the basic ideas filter into the broadest strata of our population and help to form the dominant mood of our day. Even the simplest soldier suspects that it is unpopular today to be burdened with guilt. Everyone from his pastor to his doctor is likely, if he brings up feelings that oppress him, to urge him to "forget it." Precisely this is what he often longs to hear, and, so, forgetting becomes such a disquieting phenomenon of the modern mind.

In war itself, the most potent quieters of conscience are evidently the presence of others who are doing the same things and the consciousness of acting under the orders of people "higher up" who will answer for one's deeds. So long as the soldier thinks of himself as one among many and identifies himself with his unit, army, and nation, his conscience is unlikely to waken and feel the need to respond. All awareness of guilt presupposes the capacity to respond as an individual to the call of conscience. I am using the term "respond" in its original meaning of answer to a question or a demand made on the self. We respond to conscience only when we can separate ourselves from others and become conscious, often painfully so, of our differentness. Though the call of conscience may seem to be an impersonal voice outside of one, the response is peculiarly within the individual self. Why did *you* do this? Why did *you* not do that? If we hear at all and if we attempt to answer, the response must begin with the first person singular pronoun. I must begin with myself as I was:

> My conscience seems to become little by little sooted. . . . If I can soon get out of this war and back on the soil where the clean earth will wash away these stains! I have also other things on my conscience. . . . [A man named H., accused of being the local Gestapo agent in one small town] was an old man of seventy. His wife and he looked frightened and old and miserable. . . . I was quite harsh to him and remember threatening him with an investigation when I put him under house arrest. . . . Day before yesterday word came that he and his

wife had committed suicide by taking poison. Fain and I went back and found them dead in their beds, he lying on his back and reminding me, gruesomely enough, of my father, she twisted over on her side with her face concealed. At the bedside was a card on which he had scrawled: *"Wir müssen elend zu Grunde gehen. Der Herr Gott verzeihe uns. Wir haben niemandem leid getan."*. . . [We must perish miserably. God forgive us. We have done no one any harm.] The incident affected me strongly and still does. I was directly or indirectly the cause of their death. . . . I hope it will not rest too hard on my conscience, and yet if it does not I shall be disturbed also.

Since conscience normally awakens in guilt in the sense that a troubled conscience is usually our first indication of its existence, it is clear that an important function of guiltiness is to make us aware of our selves. Whatever his response, the person who hears the call of conscience is aware of freedom in the form of a choice. He could have performed differently than he did; an act of his might have been different. The whole realm of the potential in human action is opened to him and with it the fateful recognition that he is in charge of his own course. Conscience is thus in the first instance a form of self-consciousness. It is that form that gives to us an unmistakable sense of free individuality and separates for us the domains of the actual and the ideal. Therewith the life of reflection begins, and the inner history of the individual no longer corresponds to his outer fate.

But the individual need not waken, and, indeed, everything in warfare conspires against such response to the call of freedom. Enemy and ally enclose his little life, and there is little privacy or escape from their presence. Loyalty to his unit is instilled by conscious and unconscious means; the enemy is seeking to destroy that unity and must be prevented from doing so at all costs. He is one with the others in a fraternity of exposure and danger. His consciousness of the others may be vague but is an omnipresent reality; it has much similarity to dream awareness. Directly, he is aware of his pals, the half-dozen or more men he knows relatively well, with a few dozen more who are on the periphery of his consciousness. Beyond them there are thousands who encircle him, whose presence he senses. There is a vast assemblage of unknown "friends" confronting an equally vast mass of unknown "enemies," and he is in the midst of all of them. Their presence makes his situation endurable, for they help to conquer the loneliness that oppresses him in the face of death, actual or possible. Something within him responds powerfully to the appeal of the communal. The orders that he receives from those in charge of his fate hold him where he is in the midst of disorder. He is compelled and controlled as though by invisible threads through the unseen presence of the others, friend and foe.

In an exposed position on the battlefield during action his consciousness of being a part of an organism is likely to plunge him into contradictory feelings of power and impotence which succeed one another rapidly. "If I don't hit that guy out there or man this machine gun to the last, my buddies will be killed and I'll be the cause of their death. Everything depends on me." A few minutes later he is likely to ask himself what one rifle or machine gun on one tiny portion of the field can possibly matter to the final outcome. His place in the whole complex is lost to sight, and he is in danger of feeling how absolute is his dependence. All the time, he acts as he feels he must, swept by moods of exultation, despair, loyalty, hate, and many others. Much of the time he is out of himself, acting simply as a representative of the others, as part of a superpersonal entity, on orders from elsewhere. He kills or fails to kill, fights courageously or runs away in the service of this unit and unity. Afterward, he hears no voice calling him to account for his actions, or, if he does hear a voice, feels no need to respond.

In less sophisticated natures, this presence of the others is projected also into the weapons and instruments of war. They become personalized, and the soldier becomes attached to them as an extension of himself. They afford him a vast comfort in difficult positions as a protection and a shield, a second skin. On the one hand, these weapons help to prevent the soldier from feeling responsible for the lives he takes. "I did not kill, my gun or grenade did it" is the subconscious suggestion. On the other hand, guns help to fill the intermediate spaces between him and the others. They help to cement the wall of comradeship that encloses him and ties him to his own side while at the same time preventing the enemy from becoming too real. Unless he is caught up in murderous ecstasy, destroying is easier when done at a little remove. With every foot of distance there is a corresponding decrease in reality. Imagination flags and fails altogether when distances become too great. So it is that much of the mindless cruelty of recent wars has been perpetrated by warriors at a distance, who could not guess what havoc their powerful weapons were occasioning. . . .

Though the above may be a correct, external description of the response or lack of response on the part of most soldiers to individual guilt in waging war, it nevertheless misses all the subtle ways in which guilt is incurred in conflict and made present to the conscience of the minority. There are degrees and kinds of guilt, and not merely a formal declaration of simple guilt or innocence by the inner tribunal. Those soldiers who do respond to the call of conscience find themselves involved in the most baffling situations, in which any action they could take is inappropriate. They learn soon that nearly any of the individual's relations to the world about him can involve him in guilt of some kind, particularly in warfare. It is as pervasive in life and reflection as is human freedom itself. Awakened to his personal responsibility in one aspect of combat action, the soldier is not necessarily awakened to finer nuances of guilt. Yet it sometimes happens that the awakening is thorough and absolute in character, demanding of the subject an entirely different set of relations to friend and enemy.

It is a crucial moment in a soldier's life when he is ordered to perform a deed that he finds completely at variance with his own notions of right and good. Probably for the first time, he discovers that an act someone else thinks to be necessary is for him criminal. His whole being rouses itself in protest, and he may well be forced to choose in this moment of awareness of his freedom an act involving his own life or death. He feels himself caught in a situation that he is powerless to change yet cannot himself be part of. The past cannot be undone and the present is inescapable. His only choice is to alter himself, since all external features are unchangeable.

What this means in the midst of battle can only inadequately be imagined by those who have not experienced it themselves. It means to set oneself against others and with one stroke lose their comforting presence. It means to cut oneself free of doing what one's superiors approve, free of being an integral part of the military organism with the expansion of the ego that such belonging brings. Suddenly the soldier feels himself abandoned and cast off from all security. Conscience has isolated him, and its voice is a warning. If you do this, you will not be at peace with me in the future. You can do it, but you ought not. You must act as a man and not as an instrument of another's will. . . .

There is a kind of guilt that transcends the personal responsibility of the sensitive conscience and burdens that soldier particularly who retains faith in the cause and the country for which he is fighting. It is the guilt the individual shares as a member of a military unit, a national fighting force, a people at war. We may call it social or political or collective guilt; it is not essentially different for the civilian than for the soldier, and it is inescapable. No matter how self-contained and isolated in spirit the man of conscience may feel, he cannot avoid the realization that he is a participant in a system and an enterprise whose very essence is violence and whose spirit is to win at whatever cost. For the soldier, it is his squad or company or division that performs deeds abhorrent to him. No matter how strongly he abjures personal responsibility for this or that deed, he cannot escape social responsibility. So long as he wears the same uniform as his fellows, he will be regarded by outsiders as one of them. His fellows, too, treat him as a member of the fraternity of men at arms. The conscience within him may be more and more appalled by the heedlessness of group behavior and the mechanical ruthlessness of an organization whose dedication to violence gives it an unholy character. I was appalled and yet I could not escape it. I wrote in my journal one day at the height of the war:

> Yesterday we caught two spies, making our recent total five. We are getting a reputation as a crack detachment. One had to be severely beaten before he confessed. It was pretty horrible, and I kept away from the room where it was done . . . though I could not escape his cries of pain. . . . I lay awake until three o'clock this morning. . . . I thought of the Hamlet line as most appropriate, " 'Tis bitter cold and I am sick at heart."

A soldier with an awakened conscience who is a member of such a community, coarse, vulgar, heedless, violent, realizes with overpowering clarity the possibility of being alienated from his own kind. This uniformed, machine-like monster, the combat unit, drives him back into himself and repels him utterly. Toward individuals who make it up, he can gain many relationships, but the collectivity itself chokes him without mercy.

Toward his nation as a nation he may well come to experience in his innermost self the same lack of relationship. A state at war reveals itself to the penetrating eye in its clearest light and the spectacle is not beautiful. Nietzsche's likeness of it to a cold snake is, from one perspective, not greatly exaggerated. The awakened conscience will recognize a part of this spirit of the nation in the hate-filled speeches of politician-patriots, in the antipathy toward dissenting opinions about the utter virtue of its cause, in the ruthlessness with which the individual is sacrificed for real or alleged national advantages. It will despise the fanaticism with which this state makes morally dubious and historically relative ends into absolutes, its perversity in maintaining pride at whatever price in human misery.

At the same time, justice will force this soldier to admit that these are his people, driven by fear and hatred, who are directing this vast mechanism. If he is honest with himself he will admit that he, too, is a violent man on occasion and capable of enjoying the fruits of violence. Legally, and more than legally, he belongs to the community of soldiers and to the state. At some level of his being he can understand why they perform as they do and can find it in his heart to feel sorry for some of the politicians and higher officers. In their place he wonders if he would do any better than they. He is bound to reflect that his nation has given him refuge and sustenance, provided him whatever education and property he calls his own. He belongs and will always belong to it in some sense, no matter where he goes or how hard he seeks to alter his inheritance. The crimes, therefore, that his nation or one of its units commits cannot be indifferent to him. He shares the guilt as he shares the satisfaction in the generous deeds and worthy products of nation or army. Even if he did not consciously will them and was unable to prevent them, he cannot wholly escape responsibility for collective deeds.

He belongs and yet he does not belong. "I did not ask to be born," he is likely to tell himself while struggling with his responsibility for collective deeds, "and I did not choose my nation. Had I been given a choice of places to grow up at various stages in my education I might have chosen other than the nation in which I was accidentally born. I am, of course, a citizen of this nation and am willing to expose my life in its defense. But in my inner being I belong only to the community that I have freely chosen, my friends, my club, my church, my profession. All other associations of mine are external and accidental, however little I may have realized it earlier. This does not free me from the guilt that this nation is heaping upon itself, so long as I participate in its defense. I shall always be guilty as long as I belong to a nation at all. Yet there is no good life apart from some nation or other."

It is clear to him that his political guilt is of a different sort from the personal, since the latter stems from his freedom in a direct way, the former only in part. The nation was in being long before him and will presumably continue in being after his death. Hence his capacity to change its course is immeasurably limited by its history as well as by his own powers. For the politically conscious soldier, this does not mean, however, that it is negligible. Insofar as his political guilt is in direct relation to his freedom, he will become conscious of what he has done or failed to do to promote or hinder the humanizing of military or political means and objectives. He will be certain at all events that he has not done enough. On this or that occasion he has been silent when he should have spoken out. In his own smaller or larger circle of influence he has not made his whole weight felt. Had he brought forth the civil courage to protest in time, some particular act of injustice might have been avoided. Whatever the level of influence the soldier commands, from the squad or platoon to the command of armies, in some manner he is able to affect the course of group action.

When the nation for which he is fighting has enjoyed a free government and been previously responsive to its citizens' wishes, he will be conscious of greater responsibility than will the soldier whose government is authoritarian or totalitarian. The greater the possibility of free action in the communal sphere, the greater the degree of guilt for evil deeds done in the name of everyone. Still, the degrees of guilt are impossible to assess for anyone else, and hardly any two people share an equal burden of communal guilt. The soldier may have been too young as a civilian to have exerted much influence on events or he may have been too poorly informed or confused to know where his political duty lay. As a soldier, he may be in too isolated or insignificant a location to make effective use of his freedom. No citizen of a free land can justly accuse his neighbor, I believe, of political guilt, of not having done as much as he should to prevent the state of war or the commission of this or that state crime. But each can—and the man of conscience will—accuse himself in proportion to the freedom he had to alter the course of events.

The peculiar agony of the combat soldier's situation is that, even more than in his struggle with his own ideal self, he is aware of the puniness of his individual powers to effect a change. War not only narrows the limits of personal freedom, but it likewise constricts the individual's communal liberty, his capacity to make his power felt in significant ways. The sense of impotence will weigh upon him day after day. Though the man of awakened conscience will hardly believe that the war is a natural catastrophe, he will not know how any individual can alter its seemingly inexorable course. Personal guilt can be in some measure atoned and the struggle to improve can be taken up every morning anew. But communal guilt comes upon him in ever increasing measure in any war, and he is likely to feel utterly inadequate either to atone for it or prevent its accumulation.

For instance, when the news of the atomic bombing of Hiroshima and Nagasaki came, many an American soldier felt shocked and ashamed. The combat soldier knew better than did Americans at home what those bombs meant in suffering and injustice. The man of conscience wherever he was realized intuitively that the vast majority of the Japanese in both cities were no more, if no less, guilty of the war than were his own parents, sisters, or brothers. In his shame, he may have said to himself, as some of us did: "The next atomic bomb, dropped in anger, will probably fall on my own country and we will have deserved it." Such a conviction will hardly relieve him of the heavy sense of wrong that his nation committed and the responsibility for which he must now in some measure share. All the arguments used in justification—the shortening of the war by many months and the thousands of American lives presumably saved—cannot alter the fact that his government was the first to use on undefended cities, without any warning, a monstrous new weapon of annihilation.

Worst of all about such deeds is that millions accepted and felt relief. Hearing this near-exultation in the enemy's annihilation, one can only conclude that political guilt has another source than the freedom of the individual to affect group action. It lies in the degree of his identification with the goals and the means of realizing them that his nation adopts. The person who inwardly approves an immoral action of his

government or military unit testifies to his own probable decision had he possessed the freedom and opportunity of the
actors. Freedom is possible, therefore, not only in the power
to do or prevent, but also in inner assent and consent to action
by others. With a relative criterion like this it is, of course,
impossible to be exact in estimating even one's own guilt. Yet
the jubilation in evil deeds allows little room for doubt that
inner consent is often forthcoming. So do thousands of people
increase their political guilt in wartime beyond the range of
their direct action. . . .

I find it hard to believe that in the wars of our day any
great number of soldiers attain the possibilities that lie in the
acceptance of guilt. As I indicated earlier, the reasons appear
to lie in a dominant mood of our times and in the different
nature of warfare. Yet it is hard to be sure, for few people
care to admit the guilt they sometimes feel. Possibly the profound aversion to war that is widespread at the mid-century is
not entirely due to the political and economic fruitlessness of
recent wars and their unprecedented fury. Many who reveal
no outward evidence may be aware at some level of their
being that the moral issues of war are hardly resolvable on
present capital. They may realize that since wars cannot teach
nations repentance and humility, they must be abandoned if
we are not to lose our inherited humanistic culture. Cut loose
from traditional ties, *Homo furens* is seen to be too exclusively
devoted to the devastation of the natural and human soil on
which he has hitherto been nourished.

If guilt is not experienced deeply enough to cut into us,
our future may well be lost. Possibly more people realize this
than I suspect; and veterans who did not show any traces of
it as warriors may now be feeling it keenly. At all events,
there are some who have made that secret journey within the
conscience and are building their lives on principles very
different from those they knew as unawakened ones.

> Last night I lay awake and thought of all the inhumanity of
> it, the beastliness of the war. . . . I remembered all the brutal
> things I had seen since I came overseas, all the people rotting

in jail, some of whom I had helped to put there. . . . I thought of Plato's phrase about the wise man caught in an evil time who refuses to participate in the crimes of his fellow citizens, but hides behind a wall until the storm is past. And this morning when I rose, tired and distraught from bed, I knew that in order to survive this time I must love more. There is no other way. . . . (War journal, December 8, 1944)

Perhaps most of his readers don't think of him that way, but Kurt Vonnegut, Jr., happens to be, among other things, one of the great commentators on atrocity of our age. These two brief excerpts from his novel *Cat's Cradle* give us two Vonnegutian views of twentieth-century death, absurd and (in a surprisingly serious tone) more absurd.

ON DYING

Kurt Vonnegut, Jr.

LAST RITES

So I was privileged to see the last rites of the Bokononist faith.

We made an effort to find someone among the soldiers and the household staff who would admit that he knew the rites and would give them to "Papa." We got no volunteers. That was hardly surprising, with a hook and an oubliette so near.

So. Dr. von Koenigswald said that he would have a go at the job. He had never administered the rites before, but he had seen Julian Castle do it hundreds of times.

"Are you a Bokononist?" I asked him.

"I agree with one Bokononist idea. I agree that all religions, including Bokononism, are nothing but lies."

"Will this bother you as a scientist," I inquired, "to go through a ritual like this?"

"I am a very bad scientist. I will do anything to make a human being feel better, even if it's unscientific. No scientist worthy of the name could say such a thing."

And he climbed into the golden boat with "Papa." He sat in the stern. Cramped quarters obliged him to have the golden tiller under one arm.

He wore sandals without socks, and he took these off. And then he rolled back the covers at the foot of the bed, exposing "Papa's" bare feet. He put the soles of his feet against "Papa's" feet, assuming the classical position for *boko-maru*.

"*Gott mate mutt,*" crooned Dr. von Koenigswald.

"Dyot meet mat," echoed "Papa" Monzano.

"God made mud," was what they'd said, each in his own dialect. I will here abandon the dialects of the litany.

"God got lonesome," said von Koenigswald.

"God got lonesome."

"So God said to some of the mud, 'Sit up!' "

"So God said to some of the mud, 'Sit up!' "

" 'See all I've made,' said God, 'the hills, the sea, the sky, the stars.' "

" 'See all I've made,' said God, 'the hills, the sea, the sky, the stars.' "

"And I was some of the mud that got to sit up and look around."

"And I was some of the mud that got to sit up and look around."

"Lucky me, lucky mud."

"Lucky me, lucky mud." Tears were streaming down "Papa's" cheeks.

"I, mud, sat up and saw what a nice job God had done."

"I, mud, sat up and saw what a nice job God had done."

"Nice going, God!"

"Nice going, God!" "Papa" said it with all his heart.

"Nobody but You could have done it, God! I certainly couldn't have."

"Nobody but You could have done it, God! I certainly couldn't have."

"I feel very unimportant compared to You."

"I feel very unimportant compared to You."

"The only way I can feel the least bit important is to think of all the mud that didn't even get to sit up and look around."

"The only way I can feel the least bit important is to think of all the mud that didn't even get to sit up and look around."

"I got so much, and most mud got so little."

"I got so much, and most mud got so little."

"Deng you vore da on-oh!" cried von Koenigswald.

"Tz-yenk voo vore lo yon-yo!" wheezed "Papa."

What they had said was, "Thank you for the honor!"
"Now mud lies down again and goes to sleep."
"Now mud lies down again and goes to sleep."
"What memories for mud to have!"
"What memories for mud to have!"
"What interesting other kinds of sitting-up mud I met!"
"What interesting other kinds of sitting-up mud I met!"
"I loved everything I saw!"
"I loved everything I saw!"
"Good night."
"Good night."
"I will go to heaven now."
"I will go to heaven now."
"I can hardly wait . . ."
"I can hardly wait . . ."
"To find out for certain what my *wampeter* * was . . ."
"To find out for certain what my *wampeter* was . . ."
"And who was in my *karass* † . . ."
"And who was in my *karass* . . ."
"And all the good things our *karass* did for you."
"And all the good things our *karass* did for you."
"Amen."
"Amen.". . .
"History!" writes Bokonon. "Read it and weep!"

WHEN I FELT THE BULLET ENTER MY HEART

So I once again mounted the spiral staircase in my tower; once again arrived at the uppermost battlement of my castle; and once more looked out at my guests, my servants, my cliff, and my lukewarm sea.

---

* "A *wampeter* is the pivot of a *karass*. No *karass* is without a *wampeter*," Bokonon tells us, "just as no wheel is without a hub. . . . Anything can be a *wampeter*: a tree, a rock, an animal, an idea, a book, a melody, the Holy Grail."
† "If you find your life tangled up with someone else's life for no particular reasons," writes Bokonon, "that person may be a member of your *karass*. . . . Man created the checkerboard; God created the *karass* . . . a *karass* ignores national, institutional, occupational, familial, and class boundaries."

The Hoenikkers were with me. We had locked "Papa's" door, and had spread the word among the household staff that "Papa" was feeling much better.

Soldiers were now building a funeral pyre out by the hook. They did not know what the pyre was for.

There were many, many secrets that day.

Busy, busy, busy.

I supposed that the ceremonies might as well begin, and I told Frank to suggest to Ambassador Horlick Minton that he deliver his speech.

Ambassador Minton went to the seaward parapet with his memorial wreath still in its case. And he delivered an amazing speech in honor of the Hundred Martyrs to Democracy. He dignified the dead, their country, and the life that was over for them by saying the "Hundred Martyrs to Democracy" in island dialect. That fragment of dialect was graceful and easy on his lips.

The rest of his speech was in American English. He had a written speech with him—fustian and bombast, I imagine. But, when he found he was going to speak to so few, and to fellow Americans for the most part, he put the formal speech away.

A light sea wind ruffled his thinning hair. "I am about to do a very un-ambassadorial thing," he declared. "I am about to tell you what I really feel."

Perhaps Minton had inhaled too much acetone, or perhaps he had an inkling of what was about to happen to everybody but me. At any rate, it was a strikingly Bokononist speech he gave.

"We are gathered here, friends," he said, "to honor *lo Hoon-yera Mora-toorz tut Zamoo-cratz-ya,* children dead, all dead, all murdered in war. It is customary on days like this to call such lost children *men.* I am unable to call them men for this simple reason: that in the same war in which *lo Hoon-yera Mora-toorz tut Zamoo-cratz-ya* died, my own son died.

"My soul insists that I mourn not a man but a child.

"I do not say that children at war do not die like men, if

they have to die. To their everlasting honor and our ever-lasting shame they *do* die like men, thus making possible the manly jubilation of patriotic holidays.

"But they are murdered children all the same.

"And I propose to you that if we are to pay our sincere respects to the hundred lost children of San Lorenzo, that we might best spend the day despising what killed them; which is to say, the stupidity and viciousness of all mankind.

"Perhaps, when we remember wars, we should take off our clothes and paint ourselves blue and go on all fours all day long and grunt like pigs. That would surely be more appropriate than noble oratory and shows of flags and well-oiled guns.

"I do not mean to be ungrateful for the fine, martial show we are about to see—and a thrilling show it really will be . . ."

He looked each of us in the eye, and then he commented very softly, throwing it away, "And hooray say I for thrilling shows."

We had to strain our ears to hear what Minton said next.

"But if today is really in honor of a hundred children murdered in war," he said, "is today a day for a thrilling show?

"The answer is yes, on one condition: that we, the celebrants, are working consciously and tirelessly to reduce the stupidity and viciousness of ourselves and of all mankind."

He unsnapped the catches on his wreath case.

"See what I have brought?" he asked us.

He opened the case and showed us the scarlet lining and the golden wreath. The wreath was made of wire and artificial laurel leaves, and the whole was sprayed with radiator paint.

The wreath was spanned by a cream-colored silk ribbon on which was printed, "PRO PATRIA."

Minton now recited a poem from Edgar Lee Masters' *Spoon River Anthology,* a poem that must have been incomprehensible to the San Lorenzans in the audience—and to H. Lowe Crosby and his Hazel, too, for that matter, and to Angela and Frank.

I was the first fruits of the battle of Missionary Ridge.
When I felt the bullet enter my heart
I wished I had staid at home and gone to jail
For stealing the hogs of Curl Trenary,
Instead of running away and joining the army.
Rather a thousand times the county jail
Than to lie under this marble figure with wings,
And this granite pedestal
Bearing the words, "Pro Patria."
What do they mean, anyway?

"What do they mean, anyway?" echoed Ambassador Horlick Minton. "They mean, 'For one's country.'" And he threw away another line. "Any country at all," he murmured.

"This wreath I bring is a gift from the people of one country to the people of another. Never mind which countries. Think of people . . .

"And children murdered in war . . .

"And any country at all.

"Think of peace.

"Think of brotherly love.

"Think of plenty.

"Think of what paradise this world would be if men were kind and wise.

"As stupid and vicious as men are, this is a lovely day," said Ambassador Horlick Minton. "I, in my own heart and as a representative of the peace-loving people of the United States of America, pity *lo Hoon-yera Mora-toorz tut Zamoo-cratz-ya* for being dead on this fine day."

And he sailed the wreath off the parapet.

There was a hum in the air. The six planes of the San Lorenzan Air Force were coming, skimming my lukewarm sea. They were going to shoot the effigies of what H. Lowe Crosby had called "practically every enemy that freedom ever had."

Sartre here examines the French and American experiences with atrocity, and sets forth the kind of conditions that leave little room for anything *but* genocide, the conditions under which America fights in Vietnam.

ON GENOCIDE

Jean-Paul Sartre

The word "genocide" is relatively new. It was coined by the jurist Raphael Lemkin between the two world wars. But the fact of genocide is as old as humanity. To this day there has been no society protected by its structure from committing that crime. Every case of genocide is a product of history and bears the stamp of the society which has given birth to it. The one we have before us for judgment is the act of the greatest capitalist power in the world today. It is as such that we must try to analyze it—in other words, as the simultaneous expression of the economic infrastructure of that power, its political objectives and the contradictions of its present situation.

In particular, we must try to understand the genocidal intent in the war which the American government is waging against Vietnam, for Article 2 of the 1948 Geneva Convention defines genocide on the basis of intent; the Convention was tacitly referring to memories which were still fresh. Hitler had proclaimed it his deliberate intent to exterminate the Jews. He made genocide a political means and did not hide it. A Jew had to be put to death, whoever he was, not for having been caught carrying a weapon or for having joined a resistance movement, but simply *because he was a Jew.* The American government has avoided making such clear statements. It has even claimed that it was answering the call of its allies, the South Vietnamese, who had been attacked by the communists. Is it possible for us, by studying the facts objectively, to discover implicit in them such a genocidal intention? And after such an investigation, can we say that the armed forces of the United States are killing Vietnamese in Vietnam for the simple reason that they are Vietnamese?

This is something which can only be established after an historical examination: the structure of war changes right along with the infrastructures of society. Between 1860 and the present day, the meaning and the objectives of military conflicts have changed profoundly, the final stage of this metamorphosis being precisely the "war of example" which the United States is waging in Vietnam.

In 1856, there was a convention for the protection of the property of neutrals; 1864, Geneva: protection for the wounded; 1899, 1907, The Hague: two conferences which attempted to make rules for war. It is no accident that jurists and governments were multiplying their efforts to "humanize war" on the very eve of the two most frightful massacres that mankind has ever known.

Nevertheless, during the First World War a genocidal intent appeared only sporadically. As in previous centuries, the essential aim was to crush the military power of the enemy and only secondarily to ruin his economy. But even though there was no longer any clear distinction between civilians and soldiers, it was still only rarely (except for a few terrorist raids) that the civilian population was expressly made a target. Moreover, the belligerent nations (or at least those who were doing the fighting) were industrial powers. This made for a certain initial balance: against the possibility of any real extermination each side had its own deterrent force—namely the power of applying the law of "an eye for an eye." This explains why, in the midst of the carnage, a kind of prudence was maintained.

However, since 1830, throughout the last century and continuing to this very day, there have been countless acts of genocide outside Europe. Some were reflections of authoritarian political structures and the others—those which we must understand in order to comprehend the growth of American imperialism and the nature of the Vietnam War—came out of the internal structures of capitalist democracies. To export their products and their capital, the great powers, particularly England and France, set up colonial empires. The name "overseas possessions" given by the French to their conquests indicates clearly that they had been able to acquire them only by wars of aggression. The adversary was sought out in his own territory, in Africa and Asia, in the underdeveloped countries, and far from waging "total war" (which would have required an initial balance of forces), the colonial powers, because of their overwhelming superiority of firepower, found it necessary to commit only an expeditionary force. Victory was easy, at least in conventional military terms. But since this blatant aggression kindled the hatred of the civilian population, and since civilians were potentially rebels and soldiers, the colonial troops maintained their authority by terror—by perpetual massacre. These massacres were genocidal in character: they aimed at the destruction of "a part of an ethnic, national, or religious group" in order to terrorize the remainder and to wrench apart the indigenous society.

After the bloodbath of conquest in Algeria during the last century, the French imposed the *Code Civil*, with its middle-class conceptions of property and inheritance, on a tribal society where each community held land in common. Thus they systematically destroyed the economic infrastructure of the country, and tribes of peasants soon saw their lands fall into the hands of French speculators. Indeed, colonization is not a matter of mere conquest as was the German annexation of Alsace-Lorraine; it is by its very nature an act of cultural genocide. Colonization cannot take place without systematically liquidating all the characteristics of the native society—and simultaneously refusing to integrate the natives into the mother country and denying them access to its advantages. For the subject people this inevitably means the extinction of their national character, culture, customs, sometimes even language.

However, their value as an almost unpaid labor force protects them, to a certain extent, against physical genocide.

These observations enable us to understand how the structure of colonial wars underwent a transformation after the end of the Second World War. For it was at about this time that the colonial peoples, enlightened by that conflict and its impact on the "empires," and later by the victory of Mao Tsetung, resolved to regain their national independence. The characteristics of the struggle were determined from the beginning: the colonialists had the superiority in weapons, the indigenous population the advantage of numbers.

It is no accident that people's war, with its principles, its strategy, its tactics and its theoreticians, appeared at the very moment that the industrial powers pushed total war to the ultimate by the industrial production of atomic fission. Nor is it any accident that it brought about the destruction of colonialism. The contradiction which led to the victory of the FLN in Algeria was characteristic of that time; people's war sounded the death-knell of conventional warfare at exactly the same moment as the hydrogen bomb. Against partisans supported by the entire population, the colonial armies were helpless. They had only one way of escaping this demoralizing harassment which threatened to culminate in a Dien Bien Phu, and that was to "empty the sea of its water"—i.e., the civilian population.

Torture and genocide: that was the answer of the colonial powers to the revolt of the subject peoples. And that answer, as we know, was worthless unless it was thorough and total. The populace—resolute, united by the politicized and fierce partisan army—was no longer to be cowed as in the good old days of colonialism, by an "admonitory" massacre which was supposed to serve "as an example." On the contrary, this only augmented the people's hate. Thus it was no longer a question of intimidating the populace, but rather of physically liquidating it. And since that was not possible without concurrently liquidating the colonial economy and the whole colonial system, the settlers panicked, the colonial powers got tired of pouring men and money into an interminable conflict, the mass of the people in the mother country opposed the continuation of an inhuman war, and the colonies became sovereign states.

There have been cases, however, in which the genocidal re-

sponse to people's war is not checked by infrastructural contradictions. Then total genocide emerges as the absolute basis
of an anti-guerrilla strategy. And under certain conditions it
even emerges as the explicit objective—sought either immediately or by degrees. This is precisely what is happening in the
Vietnam War. We are dealing here with a new stage in the development of imperialism, a stage usually called neo-coloni-
alism because it is characterized by aggression against a former
colony which has already gained its independence, with the
aim of subjugating it anew to colonial rule. With the beginning of independence, the neo-colonialists take care to finance
a *putsch* or *coup d'état* so that the new heads of state do not
represent the interests of the masses but those of a narrow
privileged strata, and, consequently, of foreign capital.

Ngo Dinh Diem appeared—hand-picked, maintained and
armed by the United States. He proclaimed his decision to reject the Geneva Accords and to constitute the Vietnamese territory to the south of the seventeenth parallel as an independent state. What followed was the necessary consequence of
these premises: a police force and an army were created to
hunt down people who had fought against the French, and
who now felt thwarted of their victory, a sentiment which au-
tomatically marked them as enemies of the new regime. In
short, it was the reign of terror which provoked a new uprising
in the South and rekindled the people's war.

Did the United States ever imagine that Diem could nip the
revolt in the bud? In any event, they lost no time in sending
in experts and then troops, and then they were involved in the
conflict up to their necks. And we find once again almost the
same pattern of war as the one that Ho Chi Minh fought
against the French, except that at first the American government declared that it was only sending its troops out of generosity, to fulfill its obligations to an ally.

That is the outward appearance. But looking deeper, these
two successive wars are essentially different in character: the
United States, unlike France, has no economic interests in
Vietnam. American firms have made some investments, but

not so much that they couldn't be sacrificed, if necessary, without troubling the American nation as a whole or really hurting the monopolies. Moreover, since the United States government is not waging the war for reasons of a *directly* economic nature, there is nothing to stop it from ending the war by the ultimate tactic—in other words, by genocide. This is not to say that there is proof that the United States does in fact envision genocide, but simply that nothing prevents the United States from envisaging it.

In fact, according to the Americans themselves, the conflict has two objectives. Just recently, Dean Rusk stated: "We are defending ourselves." It is no longer Diem, the ally whom the Americans are generously helping out: it is the United States itself which is in danger in Saigon. Obviously, this means that the first objective is a military one: to encircle Communist China. Therefore, the United States will not let Southeast Asia escape. It has put its men in power in Thailand, it controls two thirds of Laos and threatens to invade Cambodia. But these conquests will be hollow if it finds itself confronted by a free and unified Vietnam with thirty-two million inhabitants. That is why the military leaders like to talk in terms of "key positions." That is why Dean Rusk says, with unintentional humor, that the armed forces of the United States are fighting in Vietnam "in order to avoid a third world war." Either this phrase is meaningless, or else it must be taken to mean: "in order to *win* this third conflict." In short, the first objective is dictated by the necessity of establishing a Pacific line of defense, something which is necessary only in the context of the general policies of imperialism.

The second objective is an economic one. In October, 1966, General Westmoreland defined it as follows: "We are fighting the war in Vietnam to show that guerrilla warfare does not pay." To show whom? The Vietnamese? That would be very surprising. Must so many human lives and so much money be wasted merely to teach a lesson to a nation of poor peasants thousands of miles from San Francisco? And, in particular. what need was there to attack them, provoke them into fighting and subsequently to go about crushing them, when the big American companies have only negligible interests in Vietnam? Westmoreland's statement, like Rusk's, has to be filled in. The Americans want to show others that guerrilla war does not pay: they want to show all the oppressed and exploited nations that might be tempted to shake off the American yoke by launching a people's war, at first against their own pseudo-governments, the compradors and the army, then against the United States Special Forces, and finally against the GIs. In short, they want to show Latin America first of all, and more generally, all of the Third World. To Che Guevara who said, "We need several Vietnams," the American government answers, "They will all be crushed the way we are crushing the first."

In other words, this war has above all an admonitory value, as an example for three and perhaps four continents. (After all, Greece is a peasant nation too. A dictatorship has just been set up there; it is good to give the Greeks a warning: submit or face extermination.) This genocidal example is addressed to the whole of humanity. By means of this warning, six per cent of mankind hopes to succeed in controlling the other ninety-four per cent at a reasonably low cost in money and effort. Of course it would be preferable, for propaganda purposes, if the Vietnamese would submit before being exterminated. But it is not certain that the situation wouldn't be clearer if Vietnam *were* wiped off the map. Otherwise someone might think that Vietnam's submission had been attributable to some *avoidable* weakness. But if these peasants do not weaken for an instant, and if the price they pay for their heroism is *inevitable* death, the guerrillas of the future will be all the more discouraged.

At this point in our demonstration, three facts are established: (1) What the United States government wants is to have a base against China and to set an example. (2) The first objective *can* be achieved, without any difficulty (except, of course, for the resistance of the Vietnamese), by wiping out a whole people and imposing the Pax Americana on an uninhabited Vietnam. (3) To achieve the second, the United States *must* carry out, at least in part, this extermination.

This absurdity is not undeliberate: the Americans are ingeniously formulating, without appearing to do so, a demand which the Vietnamese cannot satisfy. They do offer an alternative: Declare you are beaten or we will bomb you back to the stone age. But the fact remains that the second term of this alternative is genocide. They have said: "genocide, yes, but *conditional* genocide." Is this juridically valid? Is it even conceivable?

But let us look at this more closely and examine the nature of the two terms of the alternative. In the South, the choice is the following: villages burned, the populace subjected to massive bombing, livestock shot, vegetation destroyed by defoliants, crops ruined by toxic aerosols, and everywhere indiscriminate shooting, murder, rape and looting. This is genocide in the strictest sense: massive extermination. The other option: what is *it?* What are the Vietnamese people supposed to do to escape this horrible death? Join the armed forces of Saigon or be enclosed in strategic or today's "New Life" hamlets, two names for the same concentration camps?

We know about these camps from numerous witnesses. They are fenced in by barbed wire. Even the most elementary needs are denied: there is malnutrition and a total lack of hygiene. The prisoners are heaped together in small tents or sheds. The social structure is destroyed. Husbands are separated from their wives, mothers from their children; family life, so important to the Vietnamese, no longer exists. As families are split up, the birth rate falls; any possibility of religious or cultural life is suppressed; even work—the work which might permit people to maintain themselves and their families—is refused them. These unfortunate people are not even slaves (slavery did not prevent the Negroes in the United States from developing a rich culture) ; they are reduced to a living heap of vegetable existence. When, sometimes, a fragmented family group is freed—children with an elder sister or a young mother—it goes to swell the ranks of the subproletariat in the big cities; the elder sister or the mother, with no job and mouths to feed, reaches the last stage of her degradation in prostituting herself to the GIs.

The camps I describe are but another kind of genocide, equally condemned by the 1948 Convention:

Causing serious bodily or mental harm to members of the group.

Deliberately inflicting on the group conditions of life calculated to bring about its physical destruction in whole or in part.

Imposing measures intended to prevent births within the group.

Forcibly transferring children of the group to another group.

In other words, it is not true that the choice is between death or submission. For submission, in those circumstances, is submission to genocide. Let us say that a choice must be made between a violent and immediate death and a slow death from mental and physical degradation. Or, if you prefer, *there is no choice at all.*

Is it any different for the North?

One choice is *extermination.* Not just the daily risk of death, but the systematic destruction of the economic base of the country: from the dikes to the factories, nothing will be left standing. Deliberate attacks against civilians and, in particular, the rural population. Systematic destruction of hospitals, schools and places of worship. An all-out campaign to destroy the achievements of twenty years of socialism. The purpose may be only to intimidate the populace. But this can only be achieved by the daily extermination of an ever larger part of the group. So this intimidation itself in its psycho-social consequence is a genocide. Among the children in particular it must be engendering psychological disorders which will for years, if not permanently, "cause serious . . . mental harm."

The other choice is *capitulation*. This means that the North Vietnamese must declare themselves ready to stand by and watch while their country is divided and the Americans impose a direct or indirect dictatorship on their compatriots, in fact on members of their own families from whom the war has separated them. And would this intolerable humiliation bring an end to the war? This is far from certain. The National Liberation Front and the Democratic Republic of Vietnam, although fraternally united, have different strategies and tactics because their war situations are different. If the National Liberation Front continued the struggle, American bombs would go on blasting the Democratic Republic of Vietnam whether it capitulated or not.

If the war were to cease, the United States—according to official statements—would feel very generously inclined to help in the reconstruction of the Democratic Republic of Vietnam, and we know exactly what this means. It means that the United States would destroy, through private investments and conditional loans, the whole economic base of socialism. And this too is genocide. They would be splitting a sovereign country in half, occupying one of the halves by a reign of terror and keeping the other half under control by economic pressure. The "national group" Vietnam would not be physically eliminated, yet it would no longer exist. Economically, politically and culturally it would be suppressed.

In the North as in the South, the choice is only between two types of liquidation: collective death or dismemberment. The American government has had ample opportunity to test the resistance of the National Liberation Front and the Democratic Republic of Vietnam: by now it knows that only total destruction will be effective. The Front is stronger than ever; North Vietnam is unshakable. For this very reason, the calculated extermination of the Vietnamese people cannot really be intended to make them capitulate. The Americans offer them a *paix des braves* knowing full well that they will not accept it. And this phony alternative hides the true goal of imperialism, which is to reach, step by step, the highest stage of escalation—total genocide.

Of course, the United States government *could have* tried to reach this stage in one jump and wipe out Vietnam in a *Blitzkrieg* against the whole country. But this extermination first required setting up complicated installations—for instances, creating and maintaining air bases in Thailand which would shorten the bombing runs by 3,000 miles.

Meanwhile, the major *purpose* of "escalation" was, and still is, to prepare international opinion for genocide. From this point of view, Americans have succeeded only too well. The repeated and systematic bombings of populated areas of Haiphong and Hanoi, which two years ago would have raised violent protests in Europe, occur today in a climate of general indifference resulting perhaps more from catatonia than from apathy. The tactic has borne its fruit: public opinion now sees escalation as a slowly and continuously increasing pressure to bargain, while in reality it is the preparation of minds for the final genocide. Is such a genocide possible? No. But that is due to the Vietnamese and the Vietnamese alone; to their courage, and to the remarkable efficiency of their organization. As for the United States government, it cannot be absolved of its crime just because its victim has enough intelligence and enough heroism to limit its effects.

We may conclude that in the face of a people's war the characteristic product of our times, the answer to imperialism and the demand for sovereignty of a people conscious of its unity, there are two possible responses: either the aggressor withdraws, he acknowledges that a whole nation confronts him, and he makes peace; or else he recognizes the inefficacy of conventional strategy, and, if he can do so without jeopardizing his interests, he resorts to extermination pure and simple. There is no third alternative, but making peace is still at least *possible*.

But as the armed forces of the United States entrench themselves firmly in Vietnam, as they intensify the bombing and the massacres, as they try to bring Laos under their control, as they plan the invasion of Cambodia, there is less and less doubt that the government of the United States, despite its hypocritical denials, has chosen genocide.

The genocidal intent is implicit in the facts. It is necessarily premeditated. Perhaps in bygone times, in the midst of tribal wars, acts of genocide were perpetrated on the spur of the moment in fits of passion. But the anti-guerrilla genocide which our times have produced requires organization, military bases, a structure of accomplices, budget appropriations. Therefore, its authors must meditate and plan out their act. Does this mean that they are thoroughly conscious of their intentions? It is impossible to decide. We would have to plumb the depths of their consciences—and the Puritan bad faith of Americans works wonders.

There are probably people in the State Department who have become so used to fooling themselves that they still think they are working for the good of the Vietnamese people. However, we may only surmise that there are fewer and fewer of these hypocritical innocents after the recent statements of their spokesmen: "We are defending ourselves; even if the Saigon government begged us, we would not leave Vietnam, etc., etc." At any rate, we don't have to concern ourselves with this psychological hide-and-seek. The truth is apparent *on the battlefield* in the racism of the American soldiers.

This racism—anti-black, anti-Asiatic, anti-Mexican—is a basic American attitude with deep historical roots and which existed, latently and overtly, well before the Vietnamese conflict. One proof of this is that the United States government refused to ratify the Genocide Convention. This doesn't mean that in 1948 the United States intended to exterminate a people; what it does mean—according to the statements of the United States Senate—is that the Convention would conflict with the laws of several states; in other words, the current policymakers enjoy a free hand in Vietnam because their predecessors catered to the anti-black racism of Southern whites. In any case, since 1966, the racism of Yankee soldiers, from Saigon to the seventeenth parallel, has become more and

more marked. Young American men use torture (even including the "field telephone treatment" *), they shoot unarmed
women for nothing more than target practice, they kick
wounded Vietnamese in the genitals, they cut ears off dead
men to take home for trophies. Officers are the worst: a general boasted of hunting "VCs" from his helicopter and gunning them down in the rice paddies. Obviously, these were
not National Liberation Front soldiers who knew how to defend themselves; they were peasants tending their rice. In the
confused minds of the American soldiers, "Vietcong" and
"Vietnamese" tend increasingly to blend into one another.
They often say themselves, "The only good Vietnamese is a
dead Vietnamese," or what amounts to the same thing, "A
dead Vietnamese is a Vietcong."

For example: south of the seventeenth parallel, peasants prepare to harvest their rice. American soldiers arrive on the
scene, set fire to their houses and want to transfer them to a
strategic hamlet. The peasants protest. What else can they do,
barehanded against these Martians? They say: "The quality of
the rice is good; we want to stay to eat our rice." Nothing
more. But this is enough to irritate the young Yankees: "It's
the Vietcong who put that into your head; they are the ones
who have taught you to resist." These soldiers are so misled
that they take the feeble protests which their own violence has
aroused for "subversive" resistance. At the outset, they were
probably disappointed: they came to save Vietnam from "communist aggressors." But they soon had to realize that the Vietnamese did not want them. Their attractive role as liberators
changed to that of occupation troops. For the soldiers it was
the first glimmering of consciousness: "We are unwanted, we
have no business here." But they go no further. They simply
tell themselves that a Vietnamese is by definition suspect.

And from the neo-colonialists' point of view, this is true.
They vaguely understand that in a people's war, civilians are

---

* The portable generator for a field telephone is used as an instrument
for interrogation by hitching the two lead wires to the victim's genitals
and turning the handle.

the only visible enemies. Their frustration turns to hatred of the Vietnamese; racism takes it from there. The soldiers discover with a savage joy that they are there to kill the Vietnamese they had been pretending to save. All of them are potential communists, as proved by the fact that they hate Americans.

Now we can recognize in those dark and misled souls the truth of the Vietnam war: it meets all of Hitler's specifications. Hitler killed the Jews because they were Jews. The armed forces of the United States torture and kill men, women and children in Vietnam merely *because they are Vietnamese*. Whatever lies or euphemisms the government may think up, the spirit of genocide is in the minds of the soldiers. This is their way of living out the genocidal situation into which their government has thrown them. As Peter Martinsen, a twenty-three-year-old student who had "interrogated" prisoners for ten months and could scarcely live with his memories, said: "I am a middle-class American. I look like any other student, yet somehow I am a war criminal." And he was right when he added: "Anyone in my place would have acted as I did." His only mistake was to attribute his degrading crimes to the influence of war *in general*.

No, it is not war in the abstract: it is the greatest power on earth against a poor peasant people. Those who fight it are *living out* the only possible relationship between an overindustrialized country and an underdeveloped country, that is to say, a genocidal relationship implemented through racism— the only relationship, short of picking up and pulling out.

Total war presupposes a certain balance of forces, a certain reciprocity. Colonial wars were not reciprocal, but the interests of the colonialists limited the scope of genocide. The present genocide, the end result of the unequal development of societies, is total war waged to the limit by one side, without the slightest reciprocity.

The American government is not guilty of inventing modern genocide, or even of having chosen it from other possible and effective measures against guerrilla warfare. It is not guilty, for example, of having preferred genocide for strategic and economic reasons. Indeed, genocide presents itself as the *only possible reaction* to the rising of a whole people against its oppressors.

The American government is guilty of having preferred, and of still preferring, a policy of war and aggression aimed at total genocide to a policy of peace, the only policy which can really replace the former. A policy of peace would necessarily have required a reconsideration of the objectives imposed on that government by the large imperialist companies through the intermediary of their pressure groups. America is guilty of continuing and intensifying the war despite the fact that every day its leaders realize more acutely, from the reports of the military commanders, that the only way to win is "to free Vietnam of all the Vietnamese." The government is guilty—despite the lessons it has been taught by this unique, unbearable experience—of proceeding at every moment a little further along a path which leads it to the point of no return. And it is guilty—according to its own admissions—of consciously carrying out this admonitory war in order to use genocide as a challenge and a threat to all peoples of the world.

We have seen that one of the features of total war has been the growing scope and efficiency of communication. As early as 1914, war could no longer be "localized." It had to spread throughout the whole world. In 1967, this process is being intensified. The ties of the "One World," on which the United States wants to impose its hegemony, have grown tighter and tighter. For this reason, as the American goverment very well knows, the current genocide is conceived as an answer to people's war and perpetrated in Vietnam not against the Vietnamese alone, but against humanity.

When a peasant falls in his rice paddy, mowed down by a machine gun, every one of us is hit. The Vietnamese fight for all men and the American forces against all. Neither figuratively nor abstractly. And not only because genocide would be a crime universally condemned by international law, but because little by little the whole human race is being subjected to this genocidal blackmail piled on top of atomic blackmail, that is, to absolute, total war. This crime, carried out every day before the eyes of the world, renders all who do not denounce it accomplices of those who commit it, so that we are being degraded today for our future enslavement.

In this sense imperialist genocide can only become more complete. The group which the United States wants to intimidate and terrorize by way of the Vietnamese nation is the human group in its entirety.

A VICTORY

Jean-Paul Sartre

In 1943, in the Rue Lauriston (the Gestapo headquarters in Paris), Frenchmen were screaming in agony and pain: all France could hear them. In those days the outcome of the war was uncertain and we did not want to think about the future. Only one thing seemed impossible in any circumstances: that one day men should be made to scream by those acting in our name.

There is no such word as impossible: in 1958, in Algiers, people are tortured regularly and systematically. Everyone from M. Lacoste (Minister Resident for Algeria) to the farmers in Aveyron, knows this is so, but almost no one talks of it. At most, a few thin voices trickle through the silence. France is almost as mute as during the Occupation, but then she had the excuse of being gagged.

Abroad, the conclusion has already been drawn: some people say our decline has gone on since 1939, other say since 1918. That is too simple. I find it hard to believe in the degradation of a people; I do believe in stagnation and stupor. During the war, when the English radio and the clandestine Press spoke of the massacre of Oradour, we watched the German soldiers walking inoffensively down the street, and would say to ourselves: "They look like us. How can they act as they do?" And we were proud of ourselves for not understanding.

Today we know there was nothing to understand. The decline has been gradual and imperceptible. But now when we raise our heads and look into the mirror we see an unfamiliar and hideous reflection: ourselves.

Appalled, the French are discovering this terrible truth: that if nothing can protect a nation against itself, neither its traditions nor its loyalties nor its laws, and if fifteen years are enough to transform victims into executioners, then its behaviour is no more than a matter of opportunity and occasion. Anybody, at any time, may equally find himself victim or executioner.

Happy are those who died without ever having had to ask

themselves: "If they tear out my fingernails, will I talk?" But even happier are others, barely out of their childhood, who have not had to ask themselves that *other* question: "If my friends, fellow soldiers, and leaders tear out an enemy's fingernails in my presence, what will I do?"

Suddenly, stupor turns to despair: if patriotism has to precipitate us into dishonour; if there is no precipice of inhumanity over which nations and men will not throw themselves, then, why, in fact, do we go to so much trouble to become, or to remain, men? Inhumanity is what we really want. But if this really is the truth, if we must either terrorise or die ourselves by terror, why do we go to such lengths to live and to be patriots?

These thoughts have given us strength; false and obscure, they all unravel from the same principle: that man is inhuman. Their purpose is to convince us of our impotence. They will descend on us if we do not face them squarely. We must let other nations abroad know that our silence is not an assent. It comes from nightmares which are forced on us, sustained and guided. I have known it for a long time and have been waiting for a decisive proof.

Here it is.

A few weeks ago a book was published by Editions de Minuit: *La Question*. The author, Henri Alleg, still in prison today in Algiers, tells without unnecessary padding and with admirable precision what he underwent when "questioned." The torturers, as they themselves promised, "looked after him": torture by electricity; by drowning as in the time of Brinvilliers, but with all the perfected technique of our own time; torture by fire, by thirst, etc. It is a book one would not advise for weak stomachs. The first edition—twenty thousand copies —is sold out; in spite of a second printing produced in haste, the publishers cannot satisfy the demand: some booksellers are selling fifty to a hundred copies a day.

Torture is neither civilian nor military, nor is it specifically French; it is a plague infecting our whole era. There are brutes East as well as West. One could cite Farkas, who not so long

ago tortured the Hungarians, and the Poles who admitted that
before the Poznan riots the police often used torture. The
Khrushchev report shows conclusively what was happening
in the Soviet Union when Stalin was alive. Men who only yesterday were being "interrogated" in Nasser's prisons have subsequently been raised, still in a rather battered state, to high
places. Today there are Cyprus and Algeria. In other words,
Hitler was only a forerunner.

Disavowed—sometimes very quietly—but systematically
practised behind a façade of democratic legality; torture has
now acquired the status of a semi-clandestine institution. Does
it always have the same causes? Certainly not: but everywhere
it betrays the same sickness. But this is not our business. It is
up to us to clean out our own backyard, and try to understand
what has happened *to us,* the French.

In spite of that, the point is not altogether badly taken; it
at any rate throws light on the function of torture: *the question,* that secret or semi-secret institution, is indissolubly allied
to the secrecy of the resistance and the opposition.

Our Army is scattered all over Algeria. We have the men,
the money and the arms. The rebels have nothing but the confidence and support of a large part of the population. It is we,
in spite of ourselves, who have imposed this type of war—terrorism in the towns and ambushes in the country. With the
disequilibrium in the forces, the F.L.N. has no other means of
action. The ratio between our forces and theirs gives them no
option but to attack us by surprise. Invisible, ungraspable, un-
expected, they must strike and disappear, or be exterminated.
The elusiveness of the enemy is the reason for our disquiet. A
bomb is thrown in the street, a soldier wounded by a random
shot. People rush up and then disperse. Later, Moslems nearby
claim they saw nothing. All this fits into the pattern of a popular war of the poor against the rich, with the rebel units depending on local support. That is why the regular Army and
civilian powers have come to regard the destitute swarm of
people as a constant and numberless enemy. The occupying
troops are baffled by the silence they themselves have created;

the rich feel hunted down by the uncommunicative poor. The "forces of order," hindered by their own might, have no defence against guerillas except punitive expeditions and reprisals, no defence against terrorism but terror. Everybody, everywhere, is hiding something. They must be *made to talk*.

Torture is senseless violence, born in fear. The purpose of it is to force from one tongue, amid its screams and its vomiting up of blood, the secret of *everything*. Senseless violence: whether the victim talks or whether he dies under his agony, the secret that he cannot tell is always somewhere else and out of reach. It is the executioner who becomes Sisyphus. If he puts *the question* at all, he will have to continue for ever.

This rebellion is not merely challenging the power of the settlers, but their very being. For most Europeans in Algeria, there are two complementary and inseparable truths: the colonists are backed by divine right, the natives are sub-human. This is a mythical interpretation of a reality, since the riches of the one are built on the poverty of the other.

In this way exploitation puts the exploiter at the mercy of his victim, and the dependence itself begets racialism. It is a bitter and tragic fact that, for the Europeans in Algeria, being a man means first and foremost superiority to the Moslems. But what if the Moslem finds in his turn that his manhood depends on equality with the settler? It is then that the European begins to feel his very existence diminished and cheapened.

I am certainly not suggesting that the Algerian Europeans invented torture, nor even that they incited the authorities to practise it. On the contrary, it was the order of the day before we even noticed it. Torture was simply the expression of racial hatred. It is man himself that they want to destroy, with all his human qualities, his courage, his will, his intelligence, his loyalty—the very qualities that the coloniser claims for himself. But if the European eventually brings himself to hate his own face, it will be because it is reflected by an Arab.

In looking at these two indissoluble partnerships, the coloniser and the colonised, the executioner and his victim, we can see that the second is only an aspect of the first. And without any doubt the executioners are not the colonisers, nor are the colonisers the executioners. These latter are frequently young men from France who have lived twenty years of their life without ever having troubled themselves about the Algerian problem. But hate is a magnetic field: it has crossed over to them; corroded them and enslaved them.

What is the point then in trying to trouble the consciences of the torturers? If one of them defaults, his chiefs will quickly replace him: one lost, ten found. Perhaps the greatest merit of Alleg's book is to dissipate our last illusions. We know now that it is not a question of punishing or re-educating certain individuals, and that the Algerian war cannot be humanised. Torture was imposed here by circumstances and demanded by racial hatred. In some ways it is the essence of the conflict and expresses its deepest truth.

Borowski takes us into the realm of what I call pornographic confrontation: an absolutely stark rendition of the concentration-camp world to the point of a distilling its horror and bypassing whatever humanity might have existed. We learn that atrocity traps victimizers and victims alike in its deadly paradox.

DEADLY PARADOXES

Tadeusz Borowski

THE DEATH OF SCHILLINGER

Until 1943, First Sergeant Schillinger performed the duties of Lagerführer, or chief commanding officer of labor sector "D" at Birkenau, which was part of the enormous complex of large and small concentration camps, centrally administered from Auschwitz, but scattered throughout Upper Silesia.

Schillinger was a short, stocky man. He had a full, round face and very light blond hair, brushed flat against his head. His eyes were blue, always slightly narrowed, his lips tight, and his face was usually set in an impatient grimace. He cared little about personal appearance, and I have never heard of an incident involving his being bribed by any of the camp "bigwigs."

Schillinger reigned over sector "D" with an iron hand. Never resting for a moment, he bicycled up and down the camp roads, always popping up unexpectedly where he was least wanted.

His arm could strike a blow as hard as a metal bar; he could crack a jaw or crush the life out of a man with no apparent effort.

His vigilance was untiring. Each of his frequent visits to the other sectors of Birkenau spread panic among the women, the gypsies, or the "aristocracy" of the *Effektenkammer*, Birkenau's wealthiest section, where the riches taken from the gas victims were stored. He also supervised the Kommandos working within the great circle of the watch-towers, and without warning he would inspect the prisoners' suits, the Kapos' shoes, or the S.S. guards' sacks. Furthermore, he visited the crematoria regularly and liked to watch people being shoved into the gas chambers. His name was usually linked with the names of Palitsch, Krankenmann, and many other Auschwitz murderers who boasted that they had personally succeeded in killing with the fist, the club, or the revolver, at least ten thousand people each.

In August 1943, we heard the news that Schillinger had died suddenly in some very unusual circumstances. Various allegedly truthful but in fact conflicting versions of the incident circulated around the camp. I myself was inclined to believe the *Sonderkommando* foreman who, sitting on my bunk one afternoon while waiting for a shipment of evaporated milk to come in from the gypsy camp warehouses, told me the following story about the death of First Sergeant Schillinger:

"On Sunday, after the midday roll-call, Schillinger came to the cremo courtyard to visit our chief. The chief was busy, as the first truckloads of the Będzin transport had just been brought over from the loading ramp.

"Surely you realize, my friend, that to unload a transport, to see that everyone gets undressed and then to drive them inside the gas chamber, is hard work that requires, if I may say so, a great deal of tact. Anybody knows that until the people are safely inside, with the doors bolted, you mustn't gape at their junk, or rummage through it, or much less paw the nude women. The very fact, you see, that the women are made to strip naked alongside the men is a considerable shock to the new arrivals. Therefore you work with systematic haste, emphasizing the pressure of duties which supposedly must be performed inside the false bathhouses. And, in fact, you really do have to make it snappy if you're to gas one transport and clean away the corpses before the next one arrives."

The foreman raised himself a bit, propped a pillow under his rear-end, threw his legs over the side of the bunk, and lighting a cigarette went on:

"So, if you get the picture, my friend, we had the Będzin transport on our hands. These Jews, they knew very well what was coming. The *Sonderkommando* boys were pretty nervous too; some of them came from those parts. There have been cases of meeting relatives or friends. I myself had . . ."

"I didn't know you came from around there . . . Can't tell by the way you talk."

"I once took a teacher's training course in Warsaw. About fifteen years ago, I reckon. Then I taught at the Będzin school. I had an offer to go abroad, but I didn't want to go. Family and all that. So there you are . . ."

"So there you are."

"It was a restless transport—these weren't the traders from Holland or France who only thought of how they'd start doing business with the Auschwitz rich. Our Polish Jews knew what was up. And so the whole place swarmed with S.S., and Schillinger, seeing what was going on, drew his revolver. But everything would have gone smoothly except that Schillinger had taken a fancy to a certain body—and, indeed, she had a classic figure. That's what he had come to see the chief about, I suppose. So he walked up to the woman and took her by the hand. But the naked woman bent down suddenly, scooped up a handful of gravel and threw it in his face, and when Schillinger cried out in pain and dropped his revolver, the woman snatched it up and fired several shots into his abdomen. The whole place went wild. The naked crowd turned on us, screaming. The woman fired once again, this time at the chief, wounding his face. Then the chief as well as the S.S. men made off, leaving us quite alone. But we managed, thank God. We drove them all right into the chamber with clubs, bolted the doors and called the S.S. to administer Cyclone B: After all, we've had time to acquire some experience."

"Well, *ja,* naturally."

"Schillinger was lying face down, clawing the dirt in pain with his fingers. We lifted him off the ground and carried him—not too gently—to a car. On the way he kept groaning through clenched teeth: '*O Gott, mein Gott, was hab' ich getan, dass ich so leiden muss?*', which means—O God, my God, what have I done to deserve such suffering?"

"That man didn't understand even to the very end," I said, shaking my head. "What strange irony of fate."

"What strange irony of fate," repeated the foreman thoughtfully.

True, what strange irony of fate. When, shortly before the camp was evacuated, the same *Sonderkommando*, anticipating liquidation, staged a revolt in the crematoria, set fire to the buildings and, snipping the barbed wire, ran for the open fields, several S.S. guards turned the machine guns on them and killed every one—without exception.

I conclude with this excerpt from the end of my book on Hiroshima in order to return to the issue of ultimate technological atrocity. I want to suggest also that it is possible to draw wisdom from atrocity, and that we had better make every effort to do so.

ABSURD TECHNOLOGICAL DEATH
Robert Jay Lifton, M.D.

PSYCHIC NUMBING

The survivor's major defense against death anxiety and death guilt is the cessation of feeling. In our observations on Hiroshima we spoke of this process, in its acute form, as psychic closing-off, and in its more chronic form as psychic numbing. I would suggest now that psychic numbing comes to characterize the entire life style of the survivor. A similar tendency has been observed among concentration camp victims (one observer spoke of "affective anesthesia"), and as a general feature of "the disaster syndrome" (the "inhibition of emotional response" noted to account for the "stunned" and "dazed" behavior of victims of ordinary disasters). But what has been insufficiently noted, and what I wish to emphasize as basic to the process, is its relationship to the death encounter.

We have seen how, at the time of the encounter, psychic closing-off can serve a highly adaptive function. It does so partly through a process of denial ("If I feel nothing, then death is not taking place"), but also through interruption of the identification process, with the additional unconscious equation: "I see you dying, but I am not related to you or to your death." Further, it protects the survivor from a sense of complete helplessness, from feeling himself totally inactivated by the force invading his environment. By closing himself off, he resists being "acted upon" or altered. Concentration camp inmates, according to Bettelheim, sought to resist such alteration by protecting the "inner self": "I became convinced that these dreadful and degrading experiences were somehow not happening to 'me' as a subject, but only to 'me' as an object."

And under the combined ideological and physical pressures of Chinese thought reform (or "brainwashing"), participants developed a similar avoidance of emotional participation as a means of resisting fundamental change. In all three cases the survivor was able to attenuate his encounter with (biological or symbolic) death by limiting his psychological investment in that encounter. We may thus say that the survivor initially undergoes a radical but temporary diminution in his sense of actuality in order to avoid losing this sense completely and permanently; *he undergoes a reversible form of symbolic death in order to avoid a permanent physical or psychic death.*

Psychic closing-off also suppresses the survivor's rage, or in a broader sense his resistance, toward the forces manipulating him. In Hiroshima we observed this suppression of anger to have detrimental psychological effects. But it also was adaptive in that hostility or resistance would have meant greater exposure to the psychic assaults of the death encounter, and could have stimulated action interfering with physical survival. Within Nazi concentration camps there has been described a more definite command—sometimes overt, sometimes implicit—"Don't dare to notice!" The message was that inmates had better not "see," that is, recognize and respond to, the vicious killings and other forms of mistreatment taking place around them, since any such recognition suggested a form of resistance and a reassertion of forbidden pre-camp ethical standards. Similarly, all survivors of extreme death immersions experience the inner command "Don't dare to *feel*."

In concentration camps even prolonged forms of psychic numbing (variously called "dehumanization," "depersonalization," and "automatization of the ego") were, as Niederland put it, "highly important . . . [for] the economy of survival." And many camp survivors, when later asked, "How did you manage to survive?" answered simply, "I lost all feeling." This reminds us of similar comments of *hibakusha* ("I became insensitive to human death"), also stressing the survival value of psychic numbing.

But in both Hiroshima and Nazi camps the pattern could

drastically overstep itself. The classical example here is the *"Musselmann"* (*"Musselmänner"*) or "Moslem," the state in which prisoners became "in a literal sense, walking corpses." The term was coined by inmates themselves to suggest a fatalistic surrender to the environment, under the mistaken notion that this was characteristic of Moslem psychology. But so totally did the *Musselmann* sever his bonds of identification, so extreme was his psychic numbing, that the form of death he underwent was neither symbolic nor reversible—as an Italian survivor vividly suggests:

> . . . they, the *Musselmänner*, the drowned, form the backbone of the camp, an anonymous mass, continually renewed and always identical, of non-men who march and labor in silence, the divine spark dead within them, already too empty to really suffer. One hesitates to call them living: one hesitates to call their death death, in the face of which they have no fear, as they are too tired to understand.
>
> They crowd my memory with their faceless presences, and if I could enclose all the evil of our time in one image, I would choose this image which is familiar to me: an emaciated man, with head drooped and shoulders curved, on whose face and in whose eyes not a trace of a thought is to be seen.

Primo Levi's evocation of the *Musselmänner* as a single image of "all the evil of our time" is both a survivor's memory of ultimate horror, and a suggestion of the profound universal danger which surrounds man's tendencies to inflict exaggerated psychic numbing upon himself. Bettelheim speaks of the *Musselmänner* as having "given the environment total power over them," and because of losing their will to live, "permitted their death tendencies to flood them." These "death tendencies," I would hold, have less to do with the unhindered operation of the death instinct (as Bettelheim suggests) than with the total "desymbolization," a breakdown of inner imagery of connection, integrity, and motion, an absolute loss of the sense of human continuity.

From this perspective we can also approach the so frequently raised question of why so many Jews went, without protest, to their deaths at the hands of the Nazis. We may suspect that in response to the threat of death and (in many cases) prolonged brutalization, they experienced various degrees of psychic numbing, sometimes even approaching the *Musselmänner*'s inability to think or feel. Such is the conclusion one can draw from a description by Wiesel of a group of Jews who had just arrived the previous day at a concentration camp, but had already witnessed and heard about an interminable series of atrocities:

> Those absent no longer touched even the surface of our memories. We still spoke of them—"Who knows what may have become of them?"—but we had little concern for their fate. We were incapable of thinking of anything at all. Our senses were blunted; everything was blurred as in a fog. It was no longer possible to grasp anything. The instincts of self-preservation, of self-defense, of pride, had all deserted us. In one ultimate moment of lucidity it seemed to me that we were damned souls wandering in the half-world, souls condemned to wander through space till the generations of man came to an end, seeking their redemption, seeking oblivion—without hope of finding it.

In other words, the Jewish survivor's (he was still at that point a survivor) capacity to grasp the deaths of others and the danger to himself was destroyed by the psychic numbing already imposed upon him. In its milder form it consisted of simple denial of the possibility of being killed. But in the extreme form depicted in the above passage, including the reference to "damned souls wandering in the half-world," we have the sense of the state of "death in life" encountered in both Hiroshima survivors and *Musselmänner*, a state of such radically impaired existence that one no longer feels related to the activities and moral standards of the life process.

MISCARRIED REPAIR

In all of these harmful effects, psychic numbing comes to resemble what has been called "miscarried repair." Much like a physical process which originates in the body's efforts to protect itself from noxious stimuli and then itself turns into a deadly pathological force, psychic numbing begins as a defense against exposure to death, but ends up inundating the organism with death imagery. In Hiroshima this miscarried repair took the form of later bodily complaints, of the patterns of fatigue and restricted vitality we so frequently noted. While these are undoubtedly related to radiation fears (if not, as some believe, to physical radiation effects), one encounters very similar complaints in concentration camp survivors. There too organic impairments can be important, particularly those derived from physical injuries or from malnutrition, as can the psychological issue of the exaggerated bodily focus created by Nazi "selection" procedures in which life itself hinged upon the appearance of bodily strength. But in both groups we suspect that generalized psychic numbing is the unifying psychological factor, bound up as it is with death guilt and with the feeling that vitality is immoral.

The expression of death guilt via bodily complaints is in keeping with a recent hypothesis concerning psychosomatic phenomena, namely, that these represent "a final common pathway," a form of "entrapment of immobilization in an interpersonal field which is affectively perceived as threatening to life or [to] biological integrity." The survivor of severe death immersion, in other words, becomes permanently "entrapped" by what he symbolically perceives to be a continuous threat of death, which he is unable either to dispel or to express in any way other than the "language" of his body. In this sense his bodily complaints are a perpetuation of his original "entrapment" at the time of the death immersion. Thus, a Dutch psychiatrist has emphasized the way in which severe war stress, including that of Nazi persecution, "disturbs the existing psychosomatic homeostasis" with a resulting pattern of "pronounced psychosomatic symptoms" and a generally "neurasthenic syndrome."

Neurasthenia literally means nervous debility, and in classical psychiatry has been employed to suggest such symptoms as "weakness" or "exhaustion" of the "nervous system," easy fatigability, various aches and pains, pathological physical sensations, and inadequate functioning of practically any organ or organ system of the body. Many *hibakusha* patterns we have observed could be included under this syndrome, and it has been encountered in even more severe form in concentration camp survivors. One group of examiners, for instance, describes a recognizable pattern of "persistence of symptoms of withdrawal from social life, insomnia, nightmares, chronic depressive and anxiety reactions, and far-reaching somatization"; while another group mentions, in addition, fatigue, emotional lability, loss of initiative, and generalized personal, sexual, and social maladaptation. We thus encounter in both Hiroshima and concentration camp survivors, what can be called a pervasive tendency toward *sluggish despair*—a more or less permanent form of psychic numbing which includes diminished vitality, chronic depression, and constricted life space, and which covers over the rage and mistrust that are just beneath the surface.

The epitome of the neurasthenic "survivor syndrome," and of psychic numbing in general, is what we have referred to as the identity of the dead. We recall the guilt-saturated inner sequence of this identity (I almost died; I should have died; I did die, or at least I am not really alive; or if I am alive, it is impure of me to be so; and anything I do which affirms life is also impure and an insult to the dead, who alone are pure) ; and we can see now its suggestion of psychic numbing as itself a form of symbolic death. Hence, when survivors of both Hiroshima and concentration camps use such terms as "walking corpse," "living dead," "walking behind my own corpse," "ghosts," "not really alive," and "as if dead," they do so not only in reference to the original immersion but at least in some degree to the way they still feel themselves to be. We know the identity of the dead to be a treadmill of unresolved grief in which the "work of mourning" is never accomplished. But we also know it to be, in its own way, life-sustaining, a psychic bargain under whose terms the survivor receives (or grants himself) a form of half-life rather than either literal death or full vitality. Indeed, I suspect that some such "bargain" exists in relationship to all neurasthenic symptoms, and that more fundamental than the sexual etiology stressed by Freud is the relationship of the syndrome—in the ordinary neurotic as well as in the survivor—to unmastered death imagery. Further, the neurotic process in general, which has been historically equated with neurasthenia, may be looked upon as a manifestation of psychic numbing and restricted life space also related to death anxiety and death guilt.

The survivor, both at the time of his death immersion and later on, requires various combinations of psychic closing-off (or numbing) and openness to his environment. In Hiroshima, for instance, one could not afford to feel too much, but one had to feel things sufficiently to dislodge oneself from debris or flee from the fire. Similarly, in concentration camps one had to avoid both being reactive in a way that suggested resistance, and becoming numbed to the point of the *Mussel-mann* state; ideally psychic numbing was combined with an exquisite alertness to signals from the environment which could enable one to prepare for the next series of blows. Significantly, the capacity for cognition may be retained even under conditions of advanced numbing; what is lost is the symbolic integration which links cognition to feeling and action.

There were also situations in which doomed concentration camp prisoners could, through a sudden psychic opening-up, recover that integration and at least achieve dignity in dying. A story is told of a young woman who was singled out from among a group of naked prisoners lined up before the gas chamber they were about to enter and ordered by the commanding SS officer to dance, as he had just learned that she had been a dancer in the past. She did so, but in the course of her dance seized the officer's gun and had the satisfaction of shooting him before she too was shot to death.* Bettelheim suggests that the act of dancing permitted her to cease being "a nameless, depersonalized prisoner" and become "the dancer she used to be," so that "she responded like her old self, destroying the enemy bent on her destruction, even if she had to die in the process."

The survivor may also make efforts to break out of his psychic numbing years after the actual death immersion. We observed in Hiroshima the compensatory forms such efforts could take, as in the case of *hibakusha* who inwardly felt themselves weak and impotent but stressed the importance of a "fighting spirit" toward life; and in the urgency with which many Hiroshima and concentration camp survivors married (or remarried) and had children, seeking not only to replace the dead but to reassert vitality and biological continuity. These compensatory responses could have important recuperative significance. But they also could be unfocused and destructive—both at the time of the death encounter (we have noted the confused activity in the midst of the Hiroshima disaster), and later on in the patterns of agitation and hyperactivity which are prominent in the depressions reported among former concentration camp survivors.

As in the case of guilt there is an outward radiation of psychic closing-off, though in a more selective and complex way. The nearer one has been to the dead (and particularly to mass death), the greater the original need for a global defense mechanism and the more psychic "work" of closing-off required; the greater also the continuing struggle with guilt and the more likelihood of prolonged patterns of psychic numbing spreading to all areas of life. For those at the next remove from the dead (ordinary Japanese, for instance, rather than *hibakusha*), the closing-off process is both more complete and accomplished with a good deal less psychic work. And at still further remove from the experience (for non-Japanese, and

* A version of the incident re-created by Borowski, pp. 555–558.

particularly for Americans) there may be a near-total emotional separation from the Hiroshima experience through relatively easily accomplished psychic numbing. But we are speaking of a continuum, not of absolutely different reactions, and there remains a fundamental similarity, if very different intensity, in all of these patterns of psychic numbing. At the center as at the periphery there is retained the potential for a reopening of psychic sensitivity to the death immersion.

Strikingly analogous observations have been made on the parents of children dying of leukemia. These parents experience painful inner struggles in which they combine patterns of denial with more forthright "coping behavior" in which they open themselves to the reality of their children's imminent deaths. Whatever their blend of psychic numbing and openness, the death imprint remains strong. In contrast, relatives and friends at one further remove from the experience tend to resort to shallow reassurances and "gross degrees of denial." Numbing for them is effortlessly achieved.

Related forms of psychic numbing occur in people undergoing acute grief reactions as survivors of the deaths of family members—here vividly conveyed in a psychiatric commentary by Eric Lindemann:

A typical report is this, "I go through all the motions of living. I look after my children. I do my errands. I go to social functions, but it is like being in a play; it doesn't really concern me. I can't have any warm feelings. If I would have any feelings at all I would be angry with everybody." . . . The absence of emotional display in this patient's face and actions was quite striking. Her face had a mask-like appearance, her movements were formal, stilted, robot-like, without the fine play of emotional expression.

Lindemann emphasized (as did the woman herself) the importance of underlying hostility in these patients. But I would stress, as of even greater significance, the identification process and the retained "identity of the dead." This survivor, much like those of Hiroshima and Nazi concentration camps, has made her psychic bargain to live at a devitalized level in return for the right to live at all. Such a "bargain" is always likely to be an angry one, though we suspect that with her the restriction was more temporary, and did not require a "life of grief." In a general sense such pathological grief reactions may well be increasing in contemporary society, as Geoffrey Gorer has suggested, because of the absence of meaningful ritual for mourning. If so, we have a further reason for assuming that tendencies toward psychic numbing abound.

Gabriel Marcel tells us that "what we call 'survival' is in reality an 'under-living' . . . [in] which we advance always more bent, more torn away from ourselves toward the moment in which all will be engulfed in love." He makes clear that "under-living" refers to a loss of a sense of life's significance, and that the latter part of the quotation does not suggest a supernatural reunion but rather an elevated state of feeling in which significance has been recovered and "our existence can take on form." A related concept is a quality of despair which Leslie Farber has called "the life of suicide," by which he means the continuous contemplation of suicide until this contemplation "has a life of its own." As in the case of the Hiroshima survivor's identity of the dead, the life of suicide is a form of psychic numbing in which the thought makes the act unnecessary. Hence the apparent infrequency, or at least lack of unusual frequency, of suicidal attempts among Hiroshima and concentration camp survivors. The suicidal attempt can, in fact, represent a desperate effort to emerge from psychic numbing, to overcome inactivation by the act of killing oneself. He who takes his own life is likely to be a survivor of many "deaths," one who feels bereft of human connection; his suicide can be a way of seeking both to master death and to reassert, however magically, a form of symbolic integrity and a sense of immortality.

I shall discuss these issues as they affect mental illness in my later volume, but I would like to suggest here a view of schizophrenia as a prototype of psychic numbing in the extreme.

The various features that have been described in schizophrenia—the "split mind," autism and emotional withdrawal, impaired sense of reality, and tendencies toward concretization of ideas and extreme desymbolization—these can all be understood as a particularly pathological form of identity of the dead. Harold Searles has commented that "In working with schizophrenic patients, one soon comes to realize that many, if not all, of them are unable to experience themselves consistently as being *alive.*" He looks upon this pattern as anxiety over the fact of death: "One need not fear death so long as one feels dead anyway; one has, subjectively, nothing to lose through death." Concerning the schizophrenic's frequent fantasies and delusions of omnipotence, he points out that "the companion of omnipotence is immortality." I would suggest further that the schizophrenic requires these primitive fantasies of omnipotence and immortality precisely because of his radically impaired *symbolic* immortality—which in turn is an expression of his impaired relationships in life. For as fundamental as death anxiety is to psychic numbing, it is never death alone that one feels the need to shut out, but rather the relationship of death to one's symbolization of life.

Examining some of the larger issues surrounding psychic numbing, we recognize it as an important factor in the general neglect of the human impact of atomic bombing. I mentioned earlier my own need, in attempting to study these effects, for at least that degree of "selective numbing" that could be accomplished through focus upon my scientific task. Such numbing was, as I suggested, essential to carrying out the research, as it is to any work which deals with the problem of death, whether performing surgical operations or serving on a Red Cross rescue team. But here too there is the danger of "miscarried repair," of "professional" and "technical" identifications leading to dangerous degrees of psychic numbing. A grotesque example was provided by the Nazi physicians who conducted brutal medical experiments upon living human subjects, and by those who conducted the "selections" which directly dispensed existence and nonexistence. To the question of how a doctor could lend himself to such activities, Bettelheim replies: "By taking pride in his professional skills, irrespective of what purpose they were used for." The doctors in question *had* to focus upon these professional skills to prevent themselves from feeling. In a more indirect manner patterns of psychic numbing have surrounded the overall creation, testing, and military use (actual or planned) of nuclear weapons: a combination of technical-professional focus and perceived ideological imperative which excludes emotional perceptions of what these weapons do. It is no exaggeration to say that psychic numbing is one of the great problems of our age.

Because it is so pervasive in all of our lives, experiences which help us break out of it are greatly valued. This is another reason for the loving rumination by some Hiroshima and concentration camp survivors on painful details of their death immersions. For these memories are unique in that they enable one to transcend both the psychic numbing of the actual death encounter and the "ordinary numbing" of the moment. Similarly, those who open themselves up, even momentarily and from afar, to the actualities of death encounters, can undergo an intense personal experience which includes elements of catharsis and purification. On several occasions members of audiences I addressed on the Hiroshima experience told me later that their involvement in what they heard was so great that they resented subsequent speakers who dealt with more ordinary concerns. Their participation in the death anxiety and death guilt of those victimized had provided a highly valued moment of breakout from the universal psychic numbing toward death in general and nuclear death in particular.

Many people had similar reactions to the assassination of President Kennedy in 1963. The event made all Americans survivors (as it did practically everyone else in the world), and there were widespread grief reactions of the kind we have discussed.* To accomplish their "work of mourning," many found it necessary to remain glued to their television sets for the details of the assassination itself, the funeral, and the worldwide repercussions. A few days later, when television stations began to return to their routine programs, some felt resentful and let down: the brief interlude of exposure to death, however disturbing, was far preferable to the shallow pattern of psychic numbing encouraged by the ordinary mass-media fare. Psychic opening-up is not only necessary to the resolution of the mourning process but becomes in itself a treasured experience. It is the goal of a great variety of emotional experiments in contemporary life, and is closely related to the "expansion of consciousness" provided by psychedelic drugs.†

Psychic numbing, then, poses constant paradoxes for general issues of autonomy and survival. A way of maintaining life when confronted with unmanageable death anxiety, it threatens always to snuff out the vitality being preserved. Our deadly contemporary technologies surround the paradox with ultimate consequences, and make certain that this aspect of the survivor's struggles envelops us all.

NURTURANCE AND CONTAGION

Two themes dominate the survivor's personal relationships and general outlook—his own suspicion of counterfeit nurturance, and his perceptions of others' fear of contagion.

In discussing problems of counterfeit nurturance in *hibakusha,* I have emphasized how feelings of special need combine with great sensitivity to any reminder of weakness and create severe conflicts over autonomy. We can see now that

* There are many reasons for the intensity of this grief, but I would emphasize the great importance of the sense (among the "survivors" of the world) of Kennedy's premature death and unfulfilled life, and of perceptions of the universal consequences of that denied fulfillment.

† But it would seem that prolonged use of these drugs can result in its own form of psychic numbing.

psychic numbing further limits autonomy and cuts off potentially enriching relationships. Help offered threatens to confirm not only weakness but more fundamental devitalization.

Adding to the survivor's anticipation of the counterfeit is what we referred to before as his inevitable identification with the death-dealing force. We have noted tendencies of some *hibakusha* to ally themselves not only with America and Americans, but with the atomic bomb itself. Even more striking was the unconscious identification which led some Jewish concentration camp inmates to take on the ideology and even the mannerisms of individual Nazi guards.* We know that this resort to "identification with the aggressor" is an attempt to share the power by which one feels threatened. For the survivor, this means power over death itself. The near-dead hospital patients whom Dr. Hachiya described as suddenly revitalized by the rumor of Japan's atomic retaliation upon American cities derived their strength from the sense of being part of the force controlling life and death rather than its victims. (I shall argue in my later volume that power in general is, at bottom, power over death, so that here too the survivor is expressing a very general tendency.) Later, the very formation of a survivor identity—a group tie built around common victimization by a deadly force—becomes a more insidious psychic tie to that force. The survivor feels drawn into permanent union with the force that killed so many others around him. His death guilt is intensified, as is his sense that his own life is counterfeit.

A WORLD OF SURVIVORS

The atomic survivor, then, is both part of a historical legacy of survivorhood, and a representative of a new dimension of

---

* Bettelheim describes how "old political prisoners" (apparently Jews and non-Jews who had been in the camp for some time) went so far as to "arrogate to themselves old pieces of SS uniforms, and when that was not possible they tried to sew and mend their prison garb until it resembled the uniforms"; and to copy such SS "leisure time activities" as "games played by the guards . . . to find out who could stand being hit the longest without uttering a complaint."

death immersion. He experiences the same general psychological themes we have enumerated for all survivors of massive death immersion, but the unique features of nuclear weapons and of the world's relationship to them give a special quality to his survivorhood.

His death imprint is complicated by a sense of continuous encounter with death—extending through the initial exposure, the immediate post-bomb impact of "invisible contamination," later involvement with "A-bomb disease," and the imagery surrounding the *hibakusha* identity. Death guilt, stimulated at each of these stages, is reinforced by group patterns within a "guilty community," and further reawakened by every flexing of nuclear muscles—whether in the form of threatening words or weapons testing—anywhere in the world. Psychic closing-off is extraordinarily immediate and massive; and later psychic numbing, inseparable from radiation fears, gives rise to a particularly widespread form of psychosomatic entrapment. Suspicion of counterfeit nurturance is markedly strong, and lends itself readily to guinea-pig imagery. Contagion anxiety is similarly great because of the radiation-intensified death taint. Formulation is made profoundly difficult, both by the dimensions of the original experience, and by the complexity and threat surrounding the general nuclear problem. And here we arrive at another quality of atomic survival not unique to it but of unique importance: we all share it.

I say this not only because if Japan or Germany had developed the bomb first, I might have been either among the A-bomb dead or else the American equivalent of a *hibakusha;* just as if my grandparents had not elected to emigrate from Eastern Europe, I might have been a concentration camp victim or survivor. Such accidents of history must be kept in mind. But what I refer to is the universal psychological sharing of any great historical experience, and particularly of this one in this epoch. In a large sense history itself is a series of survivals, but in our century the theme of survival is more immediate and more ominous.

We have observed the effects of a relatively localized impact of a "small" nuclear bomb, with the existence of an "outside world" to help. There is no need to dwell on the magnification and dissemination of destructive power since Hiroshima, or on the uncertainty of there being an "outside world" to help in a future holocaust. We may simply say that Hiroshima gave new meaning to the idea of a "world war," of man making war upon his own species.

Only man, we are often reminded, "knows death," or at least knows that he will die. To which we must add: only man could invent grotesquely absurd death. Only man, through his technology, could render the meaningful totally meaningless. And more, elevate that "invention" to something in the nature of a potential destiny that stalks us all. For, after Hiroshima, we can envisage no war-linked chivalry, certainly no glory. Indeed, we can see no relationship—not even a distinction—between victimizer and victim, only the sharing in species annihilation.

Yet we know that great discoveries have in the past been made by survivors—of dying historical epochs as well as of actual catastrophes. By confronting their predicament, they have been able to break out of the numbing and stasis of unmastered survivorhood and contribute to the enlargement of human consciousness. Our present difficulty is that we can no longer be sure of this opportunity. We can no longer count upon survivor wisdom deriving from weapons which are without limit in what they destroy.

I have tried throughout this book to write with restraint about matters that make their own emotional statements. But behind that restraint has been a conviction that goes quite beyond judgments of individuals or nations, beyond even the experience of Hiroshima itself. I believe that Hiroshima, together with Nagasaki, signifies a "last chance." It is a nuclear catastrophe from which one can still learn, from which one can derive knowledge that could contribute to holding back the even more massive extermination it seems to foreshadow.

Hiroshima was an "end of the world" in all of the ways I

have described. And yet the world still exists. Precisely in this end-of-the-world quality lies both its threat and its potential wisdom. In every age man faces a pervasive theme which defies his engagement and yet must be engaged. In Freud's day it was sexuality and moralism. Now it is unlimited technological violence and absurd death. We do well to name the threat and to analyze its components. But our need is to go further, to create new psychic and social forms to enable us to reclaim not only our technologies, but our very imaginations, in the service of the continuity of life.

CONTRIBUTORS

Dr. Robert Jay Lifton is research professor of psychiatry at Yale and has written extensively on Hiroshima, nuclear weapons, and My Lai.

Dr. Gordon S. Livingston, a West Point graduate who served as a military physician in Vietnam, is now a resident in psychiatry at The Johns Hopkins University School of Medicine.

Edward M. Opton, Jr., and Robert Duckles are psychologists at the Wright Institute in Berkeley, California.

James P. Sterba has covered the Vietnam War as a correspondent for the *New York Times*.

Dr. Jerome D. Frank is professor of psychiatry at The Johns Hopkins University School of Medicine and has written extensively on psychological aspects of war and peace.

Dr. Peter G. Bourne is director of the Mental Health Unit of the Atlanta Southside Comprehensive Health Center, and has done first-hand investigations of army basic training in the United States and combat in Vietnam.

Father Daniel Berrigan, S.J., poet and former chaplain at Cornell University, is at the time of this writing imprisoned at the Federal Correctional Institution at Danbury, Connecticut, on the basis of his anti-war activism.

Arthur Miller, one of America's leading playwrights, has long been concerned with issues of political repression, guilt, and conscience.

Karl Jaspers, the German philosopher and psychiatrist, devoted much of his later career to a consideration of man's relationship to ultimate forms of holocaust.

Hannah Arendt, professor of philosophy at the New School for Social Research, has been long concerned with the ethical questions surrounding the Nazi experience.

Erik H. Erikson is professor emeritus of human development at Harvard and has been a pioneer in the application of psychoanalysis to history.

J. Glenn Gray is professor of philosophy at Colorado College.

Kurt Vonnegut, Jr., in addition to his distinction as a novelist, is one of our most astute commentators on holocaust.

Jean-Paul Sartre, the French philosopher and writer, has been, for several decades, one of the world's most influential intellectual voices.

Tadeusz Borowski, an outstanding Polish writer, was imprisoned in Auschwitz and Dachau from 1943 to 1945, and committed suicide in Warsaw in 1951.

RECOMMENDATIONS FOR FURTHER READING

Hannah Arendt, *On Violence,* New York, Harcourt, Brace and World, 1970.

Philip Berrigan, *Prison Journals of a Priest Revolutionary,* New York, Holt, Rinehart and Winston, 1970.

William J. Bosch, *Judgment on Nuremberg,* Chapel Hill, North Carolina University Press, 1970.

Peter G. Bourne, *Men, Stress, and Vietnam,* Boston, Little-Brown, 1970.

Albert Camus, *Resistance, Rebellion, and Death,* New York, Knopf, 1958.

Clergy and Laymen Concerned about Vietnam, *In the Name of America,* Annandale, Virginia, Turnpike, 1968.

John Duffett, ed., *Against the Crime of Silence: Proceedings of the Russell International War Crimes Tribunal,* Flanders, N.J., O'Hare, 1968.

Richard A. Falk, ed., *The Vietnam War and International Law,* Princeton, N.J., Princeton University Press, Vols. I and II, 1968, 1969.

Jerome D. Frank, *Sanity and Survival,* New York, Random House, 1967.

John H. E. Fried, *Vietnam and International Law,* Consultative Council, Lawyers' Committee on American Policy Toward Vietnam, 2nd rev. ed., 1968.

Willard Gaylin, *In the Service of Their Country/War Resisters in Prison,* New York, Viking, 1970.

John Gerassi, *North Vietnam: A Documentary,* Indianapolis, Bobbs-Merrill, 1968.

Richard Hammer, *One Morning in the War,* New York, Coward-McCann, 1970.

Tich Nhat Hanh, *Vietnam: Lotus in a Sea of Fire,* New York, Hill and Wang, 1967.

Seymour M. Hersh, *My Lai 4,* New York, Random House, 1970.

Edward and Elizabeth Huberman, eds., *War: An Anthology,* New York, Simon and Schuster, 1969.

Robert H. Jackson, *The Case Against the Nazi War Criminals* and *Other Documents,* New York, Knopf, 1946.

Jean Lacouture, *Vietnam: Between Two Truces,* New York, Random House, 1966.

Daniel Lang, *Casualties of War,* New York, McGraw-Hill, 1969.

Robert Jay Lifton, *History and Human Survival,* New York, Random House, 1970.

Jonathan Schell, *The Military Half,* New York, Vintage, 1968.

Jonathan Schell, *The Village of Ben Suc,* New York, Vintage, 1968.
Kurt Vonnegut, Jr., *Slaughterhouse-Five,* Seymour Lawrence, Dell, 1969.
Richard Wasserstrom, ed., *War and Morality,* Los Angeles, Wadsworth, 1970.
Gordon C. Zahn, *War, Conscience, and Dissent,* New York, Hawthorne Books, 1967.

INDEX

DATE DUE